Luminos is the open access monograph publishing program
from UC Press. Luminos provides a framework for preserving
and reinvigorating monograph publishing for the future
and increases the reach and visibility of important scholarly
work. Titles published in the UC Press Luminos model are
published with the same high standards for selection, peer
review, production, and marketing as those in our traditional
program. www.luminosoa.org

Equity, Growth, and Community

Equity, Growth, and Community

What the Nation Can Learn from
America's Metro Areas

Chris Benner and Manuel Pastor

UNIVERSITY OF CALIFORNIA PRESS

University of California Press, one of the most distinguished university presses in the United States, enriches lives around the world by advancing scholarship in the humanities, social sciences, and natural sciences. Its activities are supported by the UC Press Foundation and by philanthropic contributions from individuals and institutions. For more information, visit www.ucpress.edu.

University of California Press
Oakland, California

Benner, Chris and Pastor, Manuel. *Equity, Growth, and Community: What the Nation Can Learn from America's Metro Areas*. Oakland: University of California Press, 2015. doi: http://dx.doi.org/10.1525/luminos.6

Library of Congress Cataloging-in-Publication Data

Benner, Chris, author.
    Equity, growth, and community : what the nation can learn from America's metro areas / Chris Benner and Manuel Pastor. — First edition.
        pages cm
    Includes bibliographical references and index.
    ISBN 978-0-520-28441-8 (pbk. : alk. paper) — ISBN 0-520-28441-0 (pbk. : alk. paper) — ISBN 978-0-520-96004-6 (ebook)—ISBN 0-520-96004-1 (ebook)
    1. Economic development—Social aspects—United States. 2. Economic development projects—United States—Case studies. 3. Income distribution—United States. 4. Regional planning—United States—Case studies. 5. Cities and towns—United States—Economic policy. 6. United States—Economic conditions—2009-
I. Pastor, Manuel, 1956- author. II. Title.
    HC110.E44B46 2015
    338.973009173'2—dc23

                    2015020407

24   23   22   21   20   19   18   17   16   15
10   9   8   7   6   5   4   3   2   1

Contents

Acknowledgments

This book began with a hunch. A hunch informed by detailed data analysis and case-study research, to be sure, but just a hunch nonetheless. In a previous book, *Just Growth* (2012), we set out to explore how and why certain metropolitan regions had been able to link social inclusion and economic prosperity. We investigated employment structures and industrial composition. We examined demographic characteristics and geographical patterns of disparity. We considered patterns of education, housing, and social well-being. And we explored the political, economic, and social strategies pursued by a range of regional leaders—in the public, private, labor, and nonprofit sectors—using a careful selection of regional case studies meant to highlight different patterns of growth and equity.

In the end, as we examined all that data, what seemed most intriguing to us was not necessarily the detailed regression analysis and fancy multinomial specifications we developed (although we definitely lingered with those methods, data nerds that we are). Instead, what struck us was that several of our successful case study regions seemed to have some set of institutions that helped build particularly diverse regional leadership networks. Moreover, at the core of those diverse networks was a messy and very qualitative process of generating information and knowledge about dynamics in the region, and a joint commitment to let that knowledge, rather than ideology or partisanship, be the most important driver of regional development strategies. In short, there was something about knowing together that seemed to promote growing together.

This book represents our effort to systematically investigate that hunch—the hunch that diverse and dynamic epistemic (or knowledge) communities are an important component of building metropolitan regions that can achieve more sustainable and more equitable growth. To say that this approach—striving to blend and balance doing good and doing well—cuts against the grain of contemporary American politics is perhaps an understatement. After all, our country seems to be characterized by growing inequality dividing our fortunes, partisan rancor frustrating national solutions, and narrow-cast cable and social-media news sources fragmenting the very information base that holds our social fabric together.

But there is also a better side of American politics that seems to be in the waiting. After all, a growing number of people recognize that widening inequalities undermine not just the promise of opportunity for all but also our very economic health as a nation; understand that strength lies in our diversity and that fights over policy priorities should be carried out in a manner rooted in a sense of our common destiny; and acknowledge that a truly inclusive process must seek out the voices of the marginalized and excluded, and recognize the dangers of narrow perspectives, half-truths, and distortions.

And we know that this better side of American politics is not just imaginable but exists today—because we have seen it in places across the country. In regions as distinct as Salt Lake City and Seattle, San Antonio and Oklahoma City, leaders from diverse constituencies and divergent political perspectives are letting a commitment to place trump a commitment to ideology. Through processes sometimes obvious and sometimes hidden, sometimes deliberate and sometimes unintentional, these leaders and their constituencies have been able to weave a new metro politics that belies the individualistic and fragmented discourse that dominates the national scene. The challenge for the nation is to lift up lessons from those places where equity, growth, and community have come together—and to do so in a manner that helps inform a new national conversation about how to secure prosperity, promote inclusion, and reweave a tattered social fabric.

In researching and writing this book, we have incurred immense debt to a wide range of people that we would like to thank for their guidance and assistance. First and foremost, we want to thank the entire staff and research allies at the Program for Environmental and Regional Equity

(PERE) at the University of Southern California. Those staff members most directly involved in this project included Madeline Wander (data analysis, case studies, writing), Justin Scoggins (data analysis), Mirabai Auer (maps, data analysis, case studies), Pamela Stephens (data analysis and writing), and Rhonda Ortiz (case studies). Rachel Rosner, long-time research affiliate of PERE, also provided invaluable help with our North Carolina case studies. PERE graduate-student researchers Chad Horsford, Heddy Nam, Sheila Nem, and Hilary Wilson helped gather case-study information and provided editing support, and PERE undergraduate student Paxton Hall helped with formatting. Others on staff, including Vanessa Carter, Jennifer Ito, Jared Sanchez, and Alejandro Sanchez-Lopez, also contributed to some of the data interpretation and analysis, while Jackie Agnello Wong, Michelle Saucedo, and Lauren Portillo provided essential administrative and logistical support.

Knowledge production is a collective process, and the entire PERE team has been an important hub for collective research, thinking, and writing for many years. While one of us (Pastor) has the pleasure of working with this team on a day-to-day basis, including with some staffers for well over a decade, the other (Benner) has also worked closely with PERE staff for nearly as long, and also had the great pleasure of spending a sabbatical year at PERE while working on this book. We cannot imagine having a better crew—and certainly this book would still be just questions in our heads without their ability to keep us on task and on time.

We also want to thank the financial supporters who made this book possible. First and foremost is the Institute for New Economic Thinking, whose grant (no. 5409) enabled Benner to spend a sabbatical year at PERE and work more or less full-time on this project. The Ford Foundation and the MacArthur Foundation also provided invaluable grants to PERE that enabled this research, particularly in the creation of a standardized database to use in case-study selection and our econometric investigation of the relation between measures of inequality and the length of growth spells.

We would also like to thank all the people we interviewed in the regions we visited. The full list of interviewees is included at the end of the book, so we won't repeat it here. But we wouldn't have been able to write this book, or share their stories, without the time, knowledge, and wisdom they generously shared with us. In their own ways, they are working to build a more inclusive and successful America, and we hope we have done their efforts justice in these pages.

We have also benefitted from the intellectual insights and contributions to this research from many colleagues along the way. The Center for Regional Change at the University of California, Davis, has been an important hub for thinking about regional equity and provided valuable feedback that helped the analysis. We are particularly grateful to Jonathan London, Nancy Erbstein, Dave Campbell, Alex Karner, Teri Greenfield, Sara Watterson, Mindy Romero, and Cassie Hartzog, whose work on various aspects of regional equity has helped inform our work.

We are also thankful to the members of the Building Resilient Regions (BRR) network, funded by the MacArthur Foundation and guided by Margaret Weir of the University of California, Berkeley. BRR was an important sounding-board for the ideas in this volume as well as the proving ground for the data development. We especially thank Hal Wolman for pushing us to do better econometrics (hope we made the grade, Hal) and Margaret Weir and Todd Swanstrom for pushing us to understand the real mechanisms and challenges of policy change in regions. We want to single out Bill Lester and Sarah Reckow, both of whom started in BRR circles as graduate students and are now professors; they gently delivered (in writing and in a major journal) one of the most insightful—and apt—critiques of our previous work that we have read. It inspired us to respond with a much more nuanced rethinking and restatement of our perspective on how equity gets inserted in a regional conversation. In a way, this book is our attempt to respond to their concerns, and we hope that, with this volume, we demonstrate that we learned as much from them as they claim to have learned from us.

Thanks also to Bob Giloth, Maureen Conway, and other contributors to the book *Connecting People to Work*, who provided valuable feedback to a book chapter that helped us in formulating the overall argument of the book. Thanks as well to Jennifer Clark and other (anonymous) reviewers of this book manuscript and several related academic articles, portions of which have been included here, thanks to the permission of the publishers.

And while this particular debt may not seem as directly intellectual, we also want to give a special shout-out to Rachel Morello-Frosch for generously sharing her house in Santa Cruz for several writing retreats. The bulk of this book was written during those retreats, and the inspiration of being in her place—mere steps from the Pacific Ocean and pretty close to multiple cappuccino shops—made writing this book a true pleasure. She's also one of the smartest people we know, and we're just hoping that hanging in her place rubbed off on us.

Finally, we have written together for years and had the chance to dedicate our books to spouses and movement heroes. This one is for the kids. Tioga, Joaquín, and Anna Eliza—it's your world. We know that the spirit of collective enterprise and creativity in the name of justice that we write about in these pages is dear to your hearts, and we hope that we and others contribute to building the world of shared opportunity, civil discourse, and common-ground economics that you and your generations deserve.

CHAPTER I

Can't We All Just Get Along?

Question: If [Senator] Ted Cruz and [Speaker of the House]
John Boehner were both on a sinking ship, who would be
saved?
Answer: America.
—*Politico* columnist Roger Simon, during the federal government
shutdown, October 2013 (Simon 2013)

On the surface, the shutdown of the federal government in October
2013 was driven by a minority of members of the US House of Representatives who prioritized the defense of their ideological beliefs over the
desires of a majority of legislators, a popularly elected president, and an
increasingly frustrated electorate. This may be disturbing enough, but
dig a little deeper into the underlying layers that enabled this remarkable political stalemate, and an even more worrisome picture emerges.

After all, part of what allowed Tea Party Republicans to challenge
the implementation of Obamacare through hardball tactics, including the
threat (and reality) of a government shutdown, was their influence over
the restructuring of congressional districts following the 2010 census—
partly because of the Republican victories in 2010 national and state
races. With large majorities in state houses, conservative legislators drew
up districts so secure for those on the right that many elected officials
were more likely to face viable political opposition from a Tea Party flank
in Republican primaries than from Democrats in the general election. But
while this gerrymandering of districts reflects a sort of politics gone crazy,
it is really just one instance in a longer-term process: the spatial sorting of
the American public.

Though deeply rooted patterns of racial segregation seem to be declining slightly, broader patterns of separation by income and political
affiliation seem to be increasing. And it's not just space. Changes in our
media landscape are reinforcing the social fragmentation that results

from this sorting into more economically and politically homogeneous neighborhoods. The decline in readership of daily newspapers and the increasing narrowcasting of cable and online media sources means that a common knowledge base of what is going on in daily society is being further eroded. Not only are our political leaders in Washington unable to govern together, but increasingly large sectors of the general population can't even agree on whether the climate is changing, whether immigration helps or hurts, or any number of issues on which actual evidence might be helpful.

This fragmentation in the very knowledge base that fortifies both public life and social norms is exacerbated by the underlying increase in economic inequality. The shift in incomes and wealth toward the richest among us has created another sort of epistemological chasm, between one group on top, who believe they got there through their own efforts, and another group down the income chain, who wonder when (and if) their efforts will ever pay off (Piketty 2014; Stiglitz 2012). In the past, economic growth helped smooth over both distributional and political tensions; when all boats are rising, people are a bit less concerned about who has a yacht and who has a raft. But when the economy seems stalled—as it did in the wake of the Great Recession—a country can find itself in a vicious cycle. As Harvard economist Benjamin Friedman put it in early 2013, "we could be stuck in a perverse equilibrium in which our absence of growth is delivering political paralysis, and the political paralysis preserves the absence of growth" (quoted in Lowrey 2013).

Yet there may be lessons for the future if we look at the way in which strategies to grow the economy, address inequality, and reduce political fragmentation vary across our national landscape. After all, certain metropolitan regions have shown particular resilience even in the face of sharp economic restructuring. The reasons behind their performance are complex and often rooted in a number of structural factors, such as the sectoral mix of their regional economy, the educational level of their workforce, and the scale and role of public employment—all of which have impacts on economic growth and the distribution of income. None of these are easy to change quickly. Industrial diversity is hard to secure, educational capabilities improve slowly over time, and local public sectors, long suffering as the nation has moved toward more market-oriented strategies, are in many places still reeling from the impacts of the Great Recession.

But another element may be more susceptible to action: the development of *diverse and dynamic epistemic communities*. It's a clunky term, we know, but *epistemic community* actually has an intuitive meaning: it's what you know and who you know it with. While the evidence is still tentative (and this book is an attempt to move the ball forward on that front), our research suggests that such communities—ones that are diverse in their membership and sources of knowledge, and dynamic in their ability to withstand shocks, continuously learn, and adjust over time—can actually help construct and sustain regional social norms that facilitate the achievement of growth, resilience, and inclusion (Benner and Pastor 2012). In short, our ability to grow together may be fundamentally rooted in our ability to know together.

CRISIS AND CHALLENGE: A NATIONAL PERSPECTIVE

So what is it that we need to know? Perhaps the most important thing is that the economic and social problems we are facing as a nation go well beyond the contemporary statistics on unemployment and GDP growth rates—and the solutions therefore require going beyond the usual tinkering with tax rates, spending patterns, or even job-training funds and strategies. This is because the downturn that manifested itself in late 2008 was actually rooted in several very long-term and interrelated challenges: the jobs crisis, the inequality crisis, and the political crisis.

The Jobs Crisis

The recovery following the Great Recession was characterized, at least until 2014, as a "jobless recovery," a term that certainly resonated with the lived experience of ordinary workers. This was not a new phenomenon. Slow job growth has followed the end of the recession in the last three economic recoveries. However, from 1961 through the 1980s, job growth began immediately with the end of the recession. By three years after the beginning of the recovery, total jobs had increased by over 7 percent in all the recoveries that lasted that long, and by 10 percent in three cases. In contrast, in all three of the most recent business cycles (starting in 1991), it took more than a year into the economic recovery for job growth to begin at all. By three years into economic recovery, in no case was total job growth greater than 4 percent, and it took six full years just to recover to pre-recession employment levels from the 2008 recession—which was still less than what would be needed to keep up with the growth in the labor force.

Some analysts suggest that this experience of "jobless recovery" since the 1990s is the result of the increased diffusion of information technology throughout the economy, as higher levels of productivity have enabled companies to produce more goods and services with fewer people and more machinery, robots, and computers (Autor, Katz, and Kearney 2006; Brynjolfsson and McAfee 2011). This argument, however, ignores the widespread evidence, both in the United States and abroad, that the overall impact of technology on job and wage levels is indeterminate—that it depends on a variety of other factors, including trade patterns, exchange rates, and education policies, that shape the overall relationship between technology diffusion and job creation (Bogliacino and Vivarelli 2010; C. L. Mann 2012; Mortensen and Pissarides 1998).

It also seems clear that our economy is experiencing not simply a jobs shortfall but also a dramatic period of economic restructuring, with some evidence that this is accompanied by a long-term slowdown in economic growth rates. In the decades of the 1950s and 1960s, the US economy experienced average annual growth rates of over 4 percent. This dropped to an average of 3 percent in the 1970s, '80s, and '90s. In the 2000s, average overall economic growth was only 1.6 percent a year, while in the first four years of the 2010s, it was 2 percent a year.[1] Rapid population growth had something to do with these numbers—the baby boom was a substantial economic boost for the country in the 1950s and '60s—but even adjusting for total population, per capita growth rates in recent decades have also slipped when compared to earlier decades.

The Inequality Crisis

We have also experienced a dramatic growth in income inequality in recent decades. Using data from the Internal Revenue Service, Emmanuel Saez and Thomas Piketty have demonstrated that from the 1940s up to the late 1970s, the proportion of total income in the United States captured by the top 10 percent of income earners consistently remained in the 33–35-percent range (Piketty and Saez 2003). Starting in 1979, however, upper income earners started gaining consistently higher proportions of total income, which rose to a peak of a full 50.4 percent of all income going to the top 10 percent of income earners in 2012. And much of this was concentrated in the top 1 percent, which saw its proportion of total US income rise from roughly 10 percent, between the 1940s and 1981, to a high of 23.5 percent in 2007 (with a slight fall to 22.5 percent in 2012; Atkinson, Piketty, and Saez 2011).[2]

This growth in inequality has many roots, including excessive CEO and executive compensation at the top of the income ladder, as well as excessive financialization, leading to outsize returns in the financial sector (Stiglitz 2012). But it is also due to stagnant and declining wages for large sectors of the workforce, partly because of large shifts in returns to education. While real hourly wages grew an average of 2.6 percent per year between 1948 and 1973, they grew only 0.2 percent per year in the 1970s, 0.8 percent per year in the 1980s, 0.3 percent per year in the 1990s, and 0.9 percent per year in the 2000s.[3] Between 1973 and 2011, wages fell by more than 20 percent for workers with less than a high school degree, more than 7 percent for workers with only a high school degree, and nearly 5 percent for those with some college education. In 1973, these categories accounted for a full 95 percent of the labor force, and even by 2011, a full 66 percent of the labor force still had less than a college degree and was receiving wages that were lower in real terms than nearly 40 years previously.[4]

As Piketty (2014) has argued, the distributional problem is exacerbated by a lack of economic growth. When growth is slow but profit rates remain high, capital's share of income accumulates—and with it, the ability of capital to exercise influence in the economic policymaking process. That, in turn, exacerbates the very shifts in tax policy and financial market openness that have helped generate income and wealth inequality in the first place (Alvaredo et al. 2013). Again, we find a sort of vicious cycle—and it is one made worse by the lack of political leadership seeking to effectively address the deep crises of slow job creation and rising inequality.

The Political Crisis

Alongside these economic and distributional challenges has been a crisis in our political institutions that is nearly unparalleled in the nation's contemporary history (Mann and Ornstein 2012). Prior to the November 2014 elections, approval ratings of President Barack Obama were nearly the lowest of his term. But most striking has been the long-term decline in the percentage of the American electorate approving of the way Congress is handling its job.[5] In one poll conducted in early 2013, following the gridlock over the "fiscal cliff" and a particularly unproductive 112th congressional session, only 9 percent of respondents had a favorable opinion of Congress (Easley 2013).[6] The Gallup Poll of Americans' level of approval of Congress, probably the most reliable and consistent source of data to compare public opinion over time, found average approval ratings from 2011 to 2013 to be the lowest in the 40 years over which comparable data has been gathered, with consistently less than 15 percent of Americans approving of the way Congress was doing its job (Newport 2013).

Like the challenges facing our economy, this is not a recent phenomenon. Despite a brief surge following the 9/11 attacks, overall confidence in political institutions has declined from highs in the 1960s. Meanwhile, voter participation rates fell steadily over the two decades following the mid-1960s, with turnout of eligible voters averaging about 40 percent in mid-term elections for the past forty years (McDonald 2010). The lack of confidence—and interest—is not surprising. Rather than addressing pressing issues, our leaders seem to be stumbling from crisis to crisis, from news cycle to news cycle, from a dismal yesterday to an uncertain future.

One bit of evidence: Congress has become less and less effective at moving legislation, even as it has become more effective at partisan bickering (McCarty, Poole, and Rosenthal 2006).[7] Party-unity scores, which measure the percentage of members voting with a majority of their party, have risen from levels of roughly 75 percent in the 1970s to around 90 percent in the most recent years (Ornstein et al. 2013). The polarization grows from—and feeds directly into—what we think is the most important underlying factor: a dramatic decline in consensus on basic facts needed for policymaking, such as the role of taxation in economic growth, the impact of immigrants on society, and even the nature of global warming.

Part of the reason for that increasing fragmentation of knowledge is an increase in narrowcasting in the media. Since the 1970s, we have experienced a growing customization of media channels and fragmentation of news sources, starting first with the growth in cable television and accelerating dramatically with the growth of the Internet (Owen 2012). Readership of daily newspapers has declined across all age groups; particularly striking is that less than 30 percent of adults age 18–34 read a daily newspaper, whether in print or on the Web.[8] Meanwhile, with the acceleration and increasing sophistication of algorithm-based customization of Internet-based information—on sites as varied as Google, Facebook, Amazon, and the *New York Times*—information that is "unwanted" is increasingly filtered out without the consumer even knowing (Pariser 2011).

We have also seen an increase in spatial sorting by both partisan ideology and social class. More people seem to be moving to areas with more homogeneous political and social circumstances, and thus are exposed to less diversity of opinions in their residential life as well (Chinni and Gimpel 2011). In 1976, for example, only about a quarter of America's voters lived in a county where a presidential candidate won by a landslide (20 percent or more); by 2004, it had grown to nearly half (Bishop and Cushing 2008), and by 2012, more than half the voters lived in such landslide counties.[9] As for class isolation, in 1970, only 15 percent of families were in neighborhoods that were classified as either affluent or poor. By 2007, this had more than doubled, to 31 percent of families (Reardon and Bischoff 2011).

Information fragmentation and spatial sorting has, we believe, eroded a common base of knowledge about the very nature of the problems we face as a nation—both in the political leadership and in the broader public that elects them. For example, in a July 2012 poll by the Pew Forum on Religion and Public Life, 30 percent of Republicans said that they thought that President Obama is Muslim—nearly double the percentage who thought so four years previously.[10] Similarly, more than a third of respondents in a 2006 survey by Ohio University believed that federal officials either assisted in the 9/11 terrorist attacks or took no action to stop them so that the United States could go to war in the Middle East.[11] While these examples could make for a lighthearted chuckle about the extremes in the political spectrum, we worry that they are evidence of a deeper challenge facing the nation. When we can't agree on the basic facts, disagreement about appropriate solutions—and sharp but ill-informed ideological warfare—are sure to follow.

Connecting the Crises

Many observers seem to see the jobs crisis, the inequality crisis, and the political crisis as relatively disconnected. This implies that they could either be dealt with separately or, to the extent that they are connected, sequentially. However, we believe that these three crises are in fact deeply interconnected—and that the starting point for addressing all three has to be shrinking the epistemic distance that allows us to believe that we are living in separate and disconnected worlds in which we are each entitled to not only our own beliefs but our own facts.

There is, for example, an emerging consensus that inequality and economic stagnation, particularly in terms of employment, are linked. The new and highly influential research by Thomas Piketty (2014) suggests that more rapid growth tends to more generally rebalance power between social classes and income groups, and weaken the grip on politics of those with inherited wealth. The relative prosperity in the latter part of the Clinton administration, for example, raised workers' bargaining power and also brought a narrowing of racial wage differentials that had not been seen since the early days of the civil rights breakthroughs.

But while this notion that growth can change the power balance is somewhat familiar, a more novel concept has emerged in economic thinking in recent years: the idea that inequality might itself damage prosperity and economic sustainability. The reasons why equity might have an impact on growth are complex—but not inaccessible. For one thing, inequality may be associated with lower demand and excessive financialization of the economy, particularly as the wealthy look for more creative (and more risky) ways to hold their assets. Inequality is also corrosive to social solidarity, creating political problems when it comes time to share either burdens or benefits (Frank 2012; Stiglitz 2012).

Both slow growth and inequality are also closely linked with our political crisis. The growth part is evident—when the labor market is slack and there is less to go around, tensions can rise. But in an intriguing paper, political scientist Eric Uslaner (2012) also suggests that inequality has an impact on the ability to reach political consensus. Running a series of multivariate regressions in which measures like trust and social cohesion were considered dependent variables while various measures of inequality and other control measures were entered as the independent variables, he found that not only is rising inequality a significant predictor of low levels of trust and social cohesion, it also explains a large share of the shifts (e.g., up to a third of the decline in a generalized measure of trust between the late 1960s and the current era).

A rise in income inequality, as measured by the Gini coefficient, has also been shown to be associated with a decline of faith in government institutions, as well as a fall in the sense that different racial groups share common interests. Of course, these various trends may be moving in the same direction because of an entirely different third factor common to them all—but the relation between growing inequality and growing social distance makes intuitive sense to those who have observed the growth of gated communities, the rise of exurbia, and the continued geographic concentration of racial minorities and the poor (Kneebone, Nadeau, and Berube 2011).

Why does this matter? When everyone is far apart in terms of both income and perspective, sensible agreements on tax policy, education investments, and industrial promotion are difficult to achieve. We need to address the jobs, inequality, and political crises at the same time, but the very social distance rendered by slow growth, slipping opportunity, and polarized politics makes it hard to move forward. However, while reversing this downward spiral may seem like a tall order, we don't actually need to start from scratch. There are lessons emerging from a handful of regions across the country which, over a sustained period of time, have been able to create not just growth but *just* growth—that is, economic expansion that weds prosperity and inclusion.

And while that fortunate coincidence of enhanced output and improved distribution is certainly connected to key structural factors—labor-market tightness, locally rooted firms, and booming industries—we suggest in this volume that there is another element that often plays a complementary role: the ability of regions to foster conversation, overcome civic fragmentation, and find the policy "sweet spots" where what seem like two sides of a divide become the interdependent *yin* and *yang* of a singular whole.

COMING TOGETHER: LESSONS FROM AMERICA'S REGIONS

The idea that a better national approach can bubble up from America's metropolitan regions has gained increased currency in recent years. Part of the reason for this "rise of the region" is the idea that it is the relevant unit for an internationalized economy—the scale at which economies of scale can be achieved to lower production costs while business networks can be maximized to facilitate innovation. Another part of the reason is simply the frustration with the stasis in Washington and the willingness of regional leaders to try new ideas to spur recovery and restructuring (Katz and Bradley 2013). Finally, the variability in regional fortunes—along with some evidence that this variability has been increasing in recent decades (discussed in chapter 3 as well as by Pastor, Lester, and Scoggins 2009)—suggests that a careful attention to the processes shaping this variation might yield valuable insights for action at different scales.

Indeed, the emerging notion that inequality might actually damage economic growth seems to have gained the most ground at the metropolitan level. In certain places, key regional actors—including collaboratives of business, labor, civic, and community leaders—have become increasingly convinced that a more inclusive economic approach can actually strengthen the social consensus and human capital needed to compete in a global economy. Backing up that perspective has been a range of empirical studies, including from the Federal Reserve, showing that strategies that reduce social, geographic, and other disparities are actually correlated with broad economic success (Eberts, Erickcek, and Kleinhenz 2006; Voith 1998).

So how is this shift in economic thinking connected to the issue of political disconnection discussed above? Under what conditions do the imperatives of fairness and the need to support economic drivers come together at the metropolitan level? What are the social and political arrangements, particularly given the general lack of regional government, that allow this to happen in some regions and impede it in others? And what are the potential lessons for a nation seeking to stop the economic bleeding, shrink the distributional divisions, and, most of all, restore a sense of common fate?

Learning from the Regions

We offered an initial answer to these questions in our last book, *Just Growth* (2012). There, we relied heavily on a quantitative approach to identify those regions with above-median performance in terms of job growth and earnings increases, on the one hand, and poverty reduction and inequality improvement, on the other. We then conducted regression-style analysis to explore the demographic, political, and economic determinants behind these growth and equity patterns—and using the same database as that employed in the regression analysis, we then identified a set of seven regions for more in-depth case studies, suspecting that we might find through this a list of best practices to attain more equitable growth in metropolitan settings.

Researchers generally begin with hypotheses, and we did find some things we expected. Both the statistical and the qualitative work revealed the stabilizing effect of the public sector, the generally positive impact of deconcentrating poverty, the growth-enhancing but equity-reducing impacts of having a large immigrant population, and the important role of an influential minority middle class that can bridge an interest in prosperity with a continuing commitment to fairness. But actually spending time in the field made us aware of a factor we had never even considered, and one we explore in great depth in this volume: the importance of efforts to create shared social norms in the form of what we now call epistemic communities.

Formally, epistemic communities have been defined as like-minded networks of professionals whose authoritative claim to consensual knowledge provides them with a unique source of power in decision-making processes (Adler and Haas 1992; Haas 1992). In our earlier work, we suggested that when the members of such knowledge communities include not just the "usual suspects" of urban-growth coalitions but a broader constellation of community interests and perspectives, regional trajectories might be affected. We specifically suggested that creating a diverse regional consciousness about the problems of poverty and its impacts on growth tends to focus attention; that interjurisdictional ties can help (because, for example, suburbs that can be annexed realize rather quickly that they cannot escape the drag on regional growth of high levels of poverty in the urban core); and that all this can be pushed along by intentional leadership programs and other strategies for collaborative governance.

We will admit to being initially hesitant to stress the role of political and governance processes. We both tend to lean toward economic and structural explanations. The idea that people just talking actually makes a difference was comforting in one sense (ideas do matter!) and discomforting in another (how do you measure this?). Still, while we remained uneasy with the concept, knowledge communities—and the leadership and other networks that produced them—did seem to make a difference to both the actors and the outcomes, and so we simply reported what we saw and hoped that the ideas would be fleshed out over time.

What we didn't anticipate is that the framework would attract both some significant attention (Reynolds 2012) and some useful criticism (Lester and Reckhow 2013). Perhaps the most important of the latter emphasized our seeming failure to account for conflict. After all, in the real world, business leaders are often deeply committed to an economic perspective in which labor unions slow growth, regulation impedes efficiency, and fairness is an afterthought to be taken up in one's charitable spare time. In contrast, community and labor leaders may be steeped in a framework wherein the economy is a site of exploitation, protection against insecurity is essential, and economic growth is someone else's concern. Conflicts can all get worse when political entrepreneurs jump into the stew, seeking to advance their own partisan interests by fueling divisions in the pursuit of short-term gain.

Moreover, conflict is not necessarily antithetical to achieving the goals of prosperity and inclusion. In what we thought was a very effective (albeit sympathetic) critique of our work and that of others, Lester and Reckhow suggested that regional progress on equity, particularly in light of generally weak metropolitan governance structures, should really be seen as advancing through a series of policy skirmishes between various actors. This is also the underlying perspective of Amy Dean and David Reynolds (2009), who argue that more inclusive growth will come only through the strengthening of central labor councils and the emergence of community–labor coalitions.

Yet another shortcoming was the impression we may have given that epistemic communities necessarily lead to more equitable growth—or perhaps better put, the shortcoming was our failure to specify causal mechanisms between community making, norm formation, and changes in the economy (Schildt 2012). Of course, the connection is tentative. Intergroup understanding may facilitate growth and equity, but it is not likely to overcome the collapse of a major regional industry (although some of the cases in this volume suggest that it might stir regional action to mitigate the damage). Knowing together will not always produce growing together—but it can help.

Learning in the Regions

You don't always get a second crack at further specifying the case you are making—but sometimes life does produce such blessings. In our case, it was a grant from the Institute for New Economic Thinking that allowed us to further investigate the links between equity and growth—and the role of knowledge communities in helping foster the connection between the two in the minds of regional actors.

We report on that research in this book, once again combining quantitative and qualitative analysis in a mixed-methods approach. As we detail below, we begin by offering some novel econometric work looking at the impact of both income distribution and various measures of social distance on the sustainability of employment growth (i.e., the relationship between inequality and the jobs crisis). We then explain how we chose a series of case-study regions, partly based on "just growth" outcomes and partly based on the presence of regional knowledge communities. We then walk through a range of cases: Sacramento and Salt Lake City, as two cases where formal collaborative planning processes have been key to producing a sense of common destiny; Charlotte, Grand Rapids, and Oklahoma City, as a set of cases where regional growth strategies have been mostly elite-driven; Greensboro, Fresno, and San Antonio, as places where conflict has raged—and in one case, eventually produced collaboration; and Raleigh, Seattle, and Silicon Valley, as locales where the knowledge economy meets what we have termed knowledge communities.

So what's new this go-around? In this effort, we expand our previous analysis in three ways. We stress more the *process* of community building than the *impacts* on growth and equity; we offer a fuller account of the ways in which *conflict* and *collaboration* can go together; and we add the characteristics of *diversity* and *dynamism* that our newest case-study research suggests are key to both sustainable communities and sustainable growth. While we explore the causal chains and the role of conflict below, it is useful to start by defining what we mean by a diverse and dynamic epistemic community at the metropolitan level.[12]

Our concept of *diverse and dynamic* epistemic communities builds initially from the work done on epistemic communities per se. The concept of an epistemic community was first developed throughout the 1960s and 1970s in the context of understanding the production of scientific knowledge, primarily by the sociologist Bukart Holzner (1968; Holzner and Marx 1979), though it owes some intellectual allegiance to Ludwik Fleck's (2012) idea of a "thought collective" and Thomas Kuhn's (2012) notion of a scientific community (see also Cross 2013). John Ruggie (1972) introduced the term to the field of international relations, drawing on Foucault's (1970) notion of an *episteme* to define such a community as embodying "a dominant way of looking at social reality, a set of shared symbols and references, mutual expectations, and predictability of intention" (Ruggie 1975).

The concept gained significant attention following work by political scientist Peter Haas in the early 1990s on the challenges of coordinating international policy in light of increasing levels of complexity and uncertainty. Haas and his colleagues suggested that networks of knowledge-based experts can play an important role "in articulating cause-and-effect relationships of complex problems, helping states identify their interests, framing the issues for collective debate, proposing specific policies and identifying salient points for negotiation" (Haas 1992, 2). In their work,

Haas and his colleagues describe an epistemic community as a group of people that has four broad characteristics:

1. a shared set of normative and principled beliefs, which provide a value-based rationale for the social action of community members

2. shared causal beliefs, which are derived from their analysis of practices leading or contributing to a central set of problems in their domain and which then serve as the basis for elucidating the multiple linkages between possible policy actions and desired outcomes

3. shared notions of validity—that is, intersubjective, internally defined criteria for weighing and validating knowledge in the domain of their expertise

4. a common policy enterprise—that is, a set of common practices associated with a set of problems to which their professional competence is directed, presumably out of the conviction that human welfare will be enhanced as a consequence (Haas 1992, 3).

In understanding the evolution of such epistemic communities, uncertainty and interaction are key. Poorly understood conditions make it more difficult to know which strategies are most likely to be successful, and with established procedures lacking, existing institutions are less effective at generating appropriate information and knowledge (Cross 2013). The process of creating such knowledge together, particularly in a series of repeated interactions over extended periods of time, can help participants develop a common language and cognitive frames that allow them to communicate effectively and share new knowledge (Hakanson 2005). And while the literature does stress institutionalization and the link with a common policy enterprise, such communities are not necessarily limited to formal legislative or policy processes. As Adler and Haas (1992, 374) put it: "The policy ideas of epistemic communities generally evolve independently, rather than under the direct influence of government sources of authority." In short, epistemic communities are more about governance than about government.

Complicating the Frame

In developing our own notion of diverse and dynamic epistemic communities, we stress multiple ways of knowing. While Haas's approach privileges traditionally defined experts and theoretically oriented methods of knowledge production, we think there are at least two other broad kinds of knowledge that are valued in more diverse epistemic communities.

One of these other kinds of knowledge is action-oriented, socially productive, and ethically rooted. It is not simply the practical knowledge that comes from the application of theoretical knowledge, but is a form of knowledge that incorporates a moral dimension about the purposes toward which that applied knowledge is being put, including the creation of and debate about ideal ends. Greenwood (2008) also identifies a third kind of knowledge, which involves the design of problem-solving actions through collaboratively developed knowledge that combines the local knowledge and interpretative strategies of stakeholders with professional researchers' knowledge.

These latter two features contribute to diversity and inclusion. Creating hybrid groupings of experts and lay people broadens the information base used to address problems and reduces the privileged position of experts while incorporating the real-world insights of those most affected by the decisions (Irwin and Michael 2003; Chilvers 2008). Diversity, in this sense, refers not simply to the racial or sectoral heterogeneity of the participants in a process of knowledge sharing but also to the recognition that at least certain types of knowledge are actually dependent on the full and equal participation of non-"expert" stakeholders in the earliest stages of issue framing and agenda setting.

In this broader framework, an epistemic community is not just about consensus, and it is definitely not a conflict-free zone. Indeed, as we stress later in our case study of San Antonio, community can actually emerge from conflict—and comity does not mean the end of tensions or "skirmishes" at a regional level (Lester and Reckhow 2013). But in high-performing regions, conflicts are attenuated by the recognition of a common regional destiny—a sense of place that makes tension an important learning opportunity rather than an invitation to further a long-term "war of attrition" (as seems to have been the case in, say, Greensboro or Fresno). This requires that participants develop social norms about how to engage in conflict, including an understanding of the "rules of the debate," a commitment to repeated interactions, and a sense of the ways in which data can and should be collectively used to shape decision-making processes. In at least one place, this even has a name. The famous "Seattle process" is a region-specific, culturally embedded way to solve conflicts that is viewed by many as tedious and time-consuming but is also valued as an effective method to reach consensus, with its latest most remarkable achievement being the 2014 agreement between business, labor, and civic leaders on a $15-an-hour minimum wage.

TABLE 1.1 CLASSIFYING EPISTEMIC COMMUNITIES

	Traditional view of epistemic communities	Diverse and dynamic epistemic communities
Membership	Driven by experts and/or professionals	Driven by leadership from diverse constituencies, with broader notions of what constitutes valid knowledge
Ties that bind	Shared values/interests	Sense of a common regional destiny, often created through repeated interaction that involves skirmishes and principled conflict as well as collaboration
Ways of knowing	Common causal beliefs and shared notions of validity	Acknowledgement of legitimacy of others' viewpoints and information bases and agreed-on norms of interaction and "rules of the debate" (either explicit or implicit)
Scope of goals	Typically a common policy enterprise	Action-oriented, not just policy-oriented; may involve multiple goals and multiple fora within broader processes of regional governance
Dynamism over time	Both episodic/single issue and ongoing	Multi-issue framing and relationship building that allow regional resilience to adjust to shocks and emerging challenges over time

The idea of repeated (even conflictual) interactions and processes gets us to the issue of dynamism. While there is a sense in the literature that epistemic communities are episodic—involving getting experts together to address a single thorny policy issue—we use the term to refer to sustained groupings of regional actors. Such dynamism, in the form of repeated interactions, has been crucial to responding to shocks and longer-term structural changes in such places as Raleigh, San Antonio, Oklahoma City, and even Silicon Valley.

In the first column of Table 1.1, we summarize key characteristics of the more traditional conception of epistemic communities as originally proposed by Haas (with some elaboration).[13] In the second column, we expand upon this original conception and identify key elements of what we call diverse and dynamic epistemic communities. The differences are rather straightforward. We see diverse and dynamic epistemic communities as having a broader membership base, an ability to accommodate multiple ways of knowing, a scope of action which stretches across multiple outcomes and conversational arenas, a desire to move beyond the episodic, and a capacity to handle conflict even as they facilitate a sense of common destiny.

Structures, Norms, and Individuals

As we hope is now clear, policy frameworks, stakeholder meetings, and community engagements may be evidence of an epistemic community, but we are talking about something far deeper and more ingrained in how a region operates. Indeed, behind the governance processes we will explore are regional "cultures" that often have to strain against the national norms and institutional incentives that have produced the divisive politics and unequal labor markets described at the beginning of this chapter. Indeed, interjurisdictional collaboration goes against the grain of local government fragmentation, inequality, and the Tieboutian service-based sorting into cities segregated by race, income, and amenities that characterizes most metropolitan regions in the United States. Thus, in trying to understand how these diverse and dynamic epistemic communities form, we need to pay particularly close attention to the development of regional *social norms* as well as the institutional structures and incentives that can underpin (or undermine) them.

This in turn requires a fundamental rethinking of traditional economic assumptions about human and social behavior. After all, economics often assumes exactly the sort of atomistic individuals among whom cooperation would be short-lived, sorting would be economically efficient, and social norms would play little role in shaping agent behavior. Yet in the cases we examine we see instances in which voters go against their seeming short-term interest, supporting pre-K for disadvantaged kids in San Antonio or investment in resuscitating Oklahoma City's downtown. We discover the importance of "Michigan nice" in explaining elite commitment to broadening opportunity in Grand Rapids, and we stress how the pride that Raleigh's leaders had in racially integrating its schools may have spilled over to other concerns. We note that the stories leaders tell themselves in regions that work tend to become similar (or normative) over time: collaboration as a keyword in San Antonio, the Triple Helix as the guiding principle for development in Raleigh, the rejection of Oklahoma City as a location for a United Airlines maintenance hub as a prompt to reexamine the area's quality of life.

More broadly, then, diverse and dynamic epistemic communities are about discovering and structuring processes to recreate a sense of the commons and of the common good. This perspective builds on and contributes to the broad literature on the commons—which has proffered evidence that cooperation and reciprocity are possible but which sometimes struggles to specify the processes in which such social norms are created (Benkler 2011). In our work below, we stress roots, relationships, and reason: that is, how sinking roots in a region for the long haul, recognizing and working with diverse constituencies and multiple actors over time, and striving to resolve issues through reasoned dialogue actually creates change *within* as well as *between* the relevant actors. Transformed by interactions with each other, the very identities of actors shift: they come to see doing good and planning for the regional future as fitting a set of standards and norms they hold for themselves and others.

We should emphasize—particularly given the literature on regional collaboratives and public–private partnerships—that we are *not* necessarily talking about formally institutionalized processes of collaboration or interaction. Such formal processes may help underpin diverse epistemic communities (as in Salt Lake City and Sacramento, cases discussed below as instances of planning-driven community building), and institutional incentives and infrastructures can help either to maintain or to erode epistemic communities over time. But ultimately the processes of producing collective knowledge and common ground that we are examining are rooted in communication between people over long periods of time that may only partially and temporarily correspond to existing organizational structures and may be better characterized as "communities of practice" (Wenger 1998).

MAKE THE ROAD BY TALKING

So how do we explore this interaction between equity, growth, and community? Below, we offer a road map to the book, outlining the chapters and what we hope to accomplish in each. The chapters build logically on one another. We start by establishing the econometric plausibility of our case and then turn to describing the quantitative and qualitative methods used to select cases. After that, we walk through the cases themselves, and we close by returning to the general lessons that emerge from the research, particularly about the importance of developing a new way for communities in a region to talk together about their common future.

That said, we are also aware that some readers might not fully enjoy or appreciate the discussions of hazard ratios, Cox regressions, and z-scores that animate chapters 2 and 3. Frankly, we don't quite understand that reaction—we tend to rejoice when there is a bounty of data and methods, and we hope that this volume actually illustrates how to effectively blend quantitative and qualitative approaches. However, we do not want to lose anyone along the way, and so we offer relatively simple explanations of the statistical work in the introductory and closing sections of each of those chapters; we also include a statistical appendix that contains a data panel for each region, to which we refer more sparingly in the text itself.

In any case, chapter 2 begins our argument by trying to establish some link between the dimensions of social disconnection and growth and equity outcomes. We do this by first reviewing research on the growth–equity relationship, including studies that make the link at both the international and interregional levels. We then describe our own work on the impacts of income inequality and various measures of social distance on regional economic sustainability, stressing that the ability to sustain employment growth over time is important because it can help regions and people avoid the long-lasting social and economic disruptions that occur as a result of economic downturns.

To look at the factors associated with long-term growth, we borrow from the methodology used in a recent study by the International Monetary Fund to examine the relations between various variables and the likelihood of falling out of "spells" of growth (which we measure as increases in employment). Looking at 184 metropolitan areas between 1990 and 2011, we find that the single largest factor that seems to curtail job growth is initial inequality; not far behind in their impact are racial segregation and metropolitan fragmentation. We also find that city–suburban political polarization has a negative impact. We bring all this together to suggest that building community—that is, overcoming fragmentation—may indeed be critical for resolving regional challenges and spurring more equitable and more sustainable growth.

Chapter 3 describes the case-study selection process. As we explain, we wanted to look at both cases where equity and growth come together, to see whether an epistemic community was present, *and* cases where knowledge communities were reportedly present and were or were not yielding good results. Given that, we first worked from an extensive set of data on job and earnings growth on the one hand and income distribution and poverty reduction on the other to determine which of the largest 192 regions (by population) performed well over a thirty-year period. (We also checked this against the end points for median household income and the Gini coefficient to ensure that we weren't picking up above-average performance from an abysmal starting point that closed the period with a nearly abysmal end point.)

From a wide range of possibilities, we chose eleven metropolitan areas, including a set of three in California and a set of three in North Carolina. (This was done in the hope that it would control for state laws and politics and allow for any metro divergence in governance to be more rooted in local regional cultures. As it turns out, less was gleaned from those controls, something that suggests more regional autonomy that even we expected, a topic discussed at more length in chapter 3.) We then entered the field, after developing a protocol aimed at understanding regional social norms around collaboration and conflict as well as the particular processes of regional information sharing, knowledge development, and knowledge interpretation across diverse constituencies. In each region, we conducted interviews with leaders from a wide range of constituencies, eliciting examples of collaboration and conflict, as well as looking at whether there were broadly shared sources of information for understanding both the region's economy and broad social conditions in the region.

Chapters 4 through 7 explore what we found—and they are organized around a sort of typology of regional epistemic communities that emerged in the course of the research. Chapter 4, for example, takes up instances in which there were quite explicit planning processes meant to actually create a shared knowledge community at the metropolitan level. One of the clearest examples of this is in the Salt Lake City metro, in which a nonprofit planning group called Envision Utah has helped create a deep sense of regional consciousness about population and housing growth strategies and decisions. We also look at the Sacramento metro, a place where a "Blueprint process" was actually undertaken by the local council of governments to help the region's residents recognize their common and interconnected fate, particularly around issues of transportation, land use, and housing development.

Chapter 5 takes up a different sort of epistemic community: one in which regional stewardship is more or less driven by business elites. Here, we look at three case studies: Grand Rapids, Charlotte, and Oklahoma City. We suggest that the first two show some of the limits of this type of approach. Charlotte, for example, is home to a storied set of business leaders who were eager to make it the exemplar of the New South in terms of both race relations and economic vitality. Its very success has brought a wave of newcomers who do not appreciate the history as much, and with old norms eroding, so too are key elements of civic culture, as well as the trajectory of economic growth. Grand Rapids is among the most paternalistic of our cases. There, interviewees even spoke of the wealthy entrepreneurs who provide regional leadership as "fathers"—and while its trajectory was positive through the 1980s and 1990s, the region stumbled in the 2000s as manufacturing declined.

On the other hand, Oklahoma City shows what can happen when elite leadership decides to respond to a shock with a commitment to dynamic change. After the region suffered the indignity of a major company's turning down significant tax breaks for relocating there—primarily because the quality of life was so bad that the company's executives were worried that they would not be able to attract and keep workers—Oklahoma City leaders undertook a conscious effort to reverse the damage of suburban sprawl to the urban center and bring about a major revitalization of the downtown. The effort included a willingness to increase taxes—in a heavily Republican region—and while the drivers and deciders may have hailed from the elite, significant attention was paid to incorporating populations of higher social need and less political clout.

While all of our case studies explore the role of conflict, that is the central theme of chapter 6. Here, we consider three cases: Greensboro, Fresno, and San Antonio. In the first of these, we note how wildly divergent visions of the region—with whites hoping that Blacks would "just get over it," while Black memories of Jim Crow and Klan violence remain remarkably vivid—have conspired to limit the evolution of a diverse *and* integrated epistemic community. In Fresno, we note how both structural factors and a history of conflict have led to both poor outcomes and fragmented politics. While there are some hopeful signs in Fresno—a new general plan emerging from the city holds the promise of addressing sprawl and promoting compact development in the long-neglected urban core—these cases could be read as simply suggesting that conflict is bad for your region's economic and epistemic health. But that is not necessarily the case.

Sometimes conflict can lead to collaboration. As it turns out, this is one of the main lessons from San Antonio. The region is currently heralded (and heralds itself) as a model of collaboration—and it has recently won a slew of federal designations under the Sustainable Communities Initiative, the Promise and Choice Neighborhoods programs, and most recently the Promise Zone effort. San Antonio has also made concrete progress on improving living standards and being more inclusive, as evidenced by its record (relative to the South) on measures of growth and distribution. But it came to what now seems like a positive set of outcomes through a set of sharp challenges to traditional centers of power by a highly mobilized set of minority constituents. This suggests that diverse epistemic communities can involve skirmish and struggle as well as conversation and consensus—and it is a point worth noting, given the need to lift up difficult issues of inequality in the contemporary United States.

Chapter 7 helps us think more about these national issues by looking at three places where the new knowledge economy has also involved knowledge communities: Silicon Valley, Raleigh, and Seattle. Silicon Valley hosts a sort of poster child for regional stewardship, Joint Venture Silicon Valley; however, a recent rise in globalization, inequality, and residential separation has helped detach leaders from the region in ways that are worrisome. Raleigh, on the other hand, more or less exemplifies the notion of a diverse and dynamic epistemic community with clear norms and a shared story. Its leaders often describe its growth lodestar as the Triple Helix (of which the three strands are university, government, and business), and long-timers consider one of its crowning achievements the desegregation of the school system (something that is now under threat from newcomers to the region). We close our case-study examination with Seattle, home to a mature process of consensus building through mediated gatherings of diverse sector leaders to share and interpret data together on regional issues. Coupled with a unique focus on equity—partly stemming from a strong history of multi-ethnic and multi-racial organizing during the Civil Rights era—this "Seattle process" has led to many accomplishments, including (as we mentioned above) the city's adoption of a joint labor–business proposal for the country's highest minimum wage.

In chapter 8, we try to synthesize the lessons of the case studies. We begin with a discussion of how the processes we unveil in our cases cannot easily be understood in the confines of traditional economic thinking, particularly models based on atomistic and disconnected actors (a point touched on above). We argue for a new microfoundational approach that recognizes how social norms and identities influence behavior and inform collaboration (or a lack thereof)—and we use that framework to suggest that diverse and dynamic epistemic communities involve transformations *in* actors as well as transactions *between* actors.

We then specifically focus on the conditions under which knowledge communities emerge, including: the role of shocks (such as rejection by an outside firm in the case of Oklahoma City or the pressures of future growth in the case of Salt Lake City); the presence or absence of formal governance structures (highlighting here, for example, the difference between the role of a metropolitan planning organization in Sacramento versus the privately initiated Envision Utah); and the impact of social movements and civic culture (for example, the emergence of principled conflict in the case of San Antonio or the commitment to process and conflict resolution in Seattle). Finally, we uncover from the cases what might be termed the mechanics of community building, including the development of shared knowledge and agendas, the need to frame issues in an inclusive way, and the importance of the development of collaborative leadership with a commitment to place.

In chapter 9, we try to explore the implications of this work for future research on regional economic and social trajectories. We suggest that diverse and dynamic epistemic communities are important in and of themselves since they contribute to a sense of civic membership—and that they can also enhance growth, innovation, and inclusion at the metropolitan level. While we acknowledge that much in this causal chain remains to be specified and also stress that there is not a fail-proof path from consensus to prosperity, we also suggest that such communities at least raise the likelihood of securing positive results. We then ask how such communities can be replicated across metropolitan areas, lifting up both nonprofit efforts like those of the Brookings Institution and PolicyLink and the innovative Sustainable Communities Initiative of the Obama administration. We note that challenges to replication are several, including the fact that connecting groups in a knowledge community is aided by a sense of place (so how does that work when there are many places?) and that some metropolitan regions may be either cursed or blessed by path dependence (cooperation breeds cooperation, conflict breeds conflict, and making the turn from one road to another is difficult).

We close the book by considering how the lessons learned might inform a more productive approach to the national crises of subpar job growth, worsening inequality, and political polarization—another sort of triple helix—with which we began this introductory chapter. We argue that diverse and dynamic knowledge networks can provide exactly the norms, standards, and (place) identities that can better link equity, growth, and community. Because they can generate genuine care for others, help participants develop communicative processes to balance competing needs, and forge a lived sense of common destiny, they provide the framework for achieving "win-win" solutions rather than Social Darwinist destruction.

As Yochai Benkler insists in his path-breaking volume, *The Penguin and the Leviathan: How Cooperation Triumphs over Self-Interest* (2011), talk is not actually cheap; it requires effort, and it can help change hearts and minds in ways that encourage collaboration rather than zero-sum competition. Another world—one which fosters both innovation and inclusion, both economic growth and social justice—is indeed possible, but getting there will involve a different set of regional and national conversations. We hope this volume will contribute to that new dialogue about economic theory, policy practice, and our American future.

CHAPTER 2

Driving That Train

Can Closing the Gap Facilitate
Sustained Growth?

One of the first concepts taught in undergraduate economics is that there is a trade-off between equity and efficiency, between fairness and economic growth. Much of that argument is rooted in the stylized experience of long-term economic development, including Kaldor's (1977) argument that high levels of savings among the rich—in order to invest in industries with large sunk costs—was a prerequisite for rapid growth, as well as the infamous "Kuznets curve," which suggests that inequality will rise in the early phases of economic growth (Kuznets 1955). In either case, the message is that interfering too early to promote a less skewed distribution of income could kill the engine of economic vitality.

This has certainly been the underlying philosophy behind the celebration of tax-cutting that has dominated US economic policymaking. In this view, aggregate demand—a factor that can be positively impacted by redistribution—may play a role in closing temporary employment gaps, but it cannot really impact long-term growth. The drivers of that growth are savings and investment—and surely placing more in the hands of the high-earning and high-saving classes through tax cuts can only be good for economic performance. In short, income distribution may be a moral concern, but the route to prosperity in the long term runs through income polarization in the short term. Luckily, growth will create the resources needed to address any lingering sense of injustice—and, as Kuznets noted (1955), development itself should eventually improve income distribution.

However, a funny thing happened on the way to this supply-side nirvana: the evidence for this position has become increasingly scant. A Congressional Research Service study found no correlation between tax cuts and economic growth over the last sixty years; it was withdrawn after pressure from Senate Republicans, erasing the evidence but not the facts (Weisman 2012). But perhaps the most spectacular refutation in recent years is the long-term data collected and presented by Emmanuel Saez, Thomas Piketty, and others (Atkinson, Piketty, and Saez 2011; Piketty 2014). It essentially suggests that the amelioration in income disparities noted by Kuznets in the middle of the twentieth century was an anomaly, not the rule.

And it's not just that the automatic improvements once predicted by mainstream economics have failed to show up. Well before the recent attention to the rise in the incomes of the richest in various societies, study after study bubbling up from the developing world seemed to suggest that those countries that took off from more equitable initial distributions, in fact, seemed to grow faster—and more stably—over time. Research in the metropolitan context in the United States also seemed to tip in the direction of equity's having a positive, not a negative, impact on growth. And it is noteworthy that the year before the sharp economic and financial crisis of 2008–2010 was also a postwar peak for the share of national income accruing to the top 1 percent of the country's households—a record just short of that set in 1928, the year before the Great Depression.

What does this potential relationship between equity and growth have to do with our central topic, the development of diverse and dynamic epistemic communities at the metropolitan level? Consider that traditional economic theory essentially argues that atomistic individuals maximizing their own utility in the context of markets are likely to land on a sustained "Pareto-optimal" equilibrium in which no one can be made better off without making someone else worse off. Social equity in this case is a question of winners and losers—and if pursuing redistribution has the negative impacts on incentives and savings that some economists believe, then everyone will actually lose from slower growth (although some will lose more than others). Better to go at each other's throats in the competitive race and trust that the invisible hand of the market will eventually steer us (perhaps staring warily and bitterly across the chasms that will result) to a promised land.

But what if that very process of fragmented competition undermines cooperation and solidarity and leads to both collective underinvestment and unproductive (and ultimately destructive) squabbling over the spoils by those who feel consistently left out? What if the creation of a sense of belonging and common purpose could instead improve our output and enhance our future? What if paying attention to equity—building it in to economic strategies from the get-go—could actually help prosperity be more sustainable as well as more widespread?

In this chapter, we look directly at the relationship between equity, social fragmentation, and the length of growth spells. While the evidence we present does not directly establish a role for diverse epistemic communities in achieving just growth—and even the case studies merely establish some sense of plausibility for the linkage—it is consistent with the idea that social norms of collaboration, cooperation, and fair play can improve regional economic results. As such, it provides at least one (even if slightly indirect) large-N platform for the chapters that follow.

We start below by reviewing some of the previous research on equity and growth, focusing first on the developing-country context before turning our attention to more recent work on America's metropolitan regions. We stress the newest research in this arena, which is focused not so much on the rate of growth as on its persistence over time; in particular, we highlight recent cross-country work by researchers at the International Monetary Fund (IMF) and then demonstrate how their approach could be transferred, as with the earlier work, to examine growth patterns in the United States.

To do that, we look at changes in employment for the 184 largest regions in the United States in 1990–2011. Interestingly, the variable with the most significant negative impact in the US context on the length of a regional growth spell is the initial level of inequality, a result much in line with the findings of IMF researchers in their cross-country comparisons. Equally important for this volume are the significant other factors impacting sustained growth we examined, including various measures of social and jurisdictional fragmentation, as well as a novel set of political homogeneity and spatial-sorting measures we introduce in a sort of coda to the main findings.

The overall message of this empirical exercise is straightforward. Socio-spatial fragmentation within a region can work against economic performance as well as social cohesion. Of course, this is exploratory research and it leaves many questions unanswered about why and how equity and cohesion matter (or are created). Untangling exactly how an epistemic community comes about and how it can lead economic and social agents to see more clearly how their interests are intertwined and act accordingly cannot be easily discerned from a regression analysis. That is the task of case-study research, and reporting on that research takes up the bulk of the rest of this book. But, for now, it's regression time. So brush up on your estimating techniques and interpretive skills as we review data sets, methodological challenges, and statistical results.

CAN EQUITY FACILITATE GROWTH?
Distribution and Prosperity: An International View

One of the most deeply held beliefs in economics is the notion that raising the minimum wage has important negative impacts on employment. After all, this is what the demand curve taught in intro courses clearly suggests, and in a 1979 survey of economists, despite profuse disagreements on a wide range of other issues, 90 percent of the profession concurred with this model of the labor market driven into their very fiber by both early training and groupthink (Kearl et al. 1979). The only problem was, as David Card and Alan Krueger insisted in their book, *Myth and Measurement* (1997), the evidence for a disemployment impact of the minimum wage just wasn't there. In fact, Card and Krueger argued that the negative employment effects found in time series research actually became weaker as sample size increased, quite the opposite of what one might expect if the underlying hypothesis were true; this suggested that these studies obtained their results through specification searches that sought to find the expected effects rather than let the data tell its own story. Once the data was allowed to drive the narrative—in their case, by comparing in real time what happened when one state raised its minimum wage while a neighboring state did not—there were not negative employment impacts.

This work has had an impact, dulling the opposition to minimum-wage increases, but it raises a question: Why do such beliefs exist and persist in the face of evidence to the contrary? In essence, prior assumptions are hard to shake when they are deeply held and deeply embedded in the shared lore of a knowledge community. Indeed, one of the reasons we have characterized productive epistemic communities as "diverse and dynamic" is that we think diversity can work against the characteristics of clubbishness and insularity that can lead to analytical and other mistakes. In this regard, it is important to realize that economists have their own circles and their own priors. They may see themselves as being as rational as the economic agents they purport to model, but going against the grain can have its consequences—for careers as well as for self-conception and group acceptance (Fourcade, Ollion, and Algan 2014).

Consider, for example, the generally held belief that financial markets are well-functioning and excel at anticipating the future ("rational expectations"). It's a fundamental precept to which economists have clung despite massive over-lending to the developing world, a savings and loan crisis that shook American finance, and a binge of subprime mortgages packaged into collateralized debt obligations that ripped open the world economy in 2007–2008. In an essay aptly entitled "Never Saw It Coming," former Federal Reserve chair Alan Greenspan (2013) notes that "For decades, most economists, including me, had concluded that irrational factors could not fit into any reliable method of forecasting." Greenspan now admits that we need to change our models of human behavior, but that seems a bit like arguing for the purchase of fire insurance after watching arsonists burn the house down once again.

Another belief firmly held in economics is that redistribution could slow economic growth, particularly in the early stages of economic development. Yet this long-held view about the growth–equity trade-off was challenged by a wave of multivariate and multi-country studies conducted in the 1990s and early 2000s (see Aghion, Caroli, and García-Peñalosa 1999 for a review). Alesina and Perotti (1996), for example, argued that inequality leads to social tension and political instability, thus lowering certainty, investment, and economic growth. Meanwhile, Rodrik (1999) noted that the ability of countries to handle external shocks depends in large part on the strength of conflict-management institutions such as government, the rule of law, and social safety nets, which themselves reflect and produce certain distributions. The latter argument certainly resonates with our notion that closing social distance can help ameliorate social conflict that can get in the way of growth.

But it's not only that a more equitable distribution of income can ameliorate social conflict and forestall crisis. Both Alesina and Rodrik (1994) and Persson and Tabellini (1994) suggested that the more equitable a society's access to productive resources, the less likely that society is to seek redistributive policies that can reduce growth by introducing economic distortions, partly because the median voter may see more interest in protecting property rights. This is a sort of ironic argument, in which equity protects innovation and competition: in a society where rewards are more widely spread, the connection between higher incomes and perceived productivity is clearer, and modest disparities do not yield politics that will upset investors.

Dymski and Pastor (1991) also provided an early insight into this effect in their study of the relationship between bank lending and debt crises in Latin American countries. They found that those countries that were more unequal in their distribution of income tended to be favored by private lenders (accounting for other factors such as GDP growth and trade openness), but that those countries also tended to wind up with payments crises later on. Since all the other factors that had a positive effect on lending also had a negative effect on crises, they labeled the inequality measure a "misleading signal" and argued that strong priors about the trade-offs between equity and growth on the part of bankers (and economists) were possibly one reason why the equity–stability relationship was not recognized. We return to this point in the conclusion.

Other researchers have argued that directly targeting poverty and inequality in the developing world may actually be essential to growth, especially through policies that increase the productivity of the poor, such as spending on education and democratization of access to finance (Birdsall, Ross, and Sabot 1995; Deninger and Squire 1996). Lopez and Serven (2009) also argue that poverty more generally deters investment, which in turn lowers growth. In any case, the picture the reader should take away is simple. There's been a revolution in thinking in the development context that stresses not just the fairness aspects of inclusion but also its potential impact (albeit often through less than perfectly clear causal chains) on broader economic outcomes.

Equity and Economic Growth in America's Metropolitan Areas

While this notion of the complementarity of equity and growth has had some impact on the thinking and policies of multilateral institutions, it is only recently that the notion of a positive relationship between equity and long-term growth—beyond the usual Keynesian notions that placing money in the hands of less well-off consumers will yield a bigger economic bang for any stimulus dollar—has made its way into the discussion of the overall US economy (Boushey and Hersh 2012; Stiglitz 2012).[1] To be sure, ground has been gained for this perspective, with authors like Nobel Prize winner Joseph Stiglitz arguing that highly unequal incomes can lead to excessive financialization of the economy and rent-seeking (that is, favor-seeking) by the wealthy in their dealings with government.

But long before the potential impacts of inequality on the economy surfaced so strongly on the national level, many had been making this argument at the level of US metropolitan regions. The rationale for moving to the metropolitan level in both theorizing and practical economic planning was, as suggested in chapter 1, a growing recognition that this was an important new operative level of the world economy—a geographic unit big enough to achieve some economies of scale, while also small enough to sustain the sort of face-to-face interactions that facilitate the creation of industrial clusters, nontradable interdependencies, and the development of tacit knowledge (Storper 1997). Interestingly, this geographic and analytical shift essentially opened up the space to consider equity more deeply: if face-to-face relations really did matter, then perhaps looking across the table at a group that was frustrated and angry about being left out was more likely to lead to civil unrest (à la Los Angeles in 1992) than to a public–private partnership for central-city revitalization.

With the analytical opening available, several researchers focused on the relation between city–suburb disparities and economic outcomes. The conclusion, perhaps surprising to some, was that such geographic and social separation *within* a region actually limited growth possibilities (Barnes and Ledebur 1998; Savitch et al. 1993). In a review of the earliest studies in this vein, many of which seemed to parallel the findings in the international development field, Gottlieb (2000) rightly argued that researchers were paying insufficient attention to multivariate controls and issues of simultaneity. However, Voith (1998) and Pastor et al. (2000) attempted to address these issues by incorporating other explanatory factors *and* considering the feedback effects of growth on poverty and income distribution, and the findings remained supportive. Even in a simultaneous setting, Voith found a positive association of suburban growth with city growth, while Pastor et al. found that various measures of inequality had a negative impact on per capita income growth over the 1980s in seventy-four regions.

Examining 341 regions in the United States and controlling for other variables that should promote growth, Pastor (2006) later found that real per capita income growth was negatively affected by such distributional measures as the ratio of city to suburban poverty, the percentage of poor residents in high-poverty neighborhoods, the ratio of income at the 60th percentile to household income at the 20th percentile, and a measure of residential segregation at the metro level. Again, the results held up to challenges of simultaneity, suggesting a causal direction from equity to growth (as well as its converse). In subsequent work, Pastor and Benner (2008) found that this dragging effect of inequality on growth held even in what might be termed "weak market" metros—places where some would say that anemic growth is an excuse for effectively treating equity as an afterthought.

Federal Reserve economists conducted a similar analysis for nearly 120 metropolitan areas throughout the United States (Eberts, Erickcek, and Kleinhenz 2006). Using factor analysis, the researchers analyzed eight key variables that influence economic growth on the regional level, whether positively or negatively, including a region's skilled workforce; active small businesses; ethnic diversity and minority business ownership; level of racial inclusion; costs associated with a declining industrial base; income inequality (measured by income disparity and number of children living in poverty); quality-of-life variables (including universities, recreation, and transportation); and concentrated poverty in core cities. The results: a skilled workforce, high levels of racial inclusion, and progress on income equality correlate strongly and positively with economic growth.

It's a Matter of Time: Equity, Social Connection, and Growth Spells

While this research on US metros has looked at economic growth rates, the international literature that helped inspire the work has moved on to look at how to *sustain* economic growth. One of the striking characteristics of growth in developing countries over the last fifty years has been its lack of persistence, with frequent fits and starts that better match the trajectory of a roller coaster than the smoother path forward many countries would prefer. Thus, a growing body of literature has been looking at turning points in countries' growth patterns, trying to explain both what helps countries shift from economic decline toward economic growth and what causes an end to a growth period (Aguiar and Gopinath 2007; Hausmann, Pritchett, and Rodrik 2005; Hausmann, Rodríguez, and Wagner 2006; Jerzmanowski 2005; Jones and Olken 2008; Pattillo and Gupta 2006; Rodrik 1999).

One particularly relevant strand of work was conducted by IMF researchers looking at what explained a country's ability to sustain economic growth and forestall a downturn (Berg, Ostry, and Zettelmeyer 2012).

These authors argue that forestalling the end of growth spells is especially critical for the poor countries of the world, in which economic volatility and vulnerability to economic setbacks can be as much a problem as slow or negative overall growth. Countries with more sustained growth spells, for example, may also create an environment where investors feel more secure about the future, facilitating a virtuous cycle (Berg and Ostry 2011).

To get at the determinants of sustained growth, Berg, Ostry, and Zettlelmeyer (2012) first identify a total of 104 distinct growth spells of at least five years in a total of 140 countries (both industrial and developing) since the 1950s. They then examine a series of factors that might help explain the likelihood that a country would fall out of a growth spell, including: external shocks; political and economic institutions; inequality and fractionalization; social and physical indicators; levels of financial development; levels and types of globalization; patterns of current account, competitiveness and export structure; and patterns of macroeconomic stability.

Some of their findings reinforce previous research. For example, external shocks and macroeconomic volatility are negatively associated with the length of growth spells, while "good" political institutions are associated with longer growth spells. The authors also use a variety of indicators—including competitive exchange rates, external capital structures weighted toward foreign direct investment, and export product sophistication—that reinforce arguments about the value of export orientation and trade liberalization, especially the ability to produce more sophisticated products.

However, what is particularly interesting, and relevant to our work—and what the researchers themselves describe as a "striking" result—is that the length of growth spells is strongly related to income distribution, with more equal societies tending to be able to sustain growth over a longer period. Across their sample, a 1-percentage-point increase in the Gini coefficient of income inequality is associated with an 11-to-15-percent reduction in the expected duration of a growth spell. In a summary model that combines a range of indicators, several factors remain significant in predicting the length of growth spells, but "income inequality is among the most robust predictors of duration" (Berg, Ostry, and Zettelmeyer 2012, 160).

There may be important reasons to look at growth spells in the United States as well. After all, spells of unemployment can have lasting effects on people's lifetime earnings long after they are once again able to secure employment, as well as causing psychological distress (Daly and Delaney 2013; Mroz and Savage 2006). There is also evidence that new graduates entering the labor market during a recession experience lower earnings over the long term, compared with those entering the labor market during growth periods (Kahn 2010; Oreopoulos, von Wachter, and Heisz 2012). Moreover, to the extent that we think variables like social equity, social norms, and social connection may have an impact on growth, we would expect this effect to be longer-term rather than shorter-term—to be more associated with decades of forward progress than with a single year's surge or dive.

So in this chapter we test the relations between measures of inequality and social disconnection and the length of growth spells, essentially offering a parallel to the work of the IMF researchers but in a domestic metropolitan context. The focus on the length of growth spells, rather than simply the pace of economic growth, is admittedly novel in the US context. We have seen no studies of America's metro regions which take up this longer-term perspective other than Hill et al. (2012), although the focus there is more on testing a variety of different notions of economic resilience. Of course, just because little has been done does not mean that we or others should shy away; indeed, we hope that the quite exploratory research in this chapter will induce a new wave of work. But first things first: What do we find when we look at the relations between various measures of income inequality, social disconnection, and the duration of economic growth?

EXPLAINING SUSTAINED METROPOLITAN GROWTH IN THE UNITED STATES

Defining Growth Spells and Their Long-Term Impacts

One of the first steps in this analysis is simply to define what we mean by sustained growth. In their work, Berg, Ostry, and Zettelmeyer (2012) consider five years of annual growth the minimum threshold for a growth spell (they also consider an eight-year threshold, but most of the analysis they present winds up focusing on the five-year threshold). In our examination below, the universe consists of the largest 184 metropolitan regions in the United States (that is, all the core based statistical areas, or CBSAs, that had a population of 250,000 or more as of the 2010 census). For our measure of economic growth, we used data from the Quarterly Census of Employment and Wages, which has a consistent measure of monthly employment starting in 1990.

We look at quarterly average employment, rather than the reported month-to-month employment, mostly because of the volatility in the underlying monthly employment figures. We also calculate whether a region is growing by comparing total average employment in a particular quarter to employment in the same quarter of the previous year; the year-over-year measure was used as a way of adjusting for seasonal variations in employment. We then set a threshold such that we consider a region as experiencing a growth spell if it experienced at least twelve quarters of uninterrupted growth in this measure of quarter-to-quarter employment—and obviously, we then considered how long this growth exceeded the three-year-minimum threshold.

At the time of our analysis, we had the full set of employment data from 1990 to 2011, for a theoretical possible maximum growth spell (all job growth, all the time) of 84 quarters. While no one hit that stellar threshold, the resulting database included 324 growth spells in 181 of the 184 regions. There were three regions with no growth spell of at least 12 quarters in this time period, and while it might seem a bit cruel to call them out, here goes: Buffalo–Niagara Falls, NY; Merced, CA; and Sarasota-Bradenton-Venice, FL.[2]

Do growth spells really matter? Although we earlier highlighted some potential impacts of sustained growth (for example, the impact on the earnings trajectory of new entrants to the labor market), one might argue that the length of the period of growth is of little consequence for overall prosperity—perhaps a boom-and-bust economy is volatile, but it will deliver high employment and rebalance labor's bargaining power in a way that facilitates more rapid wage growth and hence redistribution over time. This may be why most previous research has been on overall growth rates. Another possible reason for focusing on rates is that, as we found out, assembling a database on the duration of growth is no easy matter. Our own view is that more robust or sustained growth might have a stronger and long-lasting impact on bargaining power (and we're also data masochists, so going where no researcher had gone before sounded kind of fun).

So what does the data say? As it turns out, this is a debate that may be a bit moot: the length of growth spells and the overall growth rate are actually fairly well correlated. Table 2.1 takes the 181 regions which had growth spells and breaks them into categories based on the number of quarters in the overall period that a region was in a growth spell. The categories are chosen to create bands that are non-arbitrary but somewhat similar in terms of the number of regions that falls in each band

TABLE 2.1   GROWTH SPELLS AND REGIONAL OUTCOMES

Number of quarters in growth spells	Number of regions in category	Employment growth over whole period	Growth in real weekly earnings over whole period
12–20	18	6.0%	6.5%
21–30	17	10.7%	15.1%
31–40	25	17.3%	14.0%
41–50	31	19.8%	20.2%
51–55	23	22.9%	19.1%
56–60	31	43.3%	20.6%
61–70	36	61.2%	22.1%

(the basic results are not sensitive to our particular choice of breaks for the bands). Note that the minimum is 12 quarters—one needs that to have experienced a growth spell at all—and the maximum that any region spent in growth spells over the whole period is 70 quarters. We then calculate the growth in employment and real weekly earnings (also from the Quarterly Census of Employment and Wages data) over the whole period. The data suggests that more time in growth spells generates more overall employment growth and generally higher earnings (although the earnings effect seems to taper off in the higher bands).[3]

What about the impacts on employment and earnings of the spells themselves (rather than the length of time any particular region spends in a spell)? Table 2.2 shows those results. Note that the longest single growth spell was 69 quarters (go, Ogden, Utah!) and that, as we mentioned above, there are a total of 324 growth spells which range from 12 to 69 quarters. One feature of table 2.2 is that we are also able to offer a view of performance for periods which fall out of growth before our 12-quarter threshold. There are 332 growth periods where growth occurred for less than a year. These were indeed booms, with high employment growth on an annualized basis, but since they are associated with declining earnings and immediately fell into recession (and since growth spells are associated, as seen in table 2.1, with better growth for a region over the long haul), it's hard to see why this is a desirable outcome.

On the other hand, starting from growth periods that run from 5 to 11 quarters, we see that annualized employment growth generally rises with the length of the growth spell; the increase in real earnings also improves in longer growth spells (starting from 12 quarters on), but the effect is seemingly less strong. The big takeaway from these tables is that growth spells matter, since longer spells are associated with faster

TABLE 2.2   GROWTH SPELL OUTCOMES

Lengths of growth period (in quarters)	Number of growth periods in category	Annualized employment growth	Annualized growth in real weekly earnings
1–4	332	2.7%	–0.8%
5–11	167	1.9%	1.0%
12–16	70	2.2%	0.7%
17–20	69	2.2%	0.8%
21–28	73	2.6%	0.9%
29–38	67	2.9%	1.3%
39–69	45	4.2%	1.3%
Overall		1.0%	0.7%

growth and higher employment outcomes over time, with earnings showing a similar but weaker relationship to the length of growth spells.

Methodological Approach

So, what determines the length of a growth spell? In their country-level analysis, Berg, Ostry, and Zettelmeyer (2012) look at a range of indicators, some of which—like inequality and social conditions—have direct parallels to regional economies. Others, such as those related to macroeconomic stability or level of development in financial institutions, are essentially uniform across the entire United States and thus are not appropriate for an analysis of regional growth spells. Rather than following in complete lockstep the categories, some less relevant than others, employed by Berg, Ostry, and Zettelmeyer, we categorize our variables into the following domains: external shocks and vulnerability; jurisdictional fragmentation; inequality and separation; background social indicators; and economic structure and institutions. We subsequently consider some explicitly political measures of polarization, but as we note there, inclusion of these factors seriously reduces sample size, so we add those as a bit of an exploratory postscript.

Within our domains, we include some factors, such as the education profile of the population, the legacy structure of industry, and the relative openness to exports, that are more or less structural. Of course, change in those factors can occur if there is dedicated leadership, but one of the things we are suggesting in this volume is that such leadership is harder to achieve in the context of inequality and social alienation. Thus, we pay special attention to the more social variables—and it is interesting that these are the ones that actually dominate the regression landscape in terms of consistent and statistically significant impact.

Aside from considering somewhat similar domains, another way in which our approach parallels that of Berg, Ostry, and Zettelmeyer is that this is a highly exploratory exercise. Those authors state: "We sequentially test the relevance of particular regressors of interest, while including some minimal controls. . . . At the end, we summarize by showing the results of a few parsimonious regressions that control for all or most of the variables that were found to matter during the sequential testing process" (152). We follow suit, first looking at individual regressors and then combining them and offering one more parsimonious specification at the end.

While, like that of Berg, Ostry, and Zettelmeyer, this approach is somewhat unorthodox (there is no strong model specification prior to exploration), we do offer heuristic rationales for our variables; and we view this initial work as setting the stage for future quantitative and qualitative work. Partly because of this, we report not just on the usual significance levels (.01, .05, and .10) but also note when variables achieve a significance around .20. The idea is to point to relationships for which further research will be needed.

One final wrinkle. Because we are interested in the impact of polarization on the ability to forge an epistemic community, we also consider a range of political variables, with a conclusion that is quite intriguing. It turns out that the more uniform an area is politically overall, the more likely it is to sustain growth, while the more ideologically fragmented it is by geography, the less likely it is to sustain growth. This is exactly the stuff of epistemic communities—but it turns out that the sample sizes fall considerably in this analysis (mostly because we need multiple counties to chart the political polarization *within* regions), so we offer it below as a suggestive rather than conclusive finding.

Testing Techniques and Data Sources

The testing technique specifically used in this exercise is a Cox regression, a particular type of survival analysis regression method. In our case, we are trying to see which factors are associated with an early exit from sustained growth. The reported coefficients are so-called hazard ratios that are always positive; when a coefficient is greater than 1, that means the variable being tested is associated with falling out of a

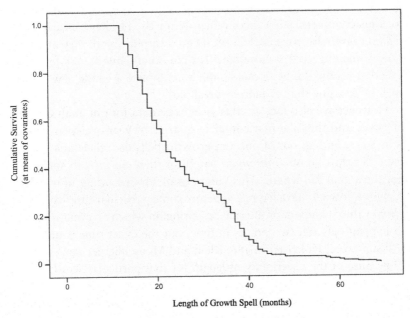

FIGURE 2.1. Survival Function for Growth Spells.

growth spell; when the coefficient is less than 1, the variable being tested is associated with staying longer in a growth spell.[4]

What do the spells look like? Figure 2.1 presents the unconditional hazard for spells of a minimum of 12 quarters, essentially showing the cumulative survival function of our growth spells. Note that no country falls out in the first 12 quarters because, by definition, one needs to have a three-year growth spell to make it into the sample. As can be discerned from the cumulative-survival dimension, there is a fairly steady fall-off of cases as we move past the 12-quarter threshold. Then the line becomes quite flat at around 45 quarters, indicating that there are much fewer cases above that level. This pattern is of course also reflected in table 2.2, although this gives a better sense of the spread as we cross the 39-quarter threshold used in that table.

We are essentially estimating the probability of falling out of that cumulative survival threshold, and one key issue in such hazard analysis is right-censoring—which occurs when an observation is terminated before the expected event occurs. All survival-analysis software is designed to handle this kind of right-censoring, and in our case only one growth spell was continuing at the end of our period of analysis. (Conveniently for the econometrics but inconveniently for the residents, nearly every region eventually got knocked off its growth path by the Great Recession. Some did recover more quickly than others, but in very few cases was there enough time in our sample to complete a whole new growth spell by crossing the 12-quarter threshold).

However, we also face another issue. The data for our analysis starts in 1990, and thus the first complete quarter of year-over-year growth is in 1991, and 29 out of our 324 growth spells date their first quarter then. We thus know a *minimum* length of these 29 growth spells, but not the actual full length. This differs from left-censoring, in which an event is known to have happened before some particular time, so a *maximum* value is known, or internal censoring, in which an event is known to happen between two points in time, but the exact time is unknown (Allison 2012; Finkelstein 1986; Klein and Moeschberger 2003).

Because of the uncertainty of length for that particular set of growth spells and a lack of clear guidance in the literature on how best to handle such cases, we ran two different sets of regressions: one in which we simply excluded those twenty-nine cases with incomplete growth lengths, and one in which we included them and treated them as regular growth spells, assuming that their growth spell did actually begin at the beginning of our time-period (which may not be problematic since the United States was coming out of a national recession in that period, so many growth spells *were* just beginning). There were only minor differences in the regression results, so we present the findings below for the entire sample.

Finally, right-hand-side variables, unless indicated, came from a database assembled for the Building Resilient Regions Network (supported by the MacArthur Foundation and organized by Margaret Weir of the University of California, Berkeley; http://brr.berkeley.edu/) that contains economic, civic, social, housing, geographic, and demographic measures for several decades for all 934 CBSAs in the United States. One special feature of the data is that CBSA boundaries have been made consistent to compare measures across the 1970, 1980, 1990, and 2000 censuses and recent versions of the American Community Survey. (Here, we just use the 1990 and 2000 data to construct the independent variables given the time period we are examining.)

REGRESSION ANALYSIS

In all of our regressions, we include dummy variables for census region (as did Hill et al. 2012), as well as regional per capita income and a measure of metro size as controls. Regional per capita income is included partly because a parallel starting income measure is used in Berg, Ostry, and Zettelmeyer; moreover, the regional economic convergence literature generally controls for initial regional income to account for convergence to the mean (see the discussion and parallel construction for growth equations in Pastor, Lester, and Scoggins 2009). The coefficients on initial income, which we do not report to conserve space, always pointed in the appropriate direction (higher per capita income is associated with shorter growth spells) and remain significant in our full specification (similar to the results in Berg, Ostry, and Zettelmeyer 2012). We included metro size, a familiar control, on the grounds that larger metros might be more resilient to shocks—and that is indeed the case in our regressions. Our measure for size, the log of the metro population normed relative to the sample, is similar to the metro-size variable used in a recent effort by Li, Campbell, and Fernandez (2013).

Note that these base variables, as well as the other variables we look at, are not allowed to vary during the time of the growth spells; indeed, what we are testing is how the initial conditions at the beginning of a spell affect the length of a spell. However, growth spells get started at different times—some in the 1990s and some in the 2000s—and we cannot assume that initial conditions are the same for those starting a decade or so apart. We therefore select the year of these variables that is the closest available data prior to the beginning of the growth spells (e.g. 1990 census data for growth spells beginning in the 1990s and 2000 census data for growth spells beginning in the 2000s). One could also simply look at the whole period and focus on 1990 starting points for every spell; that approach is more convenient in terms of computation and has its own analytical rationale. As it turns out, using only the 1990s starting points yields similar results, often with more significance for some variables; however, we believe that adjusting decadal starting points is methodologically superior, and since it works against finding significance, this is the sort of bias (if any is introduced) one wants to result from researcher choices about methods.

Building the Regression in Parts

External Shocks and Vulnerability

An external shock, such as a national recession, is one of the factors most likely to end a growth spell. But in terms of considering the durability of a growth spell, the question is whether the region's growth

TABLE 2.3   EXTERNAL SHOCKS AND VULNERABILITY

	Hazard ratio	Sig.
Percentage of growth spell in national recession	1.018	.09
Exports as percentage of gross metropolitan product	1.011	.03

NOTE: The variables are presented in a single table for convenience, but each was entered separately.

trajectory can withstand such shocks—and so we consider here the percentage of total quarters within the growth spell in which the national economy was in recession. Our notion is that the longer the spell has been impacted by the recession, the more likely it is to end—and the results for that hypothesis, reported in table 2.3, are significant at the .10 level, with the expected sign (in the tables that follow, any result that is significant at least at the .20 level is bolded). Again, recall how one should read these coefficients. The 1.018 coefficient indicates that, holding all other covariates constant, an increase of one unit (in this case a percentage-point increase in the share of the region's growth spell that the nation is in an overall recession) is associated with a nearly 2-percent *increase* in hazard (or likelihood) of growth ending (with a coefficient less than 1 indicating a similarly figured percentage *decrease* in the likelihood of growth ending).[5]

Another way to get at external shocks and regional vulnerability is to consider the potential impacts of truly external factors, such as exports. To get at this, we calculated the proportion of gross regional product accounted for by international exports with data taken from the Department of Commerce. The first year for which we had the export data was 2005, and we averaged the years 2005 to 2010 to smooth out yearly variations and instead catch the overall structure. The basic notion is that a higher level of exposure to international trade could lead to less sustained growth. While the usual economic supposition is that more trade would be good for a nation as a whole, more susceptibility of one region's industrial clusters to the rhythms of the international economy could bring risks as well as rewards. In any case, what we have is a highly imperfect measure of this trade openness, partly because it is taken from the end of the period rather than before, a failing to which we simply plead that we had no other such variable available to us for the earlier periods.[6] The direction is as expected—a higher share of exports is associated with a greater hazard of falling out of a growth spell—and it is significant at the .03 level.

Jurisdictional Fragmentation

The variables discussed above are essentially structural controls. We begin now with the first of the variables that might be consistent with notions of an epistemic community: the degree of metropolitan political fragmentation. Consistent with our focus on epistemic communities, there is now a voluminous literature suggesting that regional collaboration may be important for promoting economic competitiveness (Cooke and Morgan 1998; Martin, Kitson, and Tyler 2012; Scott 1998; Storper 1997). Even advocates for regional equity, who are generally more focused on the unfavorable terrain for the less advantaged posed by separate and unlinked jurisdictions, have suggested that the fragmentation of local government within metropolitan regions can lead to inefficient public investments—and presumably less robust growth (Rusk 2003).

Of course, not everyone is a regionalist. Some recent research has suggested that Tieboutian competition, in which governments compete to offer amenities, and residents and businesses sort across the landscape to maximize consumer well-being and firm-level profits, can be consistent with more rapid growth (Grassmueck and Shields 2010). This is the laissez-faire perspective, to be sure, that is, that a flowering of jurisdictional divisions will yield more growth, not less. In any case, both perspectives suggest that the fragmentation of metropolitan governance is implicated in growth outcomes.

Our own perspective is that fragmentation is likely to make the formation of diverse epistemic communities more difficult—and that that could have impacts on both growth and equity. But regardless of one's views, a key issue is how to measure jurisdictional separation. To do this, some researchers simply count the number of governments in a metro region, either in absolute terms or on some per capita basis (Dolan 1990; Goodman 1980; Grassmueck and Shields 2010; Ostrom, Parks, and Whitaker 1974). A second approach, most prominently represented in the Hirshmann-Herfindal Index, considers the concentration of expenditures of all governmental units in a region, and is measured as the sum of the squared percentage of each player's share of the total market (Grassmueck and Shields 2010; Scherer and Ross 2009).

A third and newer approach, developed by David Miller of the University of Pittsburgh, builds on this Hirshmann-Herfindal Index approach but also incorporates the number of jurisdictions in the region (Hamilton, Miller, and Paytas 2004; Miller and Lee 2009).[7] The resulting Metropolitan Power Diffusion Index (MPDI) is derived by using

TABLE 2.4 REGIONAL GOVERNANCE

	Hazard ratio	Sig.
Metropolitan Power Diffusion Index	1.056	.15

the square root of the percentage contribution to total regional expenditures, rather than the square, a process that gives greater mathematical value to the smaller units—and it is conveniently available for all metropolitan areas in 1987, 1997, and 2007.

When measured alone (along with the regional, per capita income, and metro-size controls), it turns out that the MPDI is associated with the shortening of growth spells—more diffuse regions are more likely to fall out of a growth spell—albeit at the .15 significance level (see table 2.4). As we will see later, the statistical significance improves slightly when the MPDI is included in regressions with a range of other indicators, suggesting that political fragmentation might be a drag on sustained growth.

Inequality and Social Separation

What about more core measures of social distance? Following Berg, Ostry, and Zettelmeyer (2012), we looked at the role of inequality in shaping growth spells, using a Gini coefficient measure derived from metropolitan household-income data from the decennial census.[8] We also looked at the size of the "minority middle class," that is, the proportion of African American and Latino households that are in the middle-income bracket for the region (first separately, then combined, although we present the results only for the combined measure to save space).[9] We also wanted to look at other issues of social separation, so we considered a standard measure of residential segregation called the dissimilarity index, in this case calculated in terms of non-Hispanic whites versus everyone else, as well as the ratio of city to suburban poverty rates.[10]

As shown in table 2.5, the Gini coefficient turns out to be extremely significant and powerful. A 1-percentage-point increase in the Gini is associated with a 21-percent increase in the likelihood that a region will fall out of the growth spell. Our various minority-middle-class variables were significant; to conserve space, we show only the combined measures, which suggest that regions with a higher percentage of minorities in middle-class income brackets are more likely to have

TABLE 2.5   INEQUALITY AND SOCIAL SEPARATION

	Hazard ratio	Sig.
Gini coefficient (initial level)	1.213	.00
Percentage minority residents in middle income brackets	0.911	.00
Dissimilarity index, non-Hispanic whites	1.010	.12
Ratio, principal city to suburban poverty rates	1.098	.23

NOTE: The variables are presented in a single table for convenience, but each was entered separately.

longer growth spells. The dissimilarity index results suggest that more segregated regions have shorter growth spells; a higher city–suburb poverty differential is also associated with shorter growth, but this result is significant only at the .23 level. This is certainly not completely convincing, but it is suggestive of a positive economic role for activities that can shrink social distance—say, by creating a metropolitan epistemic community.

Background Social Indicators

In addition to inequality and social separation, we sought to look at background social indicators such as educational attainment and levels of immigration. Our idea, reasonably enough, is that a more educated populace would yield more sustained growth. Our hypothesized effect about immigration was less clear (since a rising immigrant presence is generally thought to add energy to the economy but could also trigger growth-damaging conflict through the impacts of shifts in demographic composition on local politics; Pastor and Mollenkopf 2012). As for operationalizing these measures: for education, we looked at two variables, the proportion of the population twenty-five and older with a bachelor's degree or higher and the proportion with at least a high school diploma but less than a bachelor's degree. For immigration, we looked at the percentage of the foreign-born (immigrant) population in each region prior to the growth spell being tested.

The results are shown in table 2.6. Of our two education measures, the proportion of the population with at least a high school diploma but less than a bachelor's degree is statistically significant (at the .03 level), with regions with a larger proportion of these middle-education populations being less likely to fall out of a growth spell; recall that each of these is being entered separately, so the default category in each case is everyone else. The proportion of immigrants in the region also

TABLE 2.6 SOCIAL INDICATORS

	Hazard ratio	Sig.
Adult population with BA degree or higher	1.010	.44
Adult population with HS to AA degree	0.975	.03
Percentage of population foreign-born	1.029	.00

NOTE: The variables are presented in a single table for convenience, but each was entered separately.

has a significant (negative) relationship to the length of growth spell, perhaps reflecting the sort of "immigrant shock" to the metropolitan political and social systems discussed by Pastor and Mollenkopf (2012).

It is worth noting that some interesting differences in the roles of these background social indicators emerged when we excluded those twenty-nine growth spells of uncertain length that possibly started prior to 1990. We have not mentioned the impact of excluding these spells before since there was not much difference when they were excluded. However, when we drop the twenty-nine spells of uncertain length, our various indicators are all statistically significant, and the percentage of adult population with a bachelor's degree or higher becomes significant at a .04 level and has a hazard ratio of 1.03. This higher education variable seems to suggest that regions with a high proportion of highly educated population are more likely to fall out of a growth spell. It may be that those regions are likely to have more employment in technology and information-driven industries, which substantial research has demonstrated are significantly more volatile in their employment patterns (Brynjolfsson and Saunders 2010; Shapiro and Varian 1998). That this effect rises when we exclude growth spells that may have been started before 1991 squares with this; the high-tech effect should be stronger later in the period in question. However, our attempt to control for high-tech and high finance employment more directly through the inclusion of these labor-market shares in the regression (however imperfectly measured) does not transform higher education into having a positive impact on sustainable growth. This remains a topic for further research.

Employment Structure and Institutions

We also looked at three broad measures of industrial structure in the region, namely the percentages of the workforce employed in construction, in manufacturing, and in public administration, as well as one set

TABLE 2.7   ECONOMIC STRUCTURE AND INSTITUTIONS

	Hazard ratio	Sig.
Percentage employment in public administration	0.954	.02
Percentage employment in manufacturing	1.004	.66
Percentage employment in construction	0.971	.46
Percentage of workforce covered by a union contract	1.003	.73

NOTE: The variables are presented in a single table for convenience, but each was entered separately.

of economic institutions: the percentage of the workforce covered by unions.[11] As shown in table 2.7, the percentage of employment in public administration is associated with longer growth spells; manufacturing and construction, each entered alone, do not have a significant impact on the length of growth spells. The unionization variable seems associated with shorter growth spells (perhaps squaring with the perspective that unions introduce labor market rigidity—but it is also important to remember that unionization and manufacturing tend to be correlated in these time periods), but the result is not statistically significant.

Integrated Model

In the previous sections, we looked at each of the indicators separately, partly because of the exploratory nature of our work. Here, we enter (nearly) all our various regressors into a single regression, with the exercise offering a look into the relative power of the independent variables as well as their interaction. As with the individual regressions, we include controls for census region, per capita income, and metro size. There are several caveats to mention before looking at the results of this combined regression work.

First, we included only one educational-attainment indicator, due to obvious high levels of collinearity; we chose the one that was significant in the stand-alone regression, that is, the share of the working-age population with at least a high school diploma and no more than an AA degree. Second, in our initial integrated regression, we found that that variable, which essentially captures the share of the broadly educated middle, was actually associated with shorter growth spells, the opposite of its impact in a univariate context. Since this shift was unusual, we conducted a series of exploratory regressions in which we dropped the inequality measure. We found that with the economic-structure variables and our educational indicator alone, a broadly educated middle was associated with longer growth spells (as it was when it was entered alone), albeit only at the .20 level. The sign on education flipped when we introduced the Gini coefficient—and this is actually sensible, given that inequality is likely to be larger if there is a lower percentage of this mid-level-educated population.

To deal with this issue, we ran a simple linear regression in which the dependent variable was the original Gini coefficient and the independent variable was the share of the population with at least a high school diploma and no more than either some years of college (but not a BA) or an AA degree, that is, our main education variable with the high correlation. With the regression weighted by metro population to give a better sense of the overall relationship, we took the residuals of the regression as a sort of detrended Gini coefficient—that part of inequality not directly explained by the single educational variable we are using in this exercise (and actually probably better capturing the political economy drivers of inequality).[12]

The Cox regression results with that modified Gini coefficient are shown in table 2.8. The first set of columns include all the variables tested above, while the second set of columns drops the three least significant measures. Note first that once we have accounted for all these structural variables, the percentage of the growth spell during which the nation has been in recession is no longer significant. The export variable is also insignificant, but, as we have suggested, this measure is imperfect anyway, given its timing. However, both the Metropolitan Power Diffusion Index (a measure of jurisdictional fragmentation) and higher levels of inequality are associated with shorter growth spells—and the effects are very significant.[13]

The percentage of minorities in the middle class is not significant at all. While this may be because of competition with the two residential-segregation measures, the dissimilarity index and the city–suburb poverty ratio, it is also the case that such a measure is not really about the sort of social distance that is our main focus in this exercise but is a sort of political-coalition variable, developed and tested in previous work more specifically on growth *and* equity (Benner and Pastor 2012). Also associated with shorter growth spells were percentage foreign-born, share of the workforce in manufacturing, and with lesser significance, share of the workforce in construction; positively associated with the length of growth spells was the percentage of the population with what we have termed a middle level of education.

Although the percentage in public administration was associated with longer growth spells when entered on its own, it is now associated

TABLE 2.8   INTEGRATED MODEL WITH GINI RESIDUAL

	Full model		Parsimonious model	
	Hazard ratio	Sig.	Hazard ratio	Sig.
Percentage of growth spell in national recession	1.001	.964		
Exports as percentage of gross metropolitan product	0.996	.675		
Metropolitan Power Diffusion Index	1.096	.046	1.091	.044
Gini coefficient (residual)	1.306	.000	1.300	.000
Percentage minority middle class	1.000	.997		
Dissimilarity index, non-Hispanic white	1.012	.185	1.011	.150
Ratio, principal city to suburban poverty rates	1.166	.111	1.160	.119
Adult population with HS to AA degree	0.972	.124	0.973	.116
Percentage of population foreign-born	1.048	.004	1.046	.002
Percentage employment in public administration	1.033	.255	1.031	.269
Percentage employment in manufacturing	1.060	.001	1.057	.001
Percentage employment in construction	1.090	.128	1.085	.141
Percentage of workforce covered by a union contract	1.010	.402	1.011	.340

NOTE: Variables entered in multivariate fashion.

with shorter growth spells (although at relatively low significance). It may be that while public-sector employment can strengthen the middle class and dampen inequality and extend growth spells for that reason, when entered into a regression where inequality is a direct measure and other dynamic aspects of the economy are accounted for, a larger public sector signals a more rigid economy. A similar argument could be made for the shortening impact—albeit insignificant—of unionization (although this might also be simply because of the association of more unionization with an older industrial structure).

Of course, the big news is that the Gini coefficient remains highly significant—and, interestingly, the coefficient is essentially the same as before we did the detrending. (Every other non-education coefficient is stable as well, which makes sense since the "detrending" exercise was only done to separate out the education and Gini factors.) This suggests that inequality does indeed have a damping effect on growth spells. Moreover, one remarkable coincidence is that the time-ratio impact of the Gini measure on growth spells in the United States is almost the same as that found in the Berg, Ostry, and Zettelmeyer study on the Gini coefficient and cross-country performance.[14]

In any case, it is striking that the measures of inequality and social and political distance—metropolitan fragmentation, racial segregation, and the city–suburb poverty differential—remain significant in the multivariate specification. While one does not want to stretch too far beyond what are surely preliminary results, the findings do suggest support for the idea that building bridges between constituencies might actually be productive for sustaining economic vitality. Surely, this is the stuff of epistemic communities—and it is to more direct measures of political polarization that we now turn.

What about Politics?

As noted, one of the main findings here is essentially that social polarization—as measured by inequality, racial segregation, municipal fragmentation, and city–suburb poverty differentials—does indeed undermine sustained growth. Therefore, much of the rest of this volume is concerned with whether creating a sense of shared identity that shapes social norms, closes social distance, and helps regions overcome the tendency to atomistic, self-interested behavior can actually help inoculate a region against erratic growth.

Is there a more direct way to get at the impact of community-building and shared identity on growth trajectories? One potential way would seem to be the civic-engagement variables available in two supplements to the Current Population Survey: the volunteer supplement, which is conducted in September, and the civic-engagement supplement, which is conducted in November. These surveys have been conducted since 2002 and 2008, respectively. The volunteer supplement includes measures of amount and type of volunteer activity, along with questions about involvement in community affairs and working with other people to address neighborhood issues. The civic-engagement supplement measures participation in organizations, interaction with friends and neighbors, number of close friends, and knowledge of and participation in civic events. But there are limitations to the Current Population Survey data. It does not measure what people do when they volunteer, nor their values and motivations; nor does it measure social networks that bridge across diversity. In short, the measures tend to reflect "bonding" social capital rather than "bridging" social capital.

One, perhaps more direct, way to test the role of shared identity is to look at a measure of political polarization, particularly the degree to which voters' ideological leanings are divided by geographic lines. Our

notion is that such political polarization—possibly reflecting an epistemological polarization—could pose challenges for intraregional collaboration and perhaps say something about the challenges of forming an
epistemic community around common destinies in any particular region.

To better get at this notion, we used voting data from Dave Leip's
Atlas of U.S. Presidential Elections (www.uselectionatlas.org), a pro-
prietary dataset that is assembled from mostly primary sources (e.g.
official election agencies within each state) and includes county-level
vote counts for each candidate in presidential elections. We specifically
used data for election years 1988 and 2000, to be more or less consistent with the 1990 and 2000 decennial censuses from which many of
our other initial growth-spell covariates are taken. While we could have
used data from the 1992 election in place of 1988, we thought 1988
might be more representative of enduring political undercurrents since
both 1988 and 2000 were years in which no incumbent was running.

To derive a measure of regional political homogeneity at the metro
level, we began by summarizing votes for the Democratic and Republican candidates by CBSA. This was easy enough given that the data was
at the county level and each CBSA is either equivalent to a single county
or can be perfectly constructed by grouping two or more counties. In
this case, a bigger regional gap in voter preferences—either really "red"
or really "blue"—signals a higher level of ideological affinity. However,
because the sort of voter cohesion we were interested in capturing had
more to do with differences within a region, we also summarized the
data separately for the core county and the outlying counties in each
CBSA; we term this variable *political spatial sorting within region*.

To derive this spatial-sorting variable, we define the "core" county as
simply the county in the CBSA with the greatest population in 2010; the
"outlying" counties are simply all the others in the CBSA. In this case,
we calculated the absolute value of the difference between the percentage of the total vote that went to the Democratic candidate in the core
county and the percentage that went to the Democratic candidate in
outlying counties. The hypothesis is that a larger gap signals more political spatial sorting—that is, geographic polarization—and thus might
be associated with less cohesion and perhaps a shorter growth spell.

The fact that the voting data is not available at beneath the county
level of geography is not ideal. First, it means that our measure of political spatial sorting is not perfectly consistent with other geographic
measures we have used, such as the ratio of city to suburban poverty
rates (which compares the experience of principal cities to all other

TABLE 2.9   POLITICAL VARIABLES

	Sample 1: All CBSAs		Sample 2: Multi-county CBSAs	
	Hazard ratio	Sig.	Hazard ratio	Sig.
Regional political homogeneity	0.988	.02	0.998	.80
Political spatial sorting within region	1.023	.03	1.034	.00

locations in a metro) or the residential dissimilarity index (which offers a region-wide measure but is generated by looking at tract-level ethnic composition). Second, and perhaps more important, some of the regions included in our analysis are made up of only one county, so we cannot derive this measure of regional voter cohesion for them; indeed, among the 184 CBSAs that we consider, 52 of them cover just one county, and they account for 88 of the 324 growth spells considered above.

Because of this issue, we present results for two different samples, one that includes all CBSAs and one that includes only multi-county CBSAs. For the sample with all CBSAs, we set the spatial sorting variable to 0 for single-county CBSAs. In one set of runs, we also included a dummy variable for all single-county CBSAs to insure that that approach was not simply picking up fixed effects associated with some other characteristic of single-country metros; but since that was insignificant in all specifications, we dropped it. We should note that the single-county metros tend to be among the smallest in terms of population. Excluding these cases for sample 2 causes a loss of only about 11 percent of the total metro population in the sample.

What do we find? Table 2.9 shows the results for the two samples for a Cox regression that also includes the regional dummies as our standard size and per capita income controls. Unlike in the earlier section, we enter both variables in the same regression, mostly to save reporting space and time; the results are quite similar if we consider the results for the regional political homogeneity and political spatial sorting variables entered separately. The results are intriguing. To the extent that there is overall political homogeneity, growth spells are lengthened (although insignificantly so when we consider only the multi-county CBSAs, where we can also fully exploit the spatial sorting variable); while to the extent that there is political spatial sorting within regions, growth spells are shortened.

TABLE 2.10 INTEGRATED (PARSIMONIOUS) MODEL

	Sample 1: All CBSAs		Sample 2: Multi-county CBSAs	
	Hazard ratio	Sig.	Hazard ratio	Sig.
Metropolitan Power Diffusion Index	1.096	.036	1.041	.445
Gini coefficient (residual)	1.276	.000	1.384	.000
Dissimilarity index, non-Hispanic white	1.014	.078	1.016	.117
Ratio, principal city to suburban poverty rates	1.060	.570	0.961	.755
Adult population with HS to AA degree	0.977	.178	0.987	.639
Percentage of population foreign-born	1.056	.000	1.025	.199
Percentage employment in public administration	1.017	.557	1.049	.213
Percentage employment in manufacturing	1.057	.001	1.080	.000
Percentage employment in construction	1.120	.047	1.255	.002
Percentage of workforce covered by a union contract	1.009	.468	1.011	.492
Regional political homogeneity	0.990	.102	0.999	.873
Political spatial sorting within region	1.032	.014	1.037	.013

This is a mix of results that squares well with our notions of epistemic communities. The positive effect of political homogeneity might explain, for example, why we find in our case studies that places that are overwhelmingly Republican (Salt Lake City) or Democratic (San Antonio) can both find their way to higher levels of collaboration and steadier growth—it's not the policies of each ideological position per se as much as it is the likely consensus on analysis of problems. But there is one important nuance. As noted, those results for overall homogeneity are not statistically significant when we focus just on the multi-county CBSAs, while the political sorting is significant in both samples. In short, metropolitan fragmentation can work against collaboration and sustained growth.

What happens when we test these variables in the context of a fuller regression? We did this first with the full integrated model above and then with the parsimonious model (since the same variables—percentage of time in recession, export vulnerability, and minority middle class—were insignificant). In table 2.10, we present only the results of the parsimonious regressions, to conserve space.

There are some interaction effects with the pre-existing variables which are perhaps best seen in the regression with all CBSAs. These generally involve slight shifts in coefficient values and significance levels, but the biggest shift is the city–suburb poverty ratio, which is after all likely to be correlated with political spatial sorting.[15] We also see that as we move to the multi-county setting, several variables lose significance—not surprisingly, given the reduction in sample size. Here, the Metropolitan Power Diffusion Index has the most interesting change, losing significance in the multi-county sample. This makes intuitive sense given that it can capture fragmentation in the single-county cases included in the all-CBSA sample where the political spatial sorting variable has been set to 0, while the municipal fragmentation measure probably competes with the spatial sorting variable in the multi-county sample.

In any case, the big story is that even with controls, regional political homogeneity and spatial sorting matter. But, as with the individual regressions reported earlier, the truly critical finding is that where it really can do its job (in the more populous multi-county CBSAs), the sorting variable dominates in terms of significance. Its coefficient size and significance level are quite consistent when compared to the all-CBSA sample. Spatial and social separation matter for the length of growth spells.

We do not seek to make too much of these particular regressions. While the earlier set clearly involved exploratory work, they were a bit more solid than what we present here. After all, the political variables—degree of homogeneity and degree of sorting—are imperfect and create challenges for the sample at hand. A finer set of geographic definitions, one which allows for sorting below the county level, would be preferable. Still, the results do point in the direction that having a more like-minded regional polity—and one where that like-mindedness at a metropolitan level does not mask deep geographic divides within the metro—may be more consistent with sustained growth. We turn to the dynamic of bridging divides through epistemic communities in the case studies below.

EQUITY MATTERS

This chapter has tried to provide a platform for much of the rest of the book by considering whether social and political fragmentation matter for sustained growth. To do this, we borrowed from strategies initially developed by IMF researchers to look at GDP growth spells at the country level. In our case, we derived a measure of sustained employment growth at the metropolitan level, and then tried to see which factors are most likely to knock a region off its growth path.

In a clear parallel to the international work, we find that one of the most important factors that can shorten a growth spell is a region's initial level of inequality. We also find that measures of social cohesion, including residential segregation, fragmented metropolitan governance, and sharp difference in city–suburb poverty levels, all play a role (along with more expected covariates such as education and economic structure). Intriguingly, we also find in a supplemental set of regressions that places that have a more unified political viewpoint might be better able to sustain growth but that the more consistent and significant impact is a dragging effect on growth when political viewpoints are highly variable across geographic space.

All of this helps set the stage for case selection, a task we discuss in the next chapter. But before we turn to that, another caveat should be mentioned. Readers should remember that because of data limitations, the empirical exercise above covers only the 1990s and 2000s in metropolitan America. This is particularly important for interpreting the findings on inequality. It may well be that inequality can contribute to growth in some circumstances and retard it in others—that is, that there is a U-shaped relationship in which "perfect" equality destroys incentives and hurts economic expansion while more extreme levels of inequality manage to do the same for reasons discussed in the first few sections of this chapter.

Indeed, we think that this is likely—and we would warn progressives not to assume that we think that (or that the world works such that) any pro-equity intervention will yield improved and sustained growth. In short, the findings above may simply indicate that we have gone beyond a sort of "optimal" level of inequality in contemporary America and that we need to rebalance priorities and strategies to secure more inclusive *and* more robust growth. The first step to doing that may involving restoring a sense of common destiny—in which first metros and then the nation become more connected across income, race, and place—and it is to the exploration of that process at the metropolitan level that we turn for the remainder of the book.

CHAPTER 3

Where to Go, What to Ask

Selecting and Designing the Case Studies

We are all special cases.

—Albert Camus, *The Fall* (1956)

We are our choices.

—Jean-Paul Sartre, *Being and Nothingness* (1953)

Case-study research often walks a fine line between the particular and the abstract. This balancing act arises precisely because the very qualifier *case* in *case study* suggests that "the phenomena under investigation . . . can be found in other places. . . . The case may be unique but is not singular" (Castree 2005, 541). The iterative relationship between the concrete and the abstract, between empirical data and theoretical insights, is not only a defining feature of the approach but also the source of its analytical strength. Unlike generalization in the statistical sense, which is largely concerned with representativeness, replication, and external validity, explanations that emerge from case-study analysis involve repeated cycles of crafting theory and concepts that are "rooted in the concrete aspects of the case yet sufficiently abstract [so] that others in similar situations can see how they might apply to their own context" (Baxter 2010, 96).

Because cases are meant to be not isolated events but archetypical enough to offer insights applicable elsewhere, selection is crucial. For us, case selection was complicated because we were interested in two broad and, we hoped, interrelated phenomena. The first was the existence (or not) of diverse and dynamic regional epistemic communities—something difficult to predetermine, since that is the theoretical frame we were applying to processes others might call regional collaboration, regional networks, or regional leadership. There was, in short, no region shouting out that it had built a diverse and dynamic epistemic community, and hence no easily identifiable universe of possible cases to draw from.

The second phenomenon we were interested in was how such epistemic communities might impact social equity and economic growth. Indeed, our curiosity about epistemic communities grew from our interest in understanding whether the structure and dynamics of regional knowledge-sharing networks and the evolution of social norms over time actually shaped patterns of growth and equity—and whether the existence of diverse and dynamic regional epistemic communities could in fact help explain those instances when growth and equity go hand in hand.

In what follows, we explain the specific data we used and the analytical process we undertook to identify what ended up being eleven case studies. As it turns out, it took months for us to settle on the cases—partly because we were going at it from two contrasting directions, and partly because it was so much fun to produce typologies, maps, and data runs (although perhaps not as much fun for the research staff assisting us). We will, however, describe it in a way that's more succinct than the process—a way that we hope will explain our rationales—and then provide more details about how we conducted each case study.

CHOICE AND CONSEQUENCE

Why Regions?

Before we dive deep into the details of our case-selection process, it's important to deal with a preliminary question: Why study regions at all? In chapter 1, we emphasized some of the economic reasons for the emergence of metropolitan regions as an important element of the global economy and also stressed that the regions are one place where the equity argument has been gaining ground (with good reason, as the econometrics of chapter 2 would seem to indicate). Here, however, we want to emphasize the epistemic reasons for looking at metropolitan regions.

Economically, as a wide range of research over the past few decades has shown, regions are a critical scale for processes related to economic growth and change (Acs 2000; Scott 1998; Storper 1997). Processes of innovation, knowledge sharing, and tacit knowledge development; dynamics of growth and decline in economic clusters; efficiencies of daily commuting and goods transportation systems—these are all important processes shaping economic growth that depend on

TABLE 3.1   COEFFICIENT OF VARIATION, 192 MOST POPULOUS US
METROPOLITAN AREAS

	Coefficient of variation for the change in number of jobs	Coefficient of variation for the change in the Gini coefficient
1979–1989	0.66	0.51
1989–1999	0.62	0.41
1999–2010	0.85	0.79

SOURCE: Authors' analysis of US Bureau of Economic Analysis and American Community Survey data.

face-to-face communication and the kinds of coordination of actions that only physical proximity allows (Benner and Pastor 2012; Pastor et al. 2000; Porter 1998; Saxenian 1994). Moreover, while *causes* of social inequality are in large part shaped by regional development patterns and policies, there are promising *solutions* to these patterns of social inequity that can be achieved through addressing regional political, planning, economic policy, and governance processes; and the *political will* needed to achieve these solutions can be built at a regional scale, as the ability to have face-to-face communication helps build bridges across the racial and spatial divides that all too often constrain progress (Orfield 2002; Pastor, Benner, and Matsuoka 2011; Powell 1999; Rusk 2001).

There are also important epistemic reasons for our regional lens. In the context of the national economic, inequality, and political crises that we laid out in the first chapter, it is useful to think about regions as living laboratories, with multiple and diverse actors experimenting with how to respond to the dramatic changes we've experienced in the past thirty years. Despite (or perhaps because of) substantial variations in initial conditions and clearly different strategies and trajectories, lessons for addressing our national challenges can be gleaned from comparing the relative success or failure of different trajectories. This is particularly so because there is evidence that regional trajectories are diverging more than in the past (Drennan 2005; Scott and Storper 2003; Woo, Ross, and Boston 2015).

Table 3.1 illustrates this increasing heterogeneity among US metros by looking at the coefficient of variation for absolute percent decadal change in a measure of economic health (number of jobs) and a measure of income inequality (the Gini coefficient). The amount of variation among metros fell slightly in the 1990s, but it jumped significantly for change in employment and change in income inequality from the 1980s

TABLE 3.2   COEFFICIENT OF VARIATION, 192 MOST POPULOUS U.S.
METROPOLITAN AREAS BY CENSUS-DESIGNATED REGION

Northeast	Change in number of jobs	Change in Gini coefficient
1979–1989	0.61	0.53
1989–1999	0.70	0.32
1999–2010	0.72	0.75

Midwest	Change in number of jobs	Change in Gini coefficient
1979–1989	0.60	0.28
1989–1999	0.45	0.40
1999–2010	0.68	0.77

South	Change in number of jobs	Change in Gini coefficient
1979–1989	0.68	0.54
1989–1999	0.43	0.41
1999–2010	0.77	0.73

West	Change in number of jobs	Change in Gini coefficient
1979–1989	0.38	0.55
1989–1999	0.58	0.35
1999–2010	0.70	0.83

SOURCE: Authors' analysis of US Bureau of Economic Analysis and American Community Survey data.

to the 2000s (the higher the coefficient of variation, the more variation in regional trajectories).

Of course, part of this rising variation could be due to the experience of broader census-designated regions (i.e., Northeast, South, Midwest, and West); that is, maybe it's not that Atlanta and Denver have diverged but that the South and the West have. Table 3.2 tries to control for metro membership in the larger census region and shows that while in some cases the variation in changes in employment and inequality is lessened when restricted to the census-designated region, there is still a substantial increase in heterogeneity within broad regions of the country. This is particularly noticeable in the Midwest, where there was far more variation among changes in income inequality in the 2000s than in the 1980s and 1990s. We see a similar trend of variation in changing employment trajectories in the West. All of this is to say the following: it is clear that individual metropolitan areas are experiencing economic changes in ways that do not necessarily coincide with national or larger regional trends; that these differences are increasing over time; and there may be lessons to learn from how each region is regrouping and responding.

Choosing Regions

While all the analysis above suggests that regions are an important scale for learning, we are still left with the task of selecting cases to maximize theoretical insights and most effectively generate generalizable principles. If we could have selected regions based on the independent variable—the strength, diversity, and dynamism of regional epistemic communities—we would have used this as our criterion and investigated in those regions how these knowledge communities shape the dynamics of growth and equity. Without being able to easily identify such cases, however—and since our goal was partly to develop greater sophistication in our understanding of the very concept of diverse and dynamic epistemic communities—our case-selection process is best understood as a theoretical sampling approach, that is, an iterative process of selection with the goal of gaining a deeper, richer understanding of a concept or theory across a range of different contexts and conditions (Glaser and Strauss 1967).

Thus, we ultimately aimed to select three kinds of cases: first, regions where equity and growth came together, and where we could then investigate the nature of epistemic communities in the region and gauge what influence, if any, they might have had on those regional trajectories; second, regions with substantially below-average growth and social equity metrics, to see whether we could find evidence of a lack of diversity and dynamism in a regional epistemic community (or evidence of a thriving epistemic community despite poor concrete results, a clear counterexample to our framework); and third, regions that had reputations (from previous research by ourselves and others) of having strong, collaborative regional processes that did not necessarily show strong evidence of equity and growth going together, a pattern that might challenge our presuppositions about the positive impacts of such collaborations.

Given these various criteria, our first step in selecting case-study regions involved selecting some high performers, with the goal of eventually visiting those regions and investigating the extent to which the good results were due to structural factors, dumb luck, or the role of knowledge communities. In some ways, this was a replication of the approach taken in *Just Growth,* in which we moved strictly from data to theory. There were, however, a few modifications introduced in this exercise. The first change was that we had previously looked at patterns only in the 1980s and 1990s; for this study, we updated our analysis to include the 2000s. A second modification, which we explain in more detail below, is that we considered here the end-point as well as the trajectory; that is, we accounted for the eventual level and distribution of income as well as the shift over time in key related variables. In this way we could target regions that were truly high achievers by the end of this thirty-year period, not just regions that might have improved, albeit only slightly, over time.

Our universe of regions for consideration consisted of the US metropolitan regions that had at least 200,000 residents in 2000. Using this break, we ended up with 192 regions in our sample. To identify broad patterns of economic growth and social equity, we examined patterns over four time periods: the 1980s, the 1990s, the 2000s, and the entire thirty-year period (1980–2010). Following the methodology we developed in *Just Growth,* the indicators we used to measure economic growth were the change in employment and the change in earnings per job—because we wanted to identify not just growth in jobs but growth in *good* jobs. The indicators we used to measure equity were the change in the income gap and the change in the percentage of the population living below poverty—because it does no good to close the income gap by making everyone poorer.

To measure the income gap, or income inequality, we used the 80/20 household income ratio, which compares the 80th percentile of income earners with the 20th percentile, with higher ratios indicating more inequality. Recent attention has focused more on the tails of the income distribution, particularly the top 1 percent (Alvaredo et al. 2013). We focused on the 80/20 ratio, partly because we wanted to look at broader measures of social distance but also because calculations of a different and wider ratio (for example, the 90/10 ratio) were less reliable with the 1980 census data.[1]

While we were interested in looking at the changing dynamics over time, we also wanted to provide a snapshot of the metro regions' economic and social well-being at the end of the thirty-year period, in 2010. That is, where did they end up when all was said and done? After all, improvement from rock bottom might be impressive, but if the region remains poor and highly unequal, that's, well, a bit less impressive. To measure final economic well-being we used the median household income, and to measure equity we used the Gini coefficient for household income, a standard indicator of income inequality. These variables had the virtue of being both easily collectible and not the same variables used in the trajectory analysis, thus providing a more independent measure of the end state.

For our longitudinal analysis, we drew the economic growth variables (change in employment and earnings) from the US Bureau of Economic Analysis Personal Income Accounts Tables, and the equity variables from the American Community Survey. For our 2010 analysis—the snapshot of the economic and social well-being of metros—we used data from the American Community Survey, which we downloaded from the Missouri Census Data Center.

Making a First Cut

In order to more easily compare regional performance across these four indicators and four different time periods, we created two separate composite indices: a growth index—combining the percentage change in both employment and earnings per job—and an equity index—combining the percentage change in both poverty and the 80/20 household income ratio. While these indices were used to compare all metros, there are broad regional differences across the country, so we benchmarked all of the metros against their respective larger US census-designated region: Northeast, South, Midwest, or West. To do this, we normalized each measure into detrended z-scores: we grouped the metros by census-designated region, and for each record, we subtracted the census regional mean and divided by the census regional standard deviation.

From this process, we obtained sixteen z-scores for each region: one for each of the four variables in each of the four time periods (1980s, 1990s, 2000s, and the whole thirty-year period).[2] We then computed the growth index as the mean of the eight growth-related z-scores, and the equity index as the mean of the eight equity-related z-scores (appendix A offers an account of those indices across all 192 regions, as well as a look at some of the initial and ending variables that go into the calculations and case selection). Finally, we ranked both the growth and equity indices into terciles (best, middle, and worst) across the entire 192-region sample, and mapped the results to observe the distribution of regions based on their relative scores on these indices (map 3.1). Together, the two tercile scores form a nine-cell grid, and the upper-right-hand cell of that grid is the "best," in that it indicates both solid growth and relatively good trends in equity (meaning either actual upticks, or given the general trends in the United States during this time period, better than whatever dismal average was achieved by one's particular census region).

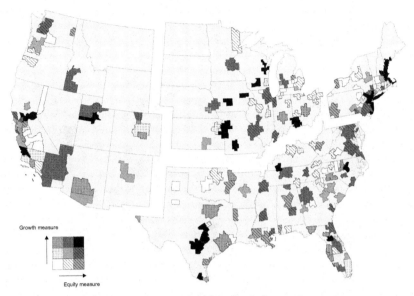

MAP 3.1. US Metro Regions by Growth and Equity Indices, 1980–2010s.

As we mentioned above, we also wanted to go beyond trends over this thirty-year period and investigate whether the ending point on income levels and distributional measures was also above average. After all, if a region started off from a particularly low point in 1980, it could appear to improve dramatically over that period but still end up substantially below average—that is, the relative acceleration in its improvement may simply reflect a process of reverting to the mean (and maybe not even getting there). So, to make sure we were capturing regions that not only posted above-average improvements over time but also ended up at above-average levels of income and equity in the end, we looked at the median household income and the Gini coefficient of household income.[3] In keeping with our trajectory analyses, we also normalized these endpoint scores by the broad census region, producing two z-scores (one for equity and one for growth) which could then be ranked into terciles. We show the results in map 3.2.

Those regions that are truly the strongest-performing in terms of both change over time and end result are in the upper-right corner of the distribution in both maps, 3.1 and 3.2. The number of regions that fall into both of those categories is interesting, but also relatively small. It includes no metro regions in the West; only Manchester-Nashua and

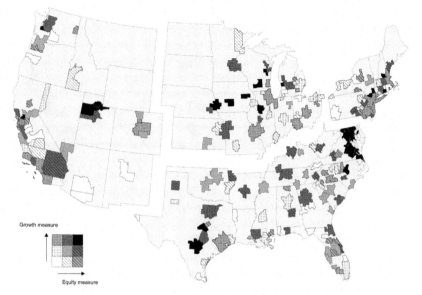

MAP 3.2. US Metro Regions: Relative Levels of Household Income and Gini Coefficient of Household Income in 2010.

New Hampshire in the Northeast; four relatively small and non-diverse regions in the Midwest (Des Moines and Cedar Rapids, Iowa, and Madison and Appleton, Wisconsin); and three regions in the South (San Antonio and Killeen–Temple–Fort Hood, Texas, and Raleigh-Cary, North Carolina). While we considered all of these regions for possible case studies (and ended up choosing two of them for our final list), we were concerned that they represented a relatively narrow experience of metropolitan regions in the United States.

Narrowing Down

Given the desire to expand the range for the case studies with positive growth and equity metrics—and knowing that it was extraordinarily difficult to actually maintain such high performance on dual criteria over multiple time periods—we decided to loosen our cutoffs for consideration on these metrics. We did this in two ways. The first was to take as successful those regions that fell into the top half—rather than the top third—in each of our growth and equity measures for both the change over time and end point. The second was to consider regions that excelled (were in the top third) in *either* growth or equity and were average or better on the *other* metric. To understand this visually, we

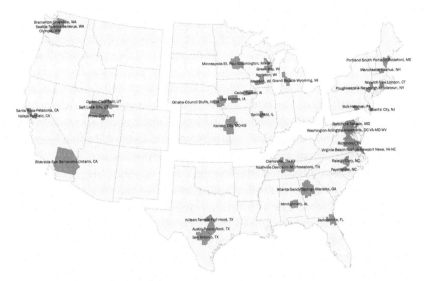

MAP 3.3. U.S. Metro Regions Scoring in Top Three Squares in Both Over-time and Endpoint Measure of Growth and Equity.

are talking about regions that are in one of the three boxes on the upper right of the three-by-three matrix in maps 3.1 and 3.2.

The second approach produced a broader set of metros, even when we required that the regional scores wind up in these top three squares for *both* our change-over-time metrics *and* our end-of-period metrics. We show the results of that approach in map 3.3.

We drew a few conclusions about possible case studies from this analysis. But first, it was comforting to know that several of the "just growth" regions studied in our earlier volume stood the test of (more) time, including Jacksonville, Kansas City, and Nashville. Another of the regions we explored in *Just Growth*, Columbus, does not make the cut in the broad map, but did when we narrowed down to a comparison with just the Rust Belt states of Pennsylvania, Ohio, Michigan, Illinois, Indiana, and Wisconsin. This suggested to us that both the method and the underlying theory might be robust to different periodization—and with that, we went more confidently ahead in this phase of the selection process.

Looking at the full set of maps, one immediately sees two regions as obvious candidates for study: San Antonio, Texas, and Raleigh-Cary, North Carolina. Both regions score in the top tercile in all of our metrics while also being large and ethnically diverse enough to provide potentially interesting lessons for a range of other metropolitan regions around the country. Another region that emerged as a candidate was Salt Lake City, Utah. While it is the neighboring region of Provo-Orem, Utah, that actually shows up most prominently in these maps, Salt Lake City does show up in map 3.3, and locals there tend to think of the region as the entire Wasatch Front, including Provo, Salt Lake City, and Ogden-Clearfield to the north. Since Salt Lake City is the urban core that drives change in this broader region, it made sense to focus on it. Finally, Seattle showed up as a top performer in terms of both trajectory and endpoint in map 3.3—so it seemed an obvious choice.

We were also interested in selecting a region within the broad Rust Belt. Once serving as the industrial heartland of the country, the area from western New York and Pennsylvania through eastern Wisconsin and Illinois has suffered some of the worst effects of the decline of manufacturing and broader economic restructuring of the past thirty years. We thought that examining a region that had weathered this transition relatively well could provide interesting insights. In looking at the patterns of change over the thirty-year period, as well as the status of income and inequality in 2010, Grand Rapids, Michigan, stood out. It was the only metropolitan region in the entire Rust Belt to score in the top three squares in our three-by-three matrix for both change over time and status in 2010 (see map 3.3), so we selected it.

As we explored these patterns, we also realized that it would be interesting theoretically to identify cases that were not just solid performers across the entire thirty-year period but had also experienced significant shifts in growth and equity during the same period. If a region were able to dramatically reverse a period of economic decline and growing inequality, and jump onto a path of faster economic growth and improving equity, it could provide important insights into the factors that shape the regional ability to recover from economic shocks. To investigate this, we created typologies describing the trends that occurred in different metros between 1980 and 2010, classifying each of the four measurements of change (change in employment, change in earnings, change in the income gap, and change in the percentage below poverty) as either "good" or "bad" in each of the four periods (1980s, 1990s, 2000s, and the thirty-year period).

Specifically, we labeled each growth measure "good" if it was *above* the median value of that measure in its respective census-designated region, and "bad" if it was below the median. Conversely, we labeled each equity measure "good" if it was *below* the median of that variable in the respective census region (i.e. relatively less inequality and poverty), and "bad" if it was above the median (i.e. relatively more inequality and poverty). Using these tags, we identified whether a metro had improved or declined in terms of growth and equity in each of the four periods, and we created a typology to categorize the metros:[4]

- *consistently good*: good in 9 of the 12 changes that occurred in the 1980s, 1990s, and 2000s (with the condition that at least three-quarters of the changes in two of the decades were good and at least one growth measure and one equity measure was good in the remaining decade)
- *thirty-year good*: good in all four changes in the thirty-year period
- *bounce back*: bad in at least three-quarters of the changes in the 1980s and 1990s and good in at least three-quarters of the changes in the 2000s, or bad in at least three-quarters of the changes in the 1980s and good in at least three-quarters of the changes in the 1990s and 2000s
- *thirty-year bad*: bad in all four changes in the thirty-year period
- *consistently bad*: bad in 9 of the 12 changes that occurred in the 1980s, 1990s, and 2000s (with the condition that at least three-quarters of the changes in two of the decades were bad and at least one growth measure and one equity measure was bad in the remaining decade)

Within this typology, the regions that had been able to recover from an economic shock and achieve positive growth and equity dynamics in subsequent periods are those in the *bounce back* category. By selecting cases of this type, we hoped to explore whether the observed bounce back was simply a function of structural factors or whether more conscious forms of knowledge generation and cross-sector collaboration—that is, the formation of an epistemic community—had played a role. Among the twenty or so candidates in this category, Oklahoma City and San Antonio were particularly interesting. San Antonio was able to turn around in enough time (going from bad in the 1980s to more promising in the 1990s and 2000s) to land in our top tier in 2010 in terms of growth and equity trajectories (map 3.3). Oklahoma City remained at the bottom, but it had moved from having bad outcomes in the 1980s and 1990s to much better ones in the 2000s, leading to curiosity about the turnaround.

As we examined these different categories in more depth, another striking feature stood out. There are very few states in the United States that had metropolitan regions that fell into *both* the best (consistently good or thirty-year good) and worst (consistently bad or thirty-year bad) categories. This may be partly a function of the state size needed for variation: California and Texas, the nation's two largest states, are among the three states that have regions that fell both into the worst *and* best categories of change over this thirty-year period. The other, however, is North Carolina, which is especially intriguing since it just makes the top ten states in terms of population. In any case, the general lack of extremes *within* states made us wonder about the role of state policy and whether it might be useful to control for similar state environments.

Considering this, we decided to develop a set of paired comparisons across two different states. Focusing on North Carolina and California, we selected regions that fell into two different categories: regions with strong patterns of both economic growth and improved social equity across the full thirty-year period (Sacramento in California—despite its dip in performance in the 1990s—and Raleigh in North Carolina); and regions that were among the worst performers in growth and equity in each state (Fresno in California and Greensboro in North Carolina). We wound up adding an additional case in each state, for reasons discussed below, so we actually had state triads, a sampling strategy that provides even more information.

Theoretically, we were also interested in identifying regions that had reputations for collaboration that might be an indicator of a diverse and dynamic epistemic community, but in which positive patterns for growth and social equity metrics failed to emerge (or were mixed). In looking at our two-state, two-region comparison, we realized that there were prime opportunities for selecting a third region in each state that met this criterion. In California, Silicon Valley's economic success has been linked to both its open, flexible, and dynamic labor markets and its particular regional culture of collaboration (Saxenian 1994). In North Carolina, Charlotte had a strong reputation in the 1980s and 1990s for regional collaboration and relatively progressive (by Southern standards) social norms, all part of repositioning the region as a central logistics and banking center for the country and an example of the New South (Pastor et al. 2000). Thus, we decided to add Silicon Valley and Charlotte as cases. Reputation for strong regional collaboration also helped reinforce our reasons for selecting Salt Lake and Sacramento, both of which were well known for regional planning processes.

Having finished this range of considerations, we wound up with a total of eleven cases—Charlotte, Fresno, Grand Rapids, Greensboro, Oklahoma City, Raleigh, Sacramento, Salt Lake City, San Antonio, San Jose/Silicon Valley, and Seattle—which fell into a series of different categories. Six regions (Grand Rapids, Raleigh, Sacramento, Salt Lake City,

San Antonio, and Seattle) were included for having positive growth and equity trajectories over the full thirty-year period of our analysis, and we added a seventh, Oklahoma City, because it was an interesting example of a "bounce back" in the latter years; here, we wanted to see whether regional culture, social norms, and epistemic communities played a role in resilience and recovery. Two regions (Fresno and Greensboro) were included because of being poor performers on both growth and equity, but being in states where other regions have thrived; here, we wanted to see whether fractious cultures played a role. Finally, two regions (Silicon Valley and Charlotte) were included because of having evidence of strong regional collaborations but growth and equity trajectories that were less positive than in two other cases (Sacramento and Salt Lake City) that also had well-known regional collaborations.

THE QUEST AND THE QUESTIONS

Once we had selected the regions to study, we began to assemble a broad range of data about them, as well as a list of possible people and organizations to interview in each region (data profiles for each of the cases are offered in appendix B, and a list of the eventual interviewees is offered in appendix C). Because we were interested in not just the outcomes but also the process of community building and knowledge creation, we focused on the most prominent organizations in four types of key constituencies: the private sector, particularly the largest chamber of commerce in each region and other major business associations; the public sector, particularly the regional planning organization and other prominent public-sector officials; labor organizations, particularly the regional labor council and prominent individual union leaders, where they existed; and nonprofit organizations, including community-based organizations and major philanthropic entities.

We then scheduled multi-day visits to all the case-study regions, interviewing as many people in each of our four broad sectors as we could fit into our (and their) schedules. In some regions, respondents were not available in person, but made themselves available for phone calls either before or after the visit. For both the in-person and the phone-call interviews, we developed a detailed interview protocol that guided our discussions. The protocol was designed to help us better understand the nature of regional knowledge networks, including mechanisms of knowledge generation, social norms about collaboration and conflict within regional governance processes, underlying factors that either contributed to collaboration or mediated conflict, and whether and how interactions between actors were extended over long periods of time.

The specific number of interviews conducted in each region varied from 11 to 19, with a total of 172 interviewed and each interview lasting between one and two hours; again, a full list of interviewees in each region is provided in appendix C. These interviews were supplemented with detailed secondary research on regional dynamics from both web-based sources and the academic literature. This additional research occurred both before the visits—to help prepare for our interviews—and afterward, since the in-person interviews inevitably raised new questions or illustrated new dynamics worth investigating in more depth.

Cultures of Conflict and Collaboration

While there are finer nuances of regional culture and knowledge sharing that we were not able to capture in the time available for each case study, our goal was not to write comprehensive historical studies of any single region. Rather, our goal was to investigate broad patterns of regional governance—particularly to understand the ways in which diverse constituencies are involved in or marginalized from regional governance processes—and how conflict and collaboration have emerged and evolved over time.

The conflict piece was particularly important since we realized that any regional process had to effectively address divergent interests; we were particularly struck by the admonition of Lester and Reckhow (2013) to understand that progress on equity was often driven by "skirmishes." To get at this, specific questions were focused on:

- *sustaining cultures of cooperation,* in which we asked respondents to identify the long-term historical processes, social factors, and interpersonal social norms that have helped shape or shred cultures of collaboration within their region
- *learning to collaborate,* in which we asked respondents to describe, against that broader backdrop, an example of successful collaboration across diverse constituencies in the region, and to share their perspectives on what contributed to the success of that collaboration
- *dealing with conflict,* in which we asked people to describe an instance of major conflict in the region between different constituencies, and to share their perspectives on what the conflicting goals and values were that shaped that conflict, how it was or was not resolved, and what lasting impact that had on regional governance processes

- *sources of knowledge,* in which we asked respondents how they obtained information and knowledge about, first, economic trends and, second, social conditions in the region, with an eye to seeing whether there was, in fact, a shared knowledge base across constituencies.

In all of the interviews in a region, we were looking for commonalities, as well as inconsistencies, in how people portrayed processes of collaboration and conflict in regional governance processes. What are the processes that help people develop a common language and cognitive frames that allow them to communicate effectively and share knowledge across diverse experiences, values, and priorities? When do such processes emerge, and how? What factors preclude those processes from developing? And who holds influence and power in regional governance processes?

Some Additional Preliminaries

In the following chapters, we present the insights that emerged from each of our case studies. Before jumping into that analysis, however, it is worth highlighting a few cross-cutting methodological issues that shaped our analysis. First, while we used the official US Census definitions of metropolitan statistical areas (called core-based statistical areas, or CBSAs) for our data analysis and case-study selection, in many of our cases respondents defined their functional region as a somewhat different geography.

In Sacramento, for example, the official CBSA is a four-county region (El Dorado, Sacramento, Placer, and Yolo Counties), but the regional council of governments covers two additional counties (Yuba and Sutter); this six-county area is the one most frequently cited in discussions of regional collaboration. Similarly, in Salt Lake City, the official CBSA consists of Salt Lake County and the sparsely populated Tooele and Summit Counties to the west and east of Salt Lake County, but most of our respondents talked more about regional integration north into neighboring Davis and Weber Counties (part of the Ogden-Clearfield Metropolitan Statistical Area) and south into Utah County (part of the Provo-Orem Metropolitan Statistical Area).

While actor perceptions of the relevant regional borders could sometimes differ from the official CBSA boundaries, in nearly all cases the patterns of growth and equity dynamics in these neighboring areas were similar enough to the data for the official CBSA that we were not concerned about gaps between our characterization of regional dynamics and the categorizations that might be offered by regional respondents. The one exception to this was in the Raleigh-Cary metro. Here, residents of the region consider the functional region to be Raleigh-Durham, but in official census designations there are two distinct CBSAs. Raleigh is a three-county metro covering Franklin, Johnston, and Wake Counties, and exhibits the strong growth and equity results that drove us to select the region, while the neighboring Durham–Chapel Hill metro covers four counties (Chatham, Durham, Orange, and Person), includes the largest concentration of African Americans in the region, and has much worse patterns of social equity than Raleigh (although its growth performance was strong).

Did this mean that Raleigh was simply shifting its problems over to neighboring Durham? To make sure our identification of Raleigh as a strong performer wasn't simply an artifact of a Census definition of the region that didn't correspond to local understandings of the functional region, we recalculated the equity and growth indices, as well as the median household income and Gini coefficient in 2010, for the combined seven-county area. As it turned out, the newly combined region still remains in the top third of both equity and growth indicators. In the statistical table we provide in appendix B about the Raleigh case study, the data is for this combined seven-county area, while for each of the other case studies, we present data for the official Census CBSA definition of the metro.

Second, as described above, our case-study selection was in part driven by consideration of the role of the state context in shaping regional dynamics. This is most obvious in our two-state, three-region paired comparison cases, but implicit in the other cases was an understanding that state policy might shape regional dynamics. In our interviews, however, it was clear that state policy had very little to do with people's understandings of regional dynamics, so we end up saying very little about it in the specific case-study descriptions. Where state policy was relevant (as in North Carolina, where new state laws have eroded the ability of local municipalities to annex and so restrain suburban fragmentation), we raise this. Overall, however, the patterns of regional development in each of our cases were primarily understood by our respondents as being driven by processes and relationships specific to the region, and this is our focus in what follows.

READY TO LAUNCH

This chapter has described the way we went about selecting regions to help us understand the relationship between epistemic communities, regional social norms, and patterns of economic growth and social equity. We essentially approached this task from two directions. On the one hand, we started from the patterns of growth and equity, identifying regions with a range of patterns (overall good, overall bad, bounce-back) and choosing a range that could help us explore the role epistemic communities might play in explaining those patterns. On the other hand, we identified regions with patterns of collaboration that might be indicative of diverse and dynamic epistemic communities but with patterns of growth and equity that diverged, including from our hypothesis that such epistemic communities should contribute to both strong growth and improved social equity.

Since our theoretical interests in the book are primarily about the nature and impact of these regional epistemic communities, we decided to group them in the chapters that follow not so much on outcomes as on processes. Thus, in the chapters that follow, the regions are clustered into the following four categories.

1. *Planning-influenced community building.* Here we include Sacramento and Salt Lake City, both places where there were very conscious efforts to bring constituencies together around regional growth and improvements (the Blueprint process for the former and Envision Utah for the latter). These cases provide insight into how formal processes can create and sustain diverse epistemic communities over time, but also how such processes—particularly in Sacramento—can leave some issues of equity to one side, but then exhibit the dynamism to be more inclusive.

2. *Elite-driven regional stewardship.* Here we include Charlotte, Grand Rapids, and Oklahoma City. As we will see, the first two cases share the characteristic that their good performance has faded, suggesting that one needs to go beyond elites and top-down approaches to be more effective and inclusive. On the other hand, the turnaround in Oklahoma City is remarkable, and there is significant evidence of attempts to widen the circle of participants in and beneficiaries from metropolitan development.

3. *Conflict-informed collaboration.* Here we examine Fresno, Greensboro, and San Antonio. It is only the latter where we actually observe conflict feeding into what later becomes well known as a culture of collaboration; in the other cases, we essentially see a continuing war of attrition between competing and distant social actors.

4. *Knowledge economies and networks.* Here we include Raleigh, Seattle, and Silicon Valley. We suggest that Silicon Valley was getting it right—but is now getting it wrong, as a more rootless group of entrepreneurs eschew the practices of what were once the region's stewards. Raleigh has woven together a seemingly coherent epistemic community. Virtually every key leader repeats the same mantra about the region's Triple Helix growth framework. Meanwhile, Seattle has made a remarkable commitment to maintaining equitable opportunity even as it is—like the others—subject to the highly disequalizing trends associated with being a center of innovation for the "new economy."

Before diving in, we want to re-emphasize one key aspect of the analysis that follows. In all of our case studies, the focus was on processes of *governance,* not formal *government* policies or the creation of new decision-making institutions. In some cases, as the literature on epistemic communities would suggest, processes of repeated interaction and knowledge sharing on a regional basis ended up being institutionalized through specific organizations that facilitate the development of regional epistemic communities. We find this in our examples of planning-influenced community building: the evolution of the Sacramento Area Council of Governments as a provider of the infrastructure for regional knowledge-sharing networks, and the development of Envision Utah, a small nonprofit organization that plays a similar role in Salt Lake City.

But even in these cases, there is no *single* institution that can be considered the true core of the regional epistemic community. In all cases, rather, there is a diversity of organizations that help facilitate more informal information sharing and knowledge development across many different constituencies. In places where this is most widely developed, there exists a philosophy of diverse knowledge-sharing across acknowledged partners, rather than a single organization that institutionalizes the diverse regional epistemic community. Thus, for example, in Grand Rapids, multiple respondents talked about the "four-legged stool," in which four distinct organizations had a well-understood division of labor in shaping regional developments, with strong cross-organization communication and collaboration.

Similarly, in Raleigh-Durham, there is no single organization underpinning the Triple Helix that regional residents identify as critical for their success, but it is exactly that frame that gets repeated over and over. In Seattle, government action is important, but the usual reference by interviewees was to the multi-stakeholder negotiations known as the Seattle process, which civic leaders go back to again and again as a way to resolve conflict. In San Antonio, the celebration of collaboration between sectors is so much a part of the region's self-presentation that it is right to worry whether the important role of political skirmishes and social movements in putting equity on the agenda will be forgotten. In short, while policies may be implemented and institutions created, the real underpinnings we found (and were searching for) have to do with the evolution of regional social norms about knowledge generation, information sharing, and conflict resolution.

None of this is as easy to measure as, say, a Gini coefficient. We are definitely aficionados of large data sets, complex metrics, and multivariate regressions (remember chapter 2?), and we did want a quantitative approach to both inform and set the stage for our case studies. But there is a sort of depth of understanding, particularly of qualitative social processes, that can only be attained with visits to the field. And so we went, with questionnaires in tow and frequent-flyer accounts in hand, as we crisscrossed the country in search of community. What we learned sometimes confirmed and sometimes surprised, but it always informed, as we looked for new ways in which leaders were sinking roots, forging relationships, and bringing reason to a conversation about our metropolitan future.

CHAPTER 4

Parks and Recreation

Planning the Epistemic Community

Information produced according to the conventional model,
by presumably neutral experts who work outside and
apart from the political and bureaucratic process through
which policy gets made, does not become embedded in
the institutions or the players' understandings. It will
become . . . shared knowledge, only if there is plenty of talk
about the meaning of the information, its accuracy, and
its implications. Information does not influence unless it
represents a socially constructed and shared understanding
created in the community of policy actors. If, however, the
meaning does emerge through such a social process, the
information changes the actors and their actions, often
without their applying it expressly to a specific decision.

—Judith Innes (1998, 56)

No one achieves anything alone.

—Leslie Knope, character on the NBC TV series
Parks and Recreation

There is a joke sometimes told in urban planning circles, involving how
many planners it takes to screw in a light bulb. The answer? None, but
it takes fifteen to prepare the plan for coping in the dark. Or, sometimes:
None, they are all too busy trying to plan the perfect light bulb. Strik-
ingly, both answers are "none," and both capture the essence of what
is often the common picture of urban planners in American cities: well-
meaning professional experts with detailed knowledge and technical
expertise, producing beautiful urban plans that all too often end up

irrelevant, ignored, or distorted in the messy political and market-driven processes that fundamentally drive urban development.

Indeed, planners themselves often lament the problems created from the largely unplanned market-driven urban sprawl that characterizes most US cities, and historical studies of metropolitan development patterns rarely point to deliberate urban planning as a prominent factor in shaping regional growth. This is not to suggest that politics and policy aren't important. To the contrary, there is a whole school of thought focused on the important role of urban growth coalitions in shaping regional development (Fulton 2001; Logan and Molotch 2007). Meanwhile, federal policies—everything from transportation spending to forms of housing subsidies and structures of local government—are critical for understanding how regions have grown (Lewis and Sprague 1997; Muro et al. 2008).

But what is clearly inadequate is the sort of technocratic, dispassionate, and disconnected "rational planning" model which has often dominated the profession. Increasingly, planners are recognizing how much their work is embedded in the broader social and political processes that shape cities. Indeed, one perspective, which we turn to in chapter 6 to help us understand conflict and collaboration in regional development processes, argues that planners should play more of an advocacy role. According to this approach, planners should explicitly articulate their values in developing planning proposals, and do so while advocating for the interests of underrepresented perspectives and constituencies (Checkoway 1994; Davidoff 1965).

While this "advocacy planning" approach occupies one sort of extreme, other planning scholars have suggested that the planner's job is mainly to help build consensus in the planning process. This can be done through a combination of providing professional advice and analysis to elected officials and the public *and* mediating between conflicting interests to develop shared goals and priorities. While this "communicative rationality" approach is also a departure from the rational-planner perspective, it is less conflictual than the messy, tense, and combative processes envisioned in advocacy planning. Instead, communicative rationality emphasizes that the *process* by which information is produced is critically important in ensuring its understanding and use by institutions (Forester 1989; Innes and Booher 1999; Innes 1998).

Linkages between this perspective and what we are terming diverse and dynamic epistemic communities are not hard to find. As reflected in the quote from Judith Innes that begins this chapter, communicative planning recognizes that it is important to consider not just what planners and regional stakeholders know but who they know it with, and how information developed in shared processes actually shapes actors and their actions (versus information generated in separate processes of technocratic planning). At the same time, there are key distinctions between notions of communicative rationality and our perspectives on epistemic communities. First, in our view, an epistemic community can include conflict and skirmish that will raise uncomfortable but important issues; and second, planners playing a leading role in epistemic communities is only one variation on a theme—only one possible way to build an epistemic community.

This chapter is all about that variation. In two of our regional case studies, the role of formal collaborative regional planning emerged as an important institutional support for the development of diverse and dynamic epistemic communities. In Sacramento, these processes were driven primarily by the public sector through the efforts of the Sacramento Area Council of Governments (SACOG) to develop long-range regional plans through broad participatory processes. These processes helped a wide range of constituencies understand the importance of an integrated land-use and transportation planning process in ensuring quality of life in the region. Initiated in the early 2000s, this "Blueprint process" was prominent in the region's efforts to recover from the economic shocks of the 1990s; it also revealed some underlying yet commonly held values around resource conservation and sustainability, helping bridge gaps between otherwise uncommon allies.

In Salt Lake City, in the midst of broadly held conservative and antigovernment sentiments, a very similar participatory process of long-range regional planning was led not by a regional government planning body but by a small nonprofit organization called Envision Utah. Despite different origins, the process of information sharing across diverse constituencies, and the generation of broadly shared goals for regional development patterns informed by like values across diverse constituencies, were quite similar to Sacramento's. Here, the inclusion of diverse constituencies in regional planning processes was (perhaps counterintuitively) also facilitated by certain characteristics of the Mormon Church and the implications they had for regional social norms.

In what follows, we look first at Salt Lake City and then Sacramento. In each case, we review the patterns of economic growth and social equity in the region, explore the processes that have brought together diverse epistemic communities, and consider *how* these processes have shaped patterns of growth and equity. In each case, we try to highlight the elements

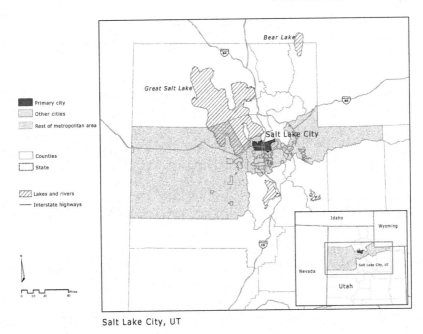

Salt Lake City, UT

MAP 4.1. Salt Lake City Region.

we raised in our framework in chapter 1: membership in regional knowledge sharing; the ties that bind different constituencies together; the ways knowledge is generated and considered valid; the focus of particular outcomes; and the dynamics of knowledge creation and interpretation over time. We conclude the chapter with some further discussion of the overall characteristics of planning-influenced community-building, setting the stage for comparison with other approaches in the chapters that follow.

SALT LAKE CITY

Our team arrived for the Salt Lake City (map 4.1) case study in three waves. The first of us, a research analyst assisting on the project, came early to spend the weekend with family; the second (Chris Benner) arrived to get the interviews started; and the last (Manuel Pastor) slipped into town in the early evening and just in time for the second day. Greeting him at the airport was Robert Grow, president and CEO of Envision Utah; he was not only enthusastic about the research visit but also eager to show off the new light rail extension that would whisk both Grow and Pastor to downtown Salt Lake.

The pride was justified—it's a nice and efficient line—but the sense of accomplishment wasn't about the quality of the trains or the smoothness of the ride. In a conservative locale usually adverse to taxes and planning, the overall system had derived its local funding from an increase in the sales tax that was approved by a remarkable two-thirds of voters in 2006. One of the more significant contributions to this success was a savvy marketing campaign by the Utah Transit Authority. Centered on the fact that the system takes 81,000 cars off the road every day and incorporating the tag-line "Even if you don't ride it, you use it," the campaign specifically marketed the benefits of transit to non-riders as well as riders. A multi-year planning effort also shifted hearts and minds, such that suburbanites who had once resisted further spending on light rail began to clamor to have lines extended to them. Most remarkable was the journey from the airport itself. Grow noted that the line was going through some of the poorest and most Hispanic neighborhoods in the city, suggested how the stations there would both promote local businesses and connect people to jobs, and then pointed out all the compact development occurring in and around the booming downtown.

The new light rail line, linking poor neighborhoods to employment opportunities while also serving the needs of elite air travelers, is a physical manifestation of the diverse membership in the region's knowledge networks. The lay clergy structure of the Church of Jesus Christ of Latter-day Saints (LDS Church) and its extensive welfare operations also contributes to these diverse connections, since it creates a systematic and personal connection between successful elites and the poor that is rare elsewhere in the country. Meanwhile, Envision Utah, a nonprofit founded in the mid-1990s, has helped the region address major growth challenges by bringing thousands of ordinary neighborhood residents together with regional business and public-sector leaders in a sustained effort of communicative planning.

To those who think that equity, growth, and sustainability must be the province of politically progressive locations, Salt Lake City might seem like an odd choice (although the central city has long had Democratic mayors, some with remarkably leftist politics).[1] But the value of a case-selection process driven at least partly by quantitative considerations is that it can yield pleasant (or at least interesting) surprises—as well as pleasant greetings and rides from the airport.

As it turns out, over the last three decades, Salt Lake City has maintained levels of inequality and poverty that remain substantially below national averages, while also creating an economic growth trajectory that is remarkable, not only in its consistent and sustained growth over a long period, but also in the relatively even distribution of that growth.

This growth has been sustained even in the most recent decade, as the historically homogeneous Salt Lake City region has experienced a dramatic growth in its non-white population, which has put it on a path to become a "majority-minority" region several years before the country as a whole.

There are several structural factors that help explain this sustained growth, including high quality of life and relatively low housing costs, both of which have helped attract people and businesses to the region. There are also several structural factors that might explain the more inclusive nature of that growth, including an improving education profile for the metro (compared to the larger Western census region). However, our main object in this case is to examine how a diverse regional knowledge community has come together, how it relates to broader social processes and norms in the region, and how this might help explain the region's patterns of growth and equity.

Below, we begin by reviewing the statistical record. We then turn to the broader institutional and cultural influence of the Mormon Church, and specifically the way this facilitates connections between communities of prosperity and poverty. We then consider the role of Envision Utah, arguing that while the longer-term culture of the region paved the way for communicative planning, the planning itself was well executed and well suited to the specificities of the region, and played an important role in faciliating connections across diverse perspectives and constituencies.

Sustained and Shared Prosperity

Between 1980 and 2010, employment in the Salt Lake metropolitan area grew by an explosive 119 percent, compared to an average of 57 percent for the top 192 metros in the United States and 73 percent for those in the West. Growth in average earnings per job was about average: 22 percent in real terms, roughly comparable to the 19-percent average for all top 192 metros and 20 percent for those in the West. What is remarkable is that the wage gains were distributed across all levels of the labor market. Between 1990 and 2010, for instance, average real earnings in the third of two-digit NAICS industries paying the highest wages grew by 23 percent, while earnings grew by 24 percent in the middle third and 28 percent in the lowest third; most American metro regions experienced earnings growth only at the top, and often declining earnings in the lower tiers of the labor market. Salt Lake City also experienced almost equal growth in low-, medium-, and high-paying industries over this time, while most metro regions either experienced an expansion in low-wage industries or a polarization of employment, with growth in low-paying and high-paying industries but not in middle-income industries.

This stronger performance in the middle of the labor market is reflected in more traditional equity measures. Salt Lake's poverty rate indeed increased from 8.6 percent in 1980 to 13.1 percent in 2010, but this still remained substantially below the 15.6-percent average for the top 192 metro areas. Inequality, as measured by the 80/20 household income ratio, increased by 8.5 percent over the three decades (from 3.7 to 4), substantially less than the 12-percent average increase across the top 192 metros. The Gini coefficient of household income inequality in Salt Lake City in 1980 was 0.37, lower than the 0.39 for the United States as a whole. Though inequality worsened in subsequent decades, the Gini coefficient in Salt Lake remained among the lowest of the top 192 metros (23rd lowest, with neighboring Ogden-Clearfield and Provo-Orem metros ranked 2nd and 15th lowest) and substantially below national averages.

The region's record in sustaining growth is also striking. The single longest unbroken growth spell of any metropolitan region between 1990 and 2011—a period of 69 quarters (more than 17 years) of unbroken annualized growth in employment—is in Ogden, Utah, just north of Salt Lake City; while this is formally a different metropolitan area, the entire Wasatch Front urbanized area, stretching from Ogden in the north to Provo in the south, is considered by residents the more accurate functional metropolitan area and is the scale of regional planning addressed by Envision Utah. Both Salt Lake City and Provo experienced short employment downturns in the 2000 recession, but with each boasting unbroken growth spells that got to 10.5 years, they still rank in the top 20 percent of metropolitan areas in the country in the maximum length of sustained growth spells.

The Book of Mormon

What explains this pattern for growth and equity? First, it is impossible to talk about development in Salt Lake without acknowledging the profound influence of the Church of Latter Day Saints (LDS Church). Though the percentage of Utah's population that is Mormon has declined with population growth, statewide, it was still an estimated

62 percent in 2012, and in Salt Lake County (the core of the CBSA) it was just over 51 percent (Canham 2012). Of course, the influence of the LDS Church goes beyond simply the percentage of the population, as it plays a substantial role in shaping the economics, politics, and culture of the region.

One of the important influences of the church has to do with its role in addressing poverty in the region. While Mormons are generally quite conservative and have a strong suspicion of centralized government programs—a sentiment embedded in the larger Utah culture—the church has developed a quite substantial internal welfare structure that was first established in the 1930s. Mormons are encouraged to fast one day a month, and to donate at least the money that was saved on two missed meals, if not more, to the local church's welfare fund. One hundred percent of these fast offerings are used to provide assistance to those in need (adminstrative costs associated with these programs are privately provided by the church through other channels). The church owns hundreds of thousands of acres of farmland and dairy operations. Food, including processed food products largely manufactured by the LDS-owned Deseret Industries and Deseret Manufacturing, are sent to the over 140 storehouses that the LDS Church operates. All told, some 10,000 volunteers work in these enterprises each year and in a range of humanitarian assistance efforts, and the total amount of humanitarian assistance provided between 1985 and 2011 was estimated at $1.4 billion.[2]

The bishop of the local ward or congregation is responsible for identifying those in need and for providing assistance to help people get back on their feet. This involves not simply allocating access to food and financial support but also advice and referrals to a range of support services provided by the LDS Church, including employment services, English as a second language assistance, social services, and clothing distribution, among others.

This important role of the local bishop highlights another feature of the LDS Church structure which becomes particularly important for our analysis: the personal contact with those less fortunate. The LDS Church has a lay clergy structure at the local level; bishops are called to service from among the members of a local congregation and serve without pay for a temporary period, typically three to seven years. Men who are called to be bishops are frequently among the more prominent and successful leaders in the community, including major business leaders.[3] Thus, as we were told by a number of our key informants, many business executives and CEOs in the region have direct experience for an extended period of time acting essentially as social workers. While most of the assistance provided through these internal welfare structures benefits Mormons, bishops also frequently provide assistance to non-Mormons, reflecting the church's commitment to helping those in need regardless of their beliefs.

The LDS Church has also contributed to a different tone around immigrant integration. This is partly because the church has such a significant international presence, but also because missionaries, who are mostly between the ages of eighteen and twenty-five, serve 18–24 months abroad and acquire a knowledge of what it means to be a stranger in a strange land. Whatever the factors, the results have been remarkable for what is clearly a conservative state. In 1999, immigrants were allowed to obtain driver's licenses using a tax number rather than a Social Security number, and since 2002, undocumented high school graduates have been allowed to pay in-state tuition at state institutions of higher education, a provision consistent with the federal-level DREAM Act—which was originally cosponsored by US Senator Orrin Hatch, from Utah.

Perhaps the most striking evidence of this different tone came in 2010 with the unveiling of the Utah Compact (www.utahcompact.com). Supported by a broad coalition of business leaders, religious groups, and politicians, the compact was a statement of principles about immigration. It was intended in part to blunt the growing anti-immigrant sentiment that was seeping its way from Arizona into Utah politics and that was accelerated when Arizona state Senator (and member of the Mormon Church) Russell Pearce became the primary sponsor of Arizona's infamous anti-immigrant bill, SB 1070. In contrast to the sentiments expressed in Arizona, the principles of the Utah Compact include celebrating the importance of immigrants to Utah's economy, recognizing the integration of immigrants into communities across the state, and opposing policies that unnecessarily separate families. The development of the pact was led by the Salt Lake City Chamber of Commerce, in close collaboration with, among others, the Catholic Diocese and the conservative Sutherland Institute, reflecting a surprising diversity of interests committed to immigrant integration. While the Mormon Church never formally signed the compact, it did issue a formal statement supporting the principles of the compact, describing it as "a responsible approach to the urgent challenge of immigration reform" that is consistent with key principles of the Mormon faith.[4]

The tone set by the Utah Compact suggests an approach one might not associate with the conservative voices representing the state in

Congress. It is a tone characterized by valuing the "other," recognizing common roots in the region, and trying to develop a civil conversation about the facts. It is this sort of regional culture that helped to set the context for and, arguably, helped facilitate the creation of one of the most impressive collaborative, consensus-based, regional planning initiatives in the country: Envision Utah.

Vision and Voice

Envision Utah originated from the creation of the Coalition for Utah's Future in 1988. The coalition, which included political, business, and civic leaders, came together because of a growing concern about losing population, particularly younger people, to more prosperous states. The economic troubles facing Salt Lake City in that era ended up being quite short-lived; by the early 1990s, unemployment had dropped to 3.5 percent and employment growth rates averaged 4–5 percent a year for four years in a row, driven in part by a technology boom.[5] Instead of population loss, by mid-decade the primary concerns were around quality-of-life issues, with growing air pollution and rapidly expanding sprawl, which was eating up farmlands and threatening neighboring canyons and mountainland.

Thus, in 1995, the coalition began the Envision Utah project, in an effort to address the challenges of population growth and sprawl along the entire Wasatch Front. It was clear from the beginning that for the initiative to have any impact it could not be predicated on the influence of government zoning or regulatory authority—that's just not how Salt Lake rolls. Rather, it had to be deeply rooted in the values of hundreds of organizations and thousands of individuals throughout the region. Thus, the process began with the creation of a hundred-person steering committee representing a wide range of influential business leaders, philanthropists, community leaders, and politicians, and the commissioning of a study of community values related to quality of life. This study ended up identifying two critical values that underpinned future efforts: the importance of Utah's scenic beauty and recreational opportunities; and the deep commitment to being a valued place for raising children and strengthening families (Envision Utah 2013; Scheer 2012).

Subsequent Envision Utah efforts included the development of alternative scenarios for long-range development in the region, and a broad public consultation process about the variety of possible future scenarios that included more than 2,000 people in fifty public workshops and some 17,500 responses over the Internet and through a mail-in newspaper survey (Envision Utah 2013). The resulting Quality Growth Strategy was not a detailed land-use plan for the region but a summary of the preferred direction and principles of growth. These included seven clear goals for future development: improving air quality, promoting housing options, creating transportation choices, encouraging water conservation, preserving critical lands, supporting efficient infrastructure, and exploring community development. These principles then became the basis for the development of more detailed implementation plans (for local jurisdictions throughout the region and regional planning bodies) that have extended through to today.

By 2012, the dean of the University of Utah's School of Architecture and Planning described the impact of the initiative's "remarkable" success in this way:

> The Salt Lake metro region has an extensive and rapidly expanding light rail and commuter rail system that is the envy of much more populous regions. The Department of Housing and Urban Development awarded a Salt Lake regional consortium the largest of its highly competitive Sustainable Communities Grants. The two metropolitan planning organizations of the region have cooperated to prepare a long-range transportation plan based on land use aspirations that include higher density. One of the largest "smart growth" planned developments in the U.S. is taking shape on 95,000 acres on Salt Lake's west side. Cities all over the region are developing plans for transit-oriented development and dense town centers, along with the policy and zoning changes needed to support them. City planners from eleven jurisdictions in Salt Lake County have come together to share data, maps, and forecasting information, with the expectation of assembling a coordinated county plan. . . . Most intriguing, data suggest that Salt Lake County is growing with more compact development and a pronounced tendency for denser housing and new jobs to locate near transit throughout the region. (Scheer 2012, 2–3)

During our site visit, informants stressed that there were a number of keys to the success of these regional planning efforts. The first was the ability to tap into values of a high quality of life, and a concern about the legacy being left to children, which was critical for helping people see the importance of long-range planning rather than in-the-moment market-driven development. The second was attention to long-range visions of the future of the region; this helped overcome contemporary divisions that would be exacerbated in discussions of specific projects *and* helped build a sense of common destiny within the region. Finally, in a place with very conservative and generally anti-government norms, it was important that this regional planning process was driven not by government but by a nonprofit, which was in turn driven by business, civic, and community leadership.

In any case, the collaborative, diverse, and consensus-driven process was critical in shaping people's understanding of complex regional processes and building long-term buy-in to a shared vision. It was not about *government* but about *governance*—and it drew boundaries around planning that crossed issue silos and gave direction to actors, such as cities, developers and agencies, who still retained their own autonomy and authority. And it was not simply about setting a static plan but about developing the capacities to react to economic and demographic shifts. Indeed, the early reasons for jump-starting the effort changed (from concerns about declining population to concerns associated with population growth), but Envision Utah continued. In short, this was almost the very definition of what we have termed a diverse and dynamic epistemic community. And while the favorable results for growth and equity have many structural and other drivers, certainly this was fertile soil being prepared by Envision Utah.

Making Sense of Salt Lake

Chapter 1 offered a frame regarding the key characteristics of a diverse and dynamic epistemic community. The first of those had to do with membership. The remarkable thing in Salt Lake is how widespread participation has been, particularly via the vehicle of Envision Utah. This has been achieved through repeated interactions and long-term communications (including through the media). It is also the case that the LDS Church reinforces norms regarding strong ties to hold the region together—and, interestingly, it also tends to unite non-Mormons into that place identity. Both Mormons and non-Mormons are seen as part of the region's future, and the strong sense of place in the Wasatch Front, along with a cross-cutting and widely held value of preserving the high quality of life in the region, helps bind these diverse constituencies together.

With respect to ways of knowing, however, the LDS Church probably has a narrowing effect on the types of knowledge that are considered legitimate in the region. After all, African Americans were barred from the Mormon priesthood until 1978 (White and White 1980), and women are still not allowed to be ordained, which arguably reflects beliefs that emphasize "distinct gender roles [that restrict] women's contributions, [assign] them to a particular sphere, and [add] to their silence and invisibility" (Cornwall 2001, 262). On the other hand, beliefs and practices of Mormons have played an invaluable role in helping build the visibility of the poor and of immigrants in the region, including those who are undocumented. Envision Utah's work has also been critical in validating the perspectives of ordinary residents in long-range planning processes that can sometimes be dominated in other places by technically sophisticated planning professionals.

One critical gap in the work of Envision Utah has been its tendency to avoid controversy (Scheer 2012). The group eschewed any stance on an important freeway project that some viewed as sprawl-inducing (or at least sprawl-reinforcing), and it also sidestepped issues raised by a massive redevelopment project undertaken by the LDS Church—one that again seemed to be pushing growth outward, and was therefore at odds with the more compact approach Envision Utah has stressed. This was not a subconscious mistake. Part of the strategy of Envision Utah has been to focus on the long term and stay "above" the day-to-day by downplaying immediate conflicts. Of course, life is made day to day, so one wonders whether Envision Utah can permanently avoid the tough conversations about more difficult topics.

Nonetheless, we don't want to pick too much on what seems to be working. The interconnections of multiple issues—from air quality to housing development to transportation, and so on—within a long-term planning process seems to have helped build and sustain wide engagement of diverse stakeholders in discussions about the region's future—and it is arguably just as dynamic, if not more so, sixteen years after it began. Though there is no guarantee of what the future will bring, the regional planning processes that have evolved in Salt Lake over the past few decades are impressive, and seem to have played some role in creating the conditions for what turns out to have been a relatively strong performance on growth and equity.

SACRAMENTO

Sacramento is another region where planning processes have been important for shaping the region's trajectory. Though sometimes derisively referred to as Cowtown—the unsophisticated inland kid sister of California's flashier coastal cities—Sacramento, the state's capital,

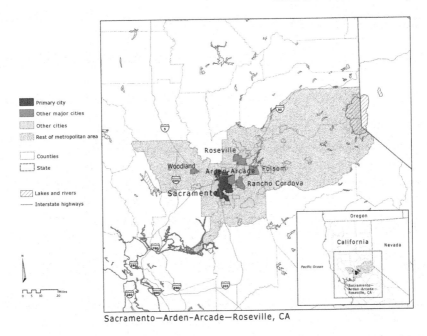

Sacramento—Arden-Arcade—Roseville, CA

MAP 4.2. Sacramento Region.

is now a dynamic region of over two million.[6] Sacramento's economy has traditionally drawn stability from its large public sector, anchored in middle-wage jobs. However, the closure of four large military bases in the late 1980s and early 1990s altered the structure of the region both economically and socially. Sacramento soon realized that weathering major economic shifts requires a broad-based strategy underpinned by a regional vision—and much of the last decade has included substantial regional initiatives intended to define and achieve that vision.

The results have been palpable. While the 1990s were not nearly as prosperous as the 1980s, the region's performance during the most recent decade demonstrated a substantial rebound. These results in the 2000s were shaped by a prominent and multifaceted "smart growth" planning process that helped create a new norm of regional collaboration, with an important role played by the local council of governments. Through its ups and downs (and ups once again), Sacramento has learned—and can teach—some essential lessons about the value of participatory regional planning.

Stumbling and Bouncing Back

Sacramento's patterns of growth and equity over the past thirty years would be the envy of many regions. The region nearly doubled in population between 1980 and 2010, and job growth in the 1980s was over 50 percent, with another 26 percent of growth in the 1990s. Earnings per job have increased consistently as well—growing 7 percent in the 1980s, 14 percent in the 1990s, and 7 percent in the 2000s. Overall patterns of equity, at least as measured by our 80/20 household income ratio, actually improved in the 1980s. Though inequality has increased in recent decades, as it did in nearly all regions in the United States, Sacramento's increases in inequality and poverty have been substantially smaller than the average in the West and in the country as a whole.

Some of Sacramento's success can be attributed to structural ingredients that generally help to shape equitable growth patterns: a strong public sector, providing a sizable and relatively stable number of middle-class jobs; a respected community college system, offering mobility and training to a diverse cross-section of students; and a near-the-Bay location that has proved attractive to some firms wishing to relocate to slightly cheaper environs. In addition to being California's capital and so hosting a range of state agencies, Sacramento's public-sector employment has also been anchored by a strong military presence.

Until the rounds of base closures in the late 1980s and 1990s, Sacramento was home to four large military bases: McClellan Air Force Base, Mather Airfield, Sacramento Army Depot, and Beale Air Force Base. McClellan was the largest of the group, dedicated to logistics and the maintenance of military aircraft. At its peak it employed over 22,000 workers (DuBois 2011). An ecosystem of military contractors and related industries grew to support the local industry, and a segment of these firms is still in operation today, including Aerojet, which designs, builds, and tests rocket engines (Benner and Pastor 2012). And since housing was affordable, unlike in California's high-cost coastal areas, the military and public-sector employees could buy homes, sink roots, and constitute the base for a broad middle class.

Housing and real estate prices were also key to attracting high-tech firms seeking affordable spaces for their operations and quality of life for their employees. Throughout the 1980s and 1990s, the region became an outpost for Silicon Valley firms, such as Hewlett Packard, Apple, and Intel. Beyond lower costs, the region's seismic stability attracted firms looking to relocate away from the earthquake-prone environments of the San Francisco Bay Area.[7] These industries contributed to a more egalitarian growth pattern by providing well-paying jobs for low- and middle-skilled workers. The defense industry, in particular, helped create a strong African American middle class in the region. At the close of the 1980s, average annual wages were relatively high, at $45,800 (inflation-adjusted to 2010 dollars), and unemployment was low, at 4.9 percent.

However, in the 1990s, the economy downshifted, partly due to post–Cold War defense spending cuts and partly due to the rise of low-wage sectors. Between 1988 and 1995, three of Sacramento's military bases closed, and California's share of defense contract expenditures fell from 24 percent of the nation's total to 14 percent in 2003 (Freedman and Ransdell 2005). Simultaneously, the region shifted toward a service-based economy anchored in low-wage jobs. Call centers, back-office operations, and financial processing firms proliferated in the area, drawn by the region's fiber optic infrastructure, the result of early government investment. These jobs partially supplanted those lost from the defense scale-back, but with less of a middle-led thrust. Jobs in high-wage industries actually declined by 14 percent in the 2000s, while low-wage sectors grew by 8 percent, and overall, the share of employment in low-wage sectors grew from 25 percent in 1990 to 30 percent in 2010. Meanwhile, African Americans and Latinos trail whites to a significant degree, with household incomes that are 63 and 73 percent of those of whites, respectively.

Yet a culture of collaboration in the region, which rose to prominence in the base-closure process, has probably helped mitigate some of the worst negative trends and build a foundation for more positive trajectories. During the base-closure process, elected officials and organizations worked across many levels of government to secure new economic development opportunities in advance of base closings and devised a plan for reskilling and repurposing the workforce, which was led by the Sacramento Employment and Training Agency. One prominent example of the success of these coordinated efforts was an initiative, spearheaded by the Sacramento Area Commerce and Trade Organization, to find new tenants for the Army Depot facility. The region was able to entice Packard Bell to relocate from its Southern California location in 1995, prompted in part by damage to its Southern California facilities caused by the 1994 Northridge earthquake (Lesher and Leeds 1997).

The decentering of the economy away from an anchor industry has nudged many organizations, local governments, and businesses toward the development of intersectoral networks and collaboration. Sacramento's increasing size and diversity—in 2010, it was home to nearly 2.15 million residents, nearly half of whom were people of color—have also contributed to the growth of new interests and alignments. Simply put, in a growing region with no stars—whether major corporations, large-scale philanthropies, or big-name individuals—people have more often had to work together to solve complex problems rather than depending on single leaders or individuals to pave the way. Through careful and thoughtful regional planning processes, Sacramento's knowledge networks, leadership structures, and decision-making processes are evolving and embracing the idea of more inclusive and more sustainable economic growth.

Planning the Future

In the absence of a pillar industry, a major philanthropic force, or a strong social movement for justice, Sacramento's regional leadership has historically been a "roving" one (a term used by one of our interviewees). Rather than individuals or institutions acting as regional conveners, collaborations tend to form around single campaigns, and the constellation of actors and interests involved is determined by the issue at hand. While this model can have its upsides—mainly that regional collaboration is not dependent on one leader or entity and thus can endure through personnel turnover—it also means that regional collaboration has no permanent home.

Yet, over the last decade in particular, signs of more institutionalized regional collaboration have emerged in an effort to plan for a more sustainable future. One key initiative has been the regional Blueprint process, a public sector–led "smart growth" planning initiative that merges some of the newest thinking around land use and development patterns. Indeed, the origins of the Blueprint are rooted in the problems wrought by earlier patterns of development. Through the 1980s, 1990s, and early 2000s, Sacramento's population and employment growth were accompanied by low-density housing development sprawling outward from the urban core. This pattern led to a severe imbalance between jobs and housing, creating high levels of car dependence and increased air pollution associated with vehicle emissions (McKeever 2011). Indeed, it was estimated that if Sacramento were to continue this pattern of unabated and rapid sprawl, which was swallowing agricultural land, the region's traffic congestion would increase by 50 percent by 2050 (Faust and Cogan 2010).

Unlike Salt Lake, in which the largely anti-government sentiment meant that regional planning was best launched from the nonprofit sector, in Sacramento the metropolitan planning organization, SACOG (Sacramento Area Council of Governments, consisting of twenty-two cities and six counties),[8] stepped up to convene regional stakeholders and address the problems arising from sprawling development patterns. Starting in 2002, SACOG began a long-range regional planning process to engage residents in helping shape how their communities grow, through a common vision for land use and transportation infrastructure through 2050. As one might imagine in a relatively diverse region, there were many opposing views about the future of Sacramento. The first main conflict was between environmentalists and builders. Environmentalists were concerned about the continued negative impact of unbridled sprawl on the region's environment and air quality, while builders were concerned about regulations that would jeopardize their livelihoods by limiting development.

A second main conflict was between urban, suburban, and rural jurisdictions. This is a common challenge in regional planning because different geographies have different economies and different land-use and transportation needs. Moreover, there are power imbalances between large urban cores and smaller rural towns, and resource allocation can be very contentious. So, not only were there long-standing interjurisdictional tensions around power and resources, all the cities and counties were concerned that SACOG's long-term regional vision and plan would overlook or even hinder the ability of each city and county to address its community's unique needs.

To facilitate collaboration and work through these deeply entrenched and often heated conflicts, SACOG took a simple yet rarely used approach: focus the conversation on the facts instead of ideology—or, as SACOG executive director Mike McKeever put it in our interview with him, "the science behind how the region operates." In short, as part of visioning for the long-term regional plan, SACOG promoted dialogue about facts to develop a "common knowledge base"—the heart of epistemic communities—rather than fights about beliefs and opinions that were not likely to change.

Using the Envision Utah model of scenario planning, SACOG spearheaded a process of comparing a base case scenario of sprawling and uncontrolled urbanization—the status quo—against other scenarios designed to promote denser development and expanded mass transit. To help with the community-outreach piece of the Blueprint process,

SACOG partnered with Valley Vision, a nonprofit organization committed to building civic engagement while addressing regional issues. SACOG was responsible for the technical and land-use planning work, while Valley Vision led the outreach effort (Faust and Cogan 2010). Throughout the region, SACOG held more than thirty neighborhood-level workshops (involving more than 1,000 community members) to discuss development scenarios. Following this, discussions were held in five of the six counties in SACOG's jurisdiction, and more than 1,400 people participated in a final regional forum on April 30, 2004.

Part of presenting the facts was providing statistics about the region. SACOG profiled the region's projected employment and population growth and other demographic information to begin a conversation about expected growth in the future. Working with groups like the Urban Land Institute and the Metro Chamber, SACOG also did a survey of housing choice preferences and demonstrated the demand for more multi-family options—which served as helpful market information for developers and builders by demonstrating the existing and future market for denser development.[9]

The other, and perhaps more important, data piece for the purpose of bringing diverse interests and geographies together was public opinion polling throughout the region. SACOG commissioned Richard Wirthlin, a well-respected polling consultant to Ronald Reagan, to test the public's attitudes toward growth and specific planning principles, such as mixed land use, walkable neighborhoods, open-space preservation, and transportation choice. He found that the region's residents were concerned about the potential downsides of growth, such as worse traffic and air quality, and that they supported regional planning and its related principles. These results were shared at an Elected Officials Summit, a large gathering of 80 local officials representing city councils and county boards across the region. At the summit, officials were asked a series of questions on regional growth and the Blueprint via live polling, and these results showed strong support for the plan's growth-management approach (SACOG 2004).

In the end, through a long and intentional process of community engagement and consensus building, the Blueprint developed a map showing different types of growth that constituents wanted to occur by 2050, guided by seven principles: housing choice and diversity, use of existing assets, compact development, natural resources conservation, high-quality design, mixed-use development, and transportation choices. As one interviewee stated, at the beginning of the Blueprint process in 2003, these principles were extremely controversial; by the final vote in 2004, they were just common sense—or, more formally put, new norms.

The planning effort was so innovative and collaborative that it would eventually garner national awards for both the outcome and the process that produced it. The Blueprint process has also served as a template for other regional planning efforts and influenced both state and national policy. In California, the Blueprint informed the development of Senate Bill 375, which sets regional greenhouse gas reduction goals, emphasizing the role of urban and regional planning strategies to curb pollution. Under the plan, regional planning bodies are required to develop a Sustainable Communities Strategy as a part of their regional transportation plan (Eaken, Horner, and Ohland 2012). It seems no coincidence that the author of the bill, Senator Darrell Steinberg, is a long-time Sacramento resident and former member of the city council. The Blueprint process also informed the development of—and plans stemming from—the US Department of Housing and Urban Development's Sustainable Communities Initiative, which provides grants to support sustainable local and regional planning efforts that integrate housing and transportation plans with land-use planning to encourage sustainable development (Chapple and Mattiuzzi 2013; ISC 2012).

From conflict to collaboration, the Blueprint process is a striking example of using the planning process to generate an epistemic community—a network with shared mechanisms of knowledge generation and knowledge integration—and to then use that newly developed, shared knowledge in decision-making processes that can create new cultural norms and further the common good. Through the process, a strong sense of regionalism emerged; communities and sectors began to view themselves as part of a broader regional puzzle, rather than stand-alone pieces.

Coming Up Short

Of course, every process has its shortcomings. The biggest gap in the Blueprint was the relative lack of attention to social equity. Equity advocates note three broad areas for improvement: better incorporation of disadvantaged communities in planning; the creation of more equity-focused planning goals; and the need to develop specific equity metrics to track performance.

Realizing the need to do better on equity—and also prodded by state law—SACOG is taking steps to incorporate equity metrics and goals, most recently within the context of their Sustainable Community Strategy—an update to the Blueprint plan. One chapter of the plan, "Equity and Choice," outlines strategies for increasing outreach, understanding affected communities, and planning for equity outcomes. In terms of outreach, SACOG has turned an eye toward refining its outreach efforts, particularly toward the environmental justice community, as well as other disadvantaged groups like new immigrants and those with limited English-speaking abilities. On the data and goals front, SACOG is working to define and map vulnerable areas and environmental justice communities, including their transportation and housing options. These baseline metrics contributed to the development of equity-related performance metrics in the plan (SACOG 2012). SACOG received feedback from several local organizations, including the Center for Regional Change at the University of California, Davis (http:// regionalchange.ucdavis.edu)—an equity-focused research center—and the Coalition on Regional Equity (CORE).

While SACOG could have done better at including equity voices in its first iterations of the Blueprint, it is also the case that the current fragmentation of equity groups and interests within the region presents a challenge. Sacramento's equity advocates include several strong issue-based groups representing various interests—from environmental justice communities to housing and human rights advocates to regional equity researchers—but there is no specific regional coalition and no shared forum for developing policy and organizing strategies around equity.

For a few years, CORE served as the focal point for organizing the region's groups on issues of equitable development, having been formed in 2007 after a number of member organizations successfully fought for one of the nation's most progressive inclusionary housing ordinances. The group went on to shine a light on residential segregation and health disparities, and the need for affordable housing and better access to healthy food. But while CORE's work was impactful, it was also short-lived, as the group dissolved over internal tensions in 2013. The nature of the tensions was actually quite classic: groups more oriented around social-change advocacy were interested in stronger action, while groups more enmeshed in the delivery of social services and housing development were worried about being too explicitly political.

In any case, the growing focus on equity, made more explicit through the Sustainable Communities Strategy process, serves as another step toward building a diverse and dynamic knowledge-sharing community in Sacramento. While the Blueprint process initially came up a bit short with regard to including equity concerns and equity actors, there is an iterative dynamism in the process—it has what one observer called a "rinse-wash-repeat" nature—and the architects of the Blueprint themselves have recognized the need to build in more metrics and goals for social equity (Pastor and Benner 2011, 102). This is of course more difficult when the equity actors are a bit fragmented, but this just presents another challenge.

Synthesizing Sacramento

Recall that our broad characteristics of diverse epistemic communities include their membership, the way they create ties that bind, the ways of knowing that are viewed as valid, the range of outcomes under discussion, and the ability to adapt over time. This historical trajectory is key, particularly since a longer set of repeated interactions can set a regional epistemic community on a better and more stable path. However, in Sacramento, the emergence of a diverse and dynamic process is relatively new, and it was largely jump-started by a formal planning mechanism.

Until the 1990s, Sacramento's regional economy and pattern of reasonably equitable development stemmed largely from a healthy public sector and a strong defense industry—so equitable outcomes were partially a byproduct of an economy producing middle-wage jobs, many of which employed people of color. With declines in defense spending in the 1990s and the appearance of the consequences of rapid and poorly planned growth, particularly sprawl and environmental degradation, the region's calling card of livability, including clean air, good jobs, affordable housing, and sensible commute times, was under threat.

The largest and most comprehensive response to this challenge was the Blueprint process, a regional planning effort advanced by SACOG. Generating a vision for regional growth required deep outreach, the use of data to cut through ideology and tensions (i.e., new "ways of knowing"), and a focus on integrating feedback and refining the plan to create buy-in. Through this process of convening, knowledge sharing, and regional goal setting, Sacramento has experienced an emergence of a form of multi-sector and multi-goal regional collaboration containing many of the elements of what could be a diverse and dynamic epistemic community in the future. Given the rather modest expectations that planners would be able to do any of this—as evidenced by the jokes at the beginning of this chapter—it is all the more remarkable that SACOG has come close.

PLANNING FOR PROGRESS

Urban and regional planning in the United States can sometimes seem to involve a mind-numbing focus on the micro-details of zoning and regulations. How many parking spots should be required for each new housing unit? What setback distance from the street is optimal for a new commercial development? What density of housing and commercial space is appropriate for particular neighborhoods? How high can new buildings rise above street level? How quickly can we end this conversation?

Communicative planning aims a bit higher. It understands that though technical details may be critically important for building better neighborhoods, cities, and regions, the most important topics involve the political processes of regional development and the role of participation in planning processes. And, as we have argued here using the cases of Salt Lake City and Sacramento, such planning can actually go beyond the technical specifications of the built environment and encourage a dialogue about norms and values and how they should shape the communities and regions in which we live.

This is exactly the stuff of building diverse and dynamic epistemic communities—and as we suggest in subsequent chapters, it can actually occur in ways that are more diffuse and multi-sector than is generally envisioned in the literature on "communicative rationality." On the other hand, sometimes planners can play an important role—and that was certainly the case in both the regions reviewed here. In Salt Lake City, Envision Utah, and in Sacramento, SACOG, managed to create a new conversation that has facilitated the emergence of a common understanding about each region's destiny.

There are three features of these cases—each rooted in regional planning efforts—that seem particularly important to stress here, and that link back to our efforts to elaborate the characteristics of diverse and dynamic epistemic communities. The first has to do with the time frame of the visioning processes, and the associated ability to maintain a dynamism of interaction over time. In both cases, discussions emphasized both long-range trends that were creating current regional challenges, and long-term visions of what future regional development patterns might look like. This long-range perspective helps regional stakeholders move beyond their immediate needs and interests, and be more open to thinking about different choices and options of future development patterns. It also enabled processes of implementation and monitoring to follow on from the initial visioning process, allowing the members of the epistemic community to adjust to changes and emerging challenges. Of course, setting aside the day-to-day to downplay critical tensions can actually work against long-term goals—conflicts still simmer. The initial emphasis on a longer time frame can also break down entrenched conflicts and help stakeholders with seemingly opposing interests understand that they may have a lot more in common than is initially apparent.

A second key feature of these collaborative long-range planning efforts was the recognition of the legitimacy of others' viewpoints and interests. All too often, in policy debates or political campaigns, the focus is on gaining a majority so that one group's preferences can prevail and then be imposed on the minority. But in these comprehensive planning processes, there was an effort to include all residents of the region, if not in the planning process, at least in the plan. It is that recognition of the legitimacy of "the other"—whether that "other" is defined by political ideology, economic interests, race, or any other dimension—that facilitates the acceptance of diversity that we think is crucial to forging a common destiny.

Finally, though tensions emerged in both regions around processes of long-term planning, the parties involved remained committed to continued engagement. Through processes of information sharing and vision setting, residents and regional leaders came to see new ways in which their futures were bound together. This sense of a common regional destiny—despite differences in interests, values, and experiences—helped each region develop coordinated responses to regional challenges, and developed new ties that bound different interests in the region together. There are certainly limits to the levels of involvement in these deliberate planning processes, with a fragmented constituency advocating for social equity still characterizing both regions. But the level of broad participation was substantial, and this helped create a new sense of the region and of the role for regional place-making.

Business Knows Best

Elite-Driven Regional Stewardship

Regional stewards are leaders who are committed to the
long-term well-being of places. They are integrators who cross
boundaries of jurisdiction, sector, and discipline to address
complex regional issues such as sprawl, equity, education,
and economic development. They see the connection between
economic, environmental, and social concerns and they know
how to "connect the dots" to create opportunities for their
regions. . . . Stewardship means the careful and responsible
management of something entrusted in our care.

—Douglas Henton and Alliance for Regional Stewardship (2000), 3–4

In May 2000, fifty business and public-sector leaders from regions
around the United States gathered in Kohler, Wisconsin, to explore creating a national network that would support regional initiatives.[1] The
result was the Alliance for Regional Stewardship. Recognizing limits
to both federal power and local activism, and building on a growing
regionalist movement across the country, the Alliance was committed
to the idea that vibrant regions are built on the connections between
an innovative economy, livable communities, social inclusion, and a
collaborative style of governance. Since its founding, the organization
has worked to develop regional leaders and support regional initiatives
that advance these integrated and diverse goals (Henton, Melville, and
Walesh 2003, 2004).

Though created in 2000, the network was building on many years
of previous experience in developing this perspective, including being
inspired in large part by the life and legacy of John W. Gardner, former
Secretary of Health, Education, and Welfare under president Lyndon

Johnson and founder of Common Cause. Gardner was a Republican who worked for a Democratic president and was committed to finding common ground across diverse constituencies in the broader public—a principle that is at the core of diverse epistemic communities. But while the Alliance for Regional Stewardship embraced multiple goals—including the three E's, economy, environment, and equity—it had its real roots in business-led and often elite-driven initiatives such as Joint Venture Silicon Valley, the organization that helped shape the consulting careers of those who helped staff its first phase. (We discuss Joint Venture in greater detail in chapter 7.) And, true to its roots, the Alliance no longer exists as a stand-alone organization but as a part of the American Chamber of Commerce Executives.

The three case-study regions in this chapter seem to particularly embody this elite-driven view of regional stewardship. In Grand Rapids, for example, it was key leaders in local, mostly privately owned companies who worked with local government to revitalize the downtown and help reverse patterns of urban decay that took hold in the 1970s. In Charlotte, executives in the area's banking industry took an enlightened approach to regional development, working, again with public-sector leaders, to transform the region from a sleepy textile town to a dynamic financial-services center with a high quality of life. In Oklahoma City, starting in the early 1990s, multiple Republican mayors worked (and continue to work) in concert with a powerful and conservative Chamber of Commerce to champion multiple rounds of voter-approved increases in regional taxes for major publicly funded development projects, transforming a dying urban core into a vibrant entertainment complex, and a revitalized downtown that stands as a symbol of a dynamic regional economy.

These are clear successes, but there are also clear limits to the levels of diversity that seem possible in this kind of elite-driven stewardship model of regional governance. Indeed, the very term *regional stewardship* reflects these limits, with its roots in the context of ecological stewardship in which enlightened environmentalists provide stewardship for nature, since nature is unable to protect itself in the face of human incursion (Cairns 1967; Knight 1998). Similarly, inherent in the notion of regional stewardship is a paternalistic ethos which is all too often reflected in processes and policies that seem to treat historically marginalized communities as subjects (not actors) in regional governance processes.

The limits of a regional-stewardship approach for the three cases we study here, Grand Rapids, Charlotte, and Oklahoma City, may also be seen in the data on outcomes. While Grand Rapids had a relatively vibrant and inclusive economy in the 1980s and 1990s, this position started to erode in the 2000s. While Charlotte had a reputation for collaborative regional leadership that helped drive investment to the central city and not just the suburbs (Pastor et al. 2000), growth in the region has not been shared broadly in recent years. And while Oklahoma City showed a significantly better record on growth and equity than comparison regions in the 2000s, this was a dramatic turnaround from its record in the 1980s and 1990s; even today, inequality, poverty, and the marginalization of the growing Latino population in Oklahoma City remain significant challenges.

Below, we track the story of these three cases, beginning with a brief review of the patterns of equity and growth that each region has experienced since 1980 and a more detailed charting of the leadership networks in each region and how they have shaped regional development. We conclude each section by analyzing the character of epistemic communities in the region and highlight some of the current challenges facing the metro in question. We conclude the chapter with some final comments on both the strength and the limits of elite-driven processes and regional stewardship models in fully addressing metropolitan challenges.

GRAND RAPIDS

Until recently, Grand Rapids was one of the better-performing regions in the Midwest.[2] There is a long history here. In the mid-nineteenth century, Grand Rapids was one of the major hubs of the country's timber industry, and the region established itself as the premier furniture manufacturing center in the country. Unlike the many other manufacturing-based regions that experienced significant deindustrialization in the 1980s, the "furniture city" was able to sustain a vibrant manufacturing sector, providing good middle-class job opportunities for non–college educated workers as late as the mid-2000s (Vande Bunte 2013). According to the Brookings Institution, while the entire nation lost almost a quarter of its manufacturing jobs between 1980 and 2005, manufacturing jobs in the Grand Rapids region increased by 28 percent (Atkins et al. 2011).[3] Other sectors—particularly health care services—also grew during this time, resulting in an overall increase in jobs of 34 percent in the 1980s and 26 percent in the 1990s. During these two decades, the region's average earnings increased by over 10 percent, and the proportion living in poverty decreased by 3 percent.

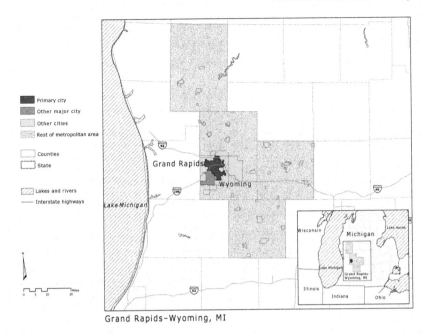

Grand Rapids-Wyoming, MI

MAP 5.1. Grand Rapids Region.

But the 2000s ushered in a painful era for many Grand Rapids families, as the flight of manufacturing jobs that had swept the country in earlier decades finally caught up with the region and office furniture manufacturing firms moved production processes overseas (Atkins et al. 2011). Average earnings also decreased over that time, and so it is not surprising that between 2000 and 2010, the percentage of people living below poverty skyrocketed. Even amidst the Great Recession, Grand Rapids stood out from the crowd. While the Midwest and the top 192 regions in the United States (by population) experienced similarly devastating increases in poverty (50 percent and 29 percent, respectively), Grand Rapids nearly doubled its poverty rate, from 9 to 16 percent. A recent Brookings book finds that the city's poverty rate grew faster than that of any other metropolitan hub in the United States during the last decade (Kneebone 2014).

But despite the recent wave of job loss and increases in poverty, Grand Rapids fared better than most over the longer thirty-year period between 1980 and 2010. A few key features of the region—in addition to the delayed shrinkage of manufacturing—contributed to this pattern. First, Grand Rapids has a small group of wealthy business leaders with deep roots in the area—indeed, many of their family histories in the region go back a century or more—who act as the "fathers" of the region. Partly because of their familial and financial commitment to place, this set of business elites have invested private money into planning and developing the city's major civic projects as part of the downtown revitalization. A strong business presence—in the areas of both governance and philanthropy—is underpinned by a largely conservative electorate who believe that the private sector, not government, should drive growth.

While there is an awareness of the importance of inclusion, it is generally believed that faith-based institutions—predominantly the Dutch Reform Church—are responsible for both providing social services and advocating on behalf of marginalized segments of the population. As the data on social equity show, that's not quite enough. As we will see, the story suggests that an epistemic community relying on elite-driven private-sector stewardship, small government, and a limited social justice organizing infrastructure—consisting of a handful of small faith-based efforts—has its limits.

The Fathers of Grand Rapids

A key feature of the history and development of Grand Rapids is the existence of a small but extremely powerful group of business elite who are deeply rooted and civically engaged in the community. Foremost among these is Grand Rapids–born Richard DeVos, who cofounded a health, beauty, and home product supplier called Amway in 1959 and whose subsequent philanthropic and business investments were key to the downtown revitalization. Other significant businessmen and families in the region have included Peter Wege and the Wege family, who founded a company in 1912 that would become Steelcase, now a global furniture manufacturer, and whose Wege Foundation has been an important philanthropic partner in creating a vibrant regional environment; the billionaire Meijer family, who in 1933 founded the privately held Meijer "hypermarket" chain combining groceries and general merchandise (now one of the twenty largest private companies in the United States) and who have also been active in Grand Rapids philanthropy; and David Frey, whose roots are in the region's banking industry and who has played a critical role in building financial support for downtown revitalization, both individually and in his leadership role in one of the region's larger family foundations, the Frey Family Foundation.

Unlike other regions such as Silicon Valley, this group of private-sector elite did not come from elsewhere; rather, they made their fortunes largely by founding and growing family businesses right in Grand Rapids. With generations in the region, they have had a commitment to being stewards of place, and this was invaluable for the revitalization of downtown Grand Rapids, a process that began in the 1970s. As the story goes, the central city then was like many others in the Midwest: a large number of the downtown businesses had either closed or followed white flight to the suburbs. But in an incident that echoes a similar realization of the empty hole in the middle on the part of the Oklahoma City elite (which we elaborate on below), business leaders had a bit of consciousness-raising in 1976 when the city wanted to throw a welcome-home parade for hometown hero Gerald Ford after he lost his presidential bid to Jimmy Carter. The problem was that there were so many vacant buildings in downtown that the Secret Service didn't have enough security personal to cover them all. The parade was only allowed to go ahead after a further mobilization of all available security personnel in the region—including off-duty sheriff's deputies and law enforcement retirees—collected enough staff to police the parade (Emrich 2008). This incident struck a nerve with the business elite, and it helped motivate their investment in downtown revitalization.[4]

Another major influence was the leadership of the city's first African American mayor, Lyman Parks, who served from 1971 to 1975. He created a committee of business and community leaders to raise funds to improve the convention center and build a music hall downtown. The committee included Amway cofounder Richard DeVos, who provided a crucial major donation to enable the creation of what is still called the DeVos Performance Hall, and who reportedly credits Mayor Parks with convincing him to purchase and renovate the aging Pantlind Hotel (with the other Amway cofounder, Jay Van Andel). These investments were the first of what became a wave of new development in downtown Grand Rapids—including the Van Andel Arena, Meijer Majestic Theatre, DeVos Place, and Michigan State University Medical School—that have completely revitalized the area (DeVos 2014).

Over time, key organizations emerged to institutionalize this individual-led philanthropic and economic development network. In 1991, DeVos convened a group of about fifty business, community, and civic leaders and founded a nonprofit called Grand Action (http://grandaction.org; originally called Grand Vision), which jumpstarted many of the downtown development projects mentioned above, including the arena in 1996 and the convention center in 2003. It also has a philanthropic arm, Grand Action Foundation, that provides large grants for civic projects throughout the city. Around the same time that DeVos convened and founded Grand Action, the Grand Rapids Area Chamber of Commerce—an extremely influential political player not only in the region but also at the state level—started an economic development initiative called The Right Place (www.rightplace.org). This program was fully funded by individuals and private companies to work on business retention, expansion, and attraction through research and training, and became an independent organization in 1997.

Since the community is fairly small and there are a limited number of players and organizations in the business elite network, these three entities—Grand Action, The Right Place, and the Chamber of Commerce—coordinate as the driving force behind regional economic development in Grand Rapids. And although government is noticeably absent from this picture, one of our private-sector interviewees called the Downtown Development Authority—the public partner in Grand Action's three major developments—the "fourth leg of the stool" underpinning local economic development.

A Pattern of "Doing the Right Thing"

While a top-down, elite-driven decision-making process generally marginalizes less advantaged groups in terms of participation, it does not preclude considering the interests of those groups (albeit with more than a bit of *noblesse oblige*). The sort of regional stewardship-based leadership network evident in Grand Rapids has indeed exhibited some concern for the less fortunate, partly because of the commitment of these business leaders to place and also due to the relatively small size of the tightly knit Grand Rapids community.

Both factors have helped facilitate a leadership norm of "doing the right thing" by addressing equity concerns. For example, when Grand Action was founded in the early 1990s, DeVos and his partners intentionally pulled in leaders from diverse sectors—business, government, academia, and community—in order to build early consensus and support for the long-term vision of recreating the downtown through civic projects. They understood that early relationship-building and buy-in would help avoid conflict later on—and the approach seems to have worked, as remarkably little conflict arose around Grand Action's major projects, specifically the arena, convention center, and baseball field.

Most recently, another project that could have raised conflict did not. The Grand Rapids Downtown Market is a multifaceted development consisting of outdoor and indoor markets featuring local food and businesses as well as classes educating residents about preparing fresh and healthy foods. Since the market is adjacent to a concentration of low-income and homeless communities in downtown Grand Rapids, Grand Action approached the missions and social service organizations in the area—rather than the other way around, which is more typical—to collaboratively figure out ways to avoid displacement and leverage the local investment to benefit existing residents. As a result, for example, Grand Action established a food stamp program at the market.[5]

An example of business more explicitly working with unlikely allies for the betterment of the community at large is the Chamber of Commerce's Leadership Grand Rapids program. This nine-month program brings together a diverse group of professionals—from sectors including financial services, education, manufacturing, health care, the arts, community organizations, and government—to expose them to community challenges and opportunities through tours, presentations, discussions, and group projects, and to help solidify their roles as "community trustees." Since its founding twenty-five years ago, Leadership Grand Rapids has produced a network of 1,500 alumni (Grand Rapids Area Chamber of Commerce 2013). While this is commendable, it also important to note that Leadership Grand Rapids is limited to "professionals" rather than those who fall within a broader definition of leadership, like neighborhood residents—which suggests a narrower base of membership in the region's epistemic community.

In any case, the norm of "doing the right thing" is present, and not just in private-sector initiatives. The regional metropolitan planning organization, the Grand Valley Metropolitan Council, engaged in a regional long-range planning process in 1993 which was very similar to the process in Sacramento (see chapter 4). This process resulted in the creation of the 1994 Metropolitan Development Blueprint, which laid out a shared vision for the region that emphasizes the protection of open space, the creation of centers of regional activity, and the promotion of compact, livable communities.

While this blueprint has had less lasting influence on planning processes in its region than Sacramento's has (Dutzik and Imus 2002), one tangible outcome was the creation of an urban utility boundary around Grand Rapids, essentially drawing a line beyond which sprawl may not proceed. This has helped promote population growth in the central city, in contrast to the trend of other large Michigan cities in the 1990s. Additionally, in the early 2000s, the Grand Valley Metropolitan Council reportedly adopted a "fix it first" policy of spending on maintenance of existing transportation infrastructure before spending on any new road building, a strategy that tends to reduce sprawl and encourage denser development.[6] A similar statewide policy was adopted in 2003, but only after community organizers and advocates, primarily in the Detroit area, organized for years to get it passed (Pastor, Benner, and Matsuoka 2009, ch. 3).

Finally, the strong presence of faith institutions—particularly the Dutch Reform Church—has played a role in raising awareness of equity concerns from the moral standpoint. Just as there is a belief that the private sector, rather than government, should drive development, there is also a belief that faith communities, rather than government, should be responsible for providing social services to those in need. Much like the Mormon Church in Salt Lake City, though not as heavily institutionalized, the strong role of faith in the Grand Rapids community helps expose business leaders to issues of social justice. For example, in the two years prior to our site visit in 2013, a Christian-based social justice advocacy organization called the Micah Center spearheaded a campaign to fight wage theft—the business practice of not compensating workers for overtime, paying less than the minimum wage, and misclassifying employees as independent contractors. Using faith as the common thread that ties business leaders, elected officials, and workers together—the eighth commandment declares, "Thou shalt not steal"—the Micah Center was able to garner support from key business leaders, like the former head of the Chamber of Commerce, and elected officials, like the Grand Rapids mayor, for a local Wage Theft Ordinance, which was passed unanimously by the City Council in November 2012.

"West Michigan Nice"

So is there a sort of epistemic community in the region that impacts governance? If by such a community we mean the norms of knowledge creation and interpretation as well as social interaction, it may be important to highlight what nearly all of our interviewees in the region characterized as a widespread regional culture: "West Michigan nice." It's a culture that actually represents a bit of a separation from the rest of the state. Interviewees were very eager to distinguish West

Michigan from East Michigan, particularly the race- and class-based conflict centered in Detroit. And it is a culture that has both an upside and a downside.

On the upside, the very reference to "West Michigan nice" reflects a strong regional identity and a desire to get along with everyone in the region. Even though we have characterized leadership in the region as elite-driven, we did see widespread concern for a diversity of interests and constituencies by regional stewards. In other parts of the country, we have found that top-down elite-driven decision-making processes receive significant pushback from advocates and organizers at the grassroots level. The relative lack of this type of conflict in Grand Rapids, combined with our review of the quantitative data showing relative equity in the region (until recently), suggests that despite the elite-driven processes, there is at least enough attention to interests of disadvantaged populations to keep any significant oppositional or confrontational movements from gaining traction.

On the other hand, stewardship for others, combined with a reluctance to face tension head-on, can reinforce a business-led top-down approach and make it difficult for equity actors to get an actual seat at the decision-making table (something suggested to us more forcefully during a subsequent visit with equity actors in 2014). Additionally, besides the few small-scale, predominantly faith-based efforts focused on social justice, there is a noticeable absence of a community organizing infrastructure to ensure that traditionally marginalized communities have a voice in decision-making processes. Thus, while the business-driven governance structure of Grand Rapids does include a consideration of equity, it is still a fairly closed process with a handful of powerful private-sector leaders at the helm.

As a result, the Grand Rapids approach may be nice, but it is also somewhat paternalistic. There is a sense of a common regional destiny and clear collaboration around downtown civic projects—but it is driven by a small group of similar professionals who call the shots. This has echoes of the more traditional epistemic community, one which is not truly diverse and so lacks some degree of dynamism. This may help explain why Grand Rapids has been less effective so far in addressing more recent economic and demographic challenges facing the region. The past decade of lower economic growth and higher inequality suggest the need to broaden the decision-making circles to more diverse sectors, such as labor and community-based organizations, in the years to come.

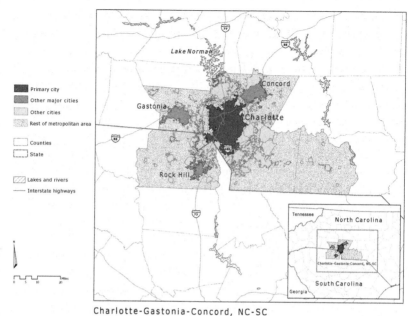

Charlotte-Gastonia-Concord, NC-SC

MAP 5.2. Charlotte Region.

CHARLOTTE

Although Charlotte was once known as a sleepy, second-tier city, today the Charlotte region epitomizes many of the qualities of the twenty-first-century Southern metro. It is anchored by a central city that has a reputation as a growing, economically and culturally vibrant hub, and its urban center, replete with a soaring and shiny skyline, well-used light rail system, and art museums, is the built representation of this retooled identity.[7] During the 1980s and 1990s, strong economic growth coupled with equity improvements underpinned Charlotte's positive transformation. Charlotte outpaced its urban counterparts in the South on many metrics and became somewhat of a "best practice" city, frequently visited by business and economic development professionals looking for ways to reinvigorate their own towns.[8]

Unfortunately, uneven growth and a poor performance on equity measures is a recent and unwelcome amendment to the once-rosy Charlotte story. Between 2000 and 2010, population growth continued, propelled by a mix of East Coast and Midwest expatriates and the growth of immigrant populations. But while aggregate employment continued to grow (although at a much lower rate than in the previous two decades), earnings per job stagnated, poverty rose, and the income gap widened significantly. During this time, the economy shed middle-class jobs, producing an hourglass employment structure, with job growth skewed toward the top and bottom of the wage spectrum.

So, what happened? How did Charlotte—a "region that works"[9]—stop working quite so well? Some of the factors are structural. For example, many of the policies that tied together city and suburb fates—such as nearly automatic annexation of developing suburbs and relatively peaceful integration of schools through bussing—have ceased to exist. But, as we review in more detail in the next section, the nature of regional leadership is also important. Much of Charlotte's development in the 1980s and 1990s was propelled by a remarkably coordinated group of corporate leaders who worked not just for the benefit of their own companies but also to stitch the region together, promote downtown development, and avoid the patterns of city–suburb division that have characterized so many other metropolitan areas.

Unfortunately, as Charlotte has expanded to become a major metropolitan region, the limits of this narrow and elite form of collaborative leadership—which lacks inclusivity and community voice—have become clearer. There have been efforts recently to bring together more diverse constituencies to address challenges in the region—to better welcome immigrants, create middle-class jobs, reduce poverty, and deal with post-annexation and bussing realities—but addressing these challenges seems likely to require a more diverse and dynamic leadership network than has existed in much of Charlotte's history over the past three decades.

Reimagining the Region: The Charlotte Way

In 1998, Charlotte-based NationsBank acquired San Francisco–based Bank of America, then promptly renamed itself after the property it had acquired. Charlotte, once a mecca of southern finance, was now quite literally a national leader. A decade later, San Francisco–based Wells Fargo bought out Charlotte-based Wachovia (which had its origins in Union National Bank, founded in 1908) for $15.1 billion and promptly renamed it Wells Fargo (DealBook 2008). The very symmetry of these two acquisitions suggests a sort of reversal of fortunes, which is evident in the data.

Charlotte has been well known for a thriving financial-services sector and strong overall growth. Employment grew by 37 percent in the 1980s and by 34 percent in the 1990s, and the finance, insurance, and real estate sector grew from 7 percent to 10 percent of total employment in the region. There were also signs of broader inclusion. The poverty rate declined from 11 percent in 1980 to 9 percent in 2000; the population with less than a high school degree dropped from 40 percent to 19 percent; and average earnings in low-wage industries actually performed better in the 1980s than in higher-wage industries, growing another 15 percent in real terms in the 1990s. But Charlotte hit a rough patch in the 2000s. Although employment and earnings per job continued to grow, they did so much more slowly than in previous decades. Total job growth over the full decade was only 13 percent, only a third of the percentage in each of the previous two decades, and earnings per job grew by only 3 percent, down from a 17-percent earnings-per-job gain in the 1980s and a 22-percent increase in the 1990s. Likewise, poverty spiked in the 2000s, and the income gap widened. But, unlike the story in many other regions, it was not a matter of salaries at the top shooting upwards; instead, everyone earned less, and the top simply suffered a smaller loss in income than those at the bottom.

Given this pattern, many have looked backward, often nostalgically, to the economic boom of the 1980s and 1990s and the iconic industry figures that helped make it happen: a select group of leaders in the corporate sector who guided the transformation of Charlotte from a sleepy textile town into a leading financial center. These city fathers, many of whom rose to prominence in the 1970s as bank, energy, real estate, and department store CEOs, were alternately called the Group, the Titans, and the White Guys (*Charlotte Magazine* 2010). Although manufacturing was far from dead in the 1970s and 1980s—still representing one-quarter of the region's employment in 1980—the Group's efforts largely excluded manufacturing and instead focused on promoting other sectors, primarily banking and finance, and downtown development (Atkins et al. 2011).

Although their direct influence is often overstated, Charlotte's business leadership worked closely and often synergistically with business organizations, city government, and foundations to shape center-city development and regional growth. The deeply rooted business leadership, many of whom lived near each other in the Myers Park neighborhood, helped steer development out of a sense of civic pride and paternalism, but also to lay the foundations for future investment. Unlike leaders in other US regions, their focus was regional, not just the city of Charlotte, a perspective facilitated by North Carolina's 1959 annexation law. This law mandated that any area taking on the character of an urban locale automatically became a candidate for annexation by the largest city in the county, which could then annex the area without requiring a vote of residents (Ubell 2004). Charlotte in particular took advantage of this law. In 1980 it annexed twenty-seven unincorporated areas totaling nearly 36 square miles of land, and in 1990 it annexed another 66 square miles, making it first in annexation among all cities in the state in both decades (Ingalls and Rassel 2005; Pastor et al. 2000, 140). As a result, fragmentation of local government was relatively low in the region, making it easier to develop regional collaboration.

Business leadership was critical in realizing this potential. In 1992, Ed Crutchfield of First Union Bank (which later became Wachovia) and Hugh McColl of NationsBank (which later became Bank of America) joined with Bill Lee of Duke Energy, Stuart Dickson of Ruddick Corporation, and John Belk of Belk department stores to create the Charlotte Regional Partnership (CRP), a public–private partnership devoted to attracting investment to the region that evolved from an older Greater Charlotte Economic Development Council. Through the CRP, the group sought to maximize regional development by creating a shared set of economic development goals and, by doing so, minimize intercounty economic development competition (Atkins et al. 2011). Meeting regularly with representatives from local jurisdictions across the region, CRP helped pool marketing resources, develop strategic partnerships around target industries, and mediate around common issues of regional competitiveness, such as transportation infrastructure and air quality.

Initially focused on finance and international business attraction, the CRP has subsequently expanded to other target industries including health, tourism, film, and a range of technology-led sectors like aerospace, energy, defense, and motor sports. But, as the Brookings Institution reports, "the major strategy employed by the private sector in Charlotte [in the 1980s and 1990s] was the aggressive expansion of the banks," including what eventually turned out to be risky strategies of acquisition and consolidation (Atkins et al. 2011, 4). For example, after Hugh McColl was named CEO of North Carolina National Bank in 1983, the bank grew in one decade from a one-state bank with 172 offices in North Carolina to a franchise with 826 offices in seven states. It acquired C&S/Sovran Corporation in 1991 and took the new name NationsBank; this organization acquired BankAmerica Corp. in 1998 and took the Bank of America name. Now operating in all 50 states, it is still headquartered in Charlotte. Similarly, Ed Crutchfield became CEO of First Union Bank in 1985, and over the following sixteen years completed more than ninety banking-related acquisitions, up to its merger in 2001 with Wachovia. By the end of this "merger craze," Charlotte was home of two of the nation's largest banks and boasted the second-most banking assets in the United States (Choi 2011; Rothacker 2010).

In addition to aggressively expanding the financial-services industry, business leadership also saw a vibrant downtown as a key ingredient for a successful future. An early planning document, the 1966 Odell Plan, called for a separation of uses downtown—a business and government hub flanked by separate high-rise residential towers areas bisected by a freeway. Over time, the business community would help champion a different vision: a 24-hour, pedestrian-friendly, mixed-use downtown. North Carolina National Bank, the predecessor to Bank of America, played a leading role here, including creating a Community Development Corporation to acquire property, provide loans, and encourage revitalization and preservation in the downtown area, paving the way for investment—and also for gentrification (Smith and Graves 2005). The Community Development Corporation has now evolved into Charlotte Center City Partners, a public–private partnership devoted to continuing the vision of Charlotte Center City as "viable, livable, memorable, and sustainable, with modern infrastructure, a tapestry of unique neighborhoods and a diversity of thriving businesses"[10] (Atkins et al. 2011).

Corporate influence also extended strongly into local philanthropy and the arts. The Foundation of the Carolinas, a local leading philanthropy, has been heavily supported by corporate donations from Bank of America and Duke Energy, which were known for their responsive and deep pockets.[11] Local museums have also benefitted. Bank of America, for example, donated a historic building to the Mint Museum of Craft and Design to house the Bank of America Gallery, a collection featuring American crafts (Nowell 1999).

While Charlotte's elite-driven structure helped expedite deals and large projects, it was not known for being particularly inclusive or democratic. "They ruled by money and insider influence," says Robert FitzPatrick, a Charlotte native and community organizer. "It was not by public participation. They didn't encourage that and they didn't respond to it very much" (St. Onge and Funk 2009). Indeed, community leaders and advocacy groups were noticeably absent from the conversation in Charlotte. Still, many argue that much of what happened behind closed doors was in the public's interest, and this is supported by data showing that the region's performance on equity measures in the 1980s and 1990s was better than that of much of the rest of the South. Leaders like Rolfe Neill, former long-time chairman and publisher of the *Charlotte Observer*, are unapologetic: "By having the top decision makers, you get instant decisions. Nobody goes to a committee. Nobody has to ask anybody's permission. . . . I don't think anybody could cite anything that we worked on that was malevolent or not in the public's interest" (St. Onge and Funk 2009).

In fact, business leadership has been progressive in Charlotte, at least by Southern standards. Business leaders were proud of a bussing plan that integrated Charlotte schools in the 1970s and generally spoke boastfully of the Charlotte Way, a combination of regional booster-ism and racial moderation (Lassiter 2004; S. S. Smith 1997). Business groups were helpful in electing the city's first African American mayor, Harvey Gantt, in 1983, and downtown and neighborhood interests have often been linked by policy as well as politics. For example, bond measures to revitalize commercial areas in Charlotte included funds for street improvements in low-income neighborhoods (Pastor, et al. 2000, 145). Similarly, Charlotte's City within a City policy, first developed in 1991, was an initiative to strategically and comprehensively address economic development and quality-of-life issues in Charlotte's poorest neighborhoods. This initiative grew out of civic and business leaders' understanding of the interdependence of the poorest neighborhoods and the rest of the region (Borgsdorf 1995).

Business leaders recognized that regional quality-of-life improvements would help pave the way for attracting a skilled workforce and new industries. They were sensitive to portraying the region as an enlightened leader of the New South, with integrated neighborhoods (and schools) and a forward-looking business class. Business leaders might have been fierce competitors, but they collaborated regularly for the good of the region. As Ed Crutchfield, former CEO of First Union Bank, said of Bank of America CEO Hugh McColl: "We made up our minds that when it came to business we'd try to kill each other, which we spent thirty years trying to do. But when it came to the good of Charlotte, anything we could do to build the city, we'd cooperate fully and completely. And we did that. We're kind of like two old generals or war horses that have a mutual respect for each other" (O'Daniel 2013).

Time of Transition: Outgrowing Paternalism

Throughout the 1980s and 1990s, under the stewardship of the region's business and public leadership, Charlotte flourished. Charlotte became known as the second-largest finance center in the United States, and a growing number of Fortune 500 companies took root in the region (Atkins et al. 2011). The US Conference of Mayors declared in 1995 that Charlotte was the most livable of any city over 100,000 people in the United States (Borgsdorf 1995), and by 2000, "small-town Charlotte" had grown into a region of over 1.3 million people.

And Charlotte was not only growing but becoming increasingly diverse, moving beyond the Black-and-white racial dynamics that had historically characterized it and many other Southern cities. The region's growing size, increasing diversity, and global integration have challenged the regional stewardship networks, at a time when many of the White Guys running the city were aging. Ed Crutchfield retired in 2000, followed by Hugh McColl in 2001. By Hugh McColl's own admission, without the region's "two rich uncles," a broader leadership effort is needed (Braunstein 2012). But while there are signs of growing diversity and vibrancy in regional leadership networks, it is clear that the region is struggling to effectively address some of these new challenges.

Part of the issue is that Charlotte's newest businesses, like its population, often have shallower roots in the region. The number of mid-size companies has proliferated, and finance and insurance executives increasingly have their main offices outside of Charlotte. One of the emblematic examples of the shifting leadership structure and global orientation is Chiquita, a company decidedly not in the financial sector and also one lacking a long history in the region. In November 2011, the company received $22 million in incentives and moved its headquarters from Cincinnati to Charlotte, a move heralded at the time as a sign of Charlotte's increasing global prominence. In addition to the incentives, the company cited Charlotte's international airport as a major attraction, providing easy access to its grower and consumer markets in South America and Europe (Portillo 2011). Barely two years later, however, the company announced that it had merged with an Irish produce company, Fyffes, and was moving its headquarters to Ireland. Apparently, it had been considering the merger even as it was accepting the incentive package in Charlotte. Such a "footloose" corporate sector is a far cry from the rooted business leadership and regional stewardship of the previous era (Portillo 2014a, 2014b).

The Charlotte Chamber of Commerce remains a strong force in the city and represents a broader, more deliberative body than the tight group of corporate CEOs who previously dominated regional decision-making. Chamber members have generally come together to support key infrastructure investments in the region, particularly transportation investments. In 1998, for example, the chamber, working in partnership with the City Council, helped lead a successful campaign to fund transportation investments, including light rail development, through an indefinite half-cent sales tax increase. Marketed as an investment in economic development, it was passed by 58 percent of Charlotte voters (Werbel and Haas 2002). Ridership exceeded projections, rail-oriented mixed-use projects took off, and in 2007, when there was a call to repeal the tax, the Chamber of Commerce worked with the City Council and the region's most prominent corporate citizens to retain the tax, a policy supported by 70 percent of the electorate (Spanberg 2007). Continued investment in light rail has continued to be an important part of economic development in the central city. The 9.6-mile Lynx light rail line, opened in 2007, cost $473 million to build. By 2010, it had already attracted at least forty-five new development projects close to station areas, totaling more than $247 million and including 1,400 new housing units and 700,000 square feet of office and retail space (Newsom 2010). Average weekly ridership, projected at 9,100, has actually been closer to 15,000 since shortly after its launch (Spanberg 2012).

But the success in rail belies a bigger regional challenge: the shrinking number of middle-wage industries and occupations. One side effect of the emphasis on finance and white-collar job growth in the Charlotte region is that little attention was given to protecting the region's substantial manufacturing base, which accounted for 25 percent of all jobs in 1980 but had shrunk to 7 percent by 2010. Many of these were good jobs, which had created a stable middle in the metro region (Atkins et al. 2011). Over the last twenty years, Charlotte's economic base has instead become an increasingly bifurcated "high-low" economy, with low- and high-wage jobs each growing by 60 percent while middle-wage jobs contracted slightly.

Addressing the growing economic separation in the region might be easier if there were a more profound sense of shared fates, but two factors that contributed to such a sense—school bussing and annexation power—have been challenged in recent years. From the mid-1970s through the 1980s, the region's school system was made up of Charlotte and the surrounding Mecklenburg County, and earned national acclaim as "the city that made desegregation work" (Morantz 1996). It wasn't a purely voluntary effort. A 1970 Supreme Court decision in *Swann v. Charlotte-Mecklenburg Board of Education* held that mandatory bussing was an appropriate remedy for the problem of racial imbalance in schools. But keeping everyone in the same system helped shore up support for public education, and when Charlotte started its bussing program in 1971 it found strong business support, in part to present the image of a New South city. As one business leader put it when the plan was later challenged (see below), "Had we taken a different course in 1972 (when schools were desegregated), then we would not be enjoying the prosperity that we now have" (Smith 2010, 189).

So why stop doing what seems to be working? It's partly because of a changing populace. The region began to experience increasing migration from the Northeast and Midwest, and by 2010, only 61 percent of Mecklenburg County residents were born in the South (compared to 73 percent in North Carolina statewide), with 15 percent from the Northeast and another 7 percent from the Midwest (Chesser 2011). One result was a decline in support for the school bussing system. The district had already started shifting away from bussing in 1992, when it introduced a managed-choice program with racial targets, allowing a portion of parents to choose local magnet schools rather than have their children bussed. In 1997, a parent sued the school system when his daughter was denied entrance into a magnet school based on race, which ultimately ended in 2002 with the school district ending mandatory bussing and implementing a more decentralized school-choice plan. The result has been a gradual resegregation of schools in the Charlotte area (Godwin et al. 2006).

North Carolina's annexation policy has also been under attack. Since the 1960s, this policy has helped minimize the "poor city–rich suburb" pattern which characterizes many regions, and has been important in maintaining the good fiscal health of Charlotte and other major cities in the state (Rusk 2006). Even though the annexation policy allows cities to annex surrounding communities without holding a vote of residents, the vast majority of annexations were voluntary—overall, only an estimated 9.6 percent of annexations in the thirty years up to 2010 were involuntary, and the portion actually declined to 7.4 percent in the most recent decade (Christensen 2011; Smith and Willse 2012).

Yet with the rise of the Tea Party and its emphasis on local power, a vocal minority opposed to involuntary annexations was able to create a powerful lobby in the state capital, resulting in laws allowing an affected area to stop an involuntary annexation if 60 percent of property owners sign a protest petition (Doran 2012). It remains to be seen what the effect of this legislation will be, but it certainly represents a step backward in terms of regional integration and building ties that bind regional residents together. It may or may not be a coincidence, but it's also the case that Charlotte, which prided itself in being relatively welcoming to immigrants, has shifted direction to a more anti-immigrant stance, partly in reaction to a rise of more conservative elements (Pastor and Mollenkopf 2012).

When the New South Gets Newer

We selected Charlotte as a case study because of a particular anomaly. While it long enjoyed a reputation for strong regional collaboration, important central city–suburban links, and a relatively decent record (by Southern standards) in economic growth and social equity (Pastor et al. 2000), it has seemed to slip in recent years. This might of course be due to structural factors—and to some degree it is, in view of the sharp shrinkage in manufacturing—but we were also curious whether the connections that had forged the Charlotte Way had frayed and whether this might have impacted the outcomes.

Fraying does seem to have occurred. One reason is the growing immigration of people from the Northeast and Midwest. These newer residents—and the newer businesses—have less sense of place and less pride in the hard-won compromises over schools. Another big shift has been the growth in the Latino population. Less than 1 percent of the region's population in 1980, Latinos grew to 5 percent in 2000 and 10 percent by 2010. This complicates what has traditionally been a sort of social bargain between white corporate leaders and Black political activists, even though Latinos remain largely invisible in regional leadership circles in the region.[12]

Incorporating the newer populations has been difficult in part because of the established leadership and political structure. What once worked to produce compromise and consensus—though within a narrow band of the White Guys—has not been able to morph enough to create forums in which "unlikely allies" can interact in sustained deliberative processes. The Chamber of Commerce, for example, has little collaboration beyond its membership and public officials, and has only recently begun reaching out to ethnic chambers and the Charlotte Business Guild (a membership association building support for businesses in Charlotte's LGBTQ community).

On the nonprofit side, many groups are creating successful coalitions with other nonprofits, but generally not across sectoral boundaries. For example, Action NC, one of the leading advocacy groups in the region, helped organize Familias Unidas, a coalition-based anti-deportation campaign that included the NAACP, the Central Labor Council, and the Latin American Coalition. But many of the civic and advocacy groups which typically call attention to the equity issues of education, good jobs, and affordable housing are noticeably absent in Charlotte leadership networks. Part of the reason is that Charlotte's nonprofit community is largely service-oriented and possesses few advocacy or community organizing–oriented groups. In fact, there is generally less tolerance of public activism, community organizing, or advocacy work. As one long-term observer told us in an interview, "*activist* is a dirty word" in Charlotte.

All of this suggests the limits to elite-driven approaches to regional governance. Charlotte's epistemic community was paternalistic, with a few strong and collaborative corporate leaders playing a critical role in stitching the region together, contributing to downtown revitalization, and supporting policies like annexation and school bussing that kept fates and fortunes interwoven. As the population of the region has shifted and new challenges have emerged, the inadequacies of this relatively narrow form of regional stewardship have become more apparent.

OKLAHOMA CITY

In the mid-to-late 1980s, Oklahoma City[13] was mired in an extended economic crisis, the result of a decline in the region's core energy businesses and damage to the region's banking and real estate sectors from the savings and loan meltdown. The region's downtown area was hit especially hard, since the legacy of classic urban-renewal policy had accelerated the hollowing-out of the urban core. By 1988, Oklahoma City councilman I. G. Purser declared: "Downtown is dead and we helped kill it. There is no major retail, no major attraction and no place to eat" (Lackmeyer and Money 2006, i).

Since the early 1990s, however, Oklahoma City has experienced a remarkable turnaround. In 2005, the *Wall Street Journal* wrote: "[T]oday Oklahoma City's downtown is thriving. The Bricktown district is buzzing with nightlife, people are moving downtown.... Add to that two successful stadiums, a performing arts center, a central library, a 'Riverwalk' type canal, clubs and restaurants, and the downtown of the once-sleepy city . . . is bustling" (Chittum 2005).

While the tailwinds of an energy boom in the 2000s are an important part of the story, the path forward has been led by a strong

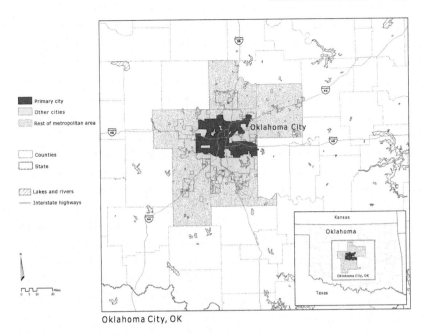

Oklahoma City, OK

MAP 5.3. Oklahoma City Region.

public–private consensus on the importance of increasing taxes to support major public expenditure on quality of life and educational improvements in the region. While this spirit of collaboration is partly rooted in strong regional integration prior to 1970, what makes the story more interesting is that the commitment to this public sector–led redevelopment effort has been headed by four successive Republican mayors and a conservative Chamber of Commerce, while the additional taxes have been supported by a majority of voters in a region who consistently vote overwhelmingly Republican.

Oklahoma City's experience suggests how a commitment to place can help leaders move beyond ideology and steer their regions off a track of negative growth and toward a more sustainable and shared growth trajectory. In the process, regional leaders explicitly made connections between unlikely allies and helped the broader public see important connections between these diverse interests in an interconnected region. While challenges remain—particularly in incorporating a growing Latino immigrant population into regional leadership processes— Oklahoma City's experience shows the potential for overcoming major economic challenges through collaborative regional efforts that bring together diverse interests, knowledge, and values.

Taking Care of Business

During the 1980s, the Oklahoma City region experienced a dramatic increase in poverty, from 11 percent of the population in 1980 to 14 percent in 1990. Employment growth for the decade, at 10 percent, was one-third that of the average metropolitan region in the South, while average earnings per job actually declined by 6 percent in real terms over the decade. Yet the subsequent decades saw a significant turnaround, as total jobs grew by 23 percent in the 1990s (despite the impact of the Federal Building bombing in 1995) and another 9 percent in the 2000s, (despite the dramatic national recession). Average earnings per job grew by 8 percent in the 1990s and another 13 percent in the 2000s.

One factor that may have helped Oklahoma City stage this rapid turnaround is a relatively centralized and integrated regional governance structure. A classic example of an "elastic city" (Rusk 1993), Oklahoma City has expanded its boundaries over time rather than let growth be captured by newly incorporated suburbs. In 1953, Oklahoma City was about 56 square miles. In 1958, the Oklahoma City Chamber of Commerce sponsored an event in partnership with the mayor, focused on "Oklahoma City's proposed metropolitan planning."[14] This conference led to a coordinated effort over the next fifteen years to rapidly annex land, with most of the increase coming quickly—by 1962 the city had encompassed more than 600 square miles. In effect, Oklahoma City created a strong regional government, similar to the city–county mergers in Nashville and Jacksonville in the 1960s, but in this case, through annexation that included expansion even beyond the county boundaries.

Interestingly, the Chamber of Commerce was a major leader in the push for this rapid annexation. Though the term *public–private partnership* began to appear in discourse in urban development only in the 1960s, and really took off only in the 1980s with the growing emphasis on market-oriented solutions to urban problems (Amdurksy 1968; Brooks, Liebman, and Schelling 1984), Oklahoma City has benefitted from public–private partnerships since its very origins in the nineteenth century. The city was essentially established in a single day, April 22, 1889, when 10,000 people settled there as part of the Oklahoma Land Rush after the Homestead Act made two million acres of public land in central Oklahoma available for settlement (Hoig 1984). The Greater Oklahoma City Chamber of Commerce (originally known as the Board of Trade) was established just three weeks later, and has had a strong influence on regional governance ever since. In essence, the chamber has operated as an arm of regional government for many years, playing a key role in the operation of multiple airports, road building, and literally contracting with the city as its economic development arm.

The chamber has also played a key role in building ties with smaller local chambers elsewhere in the region, working to build a common strategy and identity for regional development in central Oklahoma. One of the key ways it has done this is through expanding the capacity of its research department. The chamber claims to have such detailed parcel-level data in the ten-county region that after the 2013 tornado that tore through the neighboring town of Moore, the chamber was able to provide information on businesses affected along the tornado's destructive path more quickly than the regional planning body or emergency services. In addition to detailed research and information on economic dynamics, social conditions, and urban site characteristics in the central Oklahoma region, the chamber also has detailed comparison statistics for all major competitor regions. This information is readily available to all chambers in the region that agree to be part of the chamber's network for collaborative marketing of the region. Sharing information and knowledge has helped hold business leaders throughout the region together, and also helped avoid devolvement into destructive competitive bidding for outside investment—exactly the sort of epistemic community we have suggested can be so valuable.

MAPS for the Future

It was this business-led regionalism that came to the rescue when Oklahoma City received an unwelcome bit of news in the early 1990s. United Airlines was considering the city as a potential site for a major maintenance facility, with the deal partly contingent on voter approval of a series of infrastructure improvements designed to lure the airline to the region. But although Oklahoma City was offering a superior set of financial incentives, United chose Indianapolis, citing "quality of life." The rejection actually looms large as a sort of origin story for subsequent regional collaboration. It is said that United Airlines executives visited the city and simply could not conceive of their employees (or spouses) living there.

While the details of the actual event remain a bit murky, the fact that it is remembered this way suggests a deeply felt sting, which residents still recall today. Civic leaders realized the need for a major regional development effort, with the mayor supposedly thinking that "if our citizens are willing to tax themselves for somebody else, maybe they'd be willing to tax themselves for themselves" (Rosenberg 2010, 21). The result was the development of the Metropolitan Area Projects (MAPS) plan. The Chamber of Commerce took the lead in advocating a new five-year, 1-percent sales tax devoted to funding nine major projects to improve the quality of life in Oklahoma City, which voters approved with a 54-percent majority vote in December of 1993.

MAPS included a range of projects designed to cater to the needs of different constituencies while being part of a unified vision for improving quality of life in the region and renovating the urban core. Recreational projects included renovations to the Civic Center Music Hall, the Convention Center, and the Oklahoma State Fairgrounds; construction of a 20,000-seat indoor sports arena that eventually became the home of Oklahoma City's first professional sports team, the Oklahoma City Thunder basketball team; the 15,000-seat Bricktown Ballpark, home of the Triple-A affiliate of the Houston Astros and frequent host of the Big 12 baseball tournament and periodic outdoor concerts. Other developments included a new public library; a trolley transit system; construction of the Bricktown Canal, which has become a major restaurant hub and entertainment attraction; and the transformation of a seven-mile stretch of the North Canadian River—which used to be derisively referred to by locals as "the river that needs mowing" due to its being choked by grass for much of the year—into a series of river lakes bordered by landscaped areas, trails, and recreational facilities. Renamed the Oklahoma River, this area has now become an attractive site for kayaking, canoeing, and sculling, and it was the first river to receive official designation by the US Olympic Committee as an Olympic and Paralympic Training Site.[15] Funds raised by the tax over the five-year period totaled $350 million, and all the projects were completed debt-free.[16]

In 2001, voters passed a second round of sales tax increases (by a 61-percent majority vote) in a MAPS for Kids initiative that generated $514 million (along with a $180 million Oklahoma City Public Schools bond issue) for school facility improvements, technology, and transportation projects. While 70 percent of the sales tax funds were designated for the Oklahoma City Public School District, 23 other public school districts that overlap part of the land area of Oklahoma City itself received 30 percent. Indeed, the overlap of the central-city and suburban school districts provided another mechanism of stitching together the region. Civic leaders also made a point of starting the MAPS for Kids school renovations at Frederick Douglass High School, in the heart of

Oklahoma City's African American community, a move meant to show that tax revenues were being shared with disadvantaged communities in the region.

The success of the original MAPS and the MAPS for Kids programs paved the way for the passage of a third round of temporary sales tax increases, this time in 2008 (with a 54-percent majority) for the MAPS 3 initiative.[17] Projects planned under the ten-year MAPS 3 initiative include a new downtown convention center; a downtown public park; a streetcar system; improvements to the Oklahoma River and Oklahoma State Fairgrounds projects; the construction of four new state-of-the-art senior health and wellness centers, designed to serve as gathering places for active seniors; and an expanded trail system and improvements to the city's sidewalks, in efforts to promote a more walkable community. Again, the Chamber of Commerce played a strong role in advocating for the expanded taxes to support this major public investment.

While Oklahoma City is not unique in promoting major new development projects designed to attract populations and business back to the urban core, a number of the features of Oklahoma's experience are striking. One is that the projects that make up the revitalization plan were not developed and funded individually but were part of a diverse and integrated vision of transforming Oklahoma City from a hollowed-out urban core into a vibrant and dynamic place with a high quality of life and entertainment attractions. The mix of projects was designed to meet multiple constituencies' interests—when voters approved the additional taxes for these initiatives, the specific projects were listed on the ballot and voters had to vote for all or none of them. A second major feature is the diversity of projects developed under these ongoing initiatives. Projects include major renovations in schools throughout the region, substantial resources for seniors spread throughout the city, a library, and public parks and open space—along with the more typical arena, entertainment centers, and attractive restaurant districts that make up many downtown revitalization initiatives.

A third distinctive feature is the regional nature of the initiative. Much of this is driven simply by the sheer size of Oklahoma City in the region. Particularly because of the annexation powers described earlier, Oklahoma City is the third-largest city in the continental United States by land area (behind Jacksonville, Florida, and Houston, Texas). As a result, initiatives in the city immediately have a regional significance. But it's also the case that the use of a sales tax (rather than for instance a property tax) ensures that suburban residents who shop in Oklahoma

City are contributing to the core (which may be one reason why the MAPS for Kids initiative was sweetened by the inclusion of financing for suburban school districts).[18] Perhaps most remarkably, the commitment to expanded taxes for public investment in this range of projects was led by a conservative Chamber of Commerce, in close cooperation with Republican mayors, and was supported by a majority of the predominantly Republican voters of the region.

While this level of collaboration and commitment is partly due to long-standing structural features, such as annexation, multiple informants also stressed the ways in which crisis events triggered cooperation. For example, the stagnation of the overall economy of the 1980s and the sterile and hollowed-out nature of the urban core forced regional leaders to recognize the need for some coordinated response. Common identity and purpose were also forged by the 1995 bombing of the Federal Building, in which 168 lives were lost and 324 buildings in a sixteen-block radius were damaged or destroyed. Meanwhile, coordination across jurisdictions is regularly reinforced by another set of crises: regular natural disasters that arise given Oklahoma City's location in the heart of Tornado Alley.

Despite collective experiences that have united the region's residents in a unique way, it is clear that Oklahoma City still faces significant challenges around diversity and inclusion. Between 2000 and 2010, the poverty rate remained high (going from 14 to 16 percent) and inequality rose, with earnings in the region's energy sector rising dramatically against a backdrop of low-wage service-sector industries—including accommodation, food services, arts, entertainment, and recreation—that also grew, partly because of the success of the MAPS initiative. African Americans and Latinos continue to have substantially higher unemployment rates and lower educational attainment and income levels than non-Hispanic whites. While growth and equity outcomes in the past decade have outpaced those in the rest of the South, African Americans remain junior partners at best in decision-making processes, and the growing Latino population (11 percent of the region's population in 2010) has yet to achieve meaningful representation in regional governance.

Who's In, Who's Out

Despite those gaps, and even with revitalization clearly driven by an elite stratum, a variety of features of the process in Oklahoma City have ensured that a diversity of constituencies' perspectives and knowledge is included in regional considerations. Perhaps most important is the essentially regional nature of the Oklahoma City government following its aggressive annexation in the 1950s and 1960s, combined with the work of the Chamber of Commerce in collaboration with other chambers throughout the region, and the way in which the MAPS for Kids program served school districts throughout the region. All of these have helped ensure that typically suburban concerns and typically central-city concerns are tied together.

Similarly, the inclusion of many projects serving different constituencies in the various MAPS programs, along with the requirement that the projects all be voted on together as a single package, helps the broad electorate see connections between different constituencies in the region. The original projects in MAPS were developed in a process that involved broad citizen oversight. Indeed, the mayor who led the effort made a point of appointing the strongest opponent of the proposal to the head of an oversight committee, highlighting both an acceptance of disparate viewpoints and an appreciation of the value of gaining broad consensus for the program rather than a simple majority. Similarly, while putting a high school in Oklahoma City's African American neighborhood at the top of the MAPS for Kids renovation list might be criticized as simply symbolic inclusion, it also reflects a public acknowledgement of the importance of addressing African American concerns on some level in the region in a broad, public way that formed the basis for a majority vote of the entire electorate.

The ability of the region to continue the increased sales tax for multiple rounds of MAPS funding is also a tribute to the flexibility and dynamism of the leadership networks in Oklahoma City. Despite the growing anti-government and anti-tax sentiment in the Republican Party, both leaders and voters in Oklahoma City have continued to put a commitment to place above a commitment to ideology, and in the process have continued to pursue a diverse range of high-priority development projects in the region, stretching now across twenty-five years (1992–2017, when the current round of MAPS project funding expires).

We don't mean to exaggerate the diversity or inclusiveness of leadership networks in Oklahoma City. The region still struggles with high levels of poverty and inequality. The growing Latino immigrant population in the region remains largely excluded from regional decision-making processes, and our informants in community-based organizations and the African American community in the region expressed frustration at being continually marginalized by the very conservative, elite leadership network in the region. Yet the turnaround in Oklahoma City over the past twenty-five years is remarkable, and a top-down approach to regional stewardship has nonetheless linked multiple constituencies and multiple interests in an ambitious set of long-term development projects. Whether it will fall prey to "success" as in Charlotte—with new residents and businesses less aware of the history and less committed to the process—remains to be seen.

THE LIMITS OF ELITE-DRIVEN REGIONAL STEWARDSHIP

As all three of these cases underscore, paternalistic models of knowledge sharing and regional decision-making can achieve significant success in promoting economic development and facilitating some degree of inclusion. At the same time, these sorts of regional stewardship efforts have their limits. Employment and investment have flowed into each of the regions, yet none has been able to achieve long-term equity gains. Charlotte and Grand Rapids achieved both growth and improved equity in the 1980s, but equity conditions have eroded in both regions since then, starting in the 1990s in Charlotte and the 2000s in Grand Rapids. Oklahoma City continues to struggle with high poverty rates and growing inequality, despite the economic turnaround.

In each of the cases, there were few channels for community concerns to rise to the level of policymaking and institutional change. Many of the key regional decision-making groups, like Leadership Grand Rapids, are made up of traditional "professionals," not the broader leadership networks we see in other metropolitan regions. In Charlotte, paternalism has marginalized the advocacy voices, which are few and far between. As a result, many nonprofits are service-oriented, rather than focused on organizing around regional issues or policies. In Oklahoma City, efforts have been made to be inclusive economically, partly to stitch together broad support for tax-financed public investments, but large pockets of poverty remain in the African American community and the growing Latino immigrant community, which are largely unaffected by the dynamics of the new downtown.

Strong elite-driven regional decision-making processes have certain advantages, though, especially when pursued by "enlightened" regional leaders who see themselves as stewards for the region as a whole. With a strong commitment to place and deep histories in the region, dynamic business leaders in Grand Rapids, Charlotte, and Oklahoma City, working together with public officials and other allies, were able to lead processes that have been remarkable in their ability to transform formerly struggling central cities. In a period in which many regions were struggling to overcome the negative effects of suburbanization and the shift from a manufacturing to a knowledge- and services-based economy, these three regions have had an important degree of success, and elite-driven leadership collaborations have been a key part of that success.

But the norms of paternalism also assume mute acquiescence from the communities elites purport to serve. Such quiet is not likely in light of growing ethnic diversity, entrenched inequality due to bifurcated employment structures, and rising poverty in older inner-ring suburbs. Epistemic communities rooted in elite-driven regional stewardship networks may be less effective in addressing these contemporary challenges, particularly the needs to forge a more inclusive economy and polity, develop a broader and more diverse leadership base, and quickly and widely share knowledge about conditions and solutions.

At the same time, addressing the conflicts often left simmering in paternalistic regionalism can be challenging. How can both regional elites and those pushing for more equitable development lift up tough issues in a way that produces a path forward and not just permanent warfare? To understand when conflict leads to collaboration—and when it just leads to more conflict—we turn our attention in the next chapter to the cases of Greensboro, Fresno, and San Antonio.

CHAPTER 6

Struggle and the City

Conflict-Informed Collaboration

The past is never dead. It's not even past.

—William Faulkner, *Requiem for a Nun* (1951)

Power concedes nothing without a demand. It never did and
it never will.

—Frederick Douglass

Our case studies thus far have emphasized the power of collaborative
processes in which knowledge is developed, shared, and used to inform
regional decision-making and governance processes. In our planning-
influenced cases in chapter 4, we stressed how planners could drive
long-range regional visioning that helps diverse constituencies recognize
a common metropolitan destiny. In our regional-stewardship cases in
chapter 5, we emphasized the important role of elite-driven leadership
networks even as we acknowledged the limitations of such networks in
addressing equity-related challenges. In all these cases, there were conflicting values and interests—but the level of open conflict between various interest groups was quite muted, either because mutual interests were
being met (for example through MAPS in Oklahoma City or Envision
Utah in Salt Lake) or because of a regional culture (i.e., social norms) that
stressed conflict avoidance ("Michigan nice" or the "Charlotte Way").

What happens in cases where there is open conflict? Does this mean
that positive regional developments, either in terms of processes or outcomes, are not possible? One hopes that that is not the case, particularly
since equity issues are often set aside as afterthoughts by more powerful
and traditional regional actors, so community-based advocacy is key
to putting social issues squarely on the metropolitan agenda (Bollens
2003; Lester and Reckhow 2013). How does conflict and advocacy fit
into collaborative knowledge sharing—and when does it lead to inclusion becoming firmly rooted in the regional decision-making fabric?

In this chapter, we examine three regions where conflict and tension are a central part of the metropolitan dynamic: Greensboro, North Carolina; Fresno, California; and San Antonio, Texas. Two of the cases offer cautionary tales: both Greensboro and Fresno suffered poor economic performance and worsening social equity conditions throughout the 1980–2010 period. San Antonio, on the other hand, has had a somewhat remarkable record of improvements in employment, income levels, and income distribution. And we say remarkable because while there are some important differences, all three cities started from somewhat similar political economies in the early 1970s: an Anglo elite determined to check the power of growing communities of color (predominantly Latino in the cases of Fresno and San Antonio, and predominantly African American in Greensboro); simmering social-movement organizations that were getting primed to facilitate that power shift; and an economy that needed to be reorganized to generate progress.

In Greensboro, that economic shift meant diversifying from textiles, tobacco, and furniture; in Fresno, it meant diversifying away from agriculture; and in San Antonio, it meant adjusting to a sizeable military cutback. In all three places, however, what was fundamentally at stake was the need to forge a development model *not* based on cheap labor—and getting there necessitated empowering those once left behind to become part of the economy still to be born. In each case, the underlying economic struggle also meant a racial rebalancing of power. Greensboro, home to the famous lunch-counter sit-ins of the 1960s, was also a hotbed of the Black Power movement and the scene of the 1979 murder of five activists by Ku Klux Klan and Nazi Party members in what came to be known as the Greensboro Massacre. Conflict was also high in Fresno—where the United Farm Workers led national campaigns targeting Fresno-area employers—and in San Antonio, where a vibrant Alinsky-style organizing federation was targeting area banks and fighting for enhanced political representation for low-income Latino and African American residents.

Yet a visit to these regions today suggests very different trajectories of conflict and collaboration. Greensboro's experience of continued racial discord is well captured by CNN's 2011 headline in a special feature on Defining America: "After 50 years of racial strife: Why is Greensboro still so tense?" (Patterson 2011). Here is just one iconic example of the continued challenges. In the summer of 2013, there was widespread media coverage of the arrest of eleven young Black men from low-income neighborhoods near downtown—a downtown that has begun to see some signs of revitalization because of an influx of predominantly white young professionals. The incident pushed uncomfortable and simmering issues of race and class onto the front pages, amid conflicts over what downtown will look like and who will be welcome there (Killian 2013).

Similarly, in Fresno, environmental justice advocates in the region have all but given up on collaborative policy solutions to addressing the region's worst-in-the-nation air pollution, seeing adversarial lawsuits as the only meaningful pathway forward. Meanwhile, the Chamber of Commerce and local Building Industry Association leaders were strong and vocal opponents of a modest but important effort in 2012 to develop a General Plan that would attempt to revitalize downtown, promote denser development, and halt entrenched development patterns of sprawl that have contributed to inequality in the region.

But in San Antonio, the chatter is all about how well different sectors collaborate (enough to be awarded a Promise Neighborhood, a Choice Neighborhood, a Promise Zone, and a Sustainable Communities Initiative grant from the federal government). In 2012, a majority of residents voted to pass a sales-tax increase that will steer additional resources to pre-K education for the least advantaged kids—with the support not only of a progressive mayor and community groups but also the Chamber of Commerce.

Why did these regions that started with similar political economies (at least in the 1970s) end up so different? Why have key stakeholders in San Antonio been able to find ways to collaborate in the midst of conflict over competing interests and values, while in Greensboro and Fresno, the inability of stakeholders to turn conflict into a productive force has resulted in a sense of deeply rooted division and discouragement? In what follows, we review the experience of each region since the 1970s, focusing on the relationship of conflict, collaboration, and knowledge generation to regional development patterns. While (as usual) structural factors play a role in explaining the different outcomes, we stress how key differences in organizing, the presence (or lack) of key transformational leaders, and certain features of each region's civic life help us understand why Greensboro and Fresno have remained fragmented and conflicted while San Antonio has seemingly embraced collaboration in the midst of diversity.

GREENSBORO

The Greensboro region is located in the heart of North Carolina's Piedmont Triad, and is known most prominently for its manufacturing

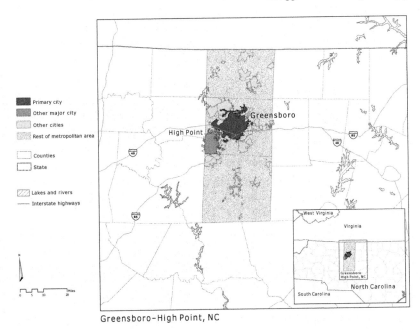

Greensboro–High Point, NC

MAP 6.1. Greensboro Region.

legacy and its civil rights struggles.[1] Although the formerly booming textile and furniture industries and the lunch-counter sit-in movement are still a source of pride for many in the region, deindustrialization and a history of social distrust and disconnection have contributed to poor performance on both growth and equity.

Economically, the region has struggled to attract or grow significant new industries in the face of a manufacturing decline that started in the 1970s. As of 1990, Greensboro still had nearly a quarter of its workforce in manufacturing, but the loss of these relatively well-paying jobs began to accelerate in the subsequent two decades, and the figure fell to 13 percent by 2010. There has been some growth in new middle- and higher-wage industries, but there has also been a steady and larger growth in low-wage service-sector industries. Overall employment in the region actually declined over the decade of the 2000s, and job growth lagged both the South and US averages for the previous two decades as well. In the 2000s, after two decades of wage growth, average earnings per job declined in real terms. Since 1990 the region has had increasing poverty, and overall income inequality has risen more, compared to either Southern or all US metros.

Although exogenous factors, such as the global and national downshifts in manufacturing, were acutely felt in the region, Greensboro was certainly not alone in facing these trends. More importantly, external shocks can, as in the case of Oklahoma City, serve to stir civic leadership into action rather than simply distress. But in Greensboro, racial tensions and inequality have impeded the ability of people and institutions in the region to come together to address regional challenges. While there have been flashpoints of open conflict, the tensions have mostly simmered just below the surface. Business leadership in the region has been relatively weak—at least when compared with the strong regional stewardship networks in places like Charlotte and Grand Rapids—and social-equity advocates have remained mostly fragmented or marginalized. The result is a disconnected region with a contested sense even of its own history.

Big Challenges, Tepid Responses

Greensboro's history is strongly rooted in its role as one of the largest textile manufacturing centers in the country. By the early 1830s, seventy-five mills were in operation and cotton material was being exported to neighboring counties and states.[2] Shortly after, furniture manufacturing would take root in neighboring High Point and the areas westward.[3] Both remained central to the local economy and employment for over a century, until the late 1990s, when the US economy shed much of its textile and apparel employment following the implementation of NAFTA (Scott 2003). According to many of our interviewees, the region has been slow to envision a broad, post-industrial future. Weak inter-regional collaboration, competition between cities, and changing leadership and organizational structures have hindered the process.

The ups and downs—and ups—of companies like Cone Denim, the country's oldest operating denim mill, shed light on the regional shifts in textile manufacturing and its role in the region's economic consciousness.[4] Founded in 1891, the company produces and supplies denim fabric to jeans manufacturers across the United States. In the 1970s, Cone was a regional economic staple, employing 2,800 loom operators, seamstresses, and patternmakers. In the ensuing decades, the company fell into decline, eventually filing for bankruptcy in 2003, as loom technology changed and production shifted to lower-wage countries. Demand has surged, however, for expensive denim, in particular for old-school, weathered-look fabrics, rejuvenating Cone's potential market.

In 2004, the company was purchased and revived by billionaire Wilbur Ross, known for his expertise in leveraged buyouts and restructuring failed companies. Today, Cone operates in a scaled-back, high-end market, producing fabric for high-end jeans using old Draper looms, but employing only 300 workers locally at its White Oak factory, a fraction of its former workforce (Burritt 2012).

Cone Denim's experience is just one example of the many challenges facing a broader business community made up of struggling manufacturing firms with few dynamic firms to replace them. For example, in 2004, cities in the region (and the state) competed heavily for Dell, a computer manufacturer. After securing over $300 million in subsidies, Dell eventually landed in nearby Winston-Salem, a city outside the official Greensboro metropolitan area but in the broader Piedmont Triad. The politicians who argued for the subsidies estimated that Dell would employ 1,500 people directly and generate another 500 related jobs, translating to a $24.5 billion economic impact over twenty years. But less than five years after arriving, Dell announced that it was shuttering the plant and laying off the 905 workers employed there (Dalesio 2009). Meanwhile, intra-regional competition, rather than cooperation, has been the practice. Two years after the initial Dell deal, the city of High Point "surprised even cynical observers" by granting incentives to La-Z-Boy to move its regional headquarters from just five miles away, in Greensboro, to within High Point city limits (Brod 2007). Our interviewees described this kind of competition as more typical than inter-regional collaboration.

Interviewees struggled to think of many examples of elite collaboration, beyond a limited number of business and governmental partnerships. Perhaps the most prominent example is the Greensboro Partnership, a multipronged entity providing business, economic, and community development in Greensboro through its member organizations: the Greensboro Economic Development Alliance (GEDA), Action Greensboro, Entrepreneur Connection, and the Greensboro Chamber of Commerce. Formed in 2005—relatively recently compared with similar groups in other regions—the Greensboro Partnership works on quality of life ("livability issues") and economic development, with a focus on downtown redevelopment. Spearheaded by local philanthropy and the public sector, the partnership has helped align the activities and plans of the GEDA and the Chamber of Commerce—and often works in tandem with the local workforce investment board. The GEDA has recently released an economic development strategy in the form of cluster analysis, which is focused on high-growth, well-paying sectors, such as aviation, the supply chain/logistics industry, the life sciences, and innovative manufacturing.[5]

The partnership has helped elevate the issues of education and training. This is critical since there are several hurdles in the way of realizing a more vibrant regional economy, including skills gaps in older workforces, low retention of recent college graduates, low rates of high school graduation, and poor preparation of children to succeed in school. Action Greensboro, the community development arm of the partnership, has played a role in education policy and program development, especially in the development of Achieve Guilford, a K-12 education advocacy collaborative. The group has come together to create a common educational agenda, which stresses a "cradle to career" approach that lifts up key programs and milestones needed at each educational level.[6] Action Greensboro is also involved in Opportunity Greensboro (http://opportunitygreensboro.com), a higher-education initiative seeking to deepen the connection between businesses and local colleges and universities and leverage the skills, resources, and talents of their 47,000 students to attract and grow industry.

Although the partnership is seeking to align the city's economic and community development goals, the process of building regional collaboration and transforming the economy is slow, and has come much later than in many other metropolitan regions—in the words of one economic development staffer, it's about a decade too late. Community groups are not often at the table, and advocacy groups often describe the relationship with business as antagonistic. Funded largely by the city, as of 2014, it wasn't even clear that the Greensboro Partnership would continue, given some of the continuing frustration about limited impact and the retirement of key executives (Carlock 2014b, 2014a).

Contesting the Past, Distrusting the Present

Greensboro is well known as a central site in the civil rights struggle. In 1960, four North Carolina A&T students asked for coffee at the Woolworth's whites-only lunch counter and gave birth to the sit-in movement in America. While these actions did result in the desegregation of department-store eateries, by 1968, civil rights organizers in Greensboro were more concerned about issues of job and educational discrimination, political underrepresentation, and poor housing, with the Black Power movement gaining adherents as issues continued to simmer.

The Greensboro Association of Poor People was founded in 1968. Relying more on direct action and confrontation, it would become one of the largest sources of community activism in the city through the mid-1970s.[7] During this time, some attempts at interracial cooperation and discussion in Greensboro were successful, including peaceful integration of the school system in 1971, the Chamber of Commerce's Community Unity Division sponsoring weekly discussion meetings on racial conciliation between 1966 and 1976, and the city's decision in the late 1970s to no longer pursue urban renewal because of its disparate impact on African Americans.[8]

As integration was taking root, however, the Greensboro Massacre shook the community to its core—and has remained an open wound. The massacre happened at a march against the Ku Klux Klan that was held on November 3, 1979. While the march was organized by the Communist Workers Party (CWP), long-time civil rights activist, founder of the Greensboro Association of Poor People, and CWP member Nelson Johnson was one of the key organizers, as the march was part of broader efforts to link together issues of race and poverty. During the demonstration, Ku Klux Klan and Nazi Party members, who had organized a counter-demonstration, opened fire and killed five protestors. The role of the police in this episode was controversial, since they were known to have anti-CWP sentiment and had only a light presence at the beginning of the march, despite knowing about the potential for violence to erupt. Though 14 KKK members were arrested for murder, a jury trial returned a not-guilty verdict in all cases (Magarrell and Wesley 2010; Waller 2002).[9]

More than two decades later, in an effort to help the region move beyond this ugly history, civil rights advocates in the region pushed for a landmark Truth and Reconciliation Commission (TRC), intended to educate and heal the community while addressing the questions and confusion that remained surrounding the event and the legal proceedings that followed. The process was funded by the Andrus Family Foundation, and a grant was awarded to the Beloved Community Center and the Greensboro Justice Center, which assembled the commission. The process, modeled after the post-apartheid TRC process in South Africa, took two years between 2004 and 2006 examining the context, causes, sequence, and consequences of the event.

Unlike the TRC process in South Africa, however, the commission was not supported by government. Greensboro's City Council voted 6–3 against endorsing the work, with the mayor at the time, Jim Melvin, also rejecting the need for a commission; the three dissenting votes were cast by African American council members. The TRC successfully completed its work and released a final report in 2006, but assessments of the ultimate impact of the process are quite mixed. Of course, original expectations of the process spanned a full spectrum, from supporters hoping that "peace and harmony should blossom in Greensboro, while at the other end of the spectrum critics foresaw greater division and dissension" (Magarrell and Wesley 2010, 207). A key goal of the TRC, as in the South African process it was modeled after, was to humanize the "other," and analysts have argued that the process went some significant way toward achieving this goal in terms of decreasing polarization in competing narratives of the events (Cunningham, Nugent, and Slodden 2010; Inwood 2012; Magarrell and Wesley 2010). Yet reactions to the TRC process shed light on the tensions that remain in the community around race and that make it difficult to come to a shared understanding of a painful past.

Overall, it seems that two key elements of regional cooperation and collaboration—trust and social capital—are in short supply in the region (Brod 2007). When asked about the culture of collaboration in Greensboro, interviewees were quick to point to high levels of distrust, and the region performs poorly on measures of social capital. Two separate Social Capital Community Benchmark Surveys were conducted by Robert Putnam of the Saguaro Institute at Harvard, one in 2000 and a follow-up study in 2006. The survey found that although residents have increasingly racially diverse personal social circles, they are not particularly trusting of others once they move beyond their immediate social circles. Also, when compared with the national sample, Greensboro residents were less trusting, and levels of trust actually declined between 2000 and 2006. And race is an important part of the story. While Blacks in the region feel strongly about what is past but not passed, whites we interviewed sometimes wondered aloud why people in the region couldn't just "get over it."

A Fragmented Future?

There are some hopeful signs that collaborative solutions to the region's challenges may be gaining more traction than in the past. The Greensboro Partnership has made some progress in developing a coordinated regional approach since its founding in 2005, and our interviewees also spoke with pride about the Downtown Greenway project (http://downtowngreenway.org), a public–private partnership between Action Greensboro and the City of Greensboro that includes a strong public process and a wide range of partners across multiple sectors, from the business community, to arts, nonprofits, and government. Once complete, the Downtown Greenway Project will be a four-mile pedestrian and bike trail encircling downtown Greensboro, connecting wealthier, Westside neighborhoods with poorer, Eastside areas in need of economic revitalization.

But despite some positive signs in recent years, Greensboro is still quite striking in its low level of collaboration across the region. It is not just that the regional epistemic community is not particularly diverse; it's that there is no such community. Some of the reasons for this are conditions that exist in many other regions: interjurisdictional economic competition, fragmented government structures, and unequal spatial distribution of poverty and economic opportunity. In Greensboro, however, these all-too-typical divides seem to be underpinned by significant racial tensions that often remain just below the surface of public discourse but are never far away.

It's hard to meet an uncertain future when the region's very history is so contested and divisive. In the context of fragmented experiences and without a common identity—are we a sleepy southern town about to stage a downtown renaissance, or a pit of racial tension that has exploded in sit-ins, a Black Power movement, and an infamous massacre?—efforts at building collaborative efforts throughout the region have been episodic and weak at best. Partly as a result, the region continues to struggle to effectively address the substantial economic challenges of the past thirty years, including persistent poverty and inequality.

FRESNO

Despite Fresno being the country's most fruitful region—literally, it is the most agriculturally productive county in the United States—it has become nationally known for its high levels of poverty and unemployment.[10] Perhaps the most striking evidence of that came when the Brookings Institution issued a post–Hurricane Katrina study trying to explain the seemingly disparate impacts by race of the storm and its aftermath. In a comparison of concentrated poverty—or the proportion of all poor people in a city who live in extreme-poverty neighborhoods—in the largest fifty cities in the United States, New Orleans was naturally quite high on the list, hitting number two. In first place: Fresno (Berube and Katz 2005, 10).

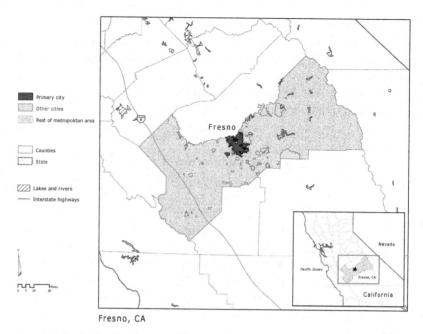

Fresno, CA

MAP 6.2. Fresno Region.

Our own data analysis confirms Fresno's reputation. While the western United States (as designated by the US Census) experienced a 45-percent increase in poverty between 1980 and 2010—about twelve percentage points more than the nation as a whole—Fresno's rate nearly doubled, from about 14 to 27 percent of residents living below the poverty level. Not surprisingly, the income gap between the 20th percentile of earners and the 80th percentile increased by nearly one-fifth during the same period. Economic growth indicators are just as dismal. While both jobs and earnings did rise, these increases happened at much lower rates in Fresno than in most US regions. The number of jobs in the West increased 73 percent between 1980 and 2010, but Fresno had less than 55-percent employment growth during that time. Similarly, while other western regions experienced a 20-percent increase in earnings per job, Fresno's workers only saw a 10-percent increase.

Despite the hardships, the region's population has grown, largely due to low-cost housing. Between 1980 and 2010, Fresno County's population nearly doubled (81 percent), bringing it to nearly a million. With this growth have come major demographic shifts. In 1980, non-Hispanic whites made up 62 percent of the region, but by 2010, they made up only one-third. Since 2000, Fresno's Latino population has grown by a third, the Asian and Pacific Islander population by nearly 40 percent, and the Black population by 12 percent; in contrast, during the same period, the region's non-Hispanic white population fell by 4 percent. By 2040, people of color will make up 75 percent of the region's total population.

It is these communities of color, however, who have suffered the most from the region's economic stagnation and skyrocketing inequality. Fresno's disparities are not just between rich and poor but between whites and people of color, too. As of 2010, the median income for Black households was only 44 percent of the median income for white households. Similarly, the median income for Latino households was only 58 percent of white households, and the median income of Asian and Pacific Islander households was 88 percent of white households, a striking finding given that Asian and Pacific Islander household income often tops that of non-Hispanic whites.

Why has Fresno—especially in its communities of color—fared so poorly over the last three decades? Many of those we interviewed point to lack of diversity in the local economy and few opportunities to move up the ladder. Others point to the deeply entrenched laissez-faire politics and policies that have allowed unfettered sprawl and hence a sharp physical separation between the rich and the poor, and between whites and people of color. Others note that economic polarization and a lack of cohesion among Fresno's various neighborhoods has left little room for marginalized communities to influence decision-making, which remains in the hands of the few business elite working with elected officials, often behind closed doors. Taken together, these regional dynamics—a highly polarized economy and region, a top-heavy political power structure perpetuating a hands-off governance approach, and a lack of collaboration (or even interaction) among diverse communities—have led to the dismal conditions we see in Fresno today.

Fresno's "Poverty–Industrial Complex"

One community organizer described Fresno as "DOA," the medical term for a patient who is found to be already clinically dead upon the arrival of professional medical assistance. But in this context, the acronym has a second—and more diagnostic—meaning. The reason for Fresno's depressed social and economic conditions, the organizer suggested, has everything to do with the overwhelming political power of business elites in Development, Oil, and Agriculture. The argument, according to activists, is that these particular (and powerful) constituencies benefit from the current arrangements and so stand in the way of reworking the economy to better serve a broad range of interests.

To understand the dynamics between these business elites and everyone else, it is important to understand how widespread and truly dominant these three industries are in Fresno's regional economy. First, development. Over the last three decades, Fresno experienced a massive real estate boom as many people priced out of California's coastal markets came to the area in search of low-cost housing. The Building Industry Association of Fresno and Madera Counties—representing builders, developers, subcontractors, and other companies related to the building industry in the two adjacent counties and referred to locally as BIA—is one of the most powerful lobbies in the region, if not *the* most powerful. For example, until recently, it was the norm for the BIA and a few of the largest developers to work directly with government staff and elected officials, behind closed doors, on local land-use planning that cleared the way for residential development on land originally zoned for agriculture. This practice resulted in unbridled suburban sprawl and the abandonment of Fresno's urban core (Arax 2009; Zuk 2013).

Second, the oil industry. Oil was first discovered in the San Joaquin Valley in the late 1800s, and more than a century later, the region still produces a vast amount. In the nearby Kern County part of the Valley, there are nearly 42,000 active wells, providing nearly 75 percent of the oil produced in California. In 2009, Fresno County had the third-highest number of active wells of any county (Los Angeles was second), with another 2,000 active wells. Fresno County is home of the Coalinga Oil Field, which was discovered in 1890 and is the eight-largest in the state in terms of cumulative production since discovery (Miller 2010).

The elephant in the room (and the A in DOA) is agriculture. As noted earlier, Fresno is the most agriculturally productive county in the nation. In 2011, Fresno's total agricultural sales were $6.9 billion, with a major focus in grapes, almonds, tomatoes, milk, and livestock. Moreover, Fresno is located at the center of one of the world's most productive agricultural hubs: the San Joaquin Valley, which has an annual gross value of more than $25 billion in agricultural production (US Environmental Protection Agency 2013). The Southern San Joaquin Valley alone—consisting of Fresno, Tulare, Kings, and Kern Counties—accounted for over 40 percent of California's total agricultural production of $43.5 billion in 2011 (California Department of Food and

Agriculture 2012), up from about a quarter in the 1970s (Bardacke 2012). Much of the production occurs on large-scale industrial agriculture enterprises. Land monopoly has characterized the San Joaquin Valley since the late 1800s (Pisani 1991). The nearly 1000-square-mile Westlands Water District in the southwest part of the valley has recently been described as "dominated by a few pioneer dynastic families" (Carter 2009, 6).

Though agricultural interests are rarely directly represented in the city of Fresno's politics, they fundamentally shape social and political dynamics in the region. Agriculture brings in large amounts of revenue, and directly provides 11 percent of the county's jobs—yet the industry predominantly provides only seasonal employment with sub-poverty wages. In 2008, for example, the western valley's 20th Congressional District had the distinction of being the poorest district in the country (Carter 2009, 7).[11] Though labor laws exist to protect the workers, many sources claim that these rules are largely ignored. Farm workers receive sub-minimum wages and experience dangerous working conditions in which they are expected to work long days in some of the country's hottest temperatures. Moreover, it is estimated that about half the agricultural workforce in California's Central Valley—of which the San Joaquin Valley is a part—are undocumented, and thus are subject to harsh levels of exploitation with no protections (National Public Radio 2002; Pastor and Marcelli 2013).

To advance a more broad-based economy, the city of Fresno and the surrounding region need to diversify and support industry clusters that pay higher wages. While there have been some sector initiatives along these lines, focusing on logistics, water technology and related manufacturing technologies, energy, and jobs related to health care, the resulting job growth has been modest at best (Chapple 2005; Montana and Nenide 2008). While this may be partly due to structural factors, such as low levels of education and inadequate systems of workforce development, some equity advocates suggest that the main economic actors in the region are so interested in cheap land (development), loose regulations (oil), and cheap labor (agriculture) that there is scant leadership for a "high road" strategy. The result is a "poverty–industrial complex"— inequity is baked right in to economic growth.

Moreover, while in Grand Rapids, Charlotte, and Oklahoma City private-sector interests set the regional agenda but seem to keep some focus on improving conditions for all, in Fresno the industrial elites seem less interested in addressing community well-being in a way that would potentially erode what they see as their competitive advantages. There are some exceptions to this generalization. The Fresno Business Council, an organization started by a few business leaders concerned about high levels of crime and blight in the early 1990s, does research on community indicators and promotes initiatives to spur community transformation through stewardship, for example efforts around school reform. Generally, however, the traditionally marginalized groups remain marginalized from most planning processes, and there is little to no room for systematic pushback against the DOA agenda.

The overall political mix has been reinforced by sprawl, a residential pattern made possible by cheap land and pushed into being by developer interests. For example, in the 1974 update to the city of Fresno's General Plan, a General Plan Citizens Committee was formed to meet the community-participation requirement for continued funding for redevelopment from the US Department of Housing and Urban Development. After due deliberation, it recommended densification strategies like urban infill to benefit the existing residents in downtown and South Fresno. In response, the Planning Commission voted to adopt a developer-supported alternative plan, channeling growth to sparsely populated North Fresno (Zuk 2013). This decision helped institutionalize sprawl as the city's planning strategy moving forward.

Corruption also played a role in accelerating northward growth over the last three decades. In the 1980s and 1990s, bribery and fraud to initiate and streamline rezoning processes that converted agricultural land to residential became widespread. In the early 1990s, a local real estate developer publicly revealed that a city councilmember in Clovis—an affluent white suburb in northeast Fresno County, and a direct byproduct of unbridled northward sprawl—had requested a campaign contribution in exchange for a rezoning permit. During a six-and-a-half-year investigation that began in 1994, the FBI uncovered a rampant practice of developers ducking local zoning requirements and environmental regulations by buying off politicians. It was so deeply entrenched as a normal business practice that one Department of Justice official speculated that it had been occurring over "decades, if not generations" (Arax 1995). In the end, Operation REZONE—named after the personalized license plate of a Fresno-based land-use consultant long suspected of working in cahoots with politicians and developers—resulted in the conviction of sixteen city council members, developers, and lobbyists in both Fresno and Clovis for "fraud, racketeering, extortion, money laundering, mail fraud and income tax violations" (Zuk 2013, 53).

Explosive residential development may have been facilitated by corruption, but it was made possible by booming population growth starting in the mid-1970s. Between 1980 and 2010, Fresno County's population nearly doubled, from a little less than 515,000 to over 930,000. As noted earlier, this was accompanied by dramatic demographic changes, including a sharp increase in the share of Latinos and Asians (including the arrival of Hmong refugees in the 1980s). With demographics changing and suburbs developing, Fresno's white residents flocked to North Fresno—and a single east-west street, Shaw Avenue, is now widely recognized as the dividing line between the affluent white residents in the north and low-income communities of color in the south. The concentration of poverty in South Fresno (part of which is physically cut off from the rest of the city by Highway 99) hinders wealth building and career advancement because of low property values and limited employment opportunities (Cytron 2009; Kneebone, Nadeau, and Berube 2011).

One interviewee described the situation as a "tale of two cities," in which the city is so segregated that rich Fresnans do not even see the poor ones, despite the region's extremely high poverty rate (George 2013). And it's not just the city but the region. Fresno's northeastern suburb of Clovis is majority-white, with a median household income of $63,983, while Huron City, in the heart of the agricultural lands to the southwest of town, is 98.5 percent Latino, with a median household income of only $21,041 and a 46-percent poverty rate.[12] The divide between rich and poor, white and non-white, north and south, exacerbates the downward spiral of economic polarization and stagnation the region has been experiencing for decades. The farther apart people grow, the less likely they are to see the value of investing in one another's communities—and the more likely it is that conflict will not help produce new understandings, only new tensions.

Fighting for Change

The entrenched poverty and striking inequality in Fresno have not gone unchallenged. Indeed, some of the most important and precedent-setting activism and organizing for workers' rights in the country has occurred in the Fresno region. The early 1970s, for example, saw a growing Chicano social movement, originally rooted in the organizing efforts of the Community Service Organization (CSO) and the subsequent labor organizing of a well-known CSO-trained organizer, Cesar Chavez. The

CSO was founded in 1947 in Los Angeles, and its first paid organizer was Fred Ross, West Coast director of the Industrial Areas Foundation, founded by Saul Alinsky. By 1954, Fresno had a CSO chapter, and Fred Ross, along with Gene Laury, was organizing in the Mexican community on Fresno's west side. Their work focused on increasing civic engagement through voter registration and citizenship classes.

The CSO played a critical role in shaping the evolution of the United Farm Workers (UFW) union as well. Cesar Chavez spent ten years organizing for the CSO, starting in 1952 and becoming executive director in 1959, before founding the National Farm Workers Association (NFWA), which eventually evolved into the UFW. In the spring of 1962, Chavez set up in Delano, which is about seventy-five miles south of Fresno, and in September of that year, the first convention of what was then called simply the Farm Workers Association was held in Fresno (Bardacke 2012; Ganz 2009). While much of the organizing was in the surrounding smaller farmworker towns, Fresno was an important regional hub and frequent site of NFWA and UFW meetings.

The year 1973 was a particularly important turning point in the UFW's history, and Fresno was at the center of the struggle. With a series of contracts expiring, and growers, including thirty fruit orchards outside Fresno, seeking to not renew contracts with the UFW, the union seemed to be facing a coordinated challenge to its strength. Its response was to try to make the Central Valley's agricultural economy ungovernable and to lay the ground for another boycott. Strikes that summer began on July 4th, and as the days wore on, strikers started turning to civil disobedience—on July 19th and 20th, more than 400 people were arrested each day. On August 3rd, at a rally in a Fresno city park, Chavez declared that the UFW would make Fresno another Selma, Alabama (or maybe Greensboro, North Carolina?) and urged allies across the country to come to Fresno and take part in mass arrests. Clergy across the state and country responded, in what Father Eugene Boyle of San Francisco later called "the largest group of religious persons ever arrested and jailed in this country" (Bardacke 2012, kindle location 9779). Polarization, albeit for a good cause, was the order of the day.

Ultimately, the strike failed, but its legacy lingered. The region has continued to experience significant organizing around immigrants' rights and other critical issues, including through a range of faith-based initiatives affiliated with PICO California.[13] In recent decades, however, the environment has become an area of significant concern and organizing. Many factors contribute to the environmental problems:

agriculture-linked industrial processes, automobiles traversing the valley between Northern and Southern California, heavy-duty diesel-fueled trucks transporting agricultural products out of the region, pesticides entering the air after use, and emissions from oil and gas fields. The resulting toxic soup has substantial health and welfare impacts (Alexeeff et al. 2012; Huang and London 2012; London, Huang, and Zagofsky 2011; Sadd et al. 2011). Indeed, in a statewide analysis of environmental burden and vulnerabilities conducted in 2013 by the California Office of Environmental Health Hazard Assessment, three of the state's five worst zip codes were in Fresno.

A range of environmental justice groups has emerged over the past two decades to try to change these dynamics. In 2004, more than seventy organizations throughout the broader region came together to form the Central Valley Air Quality Coalition (www.calcleanair.org). Despite this level of coordination, as well as extensive advocacy and litigation, the San Joaquin Air Pollution Control District and related agencies have achieved limited success in improving air quality in the region. Activists in the region attribute this to the heavy influence that dominant industrial interests have on the Air Pollution Control District's board, which is an appointed body and has historically been resistant to popular pressure.

In our interviews, environmental justice activists said that, in the face of this intransigence, their most promising path forward at this point is through adversarial lawsuits rather than collaborative policy development. This is hardly the happy stuff of a diverse and dynamic epistemic community in which clearly documented data about a problem—pollution—is shared and new solutions are collaboratively generated. Instead, tension begets tension, poverty begets poverty, and fighting for change becomes what seems to be a losing battle against contemporary political, economic, and residential landscapes characterized by polarization and inequality.

Hope Springs Eternal—but Dimly

When one considers the polarization of the regional economy, the concentration of political power in the hands of a few elites, and the lack of collaboration (or even interaction) among diverse communities, it is perhaps not surprising that traditionally disadvantaged communities have little political representation or voice in decision-making processes in Fresno. Despite the region's being 50 percent Latino and only 33 percent white in 2010, the city of Fresno has never elected a person of color as mayor. While district elections have helped ensure that both Latinos and Asians have some representation on the City Council, the city has a strong-mayor structure, and local politics are still largely driven by a relatively well-entrenched white elite and a traditionally conservative Chamber of Commerce. As a result, the region's clear problems of sprawl, segregation, and growing inequality have often been largely absent from regional conversations.

However, the tide may be turning in Fresno. In 2012, efforts that had coalesced around sustainable growth helped pushed the city to deviate from business as usual and develop a General Plan that prioritized urban infill over suburban sprawl. Called Alternative A, the plan envisioned concentrating new developments along existing major corridors and in a series of mixed-use centers surrounded by higher-density housing, while also prioritizing revitalization of the still dilapidated downtown core. Many (at least partially) credit this challenge to the region's long-standing and deeply entrenched pattern of unmitigated sprawl to the fact that South Fresno—the poorest part of town—was chosen to be a part of the California Endowment's Building Healthy Communities initiative, a ten-year place-based community development strategy in fourteen sites across the state.

Launched in 2010, the initiative seeks to build local capacity to advocate for healthier communities, with part of this strategy involving the redistribution of power through organizing communities and building their capacities to engage in decision-making (Zuk 2013). Residents came together with local agencies, community-based organizations, faith-based groups, and other leaders to suggest that one way to address health disparities was to invest in urban redevelopment rather than sprawl. These groups worked closely with staff at the city's Planning and Development Department and Downtown and Community Revitalization Department to develop expertise and share knowledge— the cornerstone of building epistemic communities—primarily through mapping demographic data and land-use scenarios to see how their city was changing and how they could direct that growth.

In the nearly two years of organizing and community participation leading up to the final vote on the city's General Plan, the majority of Building Healthy Communities funding was linked in one way or another to pushing for Alternative A—and it paid off. At the April 5, 2012, meeting for the final consideration of the different scenarios in the General Plan, the city council chambers were filled beyond capacity, with more than 350 people. A diverse group of more than 80 speakers—including

Latino children, Hmong grandmothers, neighborhood activists, farmers, pastors, doctors, public health professionals, air quality advocates, conservation groups, business representatives, developers, members of the League of Women Voters, and more—spoke in favor of the plan (Bergthold 2012). Even though the plan was opposed by the Chamber of Commerce, major local land developers, and the local Building Industry Association, it passed 5 to 2 in the council—a stark shift from the behind-closed-doors decision-making processes to which Fresno has become accustomed.

Also significant was that members of the region's farming community came out publicly in support of Alternative A—a move that made intuitive sense since rezoning has allowed suburban housing development to swallow up agricultural land over the last few decades. While this did not necessarily bridge deeply entrenched divides—namely, between industry and community—it brought together allies that had not previously worked together around a rather innovative plan for smart growth in one of the nation's capitals of sprawl. Also, as one city staffer described, this process has perhaps laid the groundwork for building a civic engagement infrastructure in Fresno to shift the status quo—something that has sorely been missing for decades.

There is also a glimmer of hope in the recent development of the Fresno Community Scorecard (www.fresnocommunityscorecard.org). Launched in the summer of 2014, this is a website presented by the Fresno Business Council and Valley Public Television that allows users to explore an array of community characteristics and see where the city stands in relation to statewide and national averages. In the spirit of creating epistemic communities, the intention of the website is to establish a central place for Fresno's stakeholders to find data and perhaps inspire collaboration among these stakeholders in identifying the solutions to the often intersecting obstacles the community faces. As a local community activist, quoted in the newspaper, put it: "Shining light and gathering data does change behavior" (Sheehan 2014).

We do not mean to exaggerate the significance of these recent efforts. The Planning Commission's decision in the 1970s to ignore citizen input in approving the General Plan paved the way (pun intended) for the subsequent three decades of urban sprawl and growing inequality. The current efforts are admirable, but it will take a decade or more of sustained collaborative efforts to turn things around. Conflict in Fresno has remained largely in a zero-sum and antagonistic framework. Business leaders have largely stuck to well-trod paths rooted in low-wage,

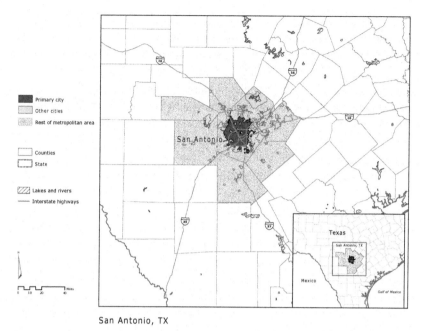

Primary city
Other cities
Rest of metropolitan area

Counties
State

Lakes and rivers
Interstate highways

San Antonio, TX

MAP 6.3. San Antonio Region.

cost-driven strategies or largely unregulated sprawl, while equity advocates have seen little reason to move from an adversarial approach. Social and economic fragmentation is reinforced by a spatial separation, and Fresno seems to lack the level of transformative leadership that is able to both maintain credibility in their own constituency while also building ties among constituencies with conflicting values and interests. A divided and fragmented region, Fresno has a level of conflict and intransigence that led many of our interviewees to be pessimistic about the future.

SAN ANTONIO

If you talk to civic leaders in San Antonio today, they proudly boast of an increasingly multifaceted economy that has been able to move beyond reliance on military spending and now boasts of vibrant tourism, medical, energy, manufacturing, and professional-services sectors.[14] They attribute that success—evident in jobs, earnings, and relative improvement in median household income and poverty—to a spirit of collaboration among government, business, universities, and community groups that has become part of the regional DNA (Benner and Pastor 2014).

What has been the record? From 1980 to 2010, jobs in the San Antonio region increased by 112 percent, and average earnings increased by 21 percent in inflation-adjusted dollars, both outperforming the averages for the top 192 metros. Part of the performance has been good fortune—or, shall we say, good energy. San Antonio is the headquarters of Tesoro and Valero, both Fortune 500 oil companies, and a range of oil-related firms have grown in recent years due to the fracking-related boom (though total oil output in Texas remains below its early 1970s peak). But San Antonio has seen employment growth across a range of other industries too, including bioscience, health care, financial services, call centers, tourism, and automobile-related manufacturing. Despite a decline in military-base employment with the closing of two of four Air Force bases in the region, military spending is still important for the region's substantial IT/cybersecurity and aerospace clusters, also significant contributors to economic dynamism (Hernandez 2011; Thomas 2013).[15]

In contrast to this current picture, San Antonio started the 1980s with a higher overall poverty level than most metro regions, and poverty worsened in that decade. But in the most recent two decades, trends in poverty in San Antonio have actually outperformed other metro regions, falling by nearly a quarter in the 1990s, and rising in the 2000s by only 8 percent (from 15.1 percent to 16.3 percent of the population), while the average increase for the top 192 metros was 30 percent over the same period (from 12.0 percent to 15.6 percent). Similarly, the region saw growing inequality in the 1980s, as the 80/20 household income ratio increased by 5 percent (from 4.19 to 4.42), compared to an average 1-percent decline for the top 192 metros (from 4.17 to 4.13). But between 1990 and 2010, the rise in that inequality measure was less than half of the average increase for the top 192 metros, a striking performance given the poor starting point.

Both the overall performance and the contemporary spirit of collaboration are far cries from where San Antonio was three decades ago. Then, the city and the region were the site of one of the country's most intense struggles to challenge stark racism in the allocation of public resources and to confront a business elite who seemed committed to marketing the region based on cheap labor (indeed, they had a plan prepared on this basis). The challenge to racism was remarkably concrete in both its subject and its strategies: working-class Latinos living on the city's poorer West Side were impacted by inadequate drainage systems that sent water and debris flowing into the streets following torrential rainstorms (Rogers 1990; Rosales 2000). As a result, the first powerful organizing efforts were focused largely on infrastructure, but the broader struggle was about tipping the political power that would be necessary to achieve change.

In short, San Antonio was an awful lot like Greensboro and Fresno. But over the past four decades, San Antonio has moved from conflict to collaboration, from stark racism and poverty to incorporation and income mobility. How has the region been able to evolve in this way? The culture of collaboration was built slowly, and often unsteadily. Conflict played an important key role in surfacing issues of equity and inclusion, but in contrast to Fresno and Greensboro, regional stakeholders were able to prevent conflict from getting in the way of continued engagement. Over time—and facilitated through the deliberate efforts of a few key bridge-building individuals—this continued engagement evolved to a growing sense of common destiny, and the broad culture and social norms of collaboration that characterize the region today.

Making Change in San Antonio

Today, the San Antonio region is nearly two-thirds people of color. The region's demographic shift was already well underway in the 1970s. San Antonio was one of the nation's first majority-minority cities (Miller 2011); by 1980, Latinos alone were 44 percent of the population. Despite popular perception, Latino growth was mainly homegrown. Even today, the share of foreign-born in San Antonio is actually lower than it is in the country as a whole. However, these US-born second- and third-generation citizens were living on the city's poorer West and South Sides, and their interests were largely ignored by long-standing Anglo elites.

The most immediate issue that surfaced as a conflict was infrastructure. The region is known for its ranches and its military bases, but also for its torrential rainstorms (Rosales 2000). In the 1970s, the resulting flooding affected all the neighborhoods, to be certain, but the downpours impacted the poor and working-class Latino neighborhoods of West San Antonio hardest, where inadequate drainage systems resulted in flooding that ruined homes and impacted public safety. When it came to infrastructure, the schools were not so hot either—literally. Many West Side schools lacked heat and proper insulation, and parents fretted about sending their kids off to a cold classroom in the winter (Rogers 1990).

These conditions in the mid-1970s provided a base for a remarkable shift over the next two decades, as a combination of broad-based community organizing and shifting electoral politics helped transform the city's fortunes. And it was two neighborhood kids from the West Side that were particularly prominent in these shifting politics: Ernesto Cortes and Henry Cisneros.

Ernie Cortes, who would become one of the country's preeminent organizers, returned home to San Antonio in the early 1970s, after gaining experience organizing with the Industrial Areas Foundation (IAF) in the Midwest. Cortes began organizing in San Antonio's West Side parishes, and in 1974 founded Communities Organized for Public Services (COPS), an IAF affiliate organization made up of faith-based leaders and their members. COPS ultimately became probably the strongest community-based organization in the IAF network, and the core of a network of seventeen affiliates working throughout the Southwest. COPS worked especially closely with a sister organization, Metro Alliance, which worked throughout the San Antonio metro area, and Cortes and other COPS leaders helped launch a Texas statewide network with a founding convention in 1990 that drew over 10,000 people (Warren 1998).

In addition to an institution-led, values-based approach, the IAF was well known for its creative direct-action tactics. COPS personified this approach. One of its early campaigns, for example, involved trying to get the City Council to pass a budget proposal that included a $100 million investment in infrastructure and increased services in poor, predominantly Latino neighborhoods. As part of the campaign, COPS activists worked to disrupt the normal operations of prominent businesses in the city, and urged business leaders to bring support of their campaign to the City Council. At Frost National Bank, a leading local institution, COPS members halted normal banking activities by exchanging dollars for pennies (and then pennies for dollars) all day long. Similarly, at Joske's department store, the women of COPS disrupted business by trying on clothes, all day long, *en masse*. In both cases, their message was the same: we will continue to throw a wrench into your day-to-day business activities until our communities' basic needs are addressed.

This disruptive and confrontational approach ultimately pushed local leadership to secure significant resources for COPS's neighborhoods, including $86 million in Community Development Block Grants between 1974 and 1981 (Marquez 1990, 360). Indeed, over its first twenty-five years, COPS reportedly directed over $1 billion in resources to the neighborhoods it represented (Warren 1998, 80). The Alinsky-inspired organizing was responsible not only for shifting significant resources within the city but also for shifting the overall economic development strategy of the region. In the early 1980s, the San Antonio Economic Development Foundation's primary strategy was attracting outside business and investment by promoting the city's low wages and unorganized labor force (Marquez 1990). Because of a major COPS-led protest of these policies, the foundation moderated its approach and worked with the city to identify other economic development strategies.

While Cortes initially took a confrontational approach, another West Side native son, Henry Cisneros, emerged to help build bridges between the disparate worlds of San Antonio's power elite and its poor Latino residents. With a strong family commitment to education, Cisneros garnered degrees from Texas A&M and Harvard, and eventually a Doctor of Public Administration from George Washington University in 1976, with doctoral research at MIT along the way. He returned to San Antonio in 1974, and in 1975, at the age of twenty-seven, was elected the youngest city councilman in the city's history. In 1981 he was elected mayor, only the second Latino mayor of a large city in the country, and he was eventually reelected another three times, serving as mayor until 1989.

Charismatic and articulate, Cisneros was comfortable straddling multiple worlds. His ability to appeal to both an Anglo old guard and the growing Latino population is perhaps best exemplified by the fact that he was initially elected as part of the (perhaps ironically titled) Good Government League slate supported by San Antonio's narrow business elite. San Antonio's elections were at-large, a system that allowed a unified city interest like business to better exercise power and control. That said, the Good Government League was aware of bubbling resentment, so it made sure to have at least one Latino and one African American on its slate, and Cisneros took one of those spots. And while that strategy reflected at least a token attempt at incorporation, the underrepresentation of minority groups in city politics led to federal pressure from the Justice Department, and in 1977 the council moved from at-large to council districts. District governments secured additional seats for Latinos, partially dismantling the structures supporting the city's Anglo power elite and paving the way for a broadening of policies, ideas, and investments.

Cisneros continued to thrive under the new system and essentially served as a transitional and transformational figure linking pro-growth business interests and the underrepresented Mexican-American community. An early supporter of COPS, Cisneros further elevated the organization's work while in office, paying attention to the neglected West Side community where he grew up (and still lives). Eventually, many members of the regional business community who had initially seen COPS as an obstructionist organization came to view it as a valued partner in the region's economic development ecosystem. Most emblematic, after suffering through COPS members' disrupting activities at his bank, Frost Bank CEO Tom Frost had bought a case of Saul Alinsky's book *Rules for Radicals* and distributed them to the power elite in San Antonio to help them be more prepared to deal with their adversaries (Warren, Defilippis, and Saegert 2008). But as he learned more about the organization, and as COPS moved out of doing only direct-action organizing to more collaborative workforce development, Frost ultimately became chair of a major COPS-initiated workforce development organization called Project QUEST.

Shocked into Collaboration

In fact, Project QUEST is a sort of poster child for the shift from conflict to collaboration, and it shows how economic shock can sometimes (as in Oklahoma City) lead to a fundamental transformation in regional governance. It was prompted by the sudden closure of San Antonio's Levi Strauss factory in 1990, a place that had employed 1,000 workers, mostly Latina women. In direct response to the closure (and against the backdrop of the other economic trends, including defense cuts that threatened civilian jobs at local military bases), Project QUEST (Quality Employment through Skills Training) was formed. Begun in 1993, the program was spearheaded by COPS and Metro Alliance, whose membership included many workers displaced from manufacturing. Importantly, QUEST brought together a diverse group: from workers to businesses and employers, the regional Private Industry Council, the governor, and the Texas Employment Commission.

Project QUEST was designed to upgrade and reskill disadvantaged workers for good jobs in high-demand occupations. It does so by targeting a cluster of in-demand, well-paying, and growing occupations, and works with the community college system to develop degree and certificate programs suited to these occupations. Unlike many workforce development programs, Project QUEST requires that participants demonstrate economic need, defined as earning less than 50 percent of the area's median household income. The organization links low-income individuals to training, but also links employers to its graduates. During the past twenty-one years, more than 80 percent of its entrants have graduated from the program, and 86 percent of those who graduated were placed into higher-paying occupations (Rodriguez 2013). Graduates enter the program with annual earnings hovering around $10,000, and leave earning on average $39,300 per year. In 2012, graduates earned an average hourly wage of $19.65.[16]

While QUEST is worthy of a long discussion (and many articles and reports have chronicled its structure and outcomes), for our purposes the important aspect of its evolution is that it highlighted the power of collaboration and also won over some leaders who were initially skeptical of COPS. But the value of paying attention to equity and collaborating for success was already being planted in the San Antonio soil. For example, the San Antonio Education Partnership (www.saedpartnership.org), formed in 1988 in a citywide effort led by then-mayor Henry Cisneros, brings together the leading Chambers of Commerce and multiple companies, COPS and Metro Alliance, and local universities, colleges, schools, and school districts. The partnership's goal was—and is—to help students graduate from high school, enroll in college, and graduate with a certificate or degree. It celebrated its twenty-fifth anniversary in 2013, and interviewees suggested that it has been an important forum not just for closing the graduation gap in underserved communities but also for coalescing disparate interests. It hasn't always been easy—respondents noted moments in which fingers were pointed and blame was cast—but the partnership moved forward, worked through challenging questions, and stayed focused on the goals of creating opportunities for all of the region's youth.

Perhaps most telling of San Antonio's collaborative progress and future orientation was the 2012 effort to pass a sales-tax increase to fund pre-K education in San Antonio's underserved communities. In addition to support from the usual suspects—the school district, the city of San Antonio, and nonprofit groups—the Chamber of Commerce joined in, not only supporting the increase but championing it as an investment in preparing a local workforce for the future economy. While the alliance of seeming odd bedfellows was striking, just as moving was the fact that the results of pre-K programming will only be revealed twenty years from now, and that the investments being made today are explicitly oriented to low-income kids whose parents are not likely to pay the bulk of the expenses. To cultivate both a long-term view and an embrace of the "other" was striking, and the tax increase passed, with 54 percent of the vote.

The region is also committed to crafting a shared vision of future regional prosperity. SA2020 is a regional visioning exercise and plan created with strong public participation (not unlike Envision Utah).[17] The visioning process was led by the Jacksonville Community Council—a nonprofit group that works on developing vision and indicators documents for several regions, including Jacksonville, Florida, and Nashville, Tennessee. Both of these regions were profiled as strong performers on growth and equity in Benner and Pastor (2012), and the Jacksonville Community Council was praised for its role in creating knowledge networks across leadership silos. The city spearheaded the initiative, but foundations, businesses, and nonprofits have also adopted the principles. Out of this long public process, the city decided to focus on several areas—education, employment, environment, and health—and the city's planning department is orienting its redevelopment plans around some of SA2020's key goals.

This is not meant to paint too rosy a picture of the San Antonio situation. For example, the business community is proud of a public–private effort to attract a Toyota manufacturing facility in the mid-2000s, which reinvigorated the regional economy and was sited relatively close to lower-income neighborhoods. But some have criticized the significant tax abatements and fee waivers, as well as the relatively secretive nature of the negotiations with the company (Morton 2013). This was indeed a case in which cards were held close to the chest (perhaps an appropriate metaphor for a Texas deal), and respondents in our interviews, including those intimately involved in the Toyota negotiations, acknowledge that a different approach might have been better.

Getting Challenged but Getting Along

Collaboration has, in some ways, become so embedded in San Antonio that for many young leaders and organizations it is a modus operandi—they report that "it's just how we do things here." The community-organizing efforts, hard-won battles, and bargains spearheaded by COPS are now viewed somewhat romantically and with a sense of nostalgia. But collaboration in San Antonio has come about only through the activities of social movements unafraid of sparking conflict and controversy, including highlighting the need for political representation of the region's significant and growing Latino community.

Particular leaders played an important role. It is a tribute to both Ernie Cortes and Tom Frost that these former adversaries could move from confrontation to collaboration, and it is clear that no story of modern-day San Antonio could be told without highlighting the way that Henry Cisneros bridged old elites and a rising new electorate. But it wasn't only these key leaders who learned that getting challenged did not preclude getting along. In contrast to the regional planning processes of Salt Lake City and Sacramento, San Antonio did not have a single unified forum in which a common future vision for the region was developed. The process in San Antonio was much messier—resembling a series of skirmishes, around multiple different issues in a variety of contexts, more than a unified process (Lester and Reckhow 2013). And yet, through repeated interactions in these multiple forums, civic leaders learned to neither patronize nor demonize the "other," and instead recognized the importance of collaborative knowledge generation and sharing.

Regional collaboration is a living and constantly changing process, and part of what makes San Antonio impressive has been its ability to continually adapt over time. But there are also signs that the current emphasis on collaboration may be leading to a sort of amnesia—forgetting that it was organizing (and conflict) that may have gotten the region to where it is. Some interviewees, for example, suggested that the poorest are being left behind and that an influx of new people masks continued challenges to mobility; others say that, even given the progress, there is still much more to be done. Unfortunately, COPS's role as an advocate and agitator has waned. Its members have, in many ways, become so thoroughly incorporated into the power structure that their role as outside agitators has lessened. COPS is also struggling to connect with and engage new constituents—young families and activists—around current issues. Likewise, Project QUEST was beset by financial mismanagement and is also struggling to find its footing. These challenges aside, San Antonio's experience clearly demonstrates that conflict indeed *can* lead eventually to collaboration and that social-movement organizing can play a critically important role in highlighting equity challenges that might otherwise be ignored by a more elite-driven process.

BEYOND "WIN-WIN": CONFLICT AND COLLABORATION

For much of the last two decades, both individually and collectively, our research has explored different aspects of regional equity and social movement building. We have been strong proponents of the important role social movements can play in shifting unequal power relationships, addressing inequality, and lifting up broader social issues that undermine the economy as a whole. But we have also stressed the need for regional collaboration and bridge-building, and the very notion that guides this particular volume—the importance of creating diverse and dynamic epistemic communities—might seem to suggest that conflict should be eschewed in favor of polite conversations, planning charrettes, and "win-win" chatter.

This chapter has tried to suggest that although conflict often remains just conflict, it can also lead to uncomfortable issues being raised and addressed in a more collaborative framework. The key question that emerges is: When does a region get stuck in entrenched differences—as in Greensboro and to some degree in Fresno—and when it is it able to move forward, as in San Antonio, to address both persistent issues (such as an undereducated populace and uneven infrastructure) and economic shocks (such as plant closures and defense cutbacks)?

In our view, one key feature of the San Antonio success story is the presence of bridge-builders—those organizations and individuals who have enough credibility on multiple sides of a conflict to help ensure ongoing communication, rather than closed minds and hardened positions. But there was also a sort of rootedness in the region—a "place pride"— that seems to have anchored commitments, including the Chamber's more recent support for a sales tax to fund pre-K. And there was also the evolution of multiple forums, including Project QUEST and now SA2020, where key actors could come together, learn to understand the "other," and find some room for common ground. These repeated interactions, often in the realm of regional knowledge generation and interpretation, are exactly what we mean by epistemic communities.

While we celebrate what has occurred in San Antonio, we do not mean to imply that conflict must shift to collaboration to achieve positive outcomes. After all, social movements for inclusion involve conflict, almost by definition. They involve groups of people making collective claims at least in part outside institutionalized channels of political and social voice. And sometimes conditions are so stark—think of the Jim Crow South—that challenge is the only path forward. Surely, in the current American moment—in which income inequality has risen dramatically, incarceration rates are racially disparate, and certain neighborhoods face a dangerous mix of inadequate employment and excessive pollution—it's right to fight.

But what we were particularly struck by in the San Antonio case is related not so much to the *balance* between conflict and collaboration but rather to a shift in *how* groups conflict, with greater efforts to develop and promote what we call *principled conflict* (Benner and Pastor 2015). In using this term, we are referring not to conflicts over principles but rather to the principles of (or norms governing) conflict: that struggles should be waged with integrity and that it is possible to directly address real conflicts in goals, objectives, and values in a way that also recognizes the need to sustain long-term relationships. The alternative is a war of attrition that can sap all sides, and the stasis in Greensboro and Fresno is suggestive of the limits of that approach.

Indeed, the very depth of the epistemic separation in those conflict-ridden regions—in which some think that Greensboro Blacks should just "get over it" or that all Fresno's problems can be swept away by moving one's family to a northern suburb—prevents a recognition that although there may be many interests, there is often but one shared destiny. But how is that sense of a shared future cultivated (or not) in those regions that are leading in America's new "knowledge economy"—and what does this point to for the nation as a whole? This is the topic to which we now turn.

CHAPTER 7

The Next Frontier

Collaboration in the New Economy

Playing together isn't just more fun; it's better business.
Collaboration connects players—plain and simple. And that
leads to more creativity and more innovation.

—Research Triangle Regional Partnership (2013)

In all of the case-study regions we've examined up to this point, we have stressed the role and evolution of epistemic communities, often against the backdrop of significant economic restructuring, growing demographic diversity, and a nationwide worsening of inequality. We've explored the differences between communities that are driven by planning, steered by elites, or wracked by conflict. We have suggested that although processes of collaboration and knowledge-sharing across diverse constituencies do not guarantee success, they may help create norms and conditions that make above-average growth and improved social equity more likely to be achieved, even in the midst of a rapidly changing economy.

With perhaps the exception of Salt Lake City, the regions we have examined so far have not been at the leading edge of the economic restructuring of the past thirty years. So, what about regions that have been at the forefront of developing the new industries and technologies that are shaping our new "knowledge economy"? What role do epistemic communities play in regions whose very economic base is rooted in the commercialization of new scientific and technological knowledge? In these areas, knowledge matters in two ways. The first is simply the products: the high-technology industries and firms we associate with the new economy rely on the advance of science and technological know-how. But just as important is the second way in which knowledge matters: research on innovation and new-technology development has demonstrated time and again that collaboration and dense information-sharing networks are key factors in explaining economic innovation (Braczyk, Cooke, and Heidenreich 1998; Brown and Duguid 2000; Saxenian 1994).

However, there is also research that argues that the sort of rapid technological change we see most dramatically in these new economy regions is associated with increasing inequality (Autor, Katz, and Kearney 2006; Brynjolfsson and McAfee 2011). For example, Silicon Valley, *the* iconic global high-tech region, has received significant public scrutiny as a place with extreme contrasts (Packer 2013)—and the spectacle of local residents protesting against buses shuttling Google employees from urban San Francisco to their suburban coding cubicles has certainly captured the public's imagination. Since we have stressed the role of knowledge and interaction in helping facilitate situations in which such disparities might receive attention, is there a contradiction in our approach? What happens when a knowledge community meets the knowledge economy?

In this chapter we examine three regions—Silicon Valley, Raleigh-Durham, and Seattle—which have large information technology industries and have built their regional economies around growth in these industries. As we'll see, the three have quite different patterns of both growth and social equity. In Silicon Valley, economic growth and social equity seemed to go together (to a certain extent) in the 1980s, but this has eroded in recent years as the region has continued to experience dramatic increases in income alongside rapidly increasing inequality and stagnant job growth. In contrast, Raleigh-Durham and Seattle have experienced substantial economic growth *and* indicators of social equity that are above average—and Seattle adopted the nation's highest municipal minimum wage ordinance in 2014, an effort to address some of the disparities that are supposedly being generated by the more dynamic parts of its regional economy.

This contrast suggests to us that there is nothing inherent in being dependent on information technology industries that condemns a region to worsening inequality, and that much depends as well on the regional norms and networks. In what follows, we first examine Silicon Valley, discussing the evolution of the region's governance from a contested but engaged business-led vision of regional stewardship, to increasing divisions and the growth of what has been called a "tale of two valleys" (Kuchler 2014). This case is a bit shorter than others in the book because the Valley has been extensively profiled elsewhere, including by

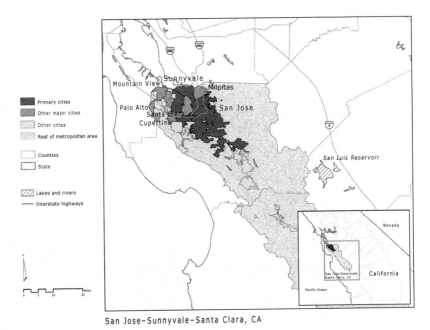

San Jose–Sunnyvale–Santa Clara, CA

MAP 7.1. Silicon Valley Region.

us (Benner 2002; Pastor et al. 2000). We then turn to Raleigh-Durham, where the Triple Helix model of regional governance, combined with a strong and networked social equity advocacy and research organization, have helped maintain the region's dynamism and relatively equitable growth. Finally, in Seattle, we explore how a culture of consensus-building and broad participation—sometimes to a fault—has contributed to a quite remarkable set of processes that certainly suggest the presence of a dynamic and diverse epistemic community.

SILICON VALLEY

Silicon Valley is well known as the global center of innovation in high-technology industries.[1] The region has managed to maintain its innovative leadership through multiple rounds of economic restructuring; it has been consistently able to develop new technological innovations even as yesterday's innovative technologies become more commoditized and globalized, and so migrate to other high-tech regions and lower-cost production centers. From the heart of the semiconductor and related integrated-circuit industry in the 1960s and 1970s, through the explosion of personal computers in the 1980s, through the software and Internet boom of the 1990s, and now into social media, the region has remained at the cutting edge of new technological innovations and related economic growth.

What has shifted over the years is the extent to which this economic growth has been associated with broad social inclusion. In the 1980s, growth and improved equity seemed to go hand in hand, and the Valley was actually home to a sizable middle-class population. More recent statistics show an erosion of these links, even as the sort of regional cohesion that led to the formation of many important collaborations, such as the Silicon Valley Manufacturing Group (1977) and Joint Venture Silicon Valley (1993), seems to have cracked in the most recent decade.

This shift is all the more remarkable because it was the strong collaboration in the Valley, epitomized by the public–private partnership Joint Venture Silicon Valley, which was held up as the premier example for a national movement of business-led regional stewardship that evolved in the late 1990s and early 2000s, and that we discussed in chapter 5 (Henton and Alliance for Regional Stewardship 2000; Henton 2003). The influence of Joint Venture has waned since the early 1990s, however, with some suggesting that the general erosion of a sense of civic responsibility is due to the spatial spreading of high-tech beyond the core of Silicon Valley (both regionally and globally). Meanwhile, to the extent that wealthy communities in Silicon Valley have concern for those who are less fortunate, it seems to be rooted in a culture of libertarian technological possibilities, rather than a sense of collective responsibility. The result has been a deepening of inequality in the region, a sense of marginalization in poorer communities, and a growing divide into "two valleys."

Drifting Apart, Drifting Away

The 1980s were good times for growth *and* equity in Silicon Valley. During that decade, employment in the San Jose metro region (the core of Silicon Valley) grew by 29 percent, slightly less than the average job growth rate for metropolitan areas in the West but above the national average of 26 percent. In the same period, average earnings grew substantially, up 18 percent, compared to 1 percent across western metros and 3 percent across the country. The region's performance on equity indicators during the 1980s was also among the best. While the West and the nation experienced 12- and 6-percent growth in poverty, respectively, during this time, Silicon Valley's poverty grew by only 4 percent. Meanwhile, household income at the 20th percentile grew dramatically in the 1980s, rising from $32,114 in 1979 to $41,146 in 1989 (in 2010 dollars). As a result, the 80/20 income ratio declined by 6 percent, better than the 5-percent decline across all metro regions in the West and substantially better than the 1-percent decline in the average US metro.

This happy combination of growth and equity began to break down in the 1990s (Benner 1996, 2002), and the decoupling accelerated following the dot-com bust in 2000. The decade of the 2000s saw a dramatic increase in inequality, as job growth stagnated and earnings at the bottom of the income structure plummeted. Even while the overall regional economy grew in the 2000s, according to statistics from the US Bureau of Economic Analysis, net employment over the decade actually declined by 12 percent. Average earnings also fell by 12 percent, poverty increased by nearly 40 percent, and inequality (as measured by the 80/20 household income ratio) grew by nearly 26 percent—all substantially worse than the average for other metros in the West and the average across the whole country. Furthermore, in the twenty-one-year period between 1990 and 2011, the longest growth spell the region was able to produce was seven years, from 1994 to 2001, putting it in the bottom half of metros in the growth-spell analysis in chapter 2. And all these dismal statistics were posted despite its being the global center of high-technology industries, the most dynamic and rapidly growing sector of the world economy during that time period.

Why didn't the economic growth of the Internet boom in the late 1990s translate into more broadly shared opportunity? Why wasn't the region better able to respond in a positive way to the economic challenges following the dot-com collapse? After all, Silicon Valley was the home to Joint Venture Silicon Valley, founded in 1993 specifically to "provide analysis and action on issues affecting [the] region's economy and quality of life."[2]

Here is one important factor in explaining the poor performance. The region's reputation for strong collaborative knowledge networks is rooted primarily in high-tech industries, rather than the region per se (Saxenian 1994; Storper 1997). In addition, the sense of place identity that seemed to dominate the high-tech industry in the 1980s and 1990s seems to have eroded, partly because of two processes that have weakened the rootedness of high tech in Silicon Valley. The first was a process of diffusion beyond the historical borders of Silicon Valley, a process which began in the 1980s and accelerated after the dot-com crash of 2000. Most obvious has been the rapid expansion of social media and other Internet media firms in San Francisco, but this was accompanied by the expansion of telecommunications firms in the north Bay Area, various manufacturing facilities on the eastern side of the Bay, and even major facilities (for Intel, Apple, and Hewlett Packard) farther east, in the Sacramento region. This led to a dilution of the high-tech industry's attention to the regional development challenges of Silicon Valley itself, such as traffic congestion, skyrocketing housing prices, and growing economic divides.

Perhaps as significantly, with the increasing diffusion of broadband Internet and associated increasing sophistication in global communication systems, new startups and other growing companies pioneered a new model of company development. Rather than historical patterns of growing initially in a company headquarters and subsequently expanding to more distant locations, companies discovered that they could be established and grow as "micro-multinationals" from the very beginning, with in fact the largest portion of their highly skilled workforce in lower-cost locations like India, China, and to a lesser extent Taiwan, and a much smaller staff in Silicon Valley itself (Copeland 2006; Varian 2011). These broad trends in the region's dominant high-tech sector worked against regional integration and cross-sector knowledge sharing.

Institutionalizing Voice

Business leadership in the region over the past three decades has been somewhat fragmented as well, further weakening the region's ability to respond to these challenges. The Silicon Valley Leadership Group (SVLG), formerly known as the Silicon Valley Manufacturing Group (which suggests something that many observers forget—there was once manufacturing in the Valley that helped develop and sustain a middle class), represents the largest employers in the region, with a strong emphasis on high-tech industries.[3] The organization was founded in 1977, when David Packard (of Hewlett-Packard fame) brought together a number of fellow CEOs with the premise that local employers should be actively working with government to find solutions to regional issues, like transportation, housing, permit streamlining, education, and the environment.[4] As of 2013, the organization had over 375 member companies, which purportedly account for one out of three private-sector jobs in the region.

The organization has been an important voice for broader regional development initiatives and was a major force in promoting affordable housing, something that helped its members' employees but also poorer residents throughout the region (Pastor et al. 2000, 136). In recent years, however, the group seems to be more narrowly aimed at the needs of the member companies. For example, its transportation work has focused on advocating for the extension of the regional mass transit system, BART, to San Jose, rather than on expansion of the more localized bus system on which poorer people in the region depend. Meanwhile, more than forty major Silicon Valley companies, including Google, Facebook, and Apple, are operating their own exclusive bus systems, and frequently using public bus stops to pick up their employees (Henderson 2013). While they benefit employees and probably reduce greenhouse-gas emissions, the private bus services have been heavily criticized for crowding out other forms of mass transit and undermining potential economic and political support for expanding a truly public transit service (Eberlein 2013; Millner 2013).

The housing policy of the SVLG seems to have narrowed in its orientation as well. The work is avowedly motivated by the barrier high housing costs create to "recruiting and retaining top talent to Silicon Valley"[5] rather than a concern for the extremely high housing-cost burden facing existing low- and moderate-income residents of the Valley. Meanwhile, those same high housing costs have contributed to levels of homelessness that are truly shocking in such a wealthy region, including a long-standing 68-acre homeless camp, dubbed the Jungle, which was widely regarded as the largest homeless camp in the country until it was cleared out in early December 2014 (Campbell and Flores 2014; Grady 2014; Nieves 2000).

While the Silicon Valley Leadership Group has become the most prominent voice for large business in the region, the San Jose Silicon Valley Chamber of Commerce remains the largest and oldest business chamber in the region. Founded in 1886, the chamber has over 1,500 members and includes many more of the region's small, medium, and family-owned businesses. Like many other chambers, it has been largely reactive and traditional in its policy stances, partly reflecting the small and local businesses that are the largest source of its membership. For example, it strongly opposed both San Jose's 1998 Living Wage Ordinance and a 2012 city-wide minimum-wage proposal, while the SVLG took a neutral stance on both campaigns. A controversial public-sector pension reform initiative on the 2012 ballot, seen by public-sector unions as a direct attack on their very existence, was also pushed by the chamber while the SVLG remained on the sidelines.[6]

As noted above, the most prominent effort at regional collaboration in Silicon Valley in the last twenty years was Joint Venture Silicon Valley. Predominantly business-led, Joint Venture also had substantial involvement from the public sector and educational institutions and showed some significant promise in addressing a wide range of concerns in the region, including social infrastructure and quality of life (JVSVN 1995). But its primary social intervention (the 21st Century Education Initiative) involved an attempt at reforming the K-12 education system, through "Renaissance teams" of varied education stakeholders. Renaissance gave way to stasis: a detailed review of the initiative noted that there was no systematic effort to track student outcomes, and found "little evidence that [the initiative] produced systemic change across Silicon Valley" (Saxenian and Dabby 2004, 13).

On broader issues of social inequality in the region, and on sustained patterns of racial discrimination, Joint Venture has been largely silent. The organization did begin to incorporate indicators of poverty and social inequality into its signature annual indicator report (Benner 1996; JVSVN 1999; Pastor, Benner, and Matsuoka 2009). But Joint Venture has failed to undertake any significant initiative that would impact large sectors of disadvantaged communities in the region. Partly as a result, labor and community allies have developed their own institutional voice, Working Partnerships USA, which has helped lead fights for a living wage, more affordable housing, and the extension of health insurance, including to undocumented children, in Santa Clara County (Benner and Dean 2000; Dean and Reynolds 2009).

This sort of a political balance—in which the business voice is countered and then coupled with labor and community concerns—could be a recipe for finding a happy medium. But rather than knowledge being pooled, the Valley has been host to competing policy reports, annual indicator measures, and data displays. The forging of a common regional identity grounded in shared processes of knowledge generation and interpretation has been elusive, particularly because one of the natural sources of civic leadership—the business community—has been globalized in its perspective and individualistic in its approach. Business leaders are far more likely to think that education alone will solve every social ill—partly because education paid off for them personally—while community leaders see the obstacles that migration status, low wages, and inadequate school spending pose to their futures.

A Tale of Two Valleys

Ultimately what has emerged is a region that our key informants almost universally described as fragmented and divided, with the high-tech community largely isolated from the broader region and particularly those parts of the region that are less fortunate. The "tale of two valleys," which had been a minor (though important) theme in media coverage and academic accounts of the Valley's development in the 1970s and 1980s, started becoming more prevalent in the 1990s and by 2013 had reached major national prominence. The Valley was highlighted in a Bill Moyers special called "The United States of Inequality,"[7] as well as in a devastating portrayal in the *New Yorker* of the high-tech industry's myopia with regard to social problems (Packer 2013).

With few opportunities for meaningful regular interaction between growth and equity constituencies—even between high-tech executives and the Latino immigrant security guards protecting their facilities—it is perhaps no surprise that the "disruptive innovations" developed out of the dominant high-tech industries in the region are not always what is most needed. As George Packer (2013) put it, entrepreneurs are "solving all the problems of being twenty years old, with cash on hand, because that is who thinks them up," rather than addressing problems challenging society at large, such as growing inequality and poverty.

That such contact can make a difference is evidenced by the transformation of Facebook cofounder Mark Zuckerberg into a campaigner for immigration reform—and not just for visas for high-tech workers. As he describes it:

> Earlier this year I started teaching a class on entrepreneurship at an after-school program in my community. . . . One day I asked my students what they thought about going to college. One of my top aspiring entrepreneurs told me he wasn't sure that he'd be able to go to college because he's undocumented. His family is from Mexico, and they moved here when he was a baby. Many students in my community are in the same situation; they moved to the United States so early in their lives that they have no memories of living anywhere else. (Zuckerberg 2013)

It is that sort of interaction with the "other" that can lead to trust, collaboration, and concern about equity and fairness. This is of course difficult in the highly atomized world of Silicon Valley, and appearances—in this case, of an easy acceptance of talented engineers from around the world—can be deceiving. Indeed, a key survey of social capital conducted in 2000 in communities across the United States found that people in Silicon Valley were more likely than in comparable regions to have friendships that crossed racial lines, but less likely than elsewhere to have friendships that crossed lines of income and class.[8]

It's an epistemic community all right, but the diversity is frequently lacking and, once again, despite appearances, so too is regional dynamism. The Valley may host Google, Apple, and Facebook (along with countless smaller companies), but the regional economy continues to be highly volatile, with the cycles of boom and bust resulting in zero net job growth between 1997 and 2013. If we want to ensure that the knowledge economy delivers in a broader and more sustained fashion, we may need to look elsewhere—and so we turn below to Raleigh and Seattle, which have taken different approaches to creating more cohesive processes of knowledge generation and interpretation.

RALEIGH-DURHAM

Raleigh-Durham provides an important comparison with Silicon Valley because it is a place where technology-driven growth and social equity have gone together in a more sustained way (though with some slippage in recent years) and where knowledge networks in and about the region seem to be more diverse and more intentional.[9] At the same time, Raleigh-Durham is home to a vibrant high-tech industry, a trio of world-class universities, and a renowned public school system, luring businesses and residents from across the country to relocate there. Indeed, over the last thirty years, Raleigh-Durham has easily outperformed its counterparts in the American South.

Between 1980 and 2010, for example, it nearly tripled the number of jobs and increased average earnings by almost 50 percent. While most regions have only experienced growth in low-wage sectors, or extreme polarization with almost zero growth in middle-class jobs, job growth in Raleigh since 1990 has occurred primarily in mid-wage industries (an 84-percent increase) and low-wage industries (a 73-percent increase), while jobs in high-wage industries increased by about one-quarter. On the other hand, while high-wage industries grew at a lower rate, these workers experienced a larger increase in earnings (56 percent) than workers in mid-wage (28 percent) and low-wage industries (23 percent). Nonetheless, the Raleigh-Durham region bolstered its middle class at a higher rate than other regions, with jobs in middle-wage industries rising from 31 percent of jobs in 1990 to 36 percent of jobs in 2010.

Indeed, while income inequality in Raleigh-Durham has increased, this happened at a much lower rate than in comparable metros between

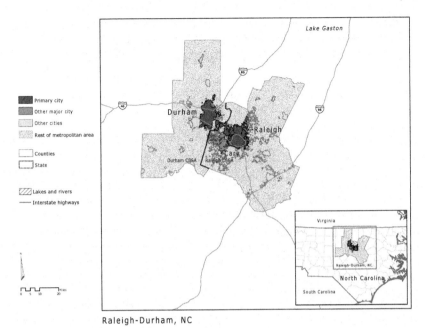

Raleigh-Durham, NC

MAP 7.2. Raleigh-Durham Region.

1980 and 2010. While the percentage living below poverty increased by nearly 14 percent in the South and by nearly 30 percent nationwide, Raleigh-Durham's increased by only 5 percent. Similarly, while the South and the nation as a whole experienced a 10-percent increase in the income gap, Raleigh-Durham's has remained nearly the same over that period. Performance was worse in the 2000s, with the region experiencing a nearly 50-percent increase in the proportion living below poverty and a 15-percent rise in the 80/20 household income ratio during the decade. But the fact that the region had done so well in the 1980s and 1990s means that over the thirty-year period, the region did substantially better than other regions in the South and the entire United States on both growth and equity metrics.

How has Raleigh-Durham been able to sustain its overall economic growth and do relatively better on some key equity measures? We think (along with many others) that the answer is partially rooted in the region's Triple Helix model of strategic information sharing and collaboration between government, business, and academia (Asheim, Cooke, and Martin 2013; Marlowe and U. of Alabama 2009). A second important feature of Raleigh-Durham is the region's seeming commitment to racial equity, which is rooted in the region's efforts to overcome the legacy of slavery and to combat racial segregation in the 1960s and 1970s. While there are many other factors involved, we suggest that these two features have not only added norms of collaboration among diverse actors to the region's DNA but have also led to a strong, almost infectious sense of collective destiny in the region as a whole.

Raleigh's Triple Helix Model of Collaboration

One thing we found striking in our various treks across the country was that many regions had an origin story: the United Airlines executives who couldn't picture living in Oklahoma and thus sparked a renaissance; the Charlotte-based business leaders who realized that racial accommodation could be their New South selling point; the various garages in Silicon Valley that gave birth to business after business. In all these places (and others), the stories were well-worn and sometimes embellished (in one telling of the United Airlines story, the executives snuck into town with their wives, who then announced they couldn't live there, a twist which sounded great but could not be verified), but they are rarely told exactly the same way by every respondent. Not so in Raleigh-Durham, where our interviewees across multiple sectors recited the same narrative describing the founding of what they now call the Research Triangle and a spirit of collaboration they term the Triple Helix.

The story traces the origins of the modern region to the 1950s, when forward-thinking leaders came together to address what they saw as the state's biggest economic problem: the brain drain. At the time, North Carolina had the second-lowest per capita income in the country, and most of the employment in the state involved low-wage jobs in farming, textiles, tobacco, and furniture (Link and Scott 2003; Learn NC n. d.). As a result, two-thirds of college graduates were reportedly leaving for higher-paying jobs elsewhere. This was an odd outcome, partly because the region had something that most did not: three top-tier research universities—Duke University in Durham, North Carolina State University in Raleigh, and University of North Carolina in Chapel Hill—which were churning out some of the country's top thinkers in the quickly growing postwar high-tech industry.

To save the region's economy from continuing down the low-wage, low-skill labor market path—which provided no opportunities for the thousands of young people graduating from these universities every year—these leaders developed a plan to funnel the outpouring of talent into a regional high-tech industry (Rohe 2011). Conveniently for this plan, located between the three universities were thousands of acres of abandoned farmland. Where better, the leaders thought, to put a physical infrastructure for a cluster of innovators and research-oriented companies than in the middle of all three universities? This way, the companies could capture a highly skilled and educated workforce as they walked out the doors of local universities.

So, in the late 1950s, business and university leaders with an economic interest in retaining talent brought local government officials, investors, and North Carolina Governor Luther Hodges on board to devote resources to the creation of Research Triangle Park (RTP). Its first tenant was the Research Triangle Institute, which started as a handful of scientists who received guidance and support from businesses, universities, and local government. Though the institute, now known as RTI International, was originally conceived of as the founding for-profit anchor tenant, it quickly converted to a nonprofit organization once leaders realized the park's potential to promote regional growth. RTI International has since grown to a staff of over 2,800 in more than 40 countries. And RTP has grown with it. Today, the 7,000-acre park houses 200 companies employing over 50,000 workers (Research Triangle Park 2014).

Since the creation of RTP, the Triple Helix model—that is, collaboration among government, business, and academia—has become, as many interviewees told us, the "lifeblood" of the region. This model involves three dynamics. First, the role of universities in innovation is emphasized, as important entrepreneurial partners to government and industry. Second, increased collaboration between the three sectors leads to interaction and the co-development of knowledge and policy. And third, each entity takes on new roles in addition to their more traditional ones (Triple Helix Research Group 2010). Indeed, the education arm of Raleigh-Durham's Triple Helix—which reaches beyond the top-tier research universities to include technical community colleges—has become central to the regional economic development strategy in that these educational institutions cater their programs and training to the changing needs of the region's high-tech industries. While the region once suffered from a brain drain, it now benefits from the coordination between businesses and educational institutions on job training and economic development policies that support innovation and offer financial incentives for companies and good jobs to locate in RTP (Research Triangle Region Partnership 2013).

An early symbol of the Triple Helix model of collaboration was the establishment of the North Carolina Board of Sciences and Technology in 1965. Now housed in the North Carolina Department of Commerce, the board was the nation's first advisory committee funded by a state legislature dedicated to growing and strengthening its science and engineering base through research grants to private and public institutions (Research Triangle Region Partnership 2013). The collaboration has been institutionalized through nongovernmental organizations, too, like the Research Triangle Regional Partnership, a public–private partnership formed with the sole purpose of keeping business, government, and educational institutions in what they define as the thirteen-county region working together to develop pipelines of trained employees and innovation. Overall, it seems generally understood that each sector is a necessary element of capitalizing on the region's assets—research and innovation—and building a sustainable economy that can weather economic ups and downs. As one of our private-sector interviewees put it, this collaboration is necessary to continue "raising the tide for everyone."

Race in the House

While Raleigh-Durham's Triple Helix model is particularly institutionalized in regional practice, in some ways it is not so different from the university–business and public–private collaborations that have contributed to Silicon Valley's growth. What distinguishes Raleigh-Durham's regional ecosystem, however, is a strong grass-roots organizing and nonprofit sector that has proven effective in lifting up the voices of traditionally marginalized communities of color. Generally, equity advocates have built coalitions that have garnered enough political power to secure a place at decision-making tables. According to a local organizer, this long-standing movement has made North Carolina the symbol of "Southern progress" throughout history—from Reconstruction to the civil rights movement, the state has led the American South in passing progressive policies that benefit traditionally marginalized groups, particularly workers and African American communities.

A pivotal moment in the region's history that helped institutionalize a commitment to social and racial equity was Raleigh's struggle—and relative success—in combating school segregation in the 1960s and 1970s. Like the rest of the country, and particularly amplified in the South, the region experienced residential segregation between Black communities, concentrated in Raleigh's urban core, and white communities, who were moving to suburban and rural areas in Wake County. The residential pattern shaped the demographic make-up of public schools and also influenced allocation of educational resources. In 1969, the US Supreme Court handed down its landmark decision in *Swann v. Charlotte-Mecklenburg Board of Education* mandating that public school districts use all means possible, including bussing, to desegregate schools; in 1971, nearly 12,000 students boarded busses in Raleigh (United States Commission on Civil Rights 1972).

This happened in Charlotte as well—indeed, the suit was filed against the school district there—but what was significant in Raleigh was the concern of some of the region's key business and community leaders that the long-term effects of segregation (especially the gap in academic achievement) would have negative impacts on the regional economy. Certainly, predominantly Black schools in the urban core felt the impact from the disappearance of educational resources that accompanied white flight to affluent suburbs, but schools in rural Wake County suffered too. Business and political leaders were also worried about the economic impacts on downtown, including several school closures. While some conservative leaders saw the remaining schools, which were overcrowded and lacked adequate resources, as inefficient and wasteful of taxpayer money, most business, community, and political leaders united behind the idea that racial equity was not only the just thing to do but also the economically sound thing to do. And to achieve this, leaders knew that integration efforts (i.e. bussing) had to go beyond city boundaries.

In 1976, despite much opposition from anti-integration residents, the city and county merged school districts to create the Wake County Public School System (McNeal and Oxholm 2009). While the merger was unprecedented, what was even more striking was the fact that Wake County adopted a diversity policy, which required that all schools be racially balanced; a later iteration of the policy required socioeconomic balance as well (Grant 2009). While the Raleigh–Wake County merger initially faced opposition from neighborhood residents—indeed, the voters passed a referendum against the merger before it happened, but state law allowed the city and county school boards to do it anyway— it is widely agreed that the region greatly benefitted in the long term. The Wake County Public School System has reduced the gap between Black and white and rich and poor students to a greater extent than any other school district in the country, and some argue that the region's school integration was key to enabling different communities to interact (Grant 2009).

A Collective Destiny?

The long history of collaboration between educational institutions, government, and industry, as well as an institutionalized commitment to racial equity in the schools, seems to have fostered a strong sense of regionalism in the Raleigh-Durham region. As one interviewee described, while each place has its unique identity—Durham is the symbol of a strong Black middle class, while Chapel Hill is the tucked-away college town—collectively, there is a strong sense of place and pride at the regional level. For instance, at a biotech conference in 2013 we were told about, the Wake County Economic Development team did not go to simply represent Wake County; rather, they partnered with economic development representatives from the other eight counties in the region to recruit businesses and industries to the Research Triangle region as a whole. This kind of collaboration is typical, and while there is indeed competition among the jurisdictions, it is described as healthy rather than adversarial. Residents seem proud of the region's high quality of life, its relative affordability, and the numerous options for employment, housing, transportation, and neighborhood type.

In addition to the strong pride in place, there is a unique commitment to knowledge sharing. Many of our interviewees credit their "open source society," in which government agencies are transparent and make data easily accessible to everyone via online tools, as key to their success. In addition to local governments, particularly those of Raleigh, Durham, Cary, and Wake County, interviewees pointed to the Regional Transportation Alliance, founded by four of the region's largest chambers of commerce as the business voice for transportation initiatives, and the Research Triangle Regional Partnership as major sources of information on economic indicators. In terms of sources of information on social conditions, most of our interviewees involved in social justice work pointed to a single central source of data and research that grounds their movement: the North Carolina Justice Center, a progressive research and advocacy organization based in Raleigh but operating at the state level. In no other region we visited could interviewees so readily identify a central clearinghouse of information on social conditions that provides legitimacy to grass-roots organizing work.

But the tides of collaboration may be changing in Raleigh. For example, in 2009, local Tea Party candidates secured four of the nine seats on the Wake County School Board, with an agenda to dismantle the diversity policy—a symbol of the region's commitment to equity and the renowned model of reducing the achievement gap—and move back to the neighborhood-schools model. In 2011, with a 5–4 vote, the school board ended bussing, or, as some describe it, initiated resegregation (Donnor and Dixson 2013). Not surprisingly, this action to dismantle a highly successful initiative caused a major community uproar, and the local NAACP chapter filed a civil rights complaint that prompted an investigation by the US Department of Education as well as re-evaluation of the school district's accreditation standing by the national accreditation agency AdvancED.

But the recent conflict around schools is a smaller indication of a seemingly larger shift that may be compromising the region's well-being and spirit of cross-sector collaboration. Since 2010, conservative legislators in North Carolina have cut unemployment compensation for 170,000 people, increased taxes on low-income and middle-class residents (while cutting them for wealthy individuals and large corporations), rejected federal Medicaid funds for half a million residents, enacted anti-abortion legislation, severely slashed education funds, and adopted the nation's strictest voter-suppression law. In response, a diverse coalition of community, labor, and faith groups, anchored by the local NAACP chapter and its leader, Reverend Doctor William Barber II, have come together in Raleigh to hold weekly Moral Monday assemblies. Over the course of eighteen weeks in 2013, the Moral Monday movement swept to other regions across the state, attracting up to 10,000 protesters per assembly, and saw about 1,000 people arrested in civil-disobedience actions (Dreier 2013).

The fight may be necessary, but it is dissonant with the diverse and dynamic epistemic community typified by the combination of a Triple Helix frame and some commitment to racial equity in education. Raleigh-Durham is rightly proud of its past as a model of multi-sector collaboration, but it will need to more effectively incorporate traditionally marginalized communities and fold equity actors into the tightly wound decision-making network that the Raleigh-Durham region has built over the last fifty years. It will also need to figure how to lead in a time in which polarization has become the political order of the day—and that will require business realizing that the immediate temptations of low taxes and less attention to inclusion hurt economic growth and quality of life in the long run. As we will see, that seems to be a lesson that has been well learned by regional leaders in our next case study, Seattle.

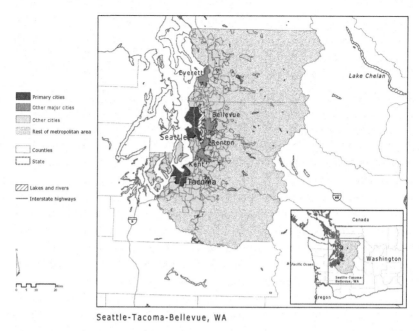

Seattle-Tacoma-Bellevue, WA

MAP 7.3. Seattle Region.

SEATTLE

We end our tour of America's high-tech regions in Seattle, the home of Microsoft, Amazon, and, as it turns out, an historical pattern of relatively inclusive growth.[10] Between 1980 and 2010, Seattle's earnings per job increased at a higher rate (29 percent) than the West as a whole (20 percent), and its income equality was substantially better than the rest of the West (though still getting worse—the 80/20 income ratio grew 5 percent between 1980 and 2010, compared to an 11-percent average for metro regions in the West). And this has happened even as Seattle has increased its global connections. Though it is only the fifteenth-largest metropolitan area in the country by population, Seattle has the sixth-highest export total, sending more than $47 billion in goods and services abroad in 2012 (Katz 2014).

Innovative industries like aerospace and technology—the engines behind those exports—have helped create a strong regional economy producing a uniquely large number of high-quality jobs. In fact, one-fourth of the region's jobs are in STEM (science, technology, engineering, and mathematics) occupations; this is the fourth-largest share of any region in the country (Rothwell 2013). While Seattle's largest increase in jobs between 1990 and 2010 was in lower-wage industries (like most places), wages in these industries increased by 37 percent (unlike most places). That Seattle has been able to maintain relatively good conditions at home while expanding its economic reach abroad sets the region apart.

How has Seattle been able to both grow faster and promote greater social equity? One obvious factor is simply the influence of a few major companies: Boeing, Microsoft, and Amazon. Boeing, the region's largest employer, has 85,000 employees in Washington, mostly in the Seattle region.[11] It has created a deeply rooted aerospace manufacturing presence that continues to provide middle-class opportunities for people without higher education—the types of jobs that have declined in many other regions of the country. Microsoft, the region's second-largest private employer, has helped catalyze Seattle as a high-tech hub, providing over 40,000 jobs statewide.[12] Similarly, Amazon has grown rapidly in the region since its founding in 1994.

But other factors beyond the presence of these large firms have contributed to the positive trends in Seattle. The region has a strong early history of worker cooperatives and radical worker organizing by the Industrial Workers of the World (also known as the Wobblies) at the beginning of the twentieth century, which is said to have instilled a deep sense of collaboration for the common good in the Seattle region (Schwantes 1994). More recently, a strong movement of multi-ethnic and multi-racial organizing emerged during the civil rights era in the late 1960s and early 1970s. In this period, four key leaders from the Filipino, American Indian, Black, and Latino communities—later known as the Four Amigos—found common ground and united as a single political force, leading to important victories for each of their communities (Santos 2005). The region's cooperative roots, its tradition of bridge-building between unlikely allies, and its largely progressive political environment seem to have led to a mature method of mediating conflict and developing shared knowledge and action that permeates decision-making across the region today and has come to be known as the "Seattle process."

The Seattle Process

In the spring of 2014, Americans had their eyes on Seattle. Not only had voters elected a socialist city council member, but this socialist was helping lead a winning fight to raise the city's minimum wage from $9.32 to $15 an hour—the highest in the country. But this wasn't simply a case of mobilizing a majority of supporters to win a new policy. Rather, Seattle

Mayor Ed Murray (who had run on a platform including a $15-an-hour minimum wage) convened a twenty-four-person task force, the Income Inequality Advisory Committee, consisting of labor leaders, business leaders, elected officials, and community advocates, to collectively devise an agreement. Their charge was to formulate a policy that would have much broader support across the entire range of stakeholders (Weise 2014). The negotiation process was contentious. Labor, community allies, and progressive city council members wanted the pay increase to happen fast, while business interests were either opposed or wanted to gradually phase in the increase and give greater leeway to small businesses, especially around tips and benefits. But by April 30—the last day before the mayor's deadline—the task force had put forth a proposal that was agreed to by 22 of the 24 members, in which small businesses will reach the $15 per hour minimum wage in seven years and large businesses will reach it in three. On June 2, 2014, Seattle's City Council adopted it into law.

While this consensus-driven, multi-stakeholder, deliberative process may have appeared unique, in fact the Seattle region has a long history of convening diverse and often adversarial parties to build consensus on how to address local and regional problems. The process involves dialogue between all relevant stakeholders—most commonly businesses, unions, nonprofits, and community residents. Municipal staff frequently play the role of convener as well as translator of relevant data and analysis for both stakeholders and decision-makers. Only when all opinions are heard and consensus is reached do municipal staff and public officials make their decision. Those in Seattle even have a name for this phenomenon: the Seattle process.

Of course, regional leaders sometimes express frustration about the Seattle process, criticizing it for being painfully slow and for placing more value on talking than on doing. A 1983 *Seattle Weekly* article, for example, called it a process of "seeking consensus through exhaustion" (Moody 2004, 66). Others criticize the process as a way of actually avoiding making decisions. As one of our informants put it, Seattleites sometimes conflate talking with action. But such deliberative processes can have real impacts on people's perceptions, knowledge, and, ultimately, their actions. And because the Seattle process of consensus building is so deeply embedded, pushing individual agendas through proposals or policies without consensus is much less common, as was illustrated in the minimum-wage debate. Rather than construct a proposal in isolation, Mayor Murphy convened a task force, allowing opposing parties to get on the same page, so that by the time a vote came around, there was very little contestation; or, as one reporter put it, "without the anger and political bloodshed that's pitted employers against workers in other cities and has stalled efforts in Congress to increase the federal minimum wage" (Weise 2014).

Another example of the Seattle process at work—and perhaps one of the best illustrations of the frustratingly slow pace at which decisions can be made—is the reconstruction of the Alaska Way Viaduct, a double-decked elevated section of State Route 99 that runs along the waterfront in downtown Seattle and carries 110,000 vehicles daily. In 1989, the Loma Prieta earthquake destroyed a similarly designed viaduct in Oakland, California, killing 42 people. After experts estimated a one-in-twenty chance that Seattle's structure would experience similar destruction, government officials agreed to replace it. What followed, however, was a negotiation process between governments (ranging from city to state), businesses, unions, and communities that lasted for eight years.

During that time, the three main options raised were to dig a tunnel for the highway, to rebuild its elevated structure, or to simply eliminate it. Seattle's local political leaders, including then-mayor Greg Nickels and both local and state-level transportation officials, supported the tunnel, arguing that it would help downtown Seattle connect to the waterfront and promote tourism and economic development. But other state officials called it a waste of resources, likening the idea to the notorious Big Dig in Boston, and argued that building a new elevated highway was the most cost-effective way of ensuring that the needed traffic and goods-movement corridor was retained. The third proposal, removing the viaduct and replacing it with surface streets, transit, and local economic development, was supported by then King County Executive Ron Sims, smart-growth advocates, and a local coalition of community members and environmentalists. Unions, however, were strongly opposed to this option, as they were interested in the high-quality construction jobs that would come with either a tunnel or a replacement highway, while transportation officials and economic development experts felt that some kind of highway corridor was essential for ensuring the free flow of goods and people in the region.

Through negotiation and stakeholder advisory council meetings, a scaled-down hybrid tunnel option was developed. The option of a tunnel or rebuilding the elevated highway was put in front of the voters of Seattle in what was purely an advisory process; neither option gained a majority of support. Public officials decided to go ahead with the tunnel and began digging in 2013. In what might be perfect symbolism of how process can stall product, the massive drill digging the tunnel (nicknamed Bertha) got stuck in place in December of that year. As of July 2015, the drill was still undergoing repairs and tunnel digging had yet to resume (www.wsdot.wa.gov/Projects/Viaduct/Schedule). Clearly, the Seattle process does not resolve all conflicts, but the widespread consultation and debate among multiple stakeholders is striking.

The Seattle process is not just applied to region-wide policies or projects; it percolates down to smaller scales, too. In the mid-2000s, CASA Latina—a nonprofit organization working to empower Latino immigrants, primarily day laborers, through educational and economic opportunities—was displaced from its trailer in the Belltown neighborhood of Seattle due to plans for reconstructing the Alaska Way Viaduct. The organization set out to find a site on which it could build a permanent worker center, and a potential site was identified: a vacant lot in southwest Seattle's Rainier Valley neighborhood, a working-class community that had suffered severe disinvestment over several decades. But some of the neighbors organized against CASA Latina, claiming that the center would bring more "riffraff" to the neighborhood rather than much-desired economic revitalization through commercial development (Jenniges 2004). On getting word that CASA Latina was considering building its worker center on the vacant lot in their neighborhood, and that the city had pledged $250,000 toward the project, the local Rainier Chamber of Commerce wrote a letter to CASA Latina and the city requesting that they find a different site.

This of course caused conflict, fraught with emotion, between neighbors and workers—some of whom also lived in Rainier Valley. In response, the city intervened, threatening to withhold promised funds from CASA Latina until it quelled neighborhood opposition. The city provided a mediator, and the two parties, CASA Latina and the Rainier Valley neighbors opposing the worker center, undertook a six-month mediation process. By the end of the discussions, a majority of the original opponents had come around. While the site ended up being too expensive for CASA Latina to purchase, those who had originally opposed the center helped the organization find a new site nearby, and the city provided the funding it had promised.

The Four Amigos

Where did this rather unique and institutionalized process of consensus-building come from? Many interviewees point to the region's Scandinavian roots. At the turn of the century, about a third of Seattle's immigrant population was from Sweden, Norway, Denmark, or Finland (Eskenazi 2001), and so, it is said, the Scandinavian norm of working in collaboration for the common good became part of the region's DNA. As hinted at earlier, other interviewees pointed to the legacy of the Wobblies—an organization founded at the turn of the twentieth century that aimed to abolish capitalism and promote a model of workplace democracy, in which workers would elect their managers—and to the presence of worker collaboratives, all of which left a legacy in which collective work was seen as leading to collective good (Saros 2009).

But a more recent period may have played an even larger role in shaping Seattle's now pervasive trend of working across difference. During the civil rights era in the 1960s, Seattle's racial and ethnic minorities all seemed to have their particular struggles. The region's Native Americans were fighting for the land and water rights promised to them by the federal government; Blacks were fighting for racial equality in schools and universities; Latinos were uniting with farmworkers by protesting local grocery stores sourcing California grapes and lettuce; and Filipinos were fighting against invasive development that threatened displacement of residents and businesses from Seattle's International District—to name just a few.

During this time, movement builders from these various struggles—ranging from the Black Panthers to the Blackfeet Indians of Montana to the Asian Coalition for Equity to the United Farm Workers—would hold meetings at St. Peter Claver Church, which allowed them to use the space cost-free (Santos 2005). As the church became a hub of civil rights activists across multiple movements, leaders from different constituencies realized that despite the specifics of their individual communities' plights, their struggle for social justice and equity was the same.[13] Four leaders in particular formed a uniquely close bond, helping unite their communities across difference. These leaders became known as the Four Amigos and included Larry Gossett, a Black student activist; Roberto Maestas, a Latino leader involved in the farmworker movement; Bob Santos, a Filipino leader in the anti-displacement movement; and Bernie Whitebear, a Native American leader in the indigenous rights movement (Santos 2005).

With the understanding that they were much stronger together than they ever were apart, showing up to each other's fights became second nature. For instance, in 1970, the federal government decided to reduce the size of the Fort Lawton army post in northwest Seattle, freeing up land that had once belonged to American Indians. Severely lacking services, the American Indian community—led by Bernie Whitebear—requested that the city dedicate a portion of the land to an Indian Cultural Center as part of the original treaty the government had used to take the land in the first place. When discussions with the city failed, Bernie Whitebear led an organized group of community members called the American Indian Fort Lawton Occupation Forces in a three-month occupation of Fort Lawton, which eventually led to a negotiation with the city—mediated by the federal government—to grant the Indians a 99-year lease on twenty acres (what eventually became Discovery Park). The city also gave $600,000 to the American Indian Women's Service League to help build a social services center (Whitebear 1994). However, there was a secret ingredient in this victory: allies outside of the American Indian community. Before the occupation, Whitebear called on his friends—the rest of the Four Amigos—to rally their communities and participate in the occupation. So, alongside the American Indians were Black students and Filipino and Chicano leaders—and even some white progressives.[14]

This is but one of many examples of how the region's disenfranchised communities formed strong coalitions to achieve victories in the 1970s. Each of the four grass-roots leaders went on to hold powerful positions in the Seattle region, mentoring other leaders along the way. Santos founded the Inter*Im community development corporation and is still a prominent leader in the International District and among Seattle's Asian American community. Whitebear founded the Seattle Indian Health Board and the United Indians of All Tribes Foundation. Maestas formed El Centro de la Raza. Gossett founded the Central Area Motivation Program and then went on to elected office as part of the King County Council. The work of the Four Amigos in the late 1960s and throughout the 1970s left a legacy not only of working across difference but also of paying attention to racial equity and social justice in the Seattle region.

The New Demographics and the Future of Collaboration

Since 1980, Seattle's population has grown by 64 percent—and, as in most American regions, much of this growth came from populations of color. In 1980, almost 90 percent of Seattleites were white; in 2010, less than 70 percent were. During this time, all racial minority groups, except American Indians, increased their proportion in the region.

In particular, Latinos grew from 2 percent of the population in 1980 to 9 percent in 2010; Asian Pacific Islanders, from 4 percent in 1980 to 12 percent in 2010; and Blacks from 4 to 5 percent of the regional population over that thirty-year period. These trends partially reflect the increasing share of immigrants making up the Seattle region. In 1980, immigrants made up 7 percent of the population; by 2010, this had more than doubled, to 16 percent. By 2040, whites will only make up 45 percent of the population—less than the projected share nationwide—with Latinos and Asian and Pacific Islanders each at about one-fifth (21 percent and 18 percent, respectively).

While these are dynamics facing much of the country, Seattle may be better poised than other regions to work its way gracefully through racial change. The legacy of multi-ethnic and multi-racial organizing has influenced the region's institutionalization of the principles of equity and social justice in its government agencies. Spearheading this work is King County. In 2010, Ron Sims, then county executive, founded the Social Justice and Equity Team. (In 1985 Sims was the first African American elected to the King County Council, and in 1997 he was the first African American elected county executive.) The initiative was primarily in response to racial disparities in the region, including education gaps between whites and Blacks as well as the disproportionate number of boys and men of color being incarcerated. But it has led to transformational efforts in many arenas.

For example, all public health department staff must participate in a two-day training on institutionalized racism. Second, the principles of "fairness and justice" are among the top priorities in the county's 2010 strategic plan. Third, the team successfully pushed an Equity and Social Justice Ordinance requiring all county departments (not just the executive branch) to consider the social justice and equity impacts of all decisions, particularly on people of color, low-income communities, and people with limited English proficiency—and if the impacts are negative, to do something about it. As part of the ordinance, the Social Justice and Equity Team developed an Equity Impact Review Tool, which is both a process and a tool "to identify, evaluate, and communicate the potential impact—both positive and negative—of a policy or program on equity" (Albetta and Valenzuela 2010).

The city of Seattle has a similar Race and Social Justice Initiative, focusing explicitly on institutionalized racism. So far, the initiative has, in good Seattle-process form, pulled together a community roundtable to strategize about ending racial inequalities; helped double the government contracts with women- and minority-owned businesses; grown community engagement in historically under-represented neighborhoods; required all city departments to provide translation and interpretation services; provided over $1 million through a Neighborhood Matching Fund; and, following the lead of the county, put 7,000 employees through institutionalized racism training and developed a Racial Equity Toolkit to ensure the consideration of equity in decision-making processes (City of Seattle 2014a). While Seattleites might take it for granted, this type of institutionalized attention toward equity at multiple levels of government is unprecedented.

This sense of inclusion extends to regional planning efforts, too. While most of the growth in the 1980s and 1990s was in the suburbs, in the 2000s, growth in the urban cores and in the suburbs was about equal: 12 percent and 14 percent, respectively. Now, low-income communities of color in more urban areas of the Seattle region face the threat of gentrification. Partly in response, local and regional government agencies, including the Puget Sound Regional Council, have collaborated to develop a Growing Transit Communities initiative, in concert with the region's voter-approved $25 billion transit build-out, in an effort to locate housing, jobs, and services close to transit, with a focus on ensuring affordability.[15] For instance, the city of Seattle is granting transit-oriented development acquisition loans that help developers purchase vacant land near light rail stations to build mixed-use projects that include affordable housing and commercial space for small businesses and community facilities (City of Seattle 2014b). Indeed, the city of Seattle has required the development of affordable housing for decades. Starting in 1981, Seattleites voted to tax themselves to fund affordable housing for low-income workers, seniors, and homeless people; through this levy, the city has funded over 10,000 affordable units (City of Seattle 2014c).

Despite this fascinating history of incorporating equity into governance and planning, we also heard concerns that regional discussions can be too shallow—able to bring stakeholders together to find common interests, but less effective in dealing with bigger substantive differences in interests or perspectives. As the region becomes less white and more racially diverse—and as that population shifts southward through the region, particularly because of high housing costs in the central city—the Seattle process will need to adapt, and broaden the leadership at the table. In addition to concerns about housing costs, transportation options, and employment opportunities, a major concern of regional leaders moving forward is the level of preparedness—or lack thereof—among Seattle-born youth to participate in the region's booming STEM sectors.[16] All that said, Seattle offers a remarkable example of a region at the leading edge of America's knowledge economy that has also built a set of knowledge communities where listening to others is valued, collaboration is second nature, and equity is at the very least an actively voiced concern.

WHAT YOU DO KNOW CAN HELP YOU

Silicon Valley, Raleigh-Durham, and Seattle are all iconic high-tech regions—places that have been relatively successful in the development of the cutting-edge technology industries that are at the core of the "new economy." Each of the three regions has also become well known for its own particular brand of collaboration. Silicon Valley's "regional advantage" has been linked to its open labor markets and collaborative culture (Saxenian 1994). Raleigh's Triple Helix of public–private–university collaboration has been celebrated for promoting innovation and growth (Research Triangle Regional Partnership 2015; Triple Helix Research Group 2010). And Seattle even has a "Seattle process" designed to ensure substantial communication among multiple stakeholders.

On the one hand, all that makes sense. As multiple authors have argued since at least the 1990s, in an economy driven by technological change, information sharing, knowledge development, and cross-sector collaboration are critical factors in economic success (Brandenburger and Nalebuff 2011; Kanter 1994; Logan and Stokes 2003; Lowitt 2013). But in two of our knowledge regions, equity has also been a fairly important concern. Leaders in Raleigh-Durham suggest that the region's school bussing plan was central to its success, and in Seattle, prominent race and social justice initiatives have been institutionalized in city, county, and regional planning processes. In Silicon Valley, in contrast, most people talked about a highly divided region, with significant limitations to the extent to which concerns about social equity find their way into regional decision-making processes.

Of course, the nature of regional communication and collaboration is not the only factor shaping growth and equity in each region; as usual, structural elements play a key role. The continued presence of Boeing and related manufacturing industries in Seattle, and the presence of the state capital and related high concentrations of public-sector employment in Raleigh-Durham, for example, have been important in ensuring relatively stable middle-income jobs in both regions; by contrast, Silicon Valley has seen its manufacturing slip away and an hourglass employment and earnings structure emerge in its place. Yet the existence of what seem to be particularly diverse and dynamic epistemic communities in Raleigh-Durham and Seattle—and the ways in which entrepreneurs in those regions seem more regionally rooted than in Silicon Valley—are, we think, factors that do help shape an environment in which growth is encouraged and equity is more achievable.

These cases also suggest that being at the cutting edge of technological change does not necessarily have to produce economic inequality or social disconnections. In both Raleigh and Seattle, public policy (education in one case; housing, transit, and minimum wage in the other) has been used to temper the economic disparities that high-tech development can produce, and communicative strategies have helped hold interests together. As such, these cases illustrate the possibilities for an America buffeted by technological change, global competition, and rising divides by skill and income. In the chapters that follow, we stand back from the details of these and the other cases to examine in more depth how such communities of concern develop, how such processes of collaboration can impact growth and equity outcomes, and what all this means for economic theory, policy practice, and national politics in the twenty-first century.

CHAPTER 8

Stepping Back

Theorizing Diverse and Dynamic Epistemic Communities

By its nature, the metropolis provides what otherwise could
be given only by traveling; namely, the strange.

—Jane Jacobs, *The Death and Life of Great American Cities*

One of the great joys of case-study work is the potential for surprise.
While we tried to rely on a rigorous combination of quantitative and
qualitative reasoning to select the cases (see chapter 3), we did not really know what we would find. Among the unexpected results on our
road trip were the Republican-led campaigns to increase taxes and
public-sector investment in Oklahoma City; the importance of merging
central-city and suburban school districts in Raleigh-Durham; support
for drivers' licenses and in-state tuition for undocumented immigrants
in Utah; a paternalism gone with diminishing benefits in Charlotte and
Grand Rapids; community organizing becoming cross-sector collaboration in San Antonio; a racial chasm in Greensboro so deep that words
failed and relationships frayed; a fabled Silicon Valley increasingly
unable to deal with sharp inequality; and, finally, a "Seattle process"
that pretty much captured everything we were trying to say with our far
clumsier concept of a diverse and dynamic epistemic community.

Obviously, spending only three days in any metropolitan region, no
matter how much it is backed up by statistical analysis and gathering of
secondary material, is not likely to give you a complete understanding
of that region's history or current political economy. But while we hope
that we have done some justice to the fuller story of these places, our
goal was narrower: to learn about tensions and collaborations between
diverse constituencies in each region; identify processes of information

sharing and knowledge generation; understand who is involved in those processes and how they shape regional dynamics; and begin to grapple with what are the key relationships, social norms, and institutions that help (or do not help) bind diverse constituencies together with a sense of common destiny in the long-term trajectory of the region.

In this chapter, we step back and talk more analytically about the concept of a diverse and dynamic epistemic community. We suggest that there are distinct social norms in the more successful regions, including a recognition of diverse constituencies with roots in the region, a commitment to maintaining relationships across those diverse constituencies despite conflict, and public discourse involving reasoned arguments informed by facts rather than solely ideology. How do these norms emerge in certain places, and what hinders their development in others? How can they affect decision-making and governance processes? Perhaps most importantly, can they actually shape positive trajectories for growth and equity, and, therefore, what are the implications for a nation seemingly as polarized as the most fragmented of our case studies?

We explore this last crucial question in more detail in the next chapter. Here, we try to elaborate our understanding of how diverse and dynamic epistemic communities develop and how the broad social norms they forge help shape regional governance processes. But we start first at the individual level, sketching how understanding people's economic motivations and transforming our view of the microfoundations of the economy can help us understand the creation of such collective norms. From there we move to a synthetic discussion of how these collective norms seemed to emerge across all our case studies and how they were sustained, and the complex interplay between these epistemic communities and regional governance processes.

INDIVIDUALS AND IDENTITIES

In recent years, the traditional economic assumption of rational but generally disconnected actors has influenced (or infected) the fields of political science and sociology. With a perspective focusing on individual actors, coalitions are understandable—short-term interests can be furthered by linking with others—but the long-term transformative communities that we suggest are present in the knowledge networks in Salt Lake, Seattle, and San Antonio necessarily disappear in the analysis: they just don't square with atomistic actors, they shouldn't really exist, and they certainly couldn't have an impact on policy.

Bowling Alone?

But is it really reasonable to think of the world as every (economic) man for himself? Economic theory suggests that this is at least a sensible way to approach modeling. Even if maximizing one's own utility is not the central object of life, people's behavior can be understood through that prism. And our preoccupation—or perhaps near-obsession—with individualized actors driving our economic models is further reinforced by (and likely helps reinforce) our national social norms and institutions. Think of everything from the American notions of rugged individualism and personal responsibility, to the institutional barriers to collective bargaining in the labor market, to the broad shift from collective pensions to individual retirement accounts. Individual risk and reward in competitive systems remains a dominant theme across American society.

So why do some regions seem to be able to go against the national grain of individual autonomy toward a more collaborative or interconnected ethos? Are they somehow specially (and randomly) composed of altruistic individuals who see their fates as intertwined with those of others? Or is there perhaps something lacking in an atomistic model of human behavior that fails to take into account real-world processes of constructing identities and, dare we say, solidarities?

We lean toward changing the model to understand the world rather than twisting the world to fit the model. Consider, for example, the findings from experimental economics in which individuals are asked to play the "ultimatum game," which goes as follows. One of two agents proposes a division of a certain amount of money. If the other agent agrees, the deal is consummated and they each get their agreed-on portion of the total. No agreement, however, and they each get nothing. Simple enough to run, test, and record, and the predictions from economic theory are quite straightforward as well. Deals that are fairly unequal—in which the proposer gets nearly all the money and there's just a bit left over for the other party—are both highly probable (since each party will look out for their own interests) and highly acceptable (since both parties will be a little better off—one will be a lot better off—than they were before).

Research does suggest that economists themselves (or at least their students) are more likely to propose such unequal deals (Carter and Irons 1991). But that might be more a matter of training than of logic. As it turns out, non-economists are likely to propose more equitable deals, mostly because the economist's alternative seems "unfair" to them and thus unacceptable—and, interestingly, the non-economists often close more deals and make more money. Moreover, in an intriguing paper, one set of authors showed that while this "irrational" splitting of the spoils is generally true of humans, the results in a similar game played by chimpanzees are actually consistent with the traditional notion of self-interested and isolated utility maximizers that dominates economic models (Jensen, Call, and Tomasello 2007).

A theory of human action that squares with the behavior of chimps, not people, may not bother traditional economic theorists, but it does bother us. Of course, a model in which "rational choice" is dominant has its appeal. It is amenable to mathematical modeling, statistical testing, and easy predictions (some of which turn out to be true, since people do after all pursue their interests, choose under constraints, and seek to maximize outcomes, *sometimes*). But there is also substantial evidence in a range of fields—including psychology, organizational sociology, political science, and even experimental economics—that many people are in fact more cooperative and behave far less selfishly than most economists and others assume (Ostrom 2000; Ostrom and Walker 2005). There are important examples of cooperative systems that are in fact more stable and more effective than equivalent incentive-based ones (Benkler 2006; Benkler 2011). The traditional theory of utility-maximizing individuals fails to fully capture deep and lasting relationships and how the formation of a sense of a self occurs in the context of those relationships—and it also fails to acknowledge how institutions and broader systems steer individuals to more or less collaborative solutions and how those solutions in turn reinforce or undermine cooperative norms.

Trying to explain our cases with traditional economic microfoundations is at best challenging and at worst impossible. Consider the impact of "Michigan nice," the pride Raleigh took in racial integration, or how the challenge to Anglo power in San Antonio eventually gave way to a broad voter commitment to pre-K education. For our case studies—and the world—to make any sense, we actually need an alternative set of microfoundations in which individuals have a sense of place, are transformed by their interactions with each other, and come to see doing good and planning for the regional future as simply fitting a set of standards and social norms they hold for themselves and others.

Identity, Norms and Community

So, if rational economic man works in theory, but not in practice, what other microfoundations can we start from? Fortunately, a different theory is possible. Nobel Prize winner George Akerlof and Rachel Kranton (2010) have developed an alternative approach in which individuals are modeled as seeking to construct identities (as well as to maximize utility); because of this, they adhere to norms consistent with those identities, and fairness therefore counts. And it is in this framework of identity formation and social norms that many of the findings of this book begin to make sense.

For example, Akerlof and Kranton specifically suggest that organizations where identity matters can use a flatter wage structure since some of the motivation is internal rather than extrinsic. Similarly, economist Samuel Bowles (2012) has been suggesting that inequality (along with fragmentation) gets in the way of developing a sense of the commons, creating coordination problems that could limit output and efficiency. This is of course exactly what we found in chapter 2, in which regional growth spells were significantly shortened by social distance and inequality. While we did not specifically trace the causal chains there, Bowles's theoretical framing does suggest one avenue in which the growth effect might result.

But the identity-economics frame is perhaps more useful in understanding why epistemic communities can actually change the way actors behave. In this framework, the norms to which people adhere are not handed down from on high but rather developed in the process of conversation and interaction—and how we structure those interactions can encourage either empathy or disdain, collaboration or competition (Benkler 2011). In short, preferences are not exogenous but endogenous—and an epistemic community can help actors see themselves in the "other," change their motivations and loyalties, and thus be potentially self-reinforcing of cooperative and empathetic behavior in powerful ways. Indeed, as Elinor Ostrom (2000, 147) argues, "a social norm, especially in a setting where there is communication between the parties, can work as well . . . at generating cooperative behavior as an externally imposed set of rules and systems of monitoring and sanctioning."

In this light, epistemic communities involve *transactions between* actors but they also involve *transformations of* actors. When campaigning for the Metropolitan Area Projects (MAPS) program, the mayor of Oklahoma City tried to persuade tax-adverse seniors by saying, "You may not like it. You may not even be around for it. But aren't your grandkids?" (Lackmeyer and Money 2006, 127). It is a direct linkage—those are *your* grandkids—but it's also an appeal to a sense of long-term pride in place and so to one's identity as a regional resident. Such an appeal was also invoked in San Antonio, and it persuaded voters to tax themselves for the education of kids that were not their own. In Raleigh, the Triple Helix frame is a convenient rhetorical device—but its repetition also changes the very story actors tell themselves and not just others. The opposite dynamic is reflected in areas that are more fragmented and less successful. Fresnans are not Fresnans but rather farmworkers, growers, suburbanites, or environmental justice advocates, while leaders in Greensboro are often decamped by color and history, and the commitment to the commons suffers as a result.

The importance of conversation and interaction in structuring identity and social norms may help explain why collaborative epistemic communities may be more likely to develop at a regional scale (or along policy or disciplinary lines) than in national governance processes, especially at a time of rapid change and uncertainty. Formal national government policy decisions may be rooted in face-to-face communication in Washington, DC, but broader involvement in national governance occurs primarily through media channels which at least until recently have been almost exclusively one-way channels of communication, rather than sites of interaction (Castells 2009). The "imagined community" (Anderson 1983) of the nation certainly includes strong elements of common identity and social norms, and these emerge through complex processes of communication. But without face-to-face contact, the sense of a national common destiny is based on symbolic representations of others, rather than direct experience.

This epistemic distance provides a poor repertoire of tools for people to deal with the kinds of rapid demographic, economic, and political changes we've experienced in the United States over the past three decades. People understandably base their perceptions of reality on prior beliefs and established patterns of interaction. When these patterns are challenged, and people are faced with new situations, they can hold on to past patterns and beliefs, essentially in an effort to restructure reality to match their imagined community (Castells 1997). But uncertainty can also lead people to reach out to others to help understand changing circumstances. The face-to-face and interactive dimensions of such knowledge-generation processes are critical for generating a more accurate understanding of social reality and knowledge development (Amin and Cohendet 2004; Brown and Duguid 1998; Maskell and Malmberg 1999; Storper 1997). It doesn't always work—witness the fragmentation of Greensboro and Fresno—but it can be a first step.

Diversity and Dynamism

So, people's identities and motivations can be driven by collective concerns, and conditions of uncertainty can contribute to a search for community. Of course, community-think could be deleterious to the capacity to adapt to changing circumstances, particularly if a group is excessively homogeneous and deviation becomes nearly inconceivable (think the Amish in America or Islamic fundamentalists in the Middle East). But when these knowledge communities are more diverse, they might be epistemically better off. This is true in scientific communities, where taking other viewpoints into account has been shown to yield better results (De Langhe 2014). In the social and political realm, diverse epistemic communities introduce members to difference, raise the possibility of understanding a different set of priorities, or provide a mechanism to see the full potential in other sub-communities and sectors. The impacts of this can be considerable. Think of the rapid evolution of views (and norms) around marriage rights for gays and lesbians in the United States, partly because of conscious efforts to increase awareness of difference (yes, your neighbor—or at least your neighbor on TV—is indeed gay) and commonality (and, yes, he and his partner, televised or not, are raising a child just as delightful as yours).

For diversity in an epistemic community to pay off, however, it isn't enough for it just to be present. Members of subordinated groups must also be empowered as epistemic agents (Daukas 2011). For this to occur, there must be a commonly understood value or norm in the community that respects differences in perspective, including the ability of people from socially marginalized groups to develop self-confidence in participating in the community, and those from socially privileged groups being appropriately humble. Thus, patterns of inclusion or exclusion in epistemic communities link closely to broader social problems, such as racism, sexism, and so on, and the ability of epistemic communities to overcome these differences helps contribute to greater epistemic validity (Daukas 2006).

Diversity can also contribute to dynamism—the ability to constantly change and adapt to new circumstances. Epistemic communities are not always dynamic—some come together as relatively ad hoc coalitions around particular policy problems, and their life is limited by the nature of that problem and its solution. Other epistemic communities, however, are more constant and have a more holistic character, engaging a broader range of issues and varied problems. Such constantly evolving epistemic communities seem to come more out of interactions rooted in social struggles, and focus as much on the establishment and perpetuation of beliefs, visions, and dominant social discourses as they do on specific policy solutions (Antoniades 2010). Dynamism has its economic benefits, especially in our contemporary era of continued change and uncertainty. Key to the learning and innovation needed in modern economies is the flexibility to rapidly move between ideas and possibilities, markets and cultures, design and production.

Consider, for example, the ability of several of our case-study regions to respond to a shock and turn things around to restore economic viability and vitality. Facing pressures (such as the threat of fast growth in Salt Lake, the collapse of a major business deal in Oklahoma City, or rising interethnic conflict in San Antonio), certain regions have the capacity to promote a conversation that will allow a regional system to adjust and regain its footing. Key is that such adjustments do not mean a return to previous equilibria—in all three of these cases, a new trajectory emerged, including a more planned Salt Lake, a more vibrant Oklahoma City, and a more inclusive San Antonio. Dynamism is not about equilibrium (or returning to equilibrium) but rather about resilience and adaptation.

JUMP-STARTING COMMUNITY

So if diverse and dynamic epistemic communities can lead to better knowledge and perhaps better adjustment to changing realities, how do such diverse and dynamic epistemic communities actually form? As noted in chapter 1, previous research on epistemic communities suggests that there are a number of conditions that contribute to the formation of such knowledge communities in general. The most important of these seem to be conditions of complexity and uncertainty in a particular subject area that lead people to recognize the value of searching beyond established networks and create a motivation for interactive processes between people to understand that complexity, interpret changing situations, and respond to unexpected dynamics. Such communities are also built around some level of expertise or specialized knowledge that is needed to effectively interpret the complex information, generally suggesting a small circle of involvement. Finally, epistemic communities tend to develop some set of processes for institutionalizing the interactions and acting on the ideas that emerge from the knowledge-generation process.

While the concept has not generally been applied to regions (as it is here), the fit seems obvious. Regional development in most regions, especially in the past thirty years, is characterized by complex and uncertain change driven by a large array of actors and factors. The result could be fragmentation or collaboration, cacophony or symphony. In some regions, as in Raleigh, knowledge communities develop that become linked by a shared story (Triple Helix over and over again), aligned strategies, and a sense of interwoven destinies (as with Raleigh's commitment to integrating its school system). In other regions, no such binding mechanism develops, and different constituencies and geographies see their futures as separate, not linked. In Fresno, for example, market-driven development contributed to wide gaps between city and suburb, agricultural dependence led to an emphasis on cheap labor, and a reliance on oil has made cleaning up some of the country's worst air pollution (something that would have widespread benefits) a political challenge.

What contributes to the development of an epistemic community focused on regional development, and what contributes to its being more or less diverse and dynamic in its membership, focus, and long-term viability? Our cases suggest at least three triggering factors: economic shocks, collaborative governance structures, and social movements. These factors are not mutually exclusive; in fact, all three may be influential in the same region at the same time, or reinforce each other sequentially (think of how Communities Organized for Public Services pushed San Antonio leaders to be more inclusive, helped shift the electoral system, then teamed with former enemies to respond to an economic downturn), but it helps to look at each factor in turn.

Economic Shocks and Opportunities

Multiple constituencies in a region are linked through the economy, whether they realize it or not. People often commute across jurisdictional boundaries; many live in one city, work in another, and shop in a third. Businesses buy goods and services from each other regardless of jurisdictional boundaries but are often interlocked in regional industrial clusters. And a significant amount of research in the past three decades has documented the increasing importance of regions for driving innovation and economic growth (Acs 2000; Berube 2007; Braczyk, Cooke, and Heidenreich 1998; de la Mothe and Paquet 1998; Katz and Bradley 2013; Scott 1998; Storper 1997).

When there is an explicit shock to the regional economy, this can be the impetus for the development of new efforts to develop and share knowledge. Think about Oklahoma City. While the longer-term economic decline of the 1980s set the background, economic development efforts in the region continued along business-as-usual lines until the shock of not winning the widely expected siting of the new United Airlines maintenance operating center. It appears that this singular event was the catalyst for the development of the MAPS program, as diverse public- and private-sector leaders in the region jointly realized the need for a more comprehensive and diverse approach to economic development.

In Silicon Valley, the economic crisis of the early 1990s was the explicit motivation for the creation of Joint Venture Silicon Valley, a group whose slogan was "collaborating to compete"—that is, working together as a region to be better positioned in the global and national economies. In Sacramento, the loss of three military bases and tens of thousands of military-linked civilian jobs in the early 1990s sparked a collaborative response, including a rethinking of land development patterns that eventually led to the Blueprint process. In Salt Lake City, economic problems in the early 1990s and the resulting out-migration of large numbers of youth stimulated regional leaders to come together in the Coalition for Utah's Future to try to collectively figure out what was happening to the regional economy and what they could do about it—and out of that grew the much-celebrated Envision Utah.

Sacramento and Salt Lake City also point to how *positive* economic shocks can trigger epistemic communities. In both cases, the economic downturn of the early 1990s was replaced by rapidly growing, and sprawling, development patterns that threatened residents' understanding of what was good about their region. In Salt Lake City, the issue was the way in which increasing sprawl ate up farmland on the urban periphery and increasingly threatened recreation areas in the foothills; this became the immediate challenge that the long-range planning under Envision Utah was intended to address. Similarly, in Sacramento, residents throughout the region became worried about growing air pollution, loss of farmland, and shrinking green space on the urban periphery; addressing this challenge became the root motivation for people coming together under the Blueprint process.

A final key point for our analysis is that it seems that shocks or opportunities that are particular to the region—the loss of military bases in Sacramento, the failure to land a United Airlines facility for Oklahoma City, or worries about the drift of younger residents out of Raleigh and Salt Lake—help sharpen attention more than sudden downturns or upswings associated with the national economy. These latter sorts of economic shocks can seem purely external (and perhaps temporary) and offer a less clear reason why coming together in a regional context is important.

Collaborative Regional Governance

Many regions have faced economic restructuring not so much as an economic shock but as more of a long-term shift. And while shock might trigger change, simmering crisis might just trigger, well, more simmering. Consider Fresno, where urban sprawl and uncontrolled growth have undermined quality of life in the region and consumed farmland on the urban periphery—but with the pressures slowly building and the constituencies very divided, little has been done to address the dilemma. On the other hand, both Raleigh and Charlotte took advantage of potential opportunities, both finding regional mechanisms (in one case through a small group of civic leaders, and in the other through a more widespread implantation of the Triple Helix in the regional DNA) to generate a consensus about how to become stellar economic examples of the New South.

So when do regional challenges (or opportunities) translate into collaborative regional governance? This partly depends on the structure of governments and governance, with the latter often influenced by regional culture. By *government*, we mean formal regional institutional arrangements or practices, whether in the form of city–county mergers or aggressive annexation policies of central cities. Clearly, the fragmented nature of metropolitan regions like Detroit and Cleveland has fostered a sense of economic isolation for both the poor and the wealthy of those regions, while the regionally integrated structures of places like Oklahoma City, Nashville, and Jacksonville have helped facilitate interconnections among different constituencies in the region.

In San Antonio, simply the size of the city relative to the region is important: moving policy and politics in the central city there is essentially moving policy and politics in the region, and that makes a single municipal government an important platform for the metro as a whole.

But beyond the formal mechanisms of government is a role for *governance*, that is, the deliberate collaborative efforts, often driven by particular individuals or groups of individuals, that help shape regional decision-making processes and development patterns. In Grand Rapids, for example, business leaders—along with the encouragement and support of the city and public officials that was eventually institutionalized in Grand Action—were critical in pulling together to revitalize downtown. In Raleigh, the Triple Helix is found in no particular location, but people are stitched together nonetheless—and a unified school district was not an accident of history but a conscious decision based in the desire to more peacefully integrate. In Salt Lake, Envision Utah has no real power other than the power of persuasion—and it has been highly persuasive.

And if governance matters, there is an important role for regional culture and norms. Again, in Grand Rapids, the efforts to consult with local homeless shelters that might be affected by development, or to put in place local hiring provisions as part of building a new arena, seemed driven more by moral values and a broad culture of "doing the right thing" than by a sense of crisis or conflict. We have also argued that the inclusive and future-looking processes in Salt Lake were rooted in a number of cultural elements, particularly the role of the Mormon Church. In Seattle, there is also a deeply rooted egalitarian streak that permeates leadership. When coupled with the aversion to conflict that also seems to be there (the region also has its own "Seattle nice"), this can result in a "Seattle process" that produces both the nation's highest minimum wage and a long-delayed road tunneling project. A simple consideration of economic interests or political structures cannot explain why conflict happens in some locations and cooperation in others; culture and the proclivity for collaborative governance matter.

Social Movements

Cooperation may also evolve from conflict, particularly if marginalized populations find that their only way to the table is by raising uncomfortable issues in uncomfortable ways. San Antonio is our most obvious example where this occurred. Organizing by COPS was a critical part of opening up opportunity structures in the regional power elite *and* of shifting regional business strategies away from a classic reliance on tax breaks and cheap labor toward a deeper investment in skills development, workforce upgrading, and a more diversified economic development strategy. The early days of conflict were later moderated, and collaboration was institutionalized in specific initiatives like Project QUEST and the San Antonio Educational Partnership, both of which brought together social-movement activists with regional private- and public-sector leadership around specific education and economic-development objectives.

There are certainly cases where social-movement activities have *not* led to the development of diverse epistemic communities. In Detroit, for example, equity advocates in the union movement, which has been dominated by the United Auto Workers, tended to focus more on holding on to whatever wage and benefit premiums they could derive from the auto industry and less on broader debates about regional development patterns. African American political activists—both those engaged in formal electoral processes and those in community organizing—have tended to focus on dynamics in the city of Detroit itself, rather than challenge white flight or organize for regional tax-base sharing, for example (Pastor and Benner 2008).[1] For social-movement activism to stimulate the development of diverse epistemic communities probably also requires some level of governance opportunity or champion to help translate between the worldviews of activists and elite leadership, a role Henry Cisneros played in San Antonio with great impact.

And while the recent shifts in Seattle have something to do with the generalized culture we refer to above, there has also been a long history there of social justice struggle (think the Four Amigos) and some brilliant strategies by labor and its allies to elect sympathetic officials and develop a new sort of collective bargaining that goes beyond union members (Rolf 2014). Against the backdrop of rising inequality in the United States, a paralyzed national political system, and emerging opportunities at the regional level, we expect far more from social-movement actors in the future. The trick will be balancing power-mapping and power-building with the sort of cooperative approach needed to grow the regional economy; the struggle to strike that balance is likely to generate discussions by activists and articles by academics for years to come.

SUSTAINING DIVERSE AND DYNAMIC EPISTEMIC COMMUNITIES

We've argued that understanding our diverse and dynamic epistemic communities requires a microfoundation that recognizes that people can be collectively motivated. We've also suggested that epistemic communities can be stimulated into formation through a range of processes, including economic shocks, regional governance opportunities, and social-movement pressures. But once they are formed, how do they evolve over time, manage to maintain a commitment to collective action and inclusion, and through those processes shift exchanges between actors toward more transformative relationships rather than simply transactional interactions? In analyzing our case studies, we have identified five specific mechanisms that seem to play a role: shared knowledge generation and agenda setting; inclusionary issue framing; collaborative leadership development; coordinated action; and demonstrating success (and hence a reason to perpetuate the knowledge community). We take these up in turn below.

Shared Knowledge Generation and Agenda Setting

The first step in agenda setting often involves the recognition of a common challenge—pressing population growth in Salt Lake, a rising Latino electorate in San Antonio, the need to retain young graduates in Raleigh, the loss of a major business opportunity in Oklahoma City, economic shifts in the Silicon Valley. Knowledge generation and interpretation—indicator projects, planning exercises, and outreach about regional data—are often used to get various actors "on the same page." In this sense, the participation is as important as the product: the data is used to facilitate a conversation that brings together unexpected interests and allies.

Perhaps the most obvious example of shared knowledge development and agenda setting in our case studies is Salt Lake City, with the work of Envision Utah. As we described in chapter 4, the explicit goal of the initiative was not to develop a detailed general plan for how the region should develop but rather to help identify the key values shared by a broad swath of Salt Lake City's population and translate that into more specific goals designed to guide regional development. The seven goals that emerged from this process—improving air quality, promoting housing options, creating transportation choices, encouraging water conservation, preserving critical lands, supporting efficient infrastructure, and exploring community development—are not particularly surprising or transformative in themselves. What is critical is that they did not come from professional planners but instead emerged from a broad consultative, knowledge-generation process that included more than 2,000 people in fifty public workshops and more than 17,000 responses to Internet and newspaper surveys. This process helped ensure that priorities for development in the region were rooted in the lived experiences and values of diverse communities and were broadly shared by leaders throughout the region.

A similar process was evident in Oklahoma City around the development of the first MAPS program. Here, the regional priorities developed in the original program were driven by more of a top-down process than in Salt Lake City, developed initially by the Chamber of Commerce and later fleshed out by city-appointed task forces operating primarily behind closed doors. However, the specific projects that were included in the original MAPS proposal were developed over a nine-month period in 1992 by a mayor-appointed Metro Area Projects Task Force consisting primarily of a range of public officials, but with project ideas also developed by various other committees consisting of city council members and civic leaders. The mayor also created a City Council committee to review the task force's work, and appointed as head of this committee the council member he thought would be the strongest *opponent* of the whole initiative. Why? In the mayor's words: "I don't want to ignore her. I'll make her top gun, and then work her through the process" (Lackmeyer and Money 2006, 112).

Initial polls showed little support for new taxes, and quite uneven support for the different project ideas being considered. Thus, a critical design component of the initiative was to develop a range of projects that met the priorities of a range of interests and then make it a single vote for all the projects so that people would be forced to consider their own priorities in light of priorities developed by other interests. In advocating new taxes to fund the package, Mayor Norick emphasized the multiple beneficiaries of the projects and the importance of focusing on the city as a whole, asking arts patrons, "Are you willing to defeat your symphony because you don't like baseball?" (Lackmeyer and Money 2006, 127).

We do not mean to exaggerate the inclusivity of the MAPS process. One of the groups opposed to the original vote, for example, was the NAACP, because of concerns that minority communities in the region would not benefit adequately from the projects. But this gap was addressed to a certain extent in the next round of increased tax funding for schools, in which the first school renovated was in the heart of Oklahoma City's African American neighborhood. The basic point here is that one way to build a community of support is through shared agenda setting.

In contrast, when a common set of regional priorities is absent, or when the priorities are developed in narrow, fragmented, or "siloed" processes, the region is not really being stitched together. In Fresno, for example, development has been primarily driven through unplanned sprawl and backroom deals between developers and elected officials (Zuk 2013). In Greensboro, the inability to even agree on how to interpret the past led to tension that held back the capacity to cooperate on the future. In both cases, a region's fragmentation has led to suboptimal outcomes, even with respect to many things on which various actors might actually agree.

Finally, the presence of a comprehensive plan does not always mean that inclusion is in the mix. For example, the efforts of the Sacramento Area Council of Governments toward long-range collaborative planning, starting first in the early 2000s with the Blueprint process and extending to more recent efforts around the Sustainable Community Strategy, have been strongest in their attention to economic growth, environmental concerns, and smart-growth principles. Social equity advocates in the region have had an uneasy relationship with these efforts, participating primarily from an outsider-advocacy position rather than from a position of full incorporation (Pastor and Benner 2011).

The gap was even manifested in the governing consortium SACOG created in 2010 to oversee implementation of its Sustainable Community Strategy participatory planning process, which received a $1.5 million grant from HUD. The consortium failed to include direct representation from either the private sector (whose interests were indirectly represented by Valley Vision, a nonprofit regional convener) or social equity advocates (whose interests were indirectly represented by the Center for Regional Change at the University of California, Davis, which included the work of one of the authors of this book). Partly as a result, when a prominent economic development initiative was launched in the following year by the Metro Chamber, the Sacramento Area Commerce and Trade Organization, and the Sacramento Area Regional Technology Association, together with Valley Vision, equity concerns—and representatives—were almost entirely absent from an effort billed as trying to build a robust strategic economic development plan for the region. SACOG is doing better than it was, but the basic lesson is that to really create community, a shared agenda must reach out to all sectors.

Inclusionary Issue Framing

As we have learned from the work of George Lakoff and others, the way issues are framed makes a significant difference in how people understand the world and how they act (Bolman and Deal 2013; Lakoff 2004; Lakoff and Johnson 2008). We are most definitely not experts on cognitive linguistics, but we were struck in our case studies by the different ways people framed issues of conflict and collaboration in their work in the region. In some places, issues were framed around a respect for difference and a sense of a common future together; in others, the frame was more about immediate interests and frustrations about lack of influence or impact.

Salt Lake City provides a number of illustrative examples of the more positive framing. In many parts of the United States, undocumented immigrants are viewed as an unwelcome alien invasion. One might expect that to be the case in Utah, one of the country's reddest (politically) and, until recently, whitest (demographically) states. However, Utah has formally allowed undocumented immigrants to have driving privileges since 1999, and undocumented students have been able to pay in-state tuition at state universities since 2002. In the words of one Mexican immigrant, "I've lived in California. I've lived in Las Vegas. No place is like this. Here, they don't think just because we don't have papers we aren't human beings" (Riley 2006). Partly because of the Mormon faith, partly because of the stress on family, and partly because of an appreciation of markets and hard work, immigrants are seen as part of the overall fabric of the state—and that framing has had a real impact on policy.

But it's not just immigration. The welfare policy of the LDS Church of providing "a hand up, not a handout" may sound like the promotion of individual responsibility and self-efficacy, but in practice it seems to also be about helping integrate suffering individuals and families into a broader long-term community. In reviewing a conflict with environmentalists over a major construction project, the head of the building trades labor council described having to figure out an agreeable solution, since both organizations are likely to be still around in the region for at least the next couple of decades. This reflects and embodies not a winner-take-all approach but rather the acknowledgement of a common future.

We see a similar framing in Oklahoma City, where mayor Mick Cornett—reelected in 2014 to an unprecedented fourth term (Crum 2014)—frequently defends the major public-sector investments made through the MAPS program, and especially through MAPS 3 under his administration, as being about creating a city where "our kids and grandkids want to live." This framing immediately connects across generations and also connects regional development to a common—almost family—destiny. Meanwhile, in San Antonio, great pride is taken in how sectors that once engaged in seeming wars of attrition are now engaged in projects of rebuilding; "collaboration" rolled off nearly every interviewee's tongue, almost to a repetitive fault, and was clearly an embedded social norm. And certainly Seattle, which seems to be trying to reconcile its egalitarian history and ethos with its current reliance on a set of high-tech industries that are driving inequality, stands out in how its government structures, including King County, stress that the "sum total of decisions" should point in the direction of social equity.

Of course, framing is not static, something that can be seen in the case of Silicon Valley. In the early 1990s, Joint Venture Silicon Valley emerged out of a process in which the first task was to diagnose the problems facing the region's economy at the time. That diagnostic process required combining "pre-existing economic data, original research . . . over 100 interviews with CEOs and civic leaders, and a broad-scale community survey" (JVSVN 1992, 3). The central storyline involved a region that was "in balance" from much of the 1950s through the 1980s but was showing warning signs of imbalance in the 1990s. A key phrase came at the end of the document—"Silicon Valley did not have to organize in the past, but today competition is too great"—and so Joint Venture called for the development of a "business plan for the regional economy" (69).

You don't generally find more explicit framing for collective action. And while Joint Venture was clearly not interested in economic inequality or poverty—in fact the word *poverty* does not appear even once in the 100-page document, and the only reference to *equity* is in relation to business concerns about the unfairness of county taxes—the group did acknowledge the problems of growing conflict in the region. For example, describing the situation at the end of the 1980s, they wrote:

> The region became increasingly filled with conflicts. Community groups identified toxic-waste hazards posed by what were thought to be "clean" high-tech industries. Resolution of those issues were expensive for all sides. Growth priorities of communities ceased to be the same as those of developers. Transportation and housing problems became a high priority for

businesses. The region's overall economic infrastructure swung from being a highly supportive asset for the region's economic engine to being a mixed blessing with uncertain prospects. (18)

As a result, Joint Venture reconciled collaboration and conflict by invoking the phrase "collaborating to compete," and stressed that the only way to come up with the right solutions was through the "community coming together."

Of course, implicit in its worldview was the notion that a recovering economy would largely do the trick in terms of creating opportunity. But by 2013, inequality in the region had worsened to the point that our interviewees framed the pressing challenges in terms of a "tale of two valleys" (the haves and the have-nots) and the isolation of the high-tech industry from the rest of the region. Interestingly, a more inclusionary frame emerged in the introduction to the 2014 version of the annual *Silicon Valley Index*, in which Joint Venture CEO Russell Hancock joined with the CEO and President of the Silicon Valley Community Foundation, Emmett Carson, to point out:

> The Index is troubling . . . because our prosperity is not widely shared. . . . The gaps and disparities are more pronounced than ever. These are the hard facts: our income gains are limited to those with ultra-high-end skills. Median wages for low- and middle-skilled workers are relatively stagnant and the share of households with mid-level incomes has fallen in Silicon Valley more than in the state and nation. Disparities by race are more persistent than ever. We also saw a sharp increase in homelessness. While job growth is important, it can never be the single measure of our region's health when it is confined to a limited number of sectors. (Massaro and Najera 2014, 3)

This is a remarkable shift in the story, and it could have a positive impact on future developments. What is also clear is that the absence of inclusionary framing in places like Fresno—where a number of respondents suggested that the problems are too large and the public too divided to actually work through solutions—can stand in the way of working together. Many in that region think that progress on equity can only be made by "standing up" to entrenched interests. That may well be, but "entrenched" also means "not going away." Eventually, conflict will need to shift to collaboration, as occurred in San Antonio, if there is to be significant impact on actual economic and social outcomes. The challenge is how to balance highlighting and challenging sharp divides in terms of income and power, *and* working to build a common regional community over the long haul.

Collaborative Leadership Development

Leaders are crucial. It's hard to understand the transformation of San Antonio without highlighting the roles of Henry Cisneros and Ernie Cortes, to fully appreciate the commitment to racial equity in Seattle without acknowledging the Four Amigos or King County Executive Ron Sims, or to recognize the skillful navigation of Envision Utah without talking about the graceful leadership of Robert Grow. But one of the keys to creating diverse and dynamic epistemic communities is to understand that although some leaders are born, many others can be made.

In our book, *Just Growth,* we cited Leadership Nashville and the Jacksonville Community Council as examples of formal programs that deliberately brought diverse constituencies together in information-sharing and knowledge-generation processes that also emphasized processes of leadership development and the resolution of differences in productive ways. In the case of the Jacksonville Community Council, this was achieved through having participants come to consensus on recommendations on how the region could solve a particular critical social and economic problem. In Leadership Nashville's case, participants told us it was the neutral learning space and the careful attention to selecting diverse cohorts that facilitated new insights and new relationships.

There are similar formal leadership programs in many of the regions we examine in this book. In Grand Rapids, for instance, the Chamber of Commerce runs a number of leadership programs, including a nine-month Leadership Grand Rapids program that is quite similar to Leadership Nashville in its structure and orientation. It has a specific emphasis on recruiting diverse participants, focusing on business, government, and nonprofits (though its representation from labor is notably much weaker than in Nashville), and giving them a more comprehensive understanding of community challenges and opportunities. In Sacramento, Charlotte, and Silicon Valley, there are strong chapters of the American Leadership Forum, a training program whose key principles include building trust and networks among diverse leaders; exploring the interconnectedness of communities, nations, and the world; and exploring, understanding, and valuing diversity. Critically, selection of participants for each cohort includes attention to bringing together leaders from constituencies that might in other contexts be at odds.

One particularly striking example of this mixing and matching—and the impact it can have—occurred in Silicon Valley in 2000, when the head of the Central Labor Council reached out to a number of key executives of prominent corporations in the region whom she had met in large part through her involvement in the American Leadership Forum. She wanted them to support unionization efforts in the region's janitorial workforce. Executives from Hewlett-Packard, Genentech, and Cisco all made public statements supporting the janitors, but the most striking intervention was by Eric Benhamou, then Chairman and CEO of 3Com, who wrote a particularly compelling editorial in the *San Jose Mercury News*, arguing that Silicon Valley was underpaying an intolerably high percentage of the population, and appealing for support of the janitors' case in part as an opportunity to make clear "which kind of a Silicon Valley we stand for" (Benhamou 2000; see also Pastor, Benner, and Matsuoka 2009, 185).

In several of our case studies, we did not find formal leadership programs, but it was clear that certain regional leaders and processes had helped generalize strong capacities in bridge-building. In San Antonio, Henry Cisneros was particularly visible and important. With roots in poor West Side communities, but reaching the highest levels of political influence in the city, he was able to garner trust and support from both sides of this divide and help strengthen a culture of collaboration that was later institutionalized even after he left the mayor's office. In Salt Lake City, we did not find a formal program to develop collaborative leadership, but the impressive success of Envision Utah's broad participatory planning processes, and the multiple constituencies involved in developing the Utah Compact, suggest cross-constituency understandings in cases where there was significant potential for heated conflict.

Collaborative leadership networks can develop in many different ways, and we have not yet developed a simple quantitative metric for assessing the strength and depth of collaborative leadership (that's our next project!). Still, we found that in regions seemingly stuck in long-range patterns of inequality and fragmentation, interviewees tended to frame power-building in us-versus-them or at least non-collaborative frameworks. In Fresno, environmental justice organizers described collaborative efforts at shifting air quality standards in the region as essentially hopeless and instead depended primarily on lawsuits and other legal channels for pursuing their goals. In Greensboro, one of the stronger and most celebrated social justice organizations in the African American community, the Beloved Community Center, has developed a reputation in the region of working largely independently rather than in collaborative efforts, even as business and other civic leaders we interviewed seemed to hope that the scars of racism would just sort of heal all on their own.

Sometimes you have to fight—and fight hard—to make sure an issue makes its way to the table. San Antonio would not be where it is today without the fierce battles and creative tactics of COPS. But making the pivot to collaborative leadership is one part of developing a diverse and dynamic epistemic community. It involves understanding that wisdom is in multiple locations, and that the role of leadership is to build bridges between diverse constituencies, identify and reconcile conflicting values and interests, and work to ensure that spirited skirmishes over policy build a base for future joint action rather than destructive and persistent conflict.

Coordinating Action

With their ability to build ties across constituencies, diverse and dynamic epistemic communities can also influence regional governance processes by facilitating coordination among different actors in the region. This goes beyond formal agreements such as those developed through institutionalized public–private partnerships or through specific collaborative initiatives like the Sustainable Community Strategy process in Sacramento or the specific planning efforts of Envision Utah. It also extends to more informal collaborative efforts that become embedded in local culture.

One of the most specific examples of this in our case studies was in Grand Rapids, where there was widespread agreement about the value of coordination by the "four-legged stool" in shaping the region's economic development trajectories: (1) Grand Action was the formal public–private partnership driving local investment and pursuing downtown revitalization efforts; (2) the Chamber of Commerce was critical in a range of leadership development, policy advocacy, and economic development initiatives; (3) The Right Place was a regional marketing entity focused on business recruitment, but also providing research, data, and indicators on regional development; and (4) Experience Grand Rapids was focused on expanding the tourism industry and marketing for conventions and related events. Even without formal collaborative agreements between these various entities, they complement each other, and with the regular sharing of information and knowledge that characterized their relationships, they all were moving in complementary directions in their programmatic work.

The Sacramento region also has a similar dynamic of coordinating action across multiple organizations in the economic development arena.

The Sacramento Area Commerce and Trade Organization focuses on external recruitment and marketing. The Metro Chamber of Commerce has focused more on internal business development and policy advocacy. Since 2001, the Sacramento Area Regional Technology Association has played a critical role in accelerating technology development in the region. And Valley Vision has been a catalyst for a number of regional economic initiatives, including the Green Capital Alliance (focusing on clean tech industries) and The Next Economy (a region-wide effort to diversify the economic base of the region). The Center for Strategic Economic Research provides critical economic data, research, and analysis of the Sacramento region's economy. In conversations with leaders from all of these organizations, it is clear that informal information sharing and communication help coordinate their actions, even when they are not involved in formal collaborative initiatives.

Similar dynamics can be seen in the ways the long-range planning efforts in Sacramento and Salt Lake City shape regional development patterns. In both cases, the entities driving the collaborative planning processes (SACOG and Envision Utah) have no statutory authority to enforce these plans (although SACOG can impact transportation funding to local jurisdictions). Instead, implementation relies on the actions of the local jurisdictions in the area, and the work of a range of other regional actors. But by creating a common knowledge base and set of principles for future work, these initiatives help coordinate action in the region toward common goals, even if undertaken in the silos that characterize regional government.

In short, diverse and dynamic epistemic communities are aimed at regional governance, not regional government—they are not about creating new Portland Metros (the elected regional council there) but about filling in the spaces so regional actors work collaboratively rather than at cross purposes. Where such spaces are not occupied, fragmentation is the order of the day. In Fresno, for example, the inability of the city and the county of Fresno to coordinate their efforts in proposing a site for a new campus of the University of California system contributed to its being established in Merced rather than Fresno, even though Fresno is by far the largest city in the San Joaquin Valley and was in many ways a much more likely home (Bender and Parman 2005). More recently, the city of Fresno's post-2012 efforts to promote downtown revitalization and reduce sprawl were being actively undermined by the county's efforts to promote new developments in surrounding unincorporated county land.

Demonstrating Success

Nothing succeeds like success—and having a real impact can shore up the confidence and continuity of knowledge communities. In Oklahoma City, for example, three different Republican mayors, in collaboration with a conservative Chamber of Commerce, have managed to convince a majority of the relatively conservative population to vote three successive times for increased taxes for major public-sector development initiatives. The result has been a transformation in Oklahoma City in a remarkably short period of time that helps reinforce the idea that stakeholder processes and civic engagement actually do make a difference. San Antonio provides another example in which cooperation has begat economic progress has begat more cooperation, including around the pre-K initiative we mentioned earlier.

But it's also the case that the power of collaboration can be demonstrated when cooperation is the path not taken. In Davis County, just north of the Salt Lake City metro, for example, development of the Legacy Parkway was pushed by the governor and the Utah Department of Transportation without collaborating with environmentalists or transit advocates. According to one of our informants, the governor and the secretary of transportation actually had a specific conversation about whether they should go through a process of consultation or simply try to go ahead with the project. The decision was to go ahead, based on an assessment of their own political strength.

What was the result? A $200 million lawsuit and nearly two years of delay on the project after it had started. Ultimately, the Sierra Club (on behalf of numerous groups opposing the parkway) signed an agreement with the state that included no trucks, no billboards, a 55 mph speed limit, and commitment to fund work to expand the transit system in the region. In contrast, along the same highway network in Salt Lake County, the Mountain View Corridor was built after extended negotiation between the Utah Department of Transportation and the Sierra Club and other environmentalists. The result was a substantial redesign of the project to include more green landscaping, expanded frontage roads with bike lanes and trails, and signalized intersections, including a new radar-activated bike turn signal to facilitate both bike and car traffic in the corridor. Oh, and no lawsuit.

In divided regions, there seem to be far fewer policies that actually get passed, and those that do are much more modest in their impact. In Fresno, for example, our informants had no problem describing multiple cases of conflict in the region with negative policy consequences. Nearly fifty years of conflict over the Darling rendering facility, for example, including tensions between environmental justice groups and the union representing workers in the plant, have failed to resolve what all agree is a noxious site near residential communities. Conflict can breed political dysfunction and policy failure—which can in turn breed further conflict.

ROOTS, RELATIONSHIPS, AND REASON

In this chapter, we have stepped back from the data and the cases to look at how diverse and dynamic epistemic communities are formed and sustained, and how they shape regional norms and behaviors. The first lesson is simple. Our findings, as interesting and surprising as they may be—Utah welcomes immigrants? Oklahoma City has rebuilt its central city? San Antonio went from cleavages as deep as the Alamo to incessant collaboration?—are not easily understood by traditional models of self-interested and individualist actors. Instead, we need a set of microfoundations in which repeated interactions, particularly around knowledge generation and interpretation, help actors recognize the "other," develop a set of social norms about regional stewardship, and find new ways to cooperate that can maximize communication and transformation.

This development of a diverse and dynamic epistemic community—one which includes multiple sectors and can adjust to change over time—can be triggered by a series of key factors, including economic shocks, governance structures and opportunity, and even social-movement forces raising issues of inclusion. We have explored the specific activities that can help build and sustain community, including shared knowledge development and agenda setting, issue framing, leadership development, coordinating action, and demonstrating success. We are not suggesting that these processes paper over conflicts, or erase key differences in priorities, values, or interests. What we are suggesting is that such processes steer participants away from a winner-take-all view in which opponents are to be vanquished and their concerns ignored, and toward a regional culture in which conflicts play out against a backdrop of long-term and repeated interactions in an interdependent world.

Our cases have suggested that leadership in building such epistemic communities and regional social norms can come from many sources: planners as in the cases of Sacramento and Utah, business as in the cases of Grand Rapids, Charlotte, Oklahoma City, and Silicon Valley, movements for justice as in the case of San Antonio, and multiple sectors as in the case of Seattle and Raleigh. In each of these cases, we have seen a tremendous pride of place—a sense of roots in the region that leads actors to believe that an investment in downtown development or pre-K education will rebound in ways that go beyond immediate interests. In some sense, it is the combination of roots in the region and relationships that are developed over time that leads to a more reasonable conversation about the metropolitan future. What difference that conversation can make for actual outcomes—and what the lessons might be for a nation where relations are strained and reason is in short supply—are the topics of our concluding chapter.

CHAPTER 9

Looking Forward

A Beloved (Epistemic) Community?

Well, it may be all right in practice, but it will never work in theory.
—Warren Buffet, letter to Berkshire Hathaway shareholders, 1984

It's always good to find firm answers, to reinforce unshakable convictions with undisputed evidence. The clarity and confidence that can result can surely provide a roadmap for policy and political change. Unfortunately, it's also the case that simply reinforcing firm prior beliefs—when, in fact, reality is a bit more complicated—can provide the combustible elements for, say, the Crusades, or more recently the Tea Party movement and its attempt to derail the workings of the federal government.

The conclusions of this volume seem to better fit the admonition of Warren Buffet quoted above. There certainly seems to be something going on, but exactly what it is may seem clearer in the field than in the realms of academic theory. Part of this is that we are, we think, pioneering new ground and there is significant work remaining to be done. For example, the regression results of chapter 2 are consistent with those reported in the international literature and suggest that equity, social cohesion, and jurisdictional alignment are strongly associated with longer growth spells, even in a multivariate setting. At the same time, we have not clearly indicated why that might be, nor have we introduced intervening variables that might explain the causal chain. Similarly, our case-selection process was rooted in a quantitative decision-making process, meaning that our range of case studies may reflect less bias than in most such enterprises. At the same time, we acknowledge that our version of theoretical sampling—in which we focused not just on places with varying quantitative outcomes but also on locales with well-known reputations for strong epistemic communities—is less analytically satisfying than a reliance on a single classification scheme.

Moreover, while all the case studies were subjected to the same preparation, interview, and write-up process, our categorizations of those regions—particularly the distinctions between planning-led, business-driven, conflict-informed, and knowledge-based—could easily be disputed by those more deeply conversant with the dynamics in those regions and so more aware of what is missing, in nuance even if not in broad theme. Meanwhile, the general conclusions we draw from those cases—that there are epistemic communities; that they are supported by a specific set of social norms and constituted through a specific set of social practices; and that they can lead to more or less favorable outcomes in terms of equity, growth, and resilience—may seem a stretch, given both the relatively small number of cases and the fact that few of the actual actors would label what they're doing the construction of a diverse and dynamic epistemic community.

So, why offer these preliminary and exploratory findings to the world now? Why not wait until the econometric evidence is even more persuasive and the microfoundations that emerge from both our hunches and our real-world examinations are spelled out in mathematical functions, complex game theory, and algebraic symbols? Why bank so much on the ideas that disconnection may be an impediment to regional alliances, that another world of knowledge and collaboration is possible, and that such collaboration could improve economic and social outcomes?

We do so because we believe that the time is short, not just for America's metros but for the nation as a whole. As we insisted at the beginning of this book, the income inequality, spatial sorting, and political polarization wracking America have grown sharper and more worrisome in recent years. While dealing with that social separation by creating shared knowledge and facilitating civil discourse will not necessarily yield a more positive direction, it is hard to see how one might forge ahead in the absence of those elements. As a result, our big challenge as a nation is not about tweaking tax rates but about building community, not about shifting policy but about recreating a polity.

This chapter eventually lifts up lessons for the national challenge, but we begin by first considering whether the sort of collaborations we discuss in this book—the diverse and dynamic epistemic communities—can actually have an impact on economic growth and social equity.

We answer this with a weak but important linkage: while there is no necessary causal chain, the mix of quantitative and qualitative evidence suggests that such communities can at least raise the probability of success in those goals through a variety of specific mechanisms we describe. We then consider issues of scaling regional epistemic communities— that is, how they might be replicated in ways that would improve communications and outcomes in multiple regions. We close by considering implications for the national picture.

IMPACTING GROWTH AND EQUITY

Epistemic communities may be good things in and of themselves—they connect people across boundaries, they develop a shared sense of destiny, and surely they appeal to a sense of identity and purpose. Celebrating these outcomes might sound a bit "soft"—and perhaps surprising for two social scientists who tend to be happiest when downloading census surveys, comparing time series, and swapping tips about how best to run fixed-effect regressions in unbalanced samples. But we think that such a focus on repairing disconnection is important and goes beyond psychic well-being; we have suggested that such sets of relationships might allow regional actors to better coordinate when faced with a sudden external or internal shock.

So, do epistemic communities actually impact economic and social outcomes—and if so, how? The econometric evidence we presented in chapter 2 suggests that the sort of social disconnection such communities try to address is important. In the hazard models presented, not only was a region's initial level of inequality strongly (negatively) associated with the ability to sustain employment growth in subsequent years, but we also found similar effects on job growth for a number of measures of social cohesion, including residential segregation, fragmented metropolitan governance, sharp differences in city–suburb poverty levels, and in a somewhat more modest (or at least complex) relationship, geographic differences in political affiliation.

This evidence certainly doesn't mean that increased social cohesion will necessarily result in greater growth and equity—but in places as diverse as Salt Lake City, San Antonio, and Raleigh, leaders seem to believe that lacking a sense of common destiny dooms that destiny to be less than it might. Formal regional collaborative initiatives have been formed, à la Envision Utah; new public–partnerships have been cemented, à la Raleigh's proclaimed Triple Helix model; and new understandings about preparing the next America have been developed, à la San Antonio's multisector commitment to fund pre-kindergarten education or Seattle's effort to balance a rapidly growing high-tech sector with the needs and hopes of a working-class population increasingly priced out of the region. None of these new collaboratives, partnerships, or understandings will *necessarily* lead to positive outcomes—structural factors, effective policy, and the capacity to implement all matter—but key economic actors seem to believe that social connection can help.

This is an important finding, albeit not entirely novel. One recent book that is close to this volume in spirit if not strategy (in some sense, we went broad to do regional comparisons while he went deep to concentrate on two cases) is Sean Safford's *Why the Garden Club Couldn't Save Youngstown* (2009). In it, Safford eloquently and powerfully analyzes why Allentown was able to fare so much better than Youngstown in dealing with the economic restructuring of the 1980s and 1990s. At the core of his argument is an understanding that regions have complex layers of identity and affiliation between individuals and organizations. When a crisis in the regional economy emerges, people draw on these social structures to help guide their actions. In his two case studies, deeply rooted crises required individuals and organizations to improvise as old familiar roles for various actors, including local government, universities, unions, civic organizations, supplier companies, and banks, were undermined and new economic possibilities were still unclear—exactly the sort of uncertainty that we argued stimulates the creation of an epistemic community.

In comparing Allentown and Youngstown, Safford argues that actors in Allentown were more successful in their collective evolution in large part because of the diversity of their social connections, not just in breadth but in the multiple economic and social dimensions of those connections:

> The latter structure—characterized by intersecting rather than overlapping multiplexity—is more robust in the face of economic change. This is true for three reasons. First, uncertainty calls for interpretation, and interpretation is facilitated by access to different sources of information. A multiplex structure in which actors are connected to each other along separate dimensions allows diverse information sources to be brought to bear on understanding the problem at hand. Second, that structure provides greater opportunities for actors to emerge who can play leadership roles. . . . It suggests that organizations that span disparate groups in a community can become places where entrepreneurs can emerge and drive change processes. Finally, the independence of relational dimensions ensures that when crisis erupts in one sphere, other spheres will be relatively protected and can therefore serve as a platform for actors to engage each other. (Kindle location 1642)

What Safford describes in his Allentown case sounds a lot like what we would call a diverse and dynamic epistemic community. With very detailed data on both interbusiness and civic ties of key leaders in each of his regions, along with a deep historical analysis of settlement patterns and leadership strategies, he argues that not just the density but the diversity of the types of ties between regional leaders in Allentown was a critical component in helping the region dynamically respond to deindustrialization. While Youngstown was never able to effectively replace the decline in traditional manufacturing industries, Allentown was able to develop significant new growth sectors in health care, certain high-tech niches, financial services, and significant new entrepreneurial activity. Through his carefully constructed paired-case comparison, Safford provides an impressive depth of understanding of the contribution of these diverse knowledge networks to economic growth.

We point to Safford's research because his intensive research methodology provides a detailed picture of some of the processes that we believe underlie the ways that diverse epistemic communities contribute to growth and equity. Our research strategy was a more extensive effort, trying first to econometrically understand the impacts on job growth from broad patterns of social connection and disconnection across the largest 192 metropolitan regions, then to turn to a sufficiently large and diverse number of case studies to help provide evidence that understanding the nature and dynamics of epistemic communities might be important beyond just a few isolated cases. What we may have lost in depth we hope to have made up in breadth and scope.

In any case, the lessons from our case studies echo the findings of Safford. The strength, diversity, and dynamic character of what we call regional epistemic communities can shape the likelihood that a region will achieve more resilience and equity in the face of economic changes. To be sure, an epistemic community, no matter how diverse, is not a single silver bullet that can explain all growth and equity outcomes or overcome deep structural challenges (even for Safford, the real question is which region did less poorly as deindustrialization gripped the Midwest). But diverse and dynamic epistemic communities can offer more fertile soil for positive outcomes.

And as with Safford's analysis, a caveat is in order: "more positive" can simply mean "less worse." After all, the economic shifts of the last thirty years have been dramatic, with the loss of industry, the rise of global competition, and rapid and disruptive technological change all constituting headwinds for any trajectory of employment growth. With median incomes falling, inequality rising, and financial sectors collapsing, it may well be that the contributions of diverse epistemic communities to outcomes in many of our cases is about moderating the overall negative trend—that is, performing better relative to the average rather than against some golden standard.

Grow, Baby, Grow

So how can knowing together contribute to growing together? We start in this section with the "growing," acknowledging first that while our frame of diverse and dynamic epistemic communities may be novel, this perspective—and its implications for the economy—really builds on earlier work about untradeable interdependencies lifted up by economic geographers (Storper 1997, 2013), as well as research suggesting that networks and other social relations are a fundamental defining feature of a new economic order (particularly in regions with strong information industries; see Castells 1996 and Benkler 2006). Those strands of research have emerged precisely because one of the new key drivers of growth is innovation—and this requires the sort of coordination that epistemic communities can provide.

Innovation is defined as the ability of firms, industries, and regions to continually translate information and knowledge into viable new products, services, and production processes in the face of changing technology and market conditions. Innovation is an interactive process which occurs through complex communication channels, both internal to and across firm boundaries. As it turns out, much of the important interaction happens within regional industry clusters and through the sort of face-to-face communication that can occur within a regional context (Clark 2013). And while many innovations incorporate important new scientific or technological developments, most innovations actually occur in more everyday processes, such as in design, marketing, business process, or other aspects of business operations that are rooted in nonscientific knowledge and in day-to-day activities (Benner 2003; Gertler 2003; Howells 2002; Lawson and Lorenz 1999; Leonard and Sensiper 1998).

Given the above, it seems reasonable to believe that diverse and dynamic epistemic communities might contribute to improved innovation as they facilitate relationships and the sharing of data and knowledge about regional realities and possibilities. More directly, our case studies have shown that such communities facilitate a collective response to shock, as in the coming together of Oklahoma City business leaders, the response of Joint Venture Silicon Valley to slippage in Silicon Valley and now to rising inequality, or the shifts in business and civic leadership in San Antonio. All of these interactions helped position regions to be more resilient—and while some of the resilience may be attributable to more structural factors, surely the collective understandings played some role.

Epistemic communities can also make sure that diversity works for a region rather than against it. Increasing diversity can contribute to economic growth through a variety of processes, including increased ethnic entrepreneurship and better ties to international markets, and there is evidence from both the United States and Europe that greater racial and cultural diversity actually contributes to economic productivity (Bellini et al. 2013; Lee 2011; Sparber 2010). Though there is also some evidence that ethnic diversity can have a negative effect on economic development, through for example reduction in investment, suboptimal provision of public goods, or declines in trust and social capital (Habyarimana et al. 2007; Montalvo and Reynal-Querol 2005), the sort of community-building we have outlined can build interethnic bridges and make it easier for regions to realize the potential economic gains of greater diversity.

Shared processes of knowledge generation and interpretation can also facilitate growth through their impact on regional workforce and economic development systems. Workforce quality depends on formal education and training programs—including community college curricula and public, private, and nonprofit workforce development and training programs—and crucial to their success is coordinating to make sure skills meet clusters (as with Project QUEST in San Antonio). Likewise, individual entrepreneurship is important, but business growth depends on access to capital, local government land-use regulations and zoning provisions, and the presence of multiple supplier companies and providers of specialized inputs ranging from customized software and technical expertise to market research, design, and advertising firms. In short, it takes a village to make a regional economy thrive, and when that economy is shifting, the more the village can work together in both recognizing and then capitalizing on positive new directions of change, the more likely it is that economic performance will be positive and sustained.

Who's In? Who's Out?

While the discussion above emphasizes the potential impacts on growth, we are even more convinced that epistemic communities have the potential for contributing to greater social equity and opportunity. In a region that is more interconnected and relational in its leadership, low-income people, and those living in poor urban neighborhoods or older suburbs, may be more likely to be aware of opportunities in more fortunate parts of the region, or have personal ties with people in better-off economic circumstances. These links may make it easier for low-income people to access better jobs and improve their social mobility over time. Indeed, a wide range of research has documented the importance of such "weak ties" and "bridging social networks" (as distinct from "bonding social networks") in facilitating improved economic outcomes (Beugelsdijk and Smulders 2009; Granovetter 1973, 1995; Johnson, Bienenstock, and Farrell 1999; Saegert, Thompson, and Warren 2001; Wial 1991).

While creating conditions that can improve individual outcomes is important, it doesn't necessarily change broader social patterns of income distribution. Shuffling who's a millionaire and who's a low-wage worker does not necessarily shift the proportion of residents in each category. But the case studies suggest that the existence of diverse epistemic communities might also create conditions in which policies that actually can reshape patterns of economic opportunity might be developed and passed. In public education, this might include efforts to equalize spending in schools, like we saw in the MAPS for Kids program in Oklahoma City, the pre-K effort in San Antonio, and the attempts to equalize educational opportunity in Raleigh. In the arena of housing, it could include the commitment to a housing levy to address affordable housing shortfalls, as we saw in Seattle. The point is that such interactions between groups in the process of knowledge generation and interpretation can impact whether key actors see equitable investments as being in the region's overall interest.

We are not naive. We understand that the interests of those who are on the bottom of the income distribution or racial hierarchy only get addressed when there are strong social movements that can articulate needs and strategize to gain decision-making power. But the workings of an epistemic community hold out the possibility that those demands and strategies to address disadvantage will be a little less contentious, a little more successful, and a little more effective over time.

SCALING EPISTEMIC COMMUNITIES

After it went through its brief stint as a family destination, Las Vegas wanted to signal its return as a place more famous for discreet mis-behavior by adults. The new slogan to highlight the shift was "What happens in Las Vegas stays in Las Vegas." Of course, Sin City was not one of our case studies—although surely there is a particular sort of knowledge being generated there. But we raise it because if diverse and dynamic epistemic communities have their benefits, if they can be identified by key characteristics, and if there are ways to jump-start them into existence—that is, to ensure that what happens in San Antonio or Salt Lake City does *not* stay there—then it would be useful to know how to replicate and scale them.

The More, the Merrier

One strategy for replication of metropolitan innovations in the past has involved connecting different metros for shared learning experiences. This was the logic of the Alliance for Regional Stewardship that we described in chapter 5, a mostly business-led effort that held a series of key conferences and eventually became a programmatic part of the American Chamber of Commerce Executives. It is also part of the intention of the Brookings Metropolitan Policy Program, which has highlighted the experiences of metro business and civic leaders, and sought to articulate a national agenda that would facilitate their work. And creating such connectivity and learning has also been the objective guiding the various Regional Equity conferences, webinars, and networks organized by PolicyLink, one of the premier equity-oriented intermediaries in the country.

Under the Obama administration, the federal government has also gotten into the act. Indeed, one of the more conscious attempts to develop regional diverse epistemic communities—not phrased that way, but it might as well have been—has been the Sustainable Communities Initiative supported by the Department of Housing and Urban Development. The initiative has two components, Regional Planning Grants and Community Challenge Planning Grants. The former are described as follows:

> Sustainable Communities Regional Planning Grants support metropolitan and multijurisdictional planning efforts that integrate housing, land use, economic and workforce development, transportation, and infrastructure investments. The Regional Planning Grant Program places a priority on investing in partnerships that direct long-term regional development and reinvestment, demonstrate a commitment to addressing issues of regional significance, utilize data to set and monitor progress toward performance goals, and engage stakeholders and citizens in meaningful decision-making roles.[1]

As of early 2015, Sustainable Communities Regional Planning grants had been awarded to 74 regional grantees in 44 states, including some of the regions mentioned in the case studies.[2] In 2010—as noted in chapter 4—Salt Lake County was awarded $5 million to continue Envision Utah's work around regional transportation and affordable housing planning; Salt Lake was one of only two regions awarded the maximum grant that year. And as mentioned in chapter 7, the Puget Sound Regional Council was awarded nearly $5 million to support its Growing Transit Communities project, which built a partnership of cities, counties, and public and nonprofit partners with a vision to connect jobs to where people live. The Sustainable Communities Initiative has included the creation of new civic conversations in metropolitan regions, annual conferences with representatives from multiple regions, and a slew of technical-assistance efforts that aim to lift up broad issues of sustainability and equity as well as economic development. This is exactly the sort of community-building we see in our cases, and it is heartening to see federal incentives for replication.

However, part of what such efforts need to do, particularly if they want epistemic communities to be diverse, dynamic, and effective, is to shore up the weak links in any particular area. When we interviewed key informants in our case-study regions, one pattern that jumped out at us was that there was often an easily identified source of economic and maybe environmental data but generally—with the exception of the North Carolina Justice Center—respondents drew a blank (or offered a very fragmented answer) when asked about any "go-to" places for information on equity and opportunity. PolicyLink is seeking to address this gap with a new website (NationalEquityAtlas.org) that includes equity indicators for America's top 150 metropolitan areas; one of the authors of this book has been actively involved in that project, while the other has been involved in the creation of a Regional Opportunity Index that measures neighborhood opportunity *within* the regions of California (interact.regionalchange.ucdavis.edu). Both of these sorts of activities (and others) can help make sure that equity concerns are an initial part of the data being used to organize regional collaboratives.

But it's not just data breadth and depth that are key. Replication of regional epistemic communities will require a better understanding of the key investments in the technical, communicative, and organizing capacities that can make them happen. As we have stressed, there is no guarantee that the widespread development of such knowledge communities will yield stronger growth, improved equity, and enhanced resilience—but it does seem that their absence is associated with decline and stagnation. And surely it is worth a try. In a world in which your economic returns are increasingly generated by association with particular co-workers, where your educational and health trajectory is affected by the neighborhood and region in which you reside, an approach which tries to more consciously capture those externalities seems helpful.

Where in the World?

Of course, replication is always easier said than done, and one of the limits to replication comes in what seems to be a special ingredient of success: place consciousness. In the cases we examined, the particular roots in a region helped forge an identity that worked to bind people to each other and to a common long-term future. Indeed, each place has its own sort of "regional narrative." We were struck by the sense in Salt Lake City that this was a place where one's children deserved the right to live and so long-term investment and good planning were key. We were amazed by how nearly everyone in Raleigh could repeat the Triple Helix mantra, echoing a sort of shared origin story that reverberated with an underlying pride that they had found just what the doctor ordered for sustainable growth. And in San Antonio—a place where the Alamo itself is seen by some as a defense of liberty and by others as an Anglo effort to maintain the rights of slave-owners—there has emerged a sort of common and quiet story of how the divisions of the past have given way to a booming downtown, a vibrant regional economy, and a secure and growing Mexican American middle class.

Fresno stands in unfortunate contrast to this picture. The region is seen as a place from which young people depart to seek a fortune beyond that available to farmworkers, partly because the civic elite has a seeming interest in maintaining poverty. One major political figure indicated that the biggest obstacle to progress is whether people believe that change is even possible. When your regional narrative is about departure, oppression, and hopelessness, it's hard to form a positive sense of place. Greensboro offered up a particularly fragmented sense of place. White leaders we talked to wondered why Black leaders could not look past the past. Actually, it's easy to understand why—when a place is infamous for lunch-counter protests and killings by the Ku Klux Klan, memories might just haunt the landscape. For our purposes, what is most significant is the divisiveness in even the *story* of the region; this bodes poorly for creating a diverse and shared epistemic community.

The importance of the sense of place was also evident where it was slipping. In Silicon Valley, respondents noted that globalization was eroding the commitment to the region that had given rise to organizations like Joint Venture Silicon Valley and the Silicon Valley Leadership Group—and that this allowed for more tolerance of inequality in a place that had once boasted of a large middle class. A similar erosion of "place-sense" seems to be underway in Charlotte, where the newcomers attracted by the booming economy have raised objections to what was once considered a symbol of Charlotte's special place in the New South: the integration of the schools via bussing policies. Meanwhile, the turnaround in Oklahoma City seems to have been driven by a sense of wounded pride. Upset emotionally as well as financially by the fact that United Airlines executives sited a maintenance facility elsewhere, civic leaders took it upon themselves to build a stadium, revitalize the downtown, and turn around the region's image.

Pride of place may seem an accident—but it can be built, and the resulting sense of identity can move people to action. The creation of geographic loyalties is embodied in the very name of Envision Utah or SA2020—people are invited to think of themselves as a part of the landscape, as rooted in the region, like the Great Salt Lake itself, or the river that ambles its way through downtown San Antonio. Critical to such identities seems to be an origin story—the historical narrative, true or not, that becomes a shared belief about why your region is now what it is. The tale of Tom Frost of San Antonio—the banker who reacted to movement organizing by distributing Alinsky's *Rules for Radicals* to other business leaders but then eventually joined the workforce development board the same organizers had willed into being—has the virtue of being true. But for many in the region, it is also an apocryphal story: it says everything you need about the pathway from conflict to cooperation in that city, and it is therefore an origin myth, even if every element of the history is true.

The implication for replication is simply that there is a point to calling on people's pride of place and sense of regional identity. We think that this can be done in productive ways, fostering not excess competition between regions (as in political leaders in Texas seeming to boast every time a business relocates there from California) but the sort of healthy crosstown rivalry that can facilitate positive outcomes for multiple teams (or regions). We're not pushing boosterism for the sake of boosterism—but it's certainly hard to forge coalitions for regional resilience when residents secretly want to live someplace else. Rootedness matters, and it can be encouraged.

The Fork in the Road

A key skill in creating and replicating diverse epistemic communities is striking the sort of balance between conflict and cooperation illustrated by the story of Tom Frost. Our earlier work has been criticized for offering too rosy a picture of regional collaboration across sectors (Lester and Reckhow 2013)—and the critics have a point. The San Antonio case, in particular, illustrates the importance of what Lester and Reckhow call "skirmishes," that is, the fights over policies and priorities that allow issues of equity to take a place in the public square. While we do not cover it here, the way in which issues of fairness have been lifted up in Los Angeles seems to have had a transformative effect on that metro (Meyerson 2013; Pastor and Prichard 2012). Concerns about both equity and growth can become second nature to a particular metro over time—think Seattle—but raising the issues of distributive justice and keeping them raised often requires a fight.

At the same time, an epistemic community needs to help create certain boundaries on these fights such that they create an opportunity to hash out difference rather than drawing the battle lines for permanent trench warfare. Of course, boundaries that are too tight can also become an excuse to avoid issues; to some degree, that's true in Salt Lake, where an aversion to conflict has led Envision Utah to steer clear of some tough and touchy issues, and in Seattle, where the infamous Seattle process can lead to issues' being talked over to the point of exhaustion and inaction. On the other hand, when every issue becomes a fight to the death, it's hard to come back to working together.

Part of what can moderate conflict is a sense that everyone is in it for the long haul. As we have stressed, this requires both vision and a set of repeated interactions that makes it more obvious that the "other," no matter how irritating he or she may be, is not leaving. This is in contrast to the kind of short-term thinking that one finds in Fresno, particularly among developers hoping that their homes will be bought before anyone notices the damage done by the suburban sprawl they facilitate. In any case, what is clear is that when actors are at each other's sides rather than at each other's throats, there are more possibilities to channel conflict into collaboration.

The challenge here is that epistemic communities are path-dependent, though not path-destined. History matters, although not absolutely. The long-standing racial conflicts in Greensboro made it harder to emulate the New South character of Raleigh and Charlotte, while the shared

Mormon history and culture helped civic leaders in Salt Lake City call for envisioning a state in which the children of current residents would also find a place. Such path dependence might simply suggest that success breeds success—but from some of the darkest circumstances a set of common understandings can emerge. Consider the community-business conflicts in San Antonio or the response of Oklahoma City when spurned by United Airlines: path dependence, in short, does not mean stasis, and it is possible to get "shocked" onto a new and more productive path.

The role of such shocks can be critical—and while one might think that the trigger would need to be an acute crisis rather than chronic underperformance, recall how Raleigh's leaders realized that a new set of industrial drivers was needed for the long-term future of the region, how Salt Lake's planners worried that population pressures would further threaten a slowly eroding quality of life, and how civic forces in Seattle are now trying to figure out how to marry a high-tech economic tiger with the imperatives of an egalitarian social ethos. You do not need to wait till your region is on fire to get started with clearing the brush of conflict and old thinking. You do not need to wait till your economy and society are sick to launch a program aimed at widespread health.

In any case, the key point here is that a diverse epistemic community is a competitive, not a natural comparative advantage; that is, it can be built, not just inherited as a factor endowment of the region. Learning more about how leaders build diverse epistemic communities through visioning exercises, leadership programs, and the like; how metro regions can facilitate it through annexation policies, reducing municipal fragmentation, and the like; and how the federal government could encourage it by shifting funds to encourage collaboration, inclusive workforce development, and the like, is a key part of a research and policy agenda for the future.

LESSONS FOR THE NEXT AMERICA

This book has explored the evolution of regional knowledge communities, the linkage between those communities and concrete economic and social outcomes, and the specific ways in which such communities are created and sustained (or eroded) over time. Partly because we are breaking relatively new ground, we have tried to deploy the most thorough and varied techniques possible: an econometric investigation of the link between social distance and sustained growth; a case-study selection process that involved theoretical sampling and quantitative criteria; a systematic approach to identifying interviewees and garnering data from the cases; and an attempt to offer some reflections on the theoretical microfoundations that are consistent with our findings.

While the results are tentative and suggestive, they do offer a platform for further research. We found, for example, that measures like inequality, residential segregation, and jurisdictional fragmentation are associated with shorter spells of employment growth—and we suggest that such measures are probably associated with epistemic distance as well. That sets up one of our core arguments: that building community at a regional level—particularly collaboratives and conversations that incorporate multiple sectors and can adjust to changing times even as they create a sense of place and stewardship—can create the conditions for more favorable outcomes.

We also realized—more along the qualitative-research way than through carefully specified hypotheses—that such regional communities are really collections of institutions rather than any particular and well-defined venue where decisions get made; that they tend to be more about new mechanisms for governance than new forms of government; and that they are rooted in underlying social norms and a deep sense of place, as well as a commitment to repeated interactions. We also learned that the overall direction of epistemic communities can come from planners, business, or civic leaders; that key leaders are frequently made and not just born; and that there may be particularly important lessons for the American future in those places where the new knowledge communities are meeting (or missing) the new knowledge economy.

Just as important, we realized what diverse epistemic communities are not. They are not simply regional collaboratives in which everyone just gets along. Indeed, one of the most important characteristics of effective diverse and dynamic epistemic communities is that skirmishes and conflict do not necessarily shred trust but can be part of building relationships. Finally, such communities are also not static things—while there is an element of path dependence in that success can indeed beget success (and often the confidence to tackle new issues), the most striking finding in the cases was that sometimes external and internal shocks can trigger an epistemic community into being.

Indeed, this is what we mean by *dynamic*: the ability to respond to circumstances and then go on to shape them, to be resilient in the face of economic uncertainty. Such dynamism is necessarily tied to diversity— by which we mean not so much ethnic diversity (although that is a part of the picture) as the ability to bridge multiple sectors, constituencies, and perspectives. For, in contrast to traditional epistemic communities, knowledge networks at the regional level need unlike-minded professionals and others if they are to truly be able to sort out the various tensions between actors that are an inevitable part of regional governance. So while the film *Casablanca* ends with a French detective telling his minions to "round up the usual suspects," dynamic and diverse epistemic communities are about bringing together unusual (and unsuspecting) allies.

All of this, we know, opens up as many questions as it answers (which could provide full employment for an army of grad students). Future research needs to include more case studies, adopt more of the in-depth analysis undertaken by Safford (2009), and develop more direct and indirect econometric evidence. Future theorizing should more formally model how preferences form, identity sticks, and trust develops. And future policy—not so much with regard to growth and equity but with regard to generating knowledge communities—should look at the potential role of formal leadership programs and strategic interventions like the Sustainable Communities Initiative.

But while replication across regions is of interest, perhaps one of the most compelling needs is for the lessons here to make their way to the national stage. The idea of scaling up metropolitan insights and practices, including those involved in building epistemic communities, has gained some ground. This is certainly the strategy of the Brookings Metropolitan Policy Program. The leaders and researchers there insist that metro America is the beating heart of the US economy and that the collaborative arrangements being crafted in regions might point the way for the nation as a whole. This sort of scaling is also reflected in the work of PolicyLink—while it once worked to organize conferences focused on Regional Equity, it now boasts of Equity Conferences (no region!) and promotes a central message, based in part on the sort of work we review in chapter 2, that "equity is the superior growth model."

All this effort to go national with regional wisdom is happening not a moment too soon. For while it would be nice to simply wait for the lessons from America's metros to bubble up to the federal level, we may need to more quickly bottle the magic elixir that leads some regions to find common ground and create the capacity to outperform others on equity and growth—and stir some of that magic into the national discourse. If we don't, we may continue to walk off multiple fiscal cliffs. If we don't, we will never get to an American Compact as rational about immigration policy as the Utah Compact is about immigrant integration. If we don't, we may not develop a long-term strategy to address the underlying issues of social disconnection and unequal life chances that hold back the entire nation from its full economic and social potential.

For this is what the next America demands. The nation is slated to become majority-minority by 2043, with the youth population likely to cross that threshold by the end of this decade. Meanwhile, the drivers of inequality, particularly globalization, technology, and shifting premiums for education, are likely to persist, meaning that this emerging population will face a less promising economic future. In the face of this simmering crisis, the country seems to be reacting to the challenge by fragmenting by political party, economic class, and geographic location. It's a recipe for the nation to become Fresno, not San Antonio; Greensboro, not Raleigh; Detroit, not Salt Lake City; Silicon Valley, not Seattle.

If ever there were a need to form a more coherent national community—to marshal identity to persuade Americans that we are in this together, to develop a shared fact base to make inequality, climate change, and other challenges undisputable, to create a set of repeated interactions in which trust is built, not eroded—that time is now. Our hope is that this book will add to the national conversation in a way that can help America move toward what has always been its promise: the achievement of individual success, to be sure, but also, and most profoundly, a more perfect union.

Regional Rankings for Growth and Equity

This appendix presents some of the basic data for the largest 192 metropolitan areas (based on 2000 population) that were used in the case-study selection process. As noted in the text, each region is defined by its corresponding metropolitan area as defined by the Office of Management and Budget's December 2003 Core Based Statistical Areas. The data used in selection included the change in total jobs and earnings per job, with both coming from the US Bureau of Economic Analysis; the change in the poverty rate and the 80/20 household income ratio; and endpoints in terms of median household income and the Gini coefficient, with all of these last four coming from the Building Resilient Regions database for the base-year (1979) values and the 2010 American Community Survey 1-year summary file for end-year (2010) values. All data has been customized to reflect consistent geographic coverage over time. See appendix B for more information on data sources.

As described in chapter 3, we wanted to recognize broad regional differences across the country, so we benchmarked all of the metros against their respective larger US census-designated region: Northeast, Midwest, South, or West. This involved normalizing each measure into detrended z-scores and calculating separately for each region. We also considered four different time periods and computed the growth index as the mean of the eight growth-related z-scores, and the equity index as the mean of the eight equity-related z-scores.

It's all too much to put in a single table, although we thought there would be interest in the scores and divergences. Thus, this appendix offers the initial level of jobs, earnings per job, poverty, and 80/20 ratio, as well as the endpoints for those measures, plus endpoints for median household income and the Gini coefficient for all 192 regions. We also provide the composite indices, with the caution that these cannot be directly calculated from the data in the table without the intervening data as well as the proper z-score procedures.

TABLE A.1   REGIONAL RANKINGS FOR GROWTH AND EQUITY

Metropolitan region (alphabetically by census region)	1979				2010				Equity index		Growth index		Gini	Median income (2010 dollars) 2010
	80/20 ratio	Poverty	Jobs (000s)	Earnings per job (2010 dollars)	80/20 ratio	Poverty	Jobs (000s)	Earnings per job (2010 dollars)	Value	Rank	Value	Rank		
Northeast														
Albany-Schenectady-Troy, NY	4.09	10%	385	$44,650	4.85	11%	533	$55,513	0.04	94	0.19	70	0.44	$55,796
Allentown-Bethlehem-Easton, PA-NJ	3.89	7%	311	$46,906	4.60	12%	418	$49,623	-0.52	169	-0.21	117	0.43	$55,630
Atlantic City, NJ	4.53	13%	100	$44,653	4.59	14%	175	$48,114	0.67	17	0.27	60	0.43	$52,571
Barnstable Town, MA	4.06	9%	74	$31,321	4.21	11%	138	$39,738	0.52	27	1.12	8	0.47	$55,294
Binghamton, NY	4.03	9%	131	$43,536	4.49	15%	133	$45,859	-0.28	141	-1.17	188	0.43	$45,959
Boston-Cambridge-Quincy, MA-NH	4.40	9%	2,214	$44,185	5.08	10%	3,078	$68,235	0.31	47	0.83	22	0.47	$68,020
Bridgeport-Stamford-Norwalk, CT	4.40	7%	443	$50,342	5.66	9%	598	$81,934	-0.51	167	0.87	19	0.54	$74,831
Buffalo-Niagara Falls, NY	4.47	10%	598	$46,867	4.96	14%	637	$48,829	0.19	64	-0.90	182	0.45	$46,420
Erie, PA	3.93	10%	138	$43,909	5.21	17%	156	$41,779	-1.05	188	-0.99	184	0.45	$42,519
Harrisburg-Carlisle, PA	3.65	8%	258	$44,852	4.04	11%	384	$52,275	0.17	70	0.20	67	0.42	$54,009
Hartford-West Hartford-East Hartford, CT	3.74	8%	615	$47,062	4.65	10%	774	$63,313	-0.37	157	0.16	73	0.45	$63,104
Lancaster, PA	3.54	8%	193	$41,755	4.11	10%	294	$44,502	0.09	84	0.01	87	0.42	$51,740
Manchester-Nashua, NH	3.73	7%	155	$39,710	3.90	7%	248	$56,658	0.82	7	0.88	18	0.41	$68,312
New Haven-Milford, CT	4.09	9%	385	$43,233	5.09	12%	476	$54,745	-0.32	151	-0.12	105	0.47	$57,056

Metro area													
New York-Northern New Jersey-Long Island, NY-NJ-PA	5.16	13%	8,178	$52,246	5.64	14%	10,837	$72,992	0.59	24	0.45	42	0.50	$61,927
Norwich-New London, CT	3.71	8%	123	$45,221	4.19	9%	168	$55,087	0.37	42	0.14	76	0.43	$62,349
Philadelphia-Camden-Wilmington, PA-NJ-DE-MD	4.48	12%	2,532	$48,507	5.14	13%	3,391	$62,206	0.34	45	0.21	64	0.47	$58,095
Pittsburgh, PA	4.33	9%	1,231	$50,865	4.82	12%	1,392	$53,715	0.30	50	−0.64	173	0.47	$46,700
Portland-South Portland-Biddeford, ME	3.53	10%	200	$38,154	4.20	10%	338	$46,381	0.29	54	0.74	26	0.43	$56,530
Poughkeepsie-Newburgh-Middletown, NY	3.97	9%	222	$43,434	4.18	9%	327	$49,388	0.60	23	0.16	74	0.42	$67,269
Providence-New Bedford-Fall River, RI-MA	4.47	10%	700	$38,115	5.43	14%	846	$50,689	−0.28	140	0.02	86	0.46	$51,935
Reading, PA	3.92	8%	164	$43,395	4.51	14%	218	$46,277	−0.60	172	−0.31	131	0.44	$51,759
Rochester, NY	4.06	9%	493	$48,357	4.68	14%	611	$50,234	−0.32	149	−0.61	168	0.45	$50,211
Scranton-Wilkes-Barre, PA	3.74	10%	266	$39,358	4.73	15%	311	$42,509	−0.47	162	−0.62	170	0.45	$42,368
Springfield, MA	4.48	12%	306	$38,767	5.49	16%	364	$45,551	−0.27	139	−0.38	136	0.45	$49,209
Syracuse, NY	4.11	10%	311	$44,861	4.99	14%	372	$49,880	−0.30	148	−0.56	158	0.46	$49,694
Trenton-Ewing, NJ	4.28	9%	180	$47,963	5.19	12%	260	$69,727	−0.32	150	1.01	12	0.47	$70,956
Utica-Rome, NY	3.82	11%	143	$39,734	4.61	15%	159	$44,151	−0.08	113	−0.69	177	0.42	$46,625
Worcester, MA	4.23	9%	311	$39,526	4.98	11%	412	$51,648	0.09	83	0.17	72	0.44	$61,212
York-Hanover, PA	3.67	7%	161	$43,981	3.88	9%	217	$46,839	0.31	49	−0.20	116	0.40	$56,368
Northeast average (unweighted)	4.08	9%	717	$43,849	4.74	12%	942	$52,946	0.00	98	0.00	96	0.45	$55,816

(Continued)

TABLE A.1 (Continued)

Metropolitan region (alphabetically by census region)	1979				2010				Equity index		Growth index		Gini	Median income (2010 dollars) 2010
	80/20 ratio	Poverty	Jobs (000s)	Earnings per job (2010 dollars)	80/20 ratio	Poverty	Jobs (000s)	Earnings per job (2010 dollars)	Value	Rank	Value	Rank		
Midwest														
Akron, OH	4.02	9%	308	$46,471	4.84	15%	396	$47,612	-0.30	144	-0.12	106	0.45	$46,521
Ann Arbor, MI	4.08	11%	166	$53,210	4.84	13%	237	$52,778	0.17	67	-0.03	95	0.46	$55,880
Appleton, WI	3.33	6%	86	$42,353	3.76	8%	145	$44,306	0.24	60	0.58	36	0.39	$55,883
Canton-Massillon, OH	3.87	9%	190	$45,975	4.21	15%	209	$40,745	0.07	89	-1.01	185	0.43	$42,365
Cedar Rapids, IA	3.60	7%	121	$43,446	3.85	9%	171	$48,715	0.73	12	0.37	49	0.41	$53,755
Champaign-Urbana, IL	4.24	12%	109	$39,523	5.52	19%	137	$46,073	-0.81	183	0.06	83	0.49	$45,845
Chicago-Naperville-Joliet, IL-IN-WI	4.34	11%	4,212	$52,787	4.79	14%	5,462	$58,895	0.44	35	0.21	65	0.47	$57,104
Cincinnati-Middletown, OH-KY-IN	4.34	11%	847	$46,155	4.77	14%	1,232	$51,616	0.45	34	0.43	45	0.46	$51,572
Cleveland-Elyria-Mentor, OH	4.31	10%	1,160	$51,405	4.90	15%	1,238	$52,499	0.00	97	-0.53	153	0.46	$46,231
Columbus, OH	3.99	11%	671	$43,659	4.92	16%	1,152	$51,116	-0.22	132	0.94	15	0.46	$51,039
Davenport-Moline-Rock Island, IA-IL	3.86	8%	207	$49,744	4.37	13%	224	$49,578	-0.18	124	-0.59	164	0.45	$46,310
Dayton, OH	4.04	10%	433	$48,050	4.58	16%	461	$48,633	-0.05	108	-0.57	161	0.44	$43,832
Des Moines, IA	3.92	8%	241	$43,506	4.01	10%	400	$52,435	0.92	2	0.93	16	0.42	$54,685
Detroit-Warren-Livonia, MI	4.54	10%	2,046	$59,329	5.11	17%	2,231	$54,120	0.03	95	-0.78	178	0.46	$48,198
Duluth, MN-WI	4.53	9%	137	$44,152	4.85	16%	156	$42,415	0.10	82	-0.57	160	0.44	$42,083
Evansville, IN-KY	4.44	10%	169	$44,059	4.64	14%	205	$47,787	0.63	19	-0.13	107	0.45	$44,319
Flint, MI	4.37	11%	209	$63,735	4.86	21%	183	$40,547	-0.30	146	-2.24	192	0.44	$38,819
Fort Wayne, IN	3.65	8%	198	$45,636	3.87	13%	246	$44,682	-0.06	111	-0.36	135	0.44	$47,004
Grand Rapids-Wyoming, MI	3.97	9%	290	$46,110	4.30	16%	455	$46,737	-0.12	116	0.29	55	0.43	$47,040

Green Bay, WI	3.85	8%	115	$41,551	4.04	11%	201	$48,044	0.70	14	0.95	14	0.41	$49,016
Holland-Grand Haven, MI	3.27	6%	74	$42,440	3.63	12%	129	$43,242	-0.49	164	0.63	35	0.43	$53,056
Indianapolis, IN	3.94	9%	655	$45,951	4.69	15%	1,087	$51,265	-0.29	143	0.76	25	0.46	$48,867
Kalamazoo-Portage, MI	4.13	11%	134	$46,462	4.82	19%	168	$46,230	-0.21	131	-0.39	139	0.46	$43,634
Kansas City, MO-KS	4.15	9%	839	$45,374	4.50	12%	1,251	$52,871	0.46	33	0.64	30	0.44	$53,919
Lansing-East Lansing, MI	3.97	11%	207	$50,249	4.73	17%	259	$46,487	-0.25	136	-0.50	151	0.43	$47,731
Lincoln, NE	3.77	8%	127	$37,634	4.47	15%	207	$43,426	-0.48	163	0.83	21	0.44	$50,091
Madison, WI	3.94	10%	233	$39,920	4.16	12%	425	$48,864	0.68	15	1.30	4	0.43	$57,594
Milwaukee-Waukesha-West Allis, WI	3.96	8%	795	$46,996	4.94	15%	959	$55,010	-0.84	186	0.11	81	0.46	$49,774
Minneapolis-St. Paul-Bloomington, MN-WI	3.87	7%	1,304	$45,951	4.18	11%	2,176	$56,377	0.18	66	1.12	9	0.44	$62,352
Omaha-Council Bluffs, NE-IA	3.81	8%	360	$42,236	4.44	12%	562	$51,231	-0.02	103	0.86	20	0.43	$54,060
Peoria, IL	3.82	8%	194	$51,913	4.31	12%	218	$51,357	0.05	93	-0.53	154	0.43	$50,983
Rockford, IL	3.72	8%	150	$48,579	4.88	18%	179	$44,814	-1.35	190	-0.62	169	0.44	$45,457
Saginaw-Saginaw Township North, MI	4.45	12%	105	$56,740	4.42	17%	101	$43,847	0.73	11	-1.54	190	0.43	$41,938
South Bend-Mishawaka, IN-MI	3.92	10%	136	$42,266	4.69	16%	163	$46,184	-0.36	156	-0.25	122	0.45	$41,991
Springfield, IL	3.92	9%	107	$42,467	4.50	13%	128	$48,931	-0.01	100	0.38	48	0.44	$50,423
Springfield, MO	4.12	13%	131	$34,604	4.49	17%	254	$38,794	0.48	31	1.22	6	0.44	$40,084
St. Louis, MO-IL	4.30	11%	1,296	$45,900	4.86	13%	1,655	$51,372	0.34	44	0.19	69	0.45	$50,912
Toledo, OH	4.40	11%	328	$47,936	4.99	17%	367	$47,565	-0.06	110	-0.61	167	0.46	$41,583
Topeka, KS	3.81	8%	113	$39,782	4.62	17%	139	$43,177	-0.82	185	-0.02	93	0.44	$45,360
Wichita, KS	3.85	9%	278	$43,611	4.48	14%	370	$48,299	-0.11	115	0.20	66	0.44	$46,131
Youngstown-Warren-Boardman, OH-PA	4.17	10%	302	$50,081	4.59	17%	278	$40,463	-0.07	112	-1.57	191	0.44	$39,240
Midwest average (unweighted)	51.04	9%	483	$46,291	52.30	15%	639	$48,028	0.00	97	0.00	93	48.29	$48,358

(Continued)

TABLE A.1 (Continued)

Metropolitan region (alphabetically by census region)	1979				2010				Equity index		Growth index		2010	
	80/20 ratio	Poverty	Jobs (000s)	Earnings per job (2010 dollars)	80/20 ratio	Poverty	Jobs (000s)	Earnings per job (2010 dollars)	Value	Rank	Value	Rank	Gini	Median income (2010 dollars)
South														
Amarillo, TX	4.04	10%	100	$42,224	4.32	16%	153	$43,441	-0.36	155	-0.56	156	0.44	$46,390
Asheville, NC	4.04	14%	135	$34,895	4.35	16%	235	$37,953	0.06	91	-0.31	130	0.44	$42,168
Atlanta-Sandy Springs-Marietta, GA	4.38	13%	1,268	$43,350	4.74	15%	3,049	$52,789	-0.11	114	0.64	32	0.46	$53,182
Augusta-Richmond County, GA-SC	4.40	17%	182	$38,800	5.10	20%	292	$44,584	-0.14	118	-0.26	123	0.46	$44,477
Austin-Round Rock, TX	4.80	15%	308	$38,277	4.70	16%	1,077	$50,429	0.67	16	1.71	1	0.46	$55,744
Baltimore-Towson, MD	4.28	12%	1,139	$44,677	4.57	11%	1,649	$58,497	0.28	56	-0.05	97	0.45	$64,812
Baton Rouge, LA	5.38	17%	268	$45,371	5.19	16%	477	$47,779	0.84	6	-0.32	133	0.46	$48,294
Beaumont-Port Arthur, TX	4.76	12%	176	$52,150	5.33	20%	206	$48,660	-0.42	160	-1.12	187	0.46	$41,291
Birmingham-Hoover, AL	5.06	16%	446	$43,494	5.13	17%	637	$50,120	0.42	37	-0.40	140	0.47	$44,216
Brownsville-Harlingen, TX	4.56	32%	78	$32,135	5.22	36%	172	$32,396	0.15	74	0.03	84	0.49	$31,736
Cape Coral-Fort Myers, FL	3.46	11%	91	$33,597	4.47	17%	286	$39,589	-1.32	189	1.05	11	0.46	$43,936
Charleston-North Charleston, SC	4.38	16%	205	$40,256	4.89	16%	387	$47,419	0.09	85	-0.04	96	0.46	$48,062
Charleston, WV	4.55	13%	155	$48,660	4.45	15%	174	$50,223	0.54	25	-0.95	183	0.44	$43,922
Charlotte-Gastonia-Concord, NC-SC	3.84	11%	504	$39,502	4.72	15%	1,055	$55,705	-0.67	176	0.77	23	0.47	$50,449
Chattanooga, TN-GA	4.20	14%	215	$41,034	4.84	16%	294	$45,184	-0.04	107	-0.57	159	0.46	$42,288
Clarksville, TN-KY	3.84	16%	84	$39,403	4.18	16%	145	$49,931	0.30	51	0.43	46	0.42	$42,262
Columbia, SC	4.26	14%	264	$37,622	4.65	16%	440	$45,476	-0.04	106	-0.06	102	0.45	$45,929

Columbus, GA-AL	4.43	19%	126	$36,700	5.34	20%	174	$45,283	-0.03	104	-0.08	104	0.51	$36,553
Corpus Christi, TX	4.62	17%	162	$45,915	4.94	20%	239	$46,710	0.21	63	-0.66	175	0.46	$41,994
Dallas-Fort Worth-Arlington, TX	4.04	10%	1,712	$45,819	4.52	15%	3,925	$56,117	-0.40	159	0.53	38	0.46	$54,449
Deltona-Daytona Beach-Ormond Beach, FL	3.90	14%	101	$32,267	4.60	16%	198	$37,621	-0.30	147	0.01	88	0.44	$41,556
Durham, NC	4.33	14%	159	$39,926	5.18	19%	362	$60,093	-0.66	175	1.05	10	0.48	$47,982
El Paso, TX	4.04	22%	207	$37,820	4.83	24%	389	$42,426	-0.15	121	0.06	82	0.47	$36,015
Fayetteville-Springdale-Rogers, AR-MO	3.86	14%	97	$31,801	4.62	15%	259	$44,929	-0.20	129	1.32	3	0.45	$45,101
Fayetteville, NC	3.58	17%	127	$39,686	4.36	18%	220	$54,793	-0.19	125	0.74	27	0.44	$43,458
Fort Smith, AR-OK	4.16	16%	95	$36,009	4.38	19%	154	$38,820	0.30	52	-0.41	143	0.45	$37,992
Gainesville, FL	5.10	23%	78	$34,997	6.17	27%	159	$44,248	-0.25	137	0.28	57	0.51	$40,274
Greensboro-High Point, NC	4.08	11%	298	$38,968	4.58	18%	424	$45,360	-0.80	182	-0.41	142	0.46	$41,120
Greenville, SC	3.84	12%	227	$37,523	4.82	16%	363	$45,474	-0.72	180	-0.17	111	0.47	$42,640
Gulfport-Biloxi, MS	4.21	18%	90	$37,127	4.46	19%	145	$44,007	0.51	29	0.03	85	0.43	$41,875
Hagerstown-Martinsburg, MD-WV	4.37	12%	77	$42,884	4.50	12%	122	$42,894	0.29	53	-0.62	171	0.43	$50,529
Hickory-Lenoir-Morganton, NC	3.22	9%	151	$34,123	4.33	16%	187	$38,894	-1.50	192	-0.67	176	0.44	$39,381
Houston-Baytown-Sugar Land, TX	3.96	10%	1,737	$52,739	4.89	17%	3,452	$63,872	-0.82	184	0.28	58	0.47	$53,942
Huntington-Ashland, WV-KY-OH	4.50	15%	130	$47,366	5.00	22%	139	$43,335	-0.20	127	-1.41	189	0.45	$36,022
Huntsville, AL	4.66	14%	127	$44,596	5.16	13%	263	$54,916	0.19	65	0.33	51	0.47	$52,384
Jackson, MS	4.96	20%	216	$37,313	4.95	18%	335	$44,603	0.79	9	-0.17	113	0.47	$42,501
Jacksonville, FL	4.62	15%	371	$41,599	4.57	15%	783	$47,387	0.43	36	0.14	78	0.46	$50,324
Killeen-Temple-Fort Hood, TX	3.71	16%	115	$38,505	3.39	13%	218	$51,181	1.24	1	0.76	24	0.40	$49,778
Kingsport-Bristol-Bristol, TN-VA	4.18	15%	133	$38,715	4.66	17%	154	$41,527	0.15	73	-0.89	181	0.48	$34,741

(Continued)

TABLE A.1 (Continued)

Metropolitan region (alphabetically by census region)	1979				2010				Equity index		Growth index			2010
	80/20 ratio	Poverty	Jobs (000s)	Earnings per job (2010 dollars)	80/20 ratio	Poverty	Jobs (000s)	Earnings per job (2010 dollars)	Value	Rank	Value	Rank	Gini	Median income (2010 dollars)
Knoxville, TN	4.60	15%	247	$39,971	4.55	14%	426	$45,202	0.75	10	-0.22	119	0.46	$43,114
Lafayette, LA	4.75	14%	102	$44,608	5.46	20%	190	$51,900	-0.16	122	-0.01	92	0.46	$46,730
Lakeland, FL	3.91	15%	149	$40,337	4.16	18%	257	$41,290	0.01	96	-0.49	150	0.43	$41,174
Lexington-Fayette, KY	4.56	14%	185	$40,403	5.23	19%	311	$46,296	-0.30	145	-0.27	126	0.46	$46,257
Little Rock-North Little Rock, AR	4.25	13%	260	$40,479	4.59	15%	424	$46,498	0.14	76	-0.18	114	0.45	$45,991
Louisville, KY-IN	4.39	12%	530	$42,965	4.63	15%	739	$48,116	0.07	90	-0.59	163	0.45	$44,678
Lubbock, TX	4.33	15%	119	$38,613	4.91	21%	168	$39,973	-0.33	153	-0.65	174	0.47	$42,126
Lynchburg, VA	3.89	11%	99	$37,502	4.70	16%	134	$39,155	-0.69	177	-0.84	180	0.44	$41,248
Macon, GA	4.66	19%	89	$37,006	5.48	23%	128	$39,360	-0.22	133	-0.60	165	0.47	$37,507
McAllen-Edinburg-Pharr, TX	4.68	35%	94	$31,279	5.52	33%	312	$34,071	0.27	58	0.98	13	0.48	$33,732
Memphis, TN-MS-AR	5.33	21%	512	$41,007	5.06	19%	775	$49,859	0.90	3	-0.05	99	0.46	$45,377
Miami-Fort Lauderdale-Miami Beach, FL	4.62	12%	1,568	$40,268	5.32	17%	3,142	$46,761	-0.51	168	0.14	77	0.50	$45,352
Mobile, AL	4.69	19%	163	$40,382	5.16	20%	227	$44,069	0.31	48	-0.58	162	0.48	$39,998
Montgomery, AL	5.10	20%	142	$38,959	5.27	18%	220	$45,394	0.61	22	-0.25	121	0.45	$45,513
Naples-Marco Island, FL	4.52	14%	44	$35,021	4.29	16%	174	$41,408	0.15	72	1.44	2	0.51	$52,730
Nashville-Davidson-Murfreesboro, TN	4.28	12%	494	$39,031	4.73	15%	994	$54,153	-0.19	126	0.63	33	0.46	$47,975
New Orleans-Metairie-Kenner, LA	5.36	17%	648	$45,882	5.45	17%	714	$52,322	0.61	21	-0.81	179	0.48	$46,134

Ocala, FL	18%	46	$31,014	3.92	20%	130	$34,507	0.34	46	0.51	39	0.44	$37,044
Oklahoma City, OK	11%	488	$42,638	4.32	16%	763	$48,087	-0.36	154	-0.39	138	0.46	$46,238
Orlando, FL	12%	397	$38,343	4.15	15%	1,248	$44,752	-0.15	120	0.91	17	0.45	$46,478
Palm Bay-Melbourne-Titusville, FL	10%	122	$43,119	3.94	13%	262	$46,758	-0.60	173	-0.03	94	0.44	$46,262
Pensacola-Ferry Pass-Brent, FL	17%	129	$42,518	4.20	17%	219	$42,263	0.12	80	-0.51	152	0.45	$43,974
Port St. Lucie-Fort Pierce, FL	16%	63	$37,688	4.02	15%	183	$36,442	0.13	77	0.19	68	0.49	$41,346
Raleigh-Cary, NC	12%	229	$37,070	4.21	13%	654	$51,875	0.26	59	1.20	7	0.44	$57,840
Richmond, VA	12%	481	$41,070	4.07	12%	758	$52,412	0.40	39	0.01	89	0.45	$55,325
Roanoke, VA	11%	142	$37,772	4.14	14%	191	$44,259	0.00	98	-0.43	145	0.44	$45,569
San Antonio, TX	18%	535	$39,442	4.19	16%	1,180	$45,923	0.51	28	0.35	50	0.45	$50,225
Sarasota-Bradenton-Venice, FL	10%	154	$34,189	3.62	14%	368	$37,979	-0.54	170	0.29	54	0.46	$45,283
Savannah, GA	18%	109	$39,598	4.63	17%	199	$44,486	0.40	40	-0.18	115	0.45	$46,755
Shreveport-Bossier City, LA	16%	177	$41,374	5.10	18%	236	$46,497	0.51	30	-0.61	166	0.48	$40,762
Spartanburg, SC	14%	105	$38,112	4.10	17%	142	$48,517	-0.28	142	-0.32	132	0.45	$41,850
Tallahassee, FL	21%	100	$36,099	6.38	26%	212	$44,072	-0.78	181	0.27	59	0.50	$41,511
Tampa-St. Petersburg-Clearwater, FL	12%	679	$38,688	4.62	15%	1,460	$47,132	-0.49	165	0.33	52	0.46	$43,547
Tulsa, OK	11%	373	$44,996	4.44	16%	553	$50,186	-0.02	102	-0.56	157	0.46	$44,519
Virginia Beach-Norfolk-Newport News, VA-NC	14%	647	$40,950	3.98	11%	993	$50,608	0.86	4	-0.05	98	0.42	$57,315
Waco, TX	17%	83	$37,400	4.55	21%	134	$42,043	0.08	87	-0.31	129	0.45	$39,143
Washington-Arlington-Alexandria, DC-VA-MD-WV	8%	2,048	$51,583	4.20	8%	3,837	$73,627	-0.15	119	0.64	31	0.43	$84,523
Wilmington, NC	17%	75	$36,033	5.04	18%	189	$41,702	0.08	88	0.45	43	0.46	$44,825
Winston-Salem, NC	12%	174	$43,068	4.58	16%	263	$47,963	-0.17	123	-0.55	155	0.47	$42,644
South average (unweighted)	15%	320	$39,927	54.90	17%	601	$46,443	0.00	97	-0.01	100	50.70	$45,364

(Continued)

TABLE A.1 (Continued)

Metropolitan region (alphabetically by census region)	1979				2010				Equity index		Growth index			Median income (2010 dollars)
	80/20 ratio	Poverty	Jobs (000s)	Earnings per job (2010 dollars)	80/20 ratio	Poverty	Jobs (000s)	Earnings per job (2010 dollars)	Value	Rank	Value	Rank	Gini	2010
West														
Albuquerque, NM	4.25	14%	248	$40,650	4.83	17%	482	$45,247	0.16	71	-0.01	91	0.46	$47,383
Anchorage, AK	4.07	8%	119	$64,741	4.32	9%	230	$63,042	0.46	32	-0.22	118	0.43	$71,490
Bakersfield, CA	4.40	13%	197	$49,315	5.04	21%	354	$53,837	-0.46	161	-0.15	110	0.45	$45,524
Boise City-Nampa, ID	4.01	11%	150	$39,574	4.32	16%	349	$44,719	0.11	81	0.21	63	0.44	$47,237
Boulder, CO	3.98	10%	110	$39,689	5.24	15%	230	$52,140	-0.59	171	0.40	47	0.49	$61,859
Bremerton-Silverdale, WA	3.76	8%	65	$50,796	3.74	11%	120	$51,279	0.40	38	-0.17	112	0.41	$56,303
Chico, CA	4.21	15%	58	$36,910	4.53	20%	100	$40,577	0.09	86	-0.26	125	0.44	$41,657
Colorado Springs, CO	3.71	10%	164	$38,613	4.75	13%	370	$48,059	-0.33	152	0.63	34	0.44	$51,683
Denver-Aurora, CO	3.87	8%	870	$46,915	4.53	13%	1,637	$58,154	-0.24	134	0.15	75	0.46	$58,732
Eugene-Springfield, OR	4.41	13%	133	$42,653	4.90	19%	184	$39,964	-0.05	109	-1.08	186	0.46	$40,276
Fort Collins-Loveland, CO	4.01	11%	72	$36,637	4.51	14%	189	$40,518	0.13	78	0.47	40	0.44	$54,154
Fresno, CA	4.47	14%	267	$43,701	5.31	27%	426	$46,369	-0.70	178	-0.44	146	0.46	$45,221
Honolulu, HI	4.08	10%	454	$44,738	4.12	9%	603	$52,446	0.72	13	-0.28	127	0.42	$68,537
Las Vegas-Paradise, NV	3.84	9%	252	$46,429	4.24	15%	1,058	$48,311	-0.20	128	1.26	5	0.44	$51,437
Los Angeles-Long Beach-Santa Ana, CA	4.53	12%	5,315	$50,459	5.13	16%	7,311	$58,042	-0.03	105	-0.42	144	0.48	$56,691
Merced, CA	3.78	15%	64	$41,193	5.05	23%	91	$45,658	-0.84	187	-0.40	141	0.49	$42,449
Modesto, CA	4.37	12%	123	$41,079	5.06	20%	209	$47,789	-0.38	158	-0.15	109	0.46	$48,044
Ogden-Clearfield, UT	3.40	8%	121	$41,791	3.58	10%	272	$40,651	0.36	43	-0.06	101	0.39	$59,171
Olympia, WA	4.02	10%	53	$44,092	4.09	10%	128	$48,325	0.80	8	0.18	71	0.40	$61,011

Oxnard-Thousand Oaks-Ventura, CA	3.71	8%	213	$42,914	4.53	11%	419	$52,867	-0.27	138	0.29	53	0.44	$71,864
Phoenix-Mesa-Scottsdale, AZ	3.93	11%	793	$43,683	4.61	16%	2,226	$49,264	-0.21	130	0.66	29	0.45	$50,385
Portland-Vancouver-Beaverton, OR-WA	4.09	9%	719	$46,305	4.32	13%	1,304	$50,695	0.14	75	-0.26	124	0.44	$53,078
Provo-Orem, UT	3.73	15%	84	$36,676	3.87	15%	254	$38,369	0.85	5	0.56	37	0.42	$54,201
Reno-Sparks, NV	3.66	7%	135	$44,762	4.80	16%	247	$48,403	-1.39	191	-0.39	137	0.47	$50,699
Riverside-San Bernardino-Ontario, CA	4.28	11%	597	$42,224	4.55	17%	1,642	$43,866	-0.01	99	0.45	44	0.43	$53,548
Sacramento-Arden-Arcade–	4.31	11%	533	$47,215	4.56	15%	1,147	$56,088	0.27	57	0.24	61	0.44	$56,233
Roseville, CA														
Salem, OR	4.07	11%	118	$38,956	4.14	18%	195	$42,927	0.12	79	-0.36	134	0.42	$45,584
Salinas, CA	3.88	11%	162	$42,890	4.36	17%	222	$52,030	-0.13	117	-0.29	128	0.45	$54,534
Salt Lake City, UT	3.71	9%	351	$42,070	4.03	13%	780	$49,537	-0.01	101	0.28	56	0.43	$57,419
San Diego-Carlsbad-San Marcos, CA	4.17	11%	951	$43,581	4.56	15%	1,822	$56,503	0.17	68	0.46	41	0.46	$59,923
San Francisco-Oakland-Fremont, CA	4.49	10%	1,895	$52,760	5.31	11%	2,691	$70,869	0.17	69	-0.07	103	0.47	$73,027
San Jose-Sunnyvale-Santa Clara, CA	3.64	7%	770	$52,345	4.91	11%	1,137	$89,221	-0.72	179	0.73	28	0.45	$83,944
San Luis Obispo-Paso Robles, CA	4.40	14%	65	$38,773	4.55	14%	149	$43,059	0.66	18	0.21	62	0.46	$53,978
Santa Barbara-Santa Maria-Goleta, CA	4.24	11%	169	$42,782	5.23	18%	248	$50,385	-0.64	174	-0.23	120	0.50	$56,767
Santa Cruz-Watsonville, CA	4.73	12%	82	$36,784	5.02	15%	139	$45,002	0.39	41	-0.06	100	0.46	$61,071
Santa Rosa-Petaluma, CA	4.16	10%	128	$40,079	4.34	13%	263	$46,539	0.24	61	0.12	80	0.44	$59,055
Seattle-Tacoma-Bellevue, WA	4.08	8%	1,123	$51,282	4.30	12%	2,148	$63,107	0.23	62	0.13	79	0.44	$63,088
Spokane, WA	4.46	11%	163	$44,281	4.40	14%	262	$44,383	0.62	20	-0.64	172	0.44	$47,039
Stockton, CA	4.71	13%	163	$45,651	4.31	19%	269	$47,479	0.53	26	-0.45	147	0.44	$50,011
Tucson, AZ	4.31	13%	225	$40,896	4.83	18%	484	$43,250	0.05	92	0.01	90	0.46	$44,274
Vallejo-Fairfield, CA	3.86	9%	95	$50,384	4.06	12%	169	$53,360	0.28	55	-0.14	108	0.41	$63,384
Visalia-Porterville, CA	3.87	16%	118	$39,794	4.79	24%	186	$43,616	-0.50	166	-0.46	148	0.45	$43,397
Yakima, WA	4.21	15%	82	$38,109	4.81	24%	119	$41,775	-0.25	135	-0.48	149	0.47	$40,648
West average (unweighted)	48.97	11%	432	$43,841	50.15	16%	764	$49,947	0.00	95	0.00	95	46.12	$54,791

Data Sources and Methods for Regional Profiles

In this appendix, we include a series of tables that offer a portrait of the demographic and economic characteristics of each region that served as a case study for this book. Unless otherwise noted, the various references to regional data in the text can be found in these tables. We may sometimes make reference in the text to values of the same variables found below summarized by census region, across the largest 192 metropolitan areas (based on 2000 population), or across the nation as a whole. However, to conserve space, those summary tables are not included; they will be made available upon request. In what follows, we describe the data and methodology used to generate these informative tables, and then present the tables themselves.

A wide variety of data sources were drawn from to create the tables; broad and detailed sources are summarized in table B.1. As noted in the text, each region is defined by its corresponding metropolitan area as defined by the Office of Management and Budget's (OMB's) December 2003 Core Based Statistical Area (CBSA) definitions. The one exception is the Raleigh-Durham region, which encompasses both the Raleigh and Durham metropolitan areas (two separate CBSAs).

One key aspect of the data presented here is that it is geographically consistent over time. Given that metropolitan boundaries can shift from one decade to the next (and even in between), data collected for the same metropolitan area in various censuses does not necessarily represent the same geographic coverage. To make the data consistent, much of it (particularly for years prior to 2003) had to be collected at more detailed levels of geography and summarized according to the December 2003 CBSA boundaries.

Fortunately for us, CBSAs are always equivalent to a single county or a grouping of counties, and given that county boundaries are far more stable, much of our data assembly boiled down to the aggregation of county data (if it was not already available at the December 2003 CBSA level, or equivalent).

TABLE B.I BROAD AND DETAILED DATA SOURCES USED TO CREATE
REGIONAL TABLES

Broad source	Detailed source
Building Resilient Regions Database	Described in Pastor, Lester, and Scoggins (2009)
Geolytics, Inc.	1980 Long Form in 2010 Boundaries
	1990 Long Form in 2010 Boundaries
	2000 Long Form in 2010 Boundaries
Integrated Public Use Microdata Series	1980 5% State Sample
	1990 5% Sample
	2000 5% Sample
	2012 5-year American Community Survey
US Department of Housing and Urban Development	State of the Cities Data Systems, Census and American Community Survey Data
US Census Bureau	1980 Census Summary Tape File 1
	1990 Census Summary Tape File 2A
	2000 Census Summary File 1
	2010 Census Summary File 1
	2010 American Community Survey 1-Year Summary File
	2012 American Community Survey 5-year Summary File
	2010 Longitudinal Employer-Household Dynamics, LODES 6
US Bureau of Economic Analysis	Gross Domestic Product by State
	Gross Domestic Product by Metropolitan Area
	Local Area Personal Income Accounts, CA30: regional economic profile
US Bureau of Labor Statistics	Quarterly Census of Employment and Wages
Woods & Poole Economics, Inc.	2011 Complete Economic and Demographic Data Source

However, not all the data we were interested in was available at the county level, so we drew several measures from two unique datasets that deserve further explanation.

The first is the Building Resilient Regions (BRR) database, a project of the Building Resilient Regions Network, funded by the John D. and Catherine T. MacArthur Foundation (Pastor et al. 2012). We were key contributors to the development of this dataset, which was assembled to support the research of the BRR network and others. It consists of hundreds of variables covering 361 metropolitan and 567 micropolitan CBSAs in the United States. In addition to using a uniform December 2003 CBSA geography (as does all the data presented in our tables here), most variables are available separately for combined principal cities and suburbs of each CBSA, based on the aggregation of census tract–level data from various years. The principal city definitions are also based on the OMB's standards, and include the largest city in each CBSA, plus additional cities that meet specific population-size and employment requirements, while the suburbs include the remainder of the CBSA. The data inputs into the BRR dataset are multiple and have been explained elsewhere (see e.g. the description in Pastor, Lester, and Scoggins 2009).

The second dataset deserving of further explanation—which we will refer to simply as the IPUMS-based dataset—was created using microdata samples (i.e. "individual-level" data) from the Integrated Public Use Microdata Series (IPUMS) for four points in time: 1980, 1990, 2000, and a 2012 five-year file, which includes data from 2008 through 2012 pooled together (Ruggles et al. 2010). The 1980 through 2000 files are based on the decennial censuses and cover about 5 percent of the US population each. More recent microdata files are based on the American Community Survey (ACS), however, and only cover about 1 percent of the US population each. Thus, we chose to use the 2012 five-year ACS file to improve statistical reliability (achieving a sample size that is comparable to that available in previous years) and because the central year of the sample is 2010, which is consistent with the last year reported for most other measures in our tables.

Compared with the more commonly used census "summary files," which include a limited set of summary tabulations of population and housing characteristics, the microdata samples provide the flexibility to create more detailed tabulations. To avoid reporting highly unreliable estimates (which, in this data exercise, really only applies to the unemployment rates by race/ethnicity), we do not report any estimates from the IPUMS microdata that are based on a universe of fewer than 100 individual survey respondents.

A key limitation of the IPUMS microdata is geographic detail. Each year of the data has a particular "lowest level" of geography associated with the individuals included, known as the Public Use Microdata Area (PUMA) or County Group in 1980. The major challenge for our purposes was that PUMAs do not neatly align with the boundaries of metropolitan areas. While several PUMAs are often entirely contained within the core of a metropolitan area, there can be a few more peripheral PUMAs straddling the metropolitan area boundary. Moreover, while the same PUMAs were used for both the 2000 and 2008–2011 microdata, the 1980, 1990, and 2012 microdata each have their own distinct PUMA geographies.

To summarize measures at the regional level, we had to first create a set of geographic crosswalks between the PUMAs and each region for each year of microdata, down-weighting appropriately when PUMAs extended beyond the regional boundary. To do this we estimated the share of each PUMA's population that fell inside each region using population data for each year from GeoLytics, at the 2010 census-block-group level of geography (2010 population information was used for the 2008–2012 geographic crosswalks). If the share was at least 50 percent, then the PUMAs were assigned to the region and included when generating our regional summary measures. For most PUMAs assigned to the region, the share was 100 percent. For some PUMAs, however, the share was somewhere between 50 and 100 percent, and this share was used to adjust the survey weights downward for individuals included in such PUMAs when estimating regional summary measures.

For the remainder of the data sources used, geographic aggregation was more straightforward, involving simply the aggregation of data across the counties included in each region. However, many of the variables themselves could use some more explanation around the specific data sources and/or methods used to generate them. Below, we walk through the data sources by variable category (e.g. demography and immigration, regional economy) and provide documentation as necessary on a variable-by-variable basis.

DEMOGRAPHY AND IMMIGRATION

Beginning with demography and immigration, data on regional population and net population growth (and by principal cities/suburbs) is from the BRR database and the US Census Bureau. The BRR database was used to get the population of principal cities and suburbs (adjusted to be consistent with official figures from the decennial census of each year). However, because the latest data point in the BRR database is a 2005–2009 average, data from the 2010 Census (SF1) was used to fill in information for 2010.

The percentage of the population by race/ethnicity, and net population growth attributable to people of color, are based on the decennial census for each year. Racial/ethnic categories are based on individual responses to two questions: one on race and the other on Hispanic or Latino origin. All racial groups (whites, Blacks, Asian and Pacific Islanders, Native Americans, and Others) are non-Hispanic—that is, they include individuals identifying the respective racial groups alone, and who do not identify as Hispanic or Latino (Other includes those identifying with a single other race not listed, or as multiracial). All persons identifying as Hispanic or Latino are treated as a separate racial group. The term *people of color* refers to everyone who does not identify as white, and *net population growth attributable to people of color* is figured as the net change in people of color divided by the net change in the total population over the past decade. Unless otherwise noted, these racial classifications apply to all other data reported in the tables. The percentages foreign (and by citizenship) are from the IPUMS-based dataset.

REGIONAL ECONOMY

Total jobs, average annual earnings per job, GDP per job, and the ratio of GDP per jobs to earnings per job are from the US Bureau of Economic Analysis (BEA). However, because the BEA does not provide county-level GDP information, and their metro area–level estimates only go back to 2001 (not to mention being based on February 2013 CBSAs), we generated our own county-level GDP estimates, which were then aggregated to December 2003 CBSAs. To do this, we relied on the BEA's state-level GDP estimates, which are available all the way back to 1963. We first made slight adjustments to make the series consistent before and after 1997, when the BEA shifted from the Standard Industrial Classification (SIC) to the North American Industry Classification System (NAICS), and then allocated GDP to the counties in each state in proportion to the total earnings of employees in each county. Finally, we adjusted the resulting county-level estimates to be consistent with the BEA's reported metro-area estimates for 2001 and later, and adjusted all estimates prior to 2001 to ensure a smooth transition at the metro level between 2000 and 2001. Unemployment rates (and by race/ethnicity) are from the IPUMS-based dataset.

INCOME AND POVERTY

Information on the poverty rate (both metro-wide and by principal cities/suburbs), the 80/20 household income ratio, and income differentials by race is from the BRR database, with data from the 2010 ACS one-year summary used to fill in values for 2010. Data from the 2011 ACS three-year summary file was also used, but only to fill in poverty data for a handful of smaller principal cities for which no data was reported in the 2010 one-year summary file.

The Gini coefficient and the percentage of households by income level are from the IPUMS-based dataset. Due to its importance to our regional selection process, however, and given the availability of single-year estimates for this measure from the ACS one-year summary file, we use the ACS one-year summary data for 2010 rather than our IPUMS-based estimate (which, as noted above, represents a 2008–2012 average). Our estimates of the Gini coefficient for household income prior to 2010 are based on all households in the microdata samples, following the standard formula with use of trapezoidal integration to estimate the area under the Lorenz curve.

The percentage of households by income level is based on an analysis that seeks to illustrate broad shifts in the household income distribution. For each region, "middle-income" households were defined in 1980 (based on 1979 income) as those in the middle 40 percent of the distribution (with upper- and lower-income households defined implicitly), and the upper and lower income values capturing them were identified. These middle-income boundary values were adjusted for each subsequent year to rise (or fall) by the same percentage as real average household income, and the share falling between the adjusted "middle-income" boundaries was calculated (along with the corresponding upper- and lower-income household shares). Thus, the percentage of middle-income households each year, for example, reflects the share of households enjoying the same relative standard of living as the middle 40 percent of households did in 1979.

SPATIAL SEGREGATION BY RACE AND INCOME

The principal cities–suburbs job distribution data is from the State of the Cities Data Systems (SOCDS), Decennial Census, and American Community Survey Data for 1980 through 2000.[1] The SOCDS data includes employment counts on a place-of-work basis for CBSAs, principal cities, and suburbs (based on the OMB's December 2003 definitions). Because the SOCDS data had not yet been updated with 2010 information at the time of writing, we drew 2010 data from the Longitudinal Employer-Household Dynamics, which uses a variety of data sources to generate estimates of total workers/jobs by census block (among other variables). We matched the block-level data to CBSAs and principal cities using GIS software to summarize the data as needed.

All spatial-segregation measures (spatial segregation by race and income, spatial poverty, and poverty concentration) were generated using data from GeoLytics, with the exception of 2010, for which we used the 2010 Census (SF1) for racial segregation, and the 2012 ACS five-year summary file for all other measures. While the GeoLytics data originates from the decennial censuses of each year, the advantage of the GeoLytics data is that it has been "reshaped" to be expressed on 2010 census-tract boundaries (the same geography used by the 2010 Census and the 2012 ACS), and so the underlying geography for our calculations is consistent over time. The census-tract boundaries of the original decennial census data change with each release, which could potentially cause a change in the value of our spatial segregation measures even if no actual change in residential segregation occurred.

Segregation by race, and the poverty dissimilarity index, are measured using the "dissimilarity index," which is calculated using two racial (or any other sort of) groups and can be construed as indicating the share of one group that would have to move to a new census tract to make the distribution of the two groups across all tracts in the region the same.[2] Our method for measuring income segregation was derived from a 2010 report, *Residential Segregation by Income, 1970–2009* (Bischoff and Reardon 2013). The only difference is that we focused on household income rather than family income so that we could generate measures of income segregation that cover the total population, including unrelated individuals, who are not included in family income measures. We organized census tracts within each region into six income categories, based on the ratio of tract-level median household income to the regional average (with the latter figured as a weighted average of the tract medians). The six income categories are defined as follows. *Poor* includes tracts with median household income of less than 67 percent of the regional average; *low income* means 67–79 percent of the regional average; *low-mid income,* 80–99 percent; *high-mid income,* 100–124 percent; *high income,* 125–149 percent; and *affluent,* income of 150 percent of the regional average or more. Once each tract's income category was determined, population was summed by income category across all tracts in each region to get the distribution shown in the tables.

The calculations for spatial poverty and poverty concentration were somewhat simpler. For spatial poverty, tracts were tagged as *high poverty* or *very high poverty* if the official federal poverty rate was above 20 or 40 percent, respectively. Within each region, the total population and the total number of persons falling below the federal poverty line residing in such tracts were determined, and divided by the respective regional total to get the figures shown in the tables.

EDUCATION AND EMPLOYMENT

The data on educational attainment is from the BRR database, with data from the 2010 ACS one-year summary file used to fill in values for 2010. Also, due to lack of detail on educational attainment in the BRR database in 1980, educational-attainment data for that year is from the IPUMS-based dataset and relies on years of schooling completed rather than degrees earned. For 1980, completing 12, 16, or 18 or more years of schooling was taken to be the equivalent of a high school diploma, bachelor's degree, or graduate or profes-sional degree, respectively, while those with schooling of 13–15 years were as-signed to the *some college* category.

Data on workers by industry is from Woods & Poole Economics. We used this data because, unlike the publicly available Quarterly Census of Employment and Wages, it provides data back to 1980, estimated for NAICS-coded industries. The industry groups shown mostly correspond to single two-digit NAICS codes, with some groupings to simplify the industry categories. The following NAICS codes were grouped together to form a single industry in the tables: agriculture (NAICS 11) and mining (NAICS 21); transportation and warehousing (NAICS 48–49) and utilities (NAICS 22); finance and insurance (NAICS 52) and real estate (NAICS 53); professional services (NAICS 54), management (NAICS 55), and administrative support (NAICS 56); and other services (NAICS 81), arts, entertainment, and recreation (NAICS 71), and ac-commodation and food services (NAICS 72).

INDUSTRY WAGE STRUCTURE

All data appearing in the Industry and Wage Structure portion of each table is based on an analysis of data from the Quarterly Census of Employment and Wages (QCEW), which only reports industry data on a NAICS basis from 1990 forward, with some minor supplementation from Woods & Poole Economics, where there were undisclosed industry data for any particu-lar region/industry. Given differences in methodology between the two data sources, it would not be appropriate to simply plug in corresponding Woods & Poole data directly to fill in the QCEW data for undisclosed industries. Our approach was to first calculate the number of jobs and total wages from undis-closed industries in each region, and then distribute those quantities across the undisclosed industries in proportion to their reported numbers in the Woods & Poole data. This was done after first making some simple adjustments to the Woods & Poole data to better align it with the QCEW, which includes only wage and salary workers rather than all workers.

Despite its only being available on a consistent NAICS basis from 1990 for-ward, the QCEW was chosen for the analysis of industry wage structure be-cause it is the most comprehensive data source for employment and wages by industry, covering 98 percent of all jobs in the United States. The analysis seeks to track shifts in regional industrial job composition and wage growth over time by industry wage level for the private sector. Using 1990 as the base year, we classified broad industries (at the two-digit NAICS level) into low-, middle-, and high-wage categories. An industry's wage category was based on its average an-nual wage, and each of the three categories contained approximately one-third of the nineteen two-digit private NAICS industries for each region.

We applied the 1990 industry wage category classification across all the years in the dataset, so that the industries within each category remained the same over time. This way, we could track the broad trajectory of jobs and wages in low-, middle-, and high-wage industries. This approach was adapted from a method used in a Brookings Institution report, *Building from Strength: Creating Opportunity in Greater Baltimore's Next Economy* (Vey 2012).

TABLE B.2 SELECT DEMOGRAPHIC AND ECONOMIC DATA FOR THE SALT LAKE
CITY REGION

Metropolitan characteristics	1980	1990	2000	2010
DEMOGRAPHY & IMMIGRATION				
Regional population	655,244	768,075	968,858	1,124,197
Principal cities	162,213	159,170	181,105	186,440
Suburbs	493,031	608,905	787,753	937,757
Regional net population growth over previous decade	–	17%	26%	16%
Principal cities	–	–2%	14%	3%
Suburbs	–	24%	29%	19%
Race/ethnicity (%)				
White	92%	90%	81%	75%
Black	1%	1%	1%	1%
Latino	5%	6%	12%	17%
Asian/Pacific Islander	1%	3%	4%	4%
Native American	1%	1%	1%	1%
Other	1%	0%	2%	2%
Net population growth attributable to people of color over previous decade	–	21%	51%	65%
Percentage foreign-born	5%	4%	10%	12%
of which, naturalized US citizen	20%	30%	21%	31%
of which, noncitizen	24%	53%	68%	69%
REGIONAL ECONOMY				
Total jobs	355,757	482,343	700,254	780,243
Job growth over previous decade	–	36%	45%	11%
Jobs-to-population ratio	0.54	0.62	0.72	0.69
Average annual earnings per job (2010 dollars)	$40,700	$38,514	$46,816	$49,537
Growth over previous decade	–	–5%	22%	6%
GDP per job (2010 dollars)	$65,018	$61,822	$74,186	$85,926
Growth over previous decade	–	–5%	20%	16%
Ratio of GDP per job to earnings per job	1.60	1.61	1.58	1.73
Unemployment rate (civilian labor force ages 25–64)	3%	4%	3%	6%
By race/ethnicity				
White	3%	3%	3%	5%
Black	–	–	–	13%
Latino	7%	7%	7%	10%
Asian/Pacific Islander	2%	5%	4%	8%
Native American	–	–	7%	13%
Other	–	–	4%	14%

(Continued)

TABLE B.2 (Continued)

Metropolitan characteristics	1980	1990	2000	2010
INCOME & POVERTY				
Poverty rate (% persons)	9%	10%	8%	13%
Principal cities	14%	16%	15%	22%
Suburbs	7%	8%	6%	11%
80/20 household income ratio	3.71	3.55	3.42	4.03
Gini coefficient (household income)	0.37	0.39	0.41	0.43
Percentage households by income level (middle class analysis)				
Lower income	30%	32%	34%	36%
Middle income	40%	39%	40%	36%
Upper income	30%	29%	26%	28%
Income differentials				
Median Black household income relative to median white household income	63%	60%	71%	64%
Median Latino household income relative to median white household income	83%	75%	74%	64%
Median Asian household income relative to median white household income	82%	85%	88%	92%
SPATIAL SEGREGATION BY RACE & INCOME				
Principal cities–suburbs job distribution				
Percentage of jobs in principal cities	60%	50%	43%	38%
Percentage of jobs in suburbs	40%	50%	57%	62%
Spatial segregation by race				
Black–white dissimilarity index	0.48	0.53	0.47	0.39
Latino–white dissimilarity index	0.31	0.33	0.42	0.43
All people of color–white dissimilarity index	0.29	0.32	0.36	0.37
Spatial segregation by income (percentage population by income level of census tract)				
Poor	13%	13%	16%	18%
Low income	6%	12%	9%	9%
Low-mid income	23%	23%	30%	26%
High-mid income	40%	30%	22%	22%
High income	13%	11%	13%	14%
Affluent	6%	12%	10%	11%
Spatial poverty				
Percentage of CBSA population in high poverty tracts (poverty rate > 20%)	6%	11%	8%	19%
Percentage of CBSA population in very high poverty tracts (poverty Rate > 40%)	0%	0%	0%	1%
Poverty concentration				
Percentage of CBSA poor in high poverty tracts (poverty rate > 20%)	17%	31%	24%	43%

TABLE B.2 (Continued)

Metropolitan characteristics	1980	1990	2000	2010
Percentage of CBSA poor in very high poverty tracts (poverty rate > 40%)	1%	2%	0%	2%
Poverty dissimilarity index	0.25	0.33	0.34	0.34

EDUCATION & EMPLOYMENT

	1980	1990	2000	2010
Educational attainment				
(Population 25 years and older)				
Less than high school	20%	15%	13%	12%
High school only	32%	27%	24%	25%
Some college	27%	35%	35%	35%
Bachelor's degree	15%	16%	18%	19%
Graduate or professional degree	7%	7%	9%	10%
Workers by industry (% distribution)				
(Total employed population 16 years and older)				
Agriculture and mining	2%	1%	1%	1%
Construction	6%	5%	7%	5%
Manufacturing	14%	11%	8%	7%
Transportation, warehousing, and utilities	5%	5%	5%	4%
Wholesale trade	6%	5%	4%	4%
Retail trade	12%	12%	11%	10%
Finance, insurance, and real estate	10%	11%	11%	13%
Professional services	9%	12%	16%	15%
Health services	5%	7%	7%	9%
Information	2%	2%	3%	2%
Education	1%	2%	1%	3%
Other services	10%	13%	13%	13%
Government – civilian	16%	14%	12%	13%
Government – military	1%	1%	0%	1%

INDUSTRY WAGE STRUCTURE

	1980	1990	2000	2010
Share of jobs by industry wage level				
Low-wage	–	35%	36%	36%
Middle-wage	–	42%	42%	42%
High-wage	–	22%	22%	22%
Job growth by industry wage level over previous decade				
Low-wage	–	–	54%	5%
Middle-wage	–	–	52%	5%
High-wage	–	–	49%	6%
Earnings growth by industry wage level over previous decade				
(Growth in real earnings per worker)				
Low-wage	–	−1%	20%	7%
Middle-wage	–	16%	16%	7%
High-wage	–	−1%	16%	6%

(Continued)

TABLE B.2 (Continued)

Metropolitan characteristics	1980	1990	2000	2010
		INDUSTRY WAGE STRUCTURE		
Average earnings per job by industry wage level	–			
Low-wage		$20,398	$24,442	$26,150
Middle-wage		$38,696	$44,853	$48,060
High-wage		$49,761	$57,743	$61,291
Total jobs by industry wage level				
		Low-Wage		
Agriculture, forestry, fishing, and hunting	–	307	395	367
Retail trade	–	46,080	64,517	66,336
Administrative and support and waste management and remediation services	–	18,683	42,854	41,770
Arts, entertainment, and recreation	–	5,767	8,404	9,657
Accommodation and food services	–	29,023	40,926	45,779
Other services (except public administration)	–	11,461	14,596	16,026
All low-wage		*111,321*	*171,692*	*179,935*
		Middle-Wage		
Construction	–	15,681	36,701	31,651
Manufacturing	–	51,261	56,735	51,592
Information	–	9,409	21,018	15,502
Finance and insurance	–	19,008	33,828	37,099
Real estate and rental and leasing	–	6,223	8,740	10,018
Education services	–	4,253	5,225	9,606
Health care and social assistance	–	27,212	39,865	56,335
All middle-wage		*133,047*	*202,112*	*211,803*
		High-Wage		
Mining	–	2,802	2,402	2,774
Utilities	–	2,688	2,270	1,738
Wholesale trade	–	21,413	27,383	28,440
Transportation and warehousing	–	18,350	26,226	24,820
Professional, scientific, and technical services	–	18,113	30,586	38,127
Management of companies and enterprises	–	6,642	15,103	13,966
All high-wage		*70,008*	*103,970*	*109,865*

NOTE: (1) Data on the 80/20 household income ratio, the Gini coefficient, and percentage households by income level for 1980–2000 are based on surveys during those years but actually reflect incomes during the year prior to the survey. Poverty-related measures rely on income from the year prior to the survey as well, but incorporate information on family composition during the survey year. (2) Certain measures reported in the 2010 column actually reflect averages across annual surveys covering 2008–2012. These include data on percentage foreign-born (and citizenship), unemployment rate (and by race/ethnicity), percentage households by income level, and all measures of segregation, spatial poverty, and poverty concentration. (3) Data on educational attainment for 1980 is estimated based on years of schooling; for other years it is based on degrees earned.

TABLE B.3 SELECT DEMOGRAPHIC AND ECONOMIC DATA FOR THE SACRAMENTO
REGION

Metropolitan characteristics	1980	1990	2000	2010
DEMOGRAPHY & IMMIGRATION				
Regional population	1,099,814	1,481,102	1,796,857	2,149,127
Principal cities	474,754	626,744	731,854	869,909
Suburbs	625,060	854,358	1,065,003	1,279,218
Regional net population growth over previous decade	–	35%	21%	20%
Principal cities	–	32%	17%	19%
Suburbs	–	37%	25%	20%
Race/ethnicity (%)				
White	79%	73%	64%	56%
Black	5%	7%	7%	7%
Latino	10%	12%	15%	20%
Asian/Pacific Islander	4%	7%	9%	12%
Native American	1%	1%	1%	1%
Other	1%	0%	4%	4%
Net population growth attributable to people of color over previous decade	–	44%	81%	85%
Percentage foreign-born	7%	10%	14%	17%
Of which, naturalized US citizen	13%	14%	15%	22%
Of which, non-citizen	16%	24%	48%	48%
REGIONAL ECONOMY				
Total jobs	544,041	837,598	1,053,509	1,146,949
Job growth over previous decade	–	54%	26%	9%
Jobs-to-population ratio	0.49	0.55	0.58	0.53
Average annual earnings per job (2010 dollars)	$44,437	$45,800	$52,197	$56,088
Growth over previous decade	–	3%	14%	7%
GDP per job (2010 dollars)	$59,398	$65,044	$70,002	$79,398
Growth over previous decade	–	10%	8%	13%
Ratio of GDP per job to earnings per job	1.34	1.42	1.34	1.42
Unemployment rate (civilian labor force ages 25–64)	7%	5%	5%	10%
By race/ethnicity				
White	6%	4%	4%	9%
Black	10%	8%	9%	17%
Latino	13%	8%	8%	12%
Asian/Pacific Islander	7%	6%	5%	9%
Native American	12%	11%	9%	10%
Other	–	–	6%	13%

(Continued)

TABLE B.3 (Continued)

Metropolitan characteristics	1980	1990	2000	2010
INCOME & POVERTY				
Poverty rate (% persons)	11%	12%	13%	15%
Principal cities	13%	14%	16%	18%
Suburbs	10%	11%	11%	13%
80/20 household income ratio	4.31	3.92	4.07	4.56
Gini coefficient (household income)	0.39	0.40	0.44	0.44
Percentage households by income level (middle class analysis)				
Lower income	30%	30%	33%	34%
Middle income	40%	42%	41%	38%
Upper income	30%	28%	26%	27%
Income differentials				
Median Black household income relative to median white household income	67%	69%	68%	63%
Median Latino household income relative to median white household income	75%	80%	75%	73%
Median Asian household income relative to median white household income	107%	86%	88%	105%
SPATIAL SEGREGATION BY RACE & INCOME				
Principal cities–suburbs job distribution				
Percentage of jobs in principal cities	48%	57%	56%	59%
Percentage of jobs in suburbs	52%	43%	44%	41%
Spatial segregation by race				
Black–white dissimilarity index	0.58	0.57	0.58	0.57
Latino–white dissimilarity index	0.37	0.38	0.41	0.39
All people of color–white dissimilarity index	0.38	0.40	0.40	0.40
Spatial segregation by income (percentage population by income level of census tract)				
Poor	12%	15%	19%	22%
Low income	9%	13%	15%	14%
Low-mid income	28%	21%	21%	18%
High-mid income	31%	26%	22%	20%
High income	15%	16%	14%	15%
Affluent	5%	8%	9%	12%

TABLE B.3 (Continued)

Metropolitan characteristics	1980	1990	2000	2010
Spatial poverty				
Percentage of CBSA population in high poverty tracts (poverty rate > 20%)	12%	16%	21%	26%
Percentage of CBSA population in very high poverty tracts (poverty rate > 40%)	0%	2%	2%	3%
Poverty concentration				
Percentage of CBSA poor in high poverty tracts (poverty rate > 20%)	27%	40%	49%	52%
Percentage of CBSA poor in very high poverty tracts (poverty rate > 40%)	1%	7%	5%	9%
Poverty dissimilarity index	0.25	0.33	0.37	0.34

EDUCATION & EMPLOYMENT

	1980	1990	2000	2010
Educational attainment				
(Population 25 years and older)				
Less than high school	22%	17%	15%	13%
High school only	30%	24%	22%	21%
Some college	28%	35%	36%	36%
Bachelor's degree	13%	16%	18%	19%
Graduate or professional degree	7%	8%	9%	10%
Workers by industry (% distribution)				
(Total employed population 16 years and older)				
Agriculture and mining	3%	2%	2%	1%
Construction	5%	7%	7%	5%
Manufacturing	5%	5%	5%	3%
Transportation, warehousing, and utilities	3%	3%	3%	3%
Wholesale trade	3%	3%	3%	2%
Retail trade	12%	11%	11%	10%
Finance, insurance, and real estate	10%	9%	9%	10%
Professional services	10%	12%	14%	15%
Health services	6%	7%	8%	11%
Information	2%	2%	2%	1%
Education	1%	1%	1%	2%
Other services	11%	13%	14%	15%
Government – civilian	27%	24%	21%	22%
Government – military	2%	1%	0%	0%

(*Continued*)

TABLE B.3 (Continued)

Metropolitan characteristics	1980	1990	2000	2010
	INDUSTRY WAGE STRUCTURE			
Share of jobs by industry wage level				
Low-wage	–	25%	28%	30%
Middle-wage	–	46%	45%	47%
High-wage	–	29%	27%	23%
Job growth by industry wage level over previous decade				
Low-wage	–	–	48%	8%
Middle-wage	–	–	25%	5%
High-wage	–	–	22%	–14%
Earnings growth by industry wage level over previous decade				
(Growth in real earnings per worker)				
Low-wage	–	9%	10%	6%
Middle-wage	–	–10%	14%	10%
High-wage	–	1%	27%	10%
Average earnings per job by industry wage level	–			
Low-wage		$21,305	$23,522	$24,944
Middle-wage		$38,027	$43,323	$47,592
High-wage		$48,155	$61,125	$67,003
Total jobs by industry wage level				
	Low-Wage			
Agriculture, forestry, fishing, and hunting	–	6,966	8,561	8,152
Administrative and support and waste management and remediation services	–	22,709	50,907	40,853
Education services	–	5,359	7,595	11,516
Arts, entertainment, and recreation	–	9,661	11,781	13,195
Accommodation and food services	–	46,158	59,516	66,766
Other services (except public administration)	–	22,549	29,455	40,807
All low-wage		113,402	167,815	181,289
	Middle-Wage			
Wholesale trade	–	24,951	26,423	26,314
Retail trade	–	80,799	89,530	87,571
Transportation and warehousing	–	13,684	21,104	19,095
Finance and insurance	–	30,666	38,375	36,376
Real estate and rental and leasing	–	11,851	13,622	12,187

TABLE B.3 (Continued)

Metropolitan characteristics	1980	1990	2000	2010
Management of companies and enterprises	–	1,387	15,001	11,654
Health care and social assistance	–	50,197	62,036	87,175
All middle-wage		*213,535*	*266,091*	*280,372*
High-Wage				
Mining	–	659	540	378
Utilities	–	2,118	1,803	2,495
Construction	–	43,779	52,221	38,344
Manufacturing	–	45,078	50,836	32,535
Information	–	15,956	18,814	15,128
Professional, scientific, and technical services	–	26,721	38,985	51,722
All high-wage		*134,311*	*163,199*	*140,602*

NOTE: (1) Data on the 80/20 household income ratio, the Gini coefficient, and percentage households by income level for 1980–2000 are based on surveys during those years but actually reflect incomes during the year prior to the survey. Poverty-related measures rely on income from the year prior to the survey as well, but incorporate information on family composition during the survey year. (2) Certain measures reported in the 2010 column actually reflect averages across annual surveys covering 2008–2012. These include data on percentage foreign-born (and citizenship), unemployment rate (and by race/ethnicity), percentage households by income level, and all measures of segregation, spatial poverty, and poverty concentration. (3) Data on educational attainment for 1980 is estimated based on years of schooling; for other years it is based on degrees earned.

TABLE B.4   SELECT DEMOGRAPHIC AND ECONOMIC DATA FOR THE GRAND
RAPIDS REGION

Metropolitan characteristics	1980	1990	2000	2010
DEMOGRAPHY & IMMIGRATION				
Regional population	577,019	645,914	740,482	774,160
Principal cities	240,731	252,401	267,733	260,165
Suburbs	336,288	393,513	472,749	513,995
Regional net population growth over previous decade	–	12%	15%	5%
Principal cities	–	5%	6%	-3%
Suburbs	–	17%	20%	9%
Race/ethnicity (%)				
White	91%	89%	83%	79%
Black	6%	7%	7%	8%
Latino	2%	3%	6%	8%
Asian/Pacific Islander	0%	1%	2%	2%
Native American	0%	0%	0%	0%
Other	0%	0%	2%	2%
Net population growth attributable to people of color over previous decade	–	28%	58%	103%
Percentage foreign-born	4%	3%	6%	7%
Of which, naturalized US citizen	25%	41%	37%	57%
Of which, non-citizen	31%	72%	119%	125%
REGIONAL ECONOMY				
Total jobs	285,097	381,137	479,152	455,445
Job growth over previous decade	–	34%	26%	-5%
Jobs-to-population ratio	0.49	0.59	0.65	0.59
Average annual earnings per job (2010 dollars)	$43,545	$42,825	$48,331	$46,737
Growth over previous decade	–	-2%	13%	-3%
GDP per job (2010 dollars)	$61,817	$63,734	$72,159	$69,489
Growth over previous decade	–	3%	13%	-4%
Ratio of GDP per job to earnings per job	1.42	1.49	1.49	1.49
Unemployment rate (civilian labor force ages 25–64)	5%	5%	4%	9%
By race/ethnicity				
White	4%	4%	3%	8%
Black	12%	13%	7%	17%
Latino	11%	12%	8%	11%
Asian/Pacific Islander	–	–	10%	8%
Native American	–	–	–	–
Other	–	–	10%	11%

TABLE B.4 (Continued)

Metropolitan characteristics	1980	1990	2000	2010
INCOME & POVERTY				
Poverty rate (% persons)	9%	10%	9%	16%
Principal cities	12%	14%	13%	27%
Suburbs	7%	7%	6%	11%
80/20 household income ratio	3.97	3.61	3.61	4.30
Gini coefficient (household income)	0.37	0.39	0.41	0.43
Percentage households by income level (middle class analysis)				
Lower income	30%	30%	33%	36%
Middle income	40%	41%	40%	36%
Upper income	30%	29%	27%	28%
Income differentials				
Median Black household income relative to median white household income	60%	57%	60%	48%
Median Latino household income relative to median white household income	77%	81%	78%	66%
Median Asian household income relative to median white household income	88%	109%	108%	83%
SPATIAL SEGREGATION BY RACE & INCOME				
Principal cities–suburbs job distribution				
Percentage of jobs in principal cities	59%	53%	44%	41%
Percentage of jobs in suburbs	41%	47%	56%	59%
Spatial segregation by race				
Black–white dissimilarity index	0.75	0.74	0.67	0.64
Latino–white dissimilarity index	0.42	0.45	0.54	0.50
All people of color–white dissimilarity index	0.58	0.57	0.53	0.49
Spatial segregation by income *(percentage population by income level of census tract)*				
Poor	10%	11%	9%	16%
Low income	9%	11%	15%	13%
Low-mid income	33%	32%	36%	29%
High-mid income	29%	29%	23%	22%
High income	14%	11%	11%	11%
Affluent	4%	6%	7%	10%
Spatial poverty				
Percentage of CBSA population in high poverty tracts (poverty rate > 20%)	8%	12%	9%	29%
Percentage of CBSA population in very high poverty tracts (poverty rate > 40%)	1%	1%	1%	5%

(Continued)

TABLE B.4 (Continued)

Metropolitan characteristics	1980	1990	2000	2010
Poverty concentration				
Percentage of CBSA poor in high poverty tracts (poverty rate > 20%)	26%	38%	28%	56%
Percentage of CBSA poor in very high poverty tracts (poverty rate > 40%)	4%	6%	4%	15%
Poverty dissimilarity index	0.31	0.36	0.33	0.34
EDUCATION & EMPLOYMENT				
Educational attainment				
(Population 25 years and older)				
Less than high school	29%	21%	16%	11%
High school only	34%	33%	31%	31%
Some college	21%	28%	31%	32%
Bachelor's degree	12%	12%	15%	18%
Graduate or professional degree	4%	6%	7%	9%
Workers by industry (% distribution)				
(Total employed population 16 years and older)				
Agriculture and mining	3%	2%	2%	2%
Construction	5%	5%	6%	4%
Manufacturing	26%	21%	20%	13%
Transportation, warehousing, and utilities	3%	2%	3%	3%
Wholesale trade	4%	6%	5%	5%
Retail trade	13%	14%	12%	10%
Finance, insurance, and real estate	7%	7%	7%	8%
Professional services	8%	10%	14%	15%
Health services	7%	8%	9%	14%
Information	2%	2%	1%	1%
Education	1%	1%	1%	3%
Other services	10%	12%	12%	14%
Government – civilian	11%	8%	8%	8%
Government – military	0%	1%	0%	0%
INDUSTRY WAGE STRUCTURE				
Share of jobs by industry wage level				
Low-wage	–	33%	34%	37%
Middle-wage	–	32%	31%	36%
High-wage	–	36%	35%	28%
Job growth by industry wage level over previous decade				
Low-wage	–	–	36%	–5%
Middle-wage	–	–	26%	2%
High-wage	–	–	26%	–29%

TABLE B.4 (Continued)

Metropolitan characteristics	1980	1990	2000	2010
Earnings growth by industry wage level over previous decade				
(Growth in real earnings per worker)				
Low-wage	–	–3%	13%	–2%
Middle-wage	–	11%	16%	–3%
High-wage	–	–2%	3%	–2%
INDUSTRY WAGE STRUCTURE				
Average earnings per job by industry wage level	–			
Low-wage		$20,657	$23,392	$22,889
Middle-wage		$41,408	$48,198	$46,937
High-wage		$52,605	$54,331	$53,481
Total jobs by industry wage level				
Low-Wage				
Agriculture, forestry, fishing, and hunting	–	2,079	3,237	3,184
Retail trade	–	43,187	46,765	36,272
Administrative and support and waste management and remediation services	–	9,533	28,870	32,611
Arts, entertainment, and recreation	–	2,808	4,335	4,006
Accommodation and food services	–	22,528	25,680	26,953
Other services (except public administration)	–	8,912	11,908	11,496
All low-wage		*89,047*	*120,795*	*114,522*
Middle-Wage				
Construction	–	13,865	18,564	12,497
Wholesale trade	–	20,637	22,574	18,773
Information	–	6,172	5,714	4,216
Finance and insurance	–	11,629	17,163	14,086
Real estate and rental and leasing	–	2,893	3,822	3,725
Education services	–	3,944	5,847	9,071
Health care and social assistance	–	27,941	36,189	49,193
All middle-wage		*87,081*	*109,873*	*111,561*
High-Wage				
Mining	–	153	154	141
Utilities	–	1,078	1,138	721
Manufacturing	–	77,368	91,636	58,261
Transportation and warehousing	–	5,550	8,558	7,986

(Continued)

TABLE B.4 (Continued)

Metropolitan characteristics	1980	1990	2000	2010
Professional, scientific, and technical services	–	9,510	14,531	14,820
Management of companies and enterprises	–	3,927	7,090	4,956
All high-wage		97,586	123,107	86,885

NOTE: (1) Data on the 80/20 household income ratio, the Gini coefficient, and percentage households by income level for 1980–2000 are based on surveys during those years but actually reflect incomes during the year prior to the survey. Poverty-related measures rely on income from the year prior to the survey as well, but incorporate information on family composition during the survey year. (2) Certain measures reported in the 2010 column actually reflect averages across annual surveys covering 2008–2012. These include data on percentage foreign-born (and citizenship), unemployment rate (and by race/ethnicity), percentage households by income level, and all measures of segregation, spatial poverty, and poverty concentration. (3) Data on educational attainment for 1980 is estimated based on years of schooling; for other years it is based on degrees earned.

TABLE B.5   SELECT DEMOGRAPHIC AND ECONOMIC DATA FOR THE
CHARLOTTE REGION

Metropolitan characteristics	1980	1990	2000	2010
DEMOGRAPHY & IMMIGRATION				
Regional population	855,482	1,024,643	1,330,448	1,758,038
Principal cities	485,668	577,781	722,390	948,385
Suburbs	369,814	446,862	608,058	809,653
Regional net population growth over previous decade	–	20%	30%	32%
Principal cities	–	19%	25%	31%
Suburbs	–	21%	36%	33%
Race/ethnicity (%)				
White	77%	76%	69%	61%
Black	22%	21%	22%	24%
Latino	1%	1%	5%	10%
Asian/Pacific Islander	0%	1%	2%	3%
Native American	0%	0%	0%	0%
Other	0%	0%	1%	2%
Net population growth attributable to people of color over previous decade	–	26%	54%	64%
Percentage foreign-born	2%	2%	7%	10%
Of which, naturalized US citizen	51%	52%	30%	37%
Of which, non-citizen	61%	92%	97%	80%
REGIONAL ECONOMY				
Total jobs	508,619	696,311	930,490	1,055,446
Job growth over previous decade	–	37%	34%	13%
Jobs-to-population ratio	0.59	0.68	0.69	0.60
Average annual earnings per job (2010 dollars)	$38,059	$44,442	$54,211	$55,705
Growth over previous decade	–	17%	22%	3%
GDP per job (2010 dollars)	$61,551	$75,178	$92,119	$104,466
Growth over previous decade	–	22%	23%	13%
Ratio of GDP per job to earnings per job	1.62	1.69	1.70	1.88
Unemployment rate (civilian labor force ages 25–64)	3%	3%	3%	9%
By race/ethnicity				
White	2%	2%	2%	7%
Black	5%	6%	6%	13%
Latino	2%	4%	6%	9%
Asian/Pacific Islander	–	3%	2%	7%
Native American	–	–	10%	8%
Other	–	–	3%	10%

(*Continued*)

TABLE B.5 (Continued)

Metropolitan characteristics	1980	1990	2000	2010
INCOME & POVERTY				
Poverty rate (% persons)	11%	10%	9%	15%
Principal cities	12%	11%	11%	18%
Suburbs	9%	8%	7%	11%
80/20 household income ratio	3.84	3.85	3.78	4.72
Gini coefficient (household income)	0.38	0.41	0.44	0.47
Percentage households by income level (middle class analysis)				
Lower income	30%	32%	35%	39%
Middle income	40%	39%	40%	35%
Upper income	30%	29%	25%	26%
Income differentials				
Median Black household income relative to median white household income	61%	59%	64%	61%
Median Latino household income relative to median white household income	68%	83%	73%	68%
Median Asian household income relative to median white household income	152%	101%	103%	85%
SPATIAL SEGREGATION BY RACE & INCOME				
Principal cities–suburbs job distribution				
Percentage of jobs in principal cities	64%	69%	69%	65%
Percentage of jobs in suburbs	36%	31%	31%	35%
Spatial segregation by race				
Black–white dissimilarity index	0.58	0.58	0.56	0.54
Latino–white dissimilarity index	0.29	0.43	0.52	0.48
All people of color–white dissimilarity index	0.55	0.54	0.51	0.47
Spatial segregation by income (percentage population by income level of census tract)				
Poor	11%	16%	18%	25%
Low income	12%	17%	17%	12%
Low-mid income	32%	27%	25%	21%
High-mid income	30%	19%	18%	17%
High income	8%	10%	12%	13%
Affluent	8%	11%	10%	12%

TABLE B.5 (Continued)

Metropolitan characteristics	1980	1990	2000	2010
Spatial poverty				
Percentage of CBSA population in high poverty tracts (poverty rate > 20%)	10%	12%	10%	23%
Percentage of CBSA population in very high poverty tracts (poverty rate > 40%)	2%	3%	1%	3%
Poverty concentration				
Percentage of CBSA poor in high poverty tracts (poverty rate > 20%)	28%	35%	27%	50%
Percentage of CBSA poor in very high poverty tracts (poverty rate > 40%)	10%	12%	3%	10%
Poverty dissimilarity index	0.30	0.36	0.34	0.35
EDUCATION & EMPLOYMENT				
Educational attainment				
(Population 25 years and older)				
Less than high school	40%	27%	19%	14%
High school only	25%	26%	25%	24%
Some college	19%	27%	29%	30%
Bachelor's degree	13%	15%	20%	22%
Graduate or professional degree	3%	5%	8%	10%
Workers by industry (% distribution)				
(Total employed population 16 years and older)				
Agriculture and mining	2%	1%	1%	1%
Construction	6%	7%	7%	5%
Manufacturing	25%	19%	12%	7%
Transportation, warehousing, and utilities	6%	6%	5%	4%
Wholesale trade	7%	7%	6%	5%
Retail trade	10%	11%	11%	10%
Finance, insurance, and real estate	7%	8%	10%	11%
Professional services	10%	12%	15%	18%
Health services	3%	4%	6%	8%
Information	3%	3%	3%	2%
Education	1%	1%	1%	2%
Other services	10%	12%	13%	15%
Government – civilian	10%	9%	10%	11%
Government – military	1%	1%	0%	0%

(Continued)

TABLE B.5 (Continued)

Metropolitan characteristics	1980	1990	2000	2010
INDUSTRY WAGE STRUCTURE				
Share of jobs by industry wage level				
Low-wage	–	30%	34%	37%
Middle-wage	–	45%	38%	33%
High-wage	–	25%	28%	29%
Job growth by industry wage level over previous decade				
Low-wage	–	–	48%	10%
Middle-wage	–	–	11%	–12%
High-wage	–	–	47%	7%
Earnings growth by industry wage level over previous decade				
(Growth in real earnings per worker)				
Low-wage	–	–2%	15%	–1%
Middle-wage	–	–10%	22%	–4%
High-wage	–	–10%	29%	12%
INDUSTRY WAGE STRUCTURE				
Average earnings per job by industry wage level	–			
Low-wage		$23,139	$26,564	$26,380
Middle-wage		$39,878	$48,470	$46,599
High-wage		$54,675	$70,803	$79,650
Total jobs by industry wage level				
Low-Wage				
Agriculture, forestry, fishing, and hunting	–	1,285	1,833	2,330
Retail trade	–	67,464	84,006	89,826
Administrative and support and waste management and remediation services	–	26,120	57,117	60,075
Arts, entertainment, and recreation	–	7,526	11,739	13,084
Accommodation and food services	–	36,289	54,102	68,267
Other services (except public administration)	–	16,225	20,368	19,276
All low-wage		*154,909*	*229,165*	*252,858*
Middle-Wage				
Mining	–	510	543	367
Construction	–	34,361	49,683	37,273
Manufacturing	–	133,486	111,761	66,018
Transportation and warehousing	–	20,901	31,484	27,729

TABLE B.5 (Continued)

Metropolitan characteristics	1980	1990	2000	2010
Real estate and rental and leasing	–	8,182	12,017	11,815
Education services	–	3,830	5,377	11,613
Health care and social assistance	–	29,419	44,357	69,405
All middle-wage		*230,689*	*255,222*	*224,220*
High-Wage				
Utilities	–	9,484	4,662	3,865
Wholesale trade	–	37,895	51,223	43,901
Information	–	16,571	25,104	21,187
Finance and insurance	–	29,610	39,242	56,736
Professional, scientific, and technical services	–	25,413	36,901	49,366
Management of companies and enterprises	–	8,193	29,570	24,571
All high-wage		*127,166*	*186,702*	*199,626*

NOTE: (1) Data on the 80/20 household income ratio, the Gini coefficient, and percentage households by income level for 1980–2000 are based on surveys during those years but actually reflect incomes during the year prior to the survey. Poverty-related measures rely on income from the year prior to the survey as well, but incorporate information on family composition during the survey year. (2) Certain measures reported in the 2010 column actually reflect averages across annual surveys covering 2008–2012. These include data on percentage foreign-born (and citizenship), unemployment rate (and by race/ethnicity), percentage households by income level, and all measures of segregation, spatial poverty, and poverty concentration. (3) Data on educational attainment for 1980 is estimated based on years of schooling; for other years it is based on degrees earned.

TABLE B.6 SELECT DEMOGRAPHIC AND ECONOMIC DATA FOR THE OKLAHOMA
CITY REGION

Metropolitan characteristics	1980	1990	2000	2010
DEMOGRAPHY & IMMIGRATION				
Regional population	871,821	971,042	1,095,421	1,252,987
Principal cities	410,716	450,651	510,136	579,999
Suburbs	461,105	520,391	585,285	672,988
Regional net population growth over previous decade	–	11%	13%	14%
Principal cities	–	10%	13%	14%
Suburbs	–	13%	12%	15%
Race/ethnicity (%)				
White	85%	80%	73%	67%
Black	9%	10%	10%	10%
Latino	2%	4%	7%	11%
Asian/Pacific Islander	1%	2%	2%	3%
Native American	3%	4%	4%	4%
Other	1%	0%	3%	4%
Net population growth attributable to people of color over previous decade	–	61%	78%	74%
Percentage foreign-born	3%	3%	6%	8%
Of which, naturalized US citizen	35%	41%	39%	49%
Of which, non-citizen	43%	71%	125%	107%
REGIONAL ECONOMY				
Total jobs	513,840	567,554	700,807	763,203
Job growth over previous decade	–	10%	23%	9%
Jobs-to-population ratio	0.59	0.58	0.64	0.61
Average annual earnings per job (2010 dollars)	$41,870	$39,380	$42,554	$48,087
Growth over previous decade	–	–6%	8%	13%
GDP per job (2010 dollars)	$67,184	$59,596	$62,645	$75,823
Growth over previous decade	–	–11%	5%	21%
Ratio of GDP per job to earnings per job	1.60	1.51	1.47	1.58
Unemployment rate (civilian labor force ages 25–64)	3%	5%	3%	5%
By race/ethnicity				
White	2%	4%	2%	4%
Black	4%	10%	7%	8%
Latino	4%	6%	5%	7%
Asian/Pacific Islander	4%	5%	3%	2%
Native American	4%	9%	4%	7%
Other	–	–	5%	8%
INCOME & POVERTY				
Poverty rate (% persons)	11%	14%	14%	16%
Principal cities	12%	16%	16%	17%
Suburbs	10%	13%	11%	15%

TABLE B.6 (Continued)

Metropolitan characteristics	1980	1990	2000	2010
80/20 household income ratio	4.32	4.23	4.17	4.73
Gini coefficient (household income)	0.39	0.42	0.45	0.46
Percentage households by income level (middle class analysis)				
Lower income	30%	31%	34%	36%
Middle income	40%	41%	40%	38%
Upper income	30%	28%	27%	26%
Income differentials				
Median Black household income relative to median white household income	64%	64%	63%	63%
Median Latino household income relative to median white household income	78%	75%	72%	68%
Median Asian household income relative to median white household income	75%	83%	86%	113%
SPATIAL SEGREGATION BY RACE & INCOME				
Principal cities–suburbs job distribution				
Percentage of jobs in principal cities	68%	65%	63%	63%
Percentage of jobs in suburbs	32%	35%	37%	37%
Spatial segregation by race				
Black–white dissimilarity index	0.70	0.61	0.56	0.51
Latino–white dissimilarity index	0.29	0.37	0.45	0.47
All people of color–white dissimilarity index	0.48	0.39	0.36	0.34
Spatial segregation by income *(percentage population by income level of census tract)*				
Poor	14%	18%	18%	23%
Low income	12%	13%	17%	13%
Low-mid income	25%	23%	21%	18%
High-mid income	27%	23%	19%	21%
High income	12%	14%	17%	12%
Affluent	10%	9%	9%	12%
Spatial poverty				
Percentage of CBSA population in high poverty tracts (poverty rate > 20%)	12%	22%	23%	29%
Percentage of CBSA population in very high poverty tracts (poverty rate > 40%)	2%	4%	3%	4%
Poverty concentration				
Percentage of CBSA poor in high poverty tracts (poverty rate > 20%)	33%	47%	48%	55%
Percentage of CBSA poor in very high poverty tracts (poverty rate > 40%)	5%	13%	9%	10%
Poverty dissimilarity index	0.32	0.33	0.34	0.34

(Continued)

TABLE B.6 (Continued)

Metropolitan characteristics	1980	1990	2000	2010
EDUCATION & EMPLOYMENT				
Educational attainment				
(Population 25 years and older)				
Less than high school	27%	21%	16%	12%
High school only	32%	28%	28%	28%
Some college	23%	30%	31%	32%
Bachelor's degree	13%	14%	16%	18%
Graduate or professional degree	6%	7%	8%	9%
Workers by industry (% distribution)				
(Total employed population 16 years and older)				
Agriculture and mining	6%	5%	4%	6%
Construction	6%	4%	5%	5%
Manufacturing	10%	8%	8%	4%
Transportation, warehousing, and utilities	4%	3%	3%	2%
Wholesale trade	5%	4%	4%	3%
Retail trade	11%	11%	11%	10%
Finance, insurance, and real estate	11%	9%	8%	8%
Professional services	8%	11%	14%	13%
Health services	6%	8%	9%	11%
Information	2%	2%	2%	2%
Education	1%	1%	1%	2%
Other services	10%	13%	14%	15%
Government – civilian	18%	19%	15%	16%
Government – military	2%	2%	0%	2%
INDUSTRY WAGE STRUCTURE				
Share of jobs by industry wage level				
Low-wage	–	36%	38%	39%
Middle-wage	–	33%	35%	37%
High-wage	–	32%	27%	24%
Job growth by industry wage level over previous decade				
Low-wage	–	–	42%	3%
Middle-wage	–	–	41%	8%
High-wage	–	–	12%	–10%
Earnings growth by industry wage level over previous decade				
(Growth in real earnings per worker)				
Low-wage	–	–1%	3%	13%
Middle-wage	–	–9%	3%	12%
High-wage	–	–3%	8%	22%

TABLE B.6 (Continued)

Metropolitan characteristics	1980	1990	2000	2010
Average earnings per job by industry wage level	–			
Low-wage		$19,966	$20,469	$23,071
Middle-wage		$36,145	$37,176	$41,752
High-wage		$46,529	$50,046	$61,189
Total jobs by industry wage level				
Low-Wage				
Agriculture, forestry, fishing, and hunting	–	2,295	3,504	3,504
Retail trade	–	49,827	62,617	60,048
Administrative and support and waste management and remediation services	–	18,661	40,356	37,010
Education services	–	3,459	4,615	6,935
Arts, entertainment, and recreation	–	6,479	6,536	6,952
Accommodation and food services	–	32,264	42,793	50,504
All low-wage		*112,985*	*160,421*	*164,953*
Middle-Wage				
Construction	–	12,973	22,555	25,272
Transportation and warehousing	–	11,950	14,762	11,802
Information	–	7,436	12,097	10,607
Finance and insurance	–	19,391	21,204	21,814
Real estate and rental and leasing	–	8,885	10,760	9,902
Health care and social assistance	–	33,359	52,862	66,385
Other services (except public administration)	–	10,117	12,818	13,417
All middle-wage		*104,111*	*147,058*	*159,199*
High-Wage				
Mining	–	11,071	9,521	16,068
Utilities	–	2,991	2,582	2,903
Manufacturing	–	48,015	52,001	30,868
Wholesale trade	–	18,662	22,436	21,942
Professional, scientific, and technical services	–	16,458	21,471	23,446
Management of companies and enterprises	–	3,210	4,211	5,891
All high-wage		*100,407*	*112,222*	*101,118*

NOTE: (1) Data on the 80/20 household income ratio, the Gini coefficient, and percentage households by income level for 1980–2000 are based on surveys during those years but actually reflect incomes during the year prior to the survey. Poverty-related measures rely on income from the year prior to the survey as well, but incorporate information on family composition during the survey year. (2) Certain measures reported in the 2010 column actually reflect averages across annual surveys covering 2008–2012. These include data on percentage foreign-born (and citizenship), unemployment rate (and by race/ethnicity), percentage households by income level, and all measures of segregation, spatial poverty, and poverty concentration. (3) Data on educational attainment for 1980 is estimated based on years of schooling; for other years it is based on degrees earned.

TABLE B.7   SELECT DEMOGRAPHIC AND ECONOMIC DATA FOR THE GREENSBORO REGION

Metropolitan characteristics	1980	1990	2000	2010
DEMOGRAPHY & IMMIGRATION				
Regional population	492,308	540,030	643,430	723,801
Principal cities	245,556	261,478	307,516	374,037
Suburbs	246,752	278,552	335,914	349,764
Regional net population growth over previous decade	–	10%	19%	12%
Principal cities	–	6%	18%	22%
Suburbs	–	13%	21%	4%
Race/ethnicity (%)				
White	78%	77%	69%	62%
Black	21%	21%	23%	25%
Latino	1%	1%	4%	8%
Asian/Pacific Islander	0%	1%	2%	3%
Native American	0%	0%	0%	0%
Other	0%	0%	1%	2%
Net population growth attributable to people of color over previous decade	–	37%	68%	97%
Percentage foreign-born	1%	2%	5%	8%
Of which, naturalized US citizen	78%	84%	40%	47%
Of which, non-citizen	95%	148%	128%	103%
REGIONAL ECONOMY				
Total jobs	296,166	373,827	437,514	424,074
Job growth over previous decade	–	26%	17%	–3%
Jobs-to-population ratio	0.60	0.69	0.68	0.58
Average annual earnings per job (2010 dollars)	$37,234	$39,769	$46,011	$45,360
Growth over previous decade	–	7%	16%	–1%
GDP per job (2010 dollars)	$56,899	$63,218	$73,370	$80,535
Growth over previous decade	–	11%	16%	10%
Ratio of GDP per job to earnings per job	1.53	1.59	1.59	1.78
Unemployment rate (civilian labor force ages 25–64)	4%	3%	3%	9%
By race/ethnicity				
White	3%	2%	2%	8%
Black	7%	6%	6%	13%
Latino	–	–	7%	8%
Asian/Pacific Islander	–	–	5%	9%
Native American	–	–	–	–
Other	–	–	3%	20%
INCOME & POVERTY				
Poverty rate (% persons)	11%	10%	11%	18%
Principal cities	12%	11%	12%	20%
Suburbs	10%	9%	9%	16%

TABLE B.7 (Continued)

Metropolitan characteristics	1980	1990	2000	2010
80/20 household income ratio	4.08	3.95	3.99	4.58
Gini coefficient (household income)	0.40	0.42	0.45	0.46
Percentage households by income level (middle class analysis)				
Lower income	30%	31%	34%	37%
Middle income	40%	42%	41%	36%
Upper income	30%	28%	25%	27%
Income differentials				
Median Black household income relative to median white household income	67%	66%	69%	62%
Median Latino household income relative to median white household income	70%	78%	72%	67%
Median Asian household income relative to median white household income	90%	92%	107%	106%
SPATIAL SEGREGATION BY RACE & INCOME				
Principal cities–suburbs job distribution				
Percentage of jobs in principal cities	62%	64%	66%	70%
Percentage of jobs in suburbs	38%	36%	34%	30%
Spatial segregation by race				
Black–white dissimilarity index	0.58	0.55	0.55	0.55
Latino–white dissimilarity index	0.28	0.39	0.45	0.41
All people of color–white dissimilarity index	0.56	0.52	0.48	0.47
Spatial segregation by income (percentage population by income level of census tract)				
Poor	11%	13%	13%	20%
Low income	12%	13%	18%	14%
Low-mid income	32%	31%	31%	24%
High-mid income	30%	28%	20%	21%
High income	8%	7%	8%	8%
Affluent	7%	7%	10%	12%
Spatial poverty				
Percentage of CBSA population in high poverty tracts (poverty rate > 20%)	14%	11%	11%	33%
Percentage of CBSA population in very high poverty tracts (poverty rate > 40%)	0%	2%	1%	5%
Poverty concentration				
Percentage of CBSA poor in high poverty tracts (poverty rate > 20%)	32%	27%	27%	57%
Percentage of CBSA poor in very high poverty tracts (poverty rate > 40%)	0%	7%	3%	14%
Poverty dissimilarity index	0.29	0.29	0.30	0.32

(Continued)

TABLE B.7 (Continued)

Metropolitan characteristics	1980	1990	2000	2010
EDUCATION & EMPLOYMENT				
Educational attainment				
(Population 25 years and older)				
Less than high school	41%	29%	22%	15%
High school only	25%	29%	29%	30%
Some college	17%	23%	26%	29%
Bachelor's degree	13%	14%	17%	18%
Graduate or professional degree	4%	5%	7%	8%
Workers by industry (% distribution)				
(Total employed population 16 years and older)				
Agriculture and mining	3%	2%	1%	1%
Construction	6%	7%	6%	5%
Manufacturing	31%	24%	19%	13%
Transportation, warehousing' and utilities	4%	4%	6%	4%
Wholesale trade	5%	6%	5%	5%
Retail trade	10%	11%	11%	10%
Finance, insurance' and real estate	7%	7%	7%	9%
Professional services	7%	9%	12%	15%
Health services	5%	6%	8%	11%
Information	2%	2%	2%	2%
Education	1%	1%	1%	2%
Other services	9%	11%	12%	14%
Government – civilian	10%	10%	9%	11%
Government – military	1%	1%	0%	0%
INDUSTRY WAGE STRUCTURE				
Share of jobs by industry wage level				
Low-wage	–	28%	31%	35%
Middle-wage	–	58%	54%	50%
High-wage	–	14%	15%	15%
Job growth by industry wage level over previous decade				
Low-wage	–	–	31%	–1%
Middle-wage	–	–	12%	–19%
High-wage	–	–	30%	–12%
Earnings growth by industry wage level over previous decade				
(Growth in real earnings per worker)				
Low-wage	–	–18%	13%	–5%
Middle-wage	–	–6%	12%	3%
High-wage	–	–13%	16%	2%

TABLE B.7 (Continued)

Metropolitan characteristics	1980	1990	2000	2010
Average earnings per job by industry wage level	–			
Low-wage		$20,592	$23,196	$22,105
Middle-wage		$38,578	$43,384	$44,622
High-wage		$48,252	$55,827	$56,777
Total jobs by industry wage level				
Low-Wage				
Agriculture, forestry, fishing, and hunting	–	384	572	600
Retail trade	–	34,860	39,700	35,062
Administrative and support and waste management and remediation services	–	12,097	24,802	26,729
Arts, entertainment, and recreation	–	2,402	3,121	3,410
Accommodation and food services	–	18,749	23,031	26,485
Other services (except public administration)	–	8,246	9,380	7,712
All low-wage		76,738	100,606	99,998
Middle-Wage				
Construction	–	16,621	18,952	13,096
Manufacturing	–	90,271	83,831	51,126
Transportation and warehousing	–	9,189	19,562	14,255
Finance and insurance	–	12,055	14,062	16,449
Real estate and rental and leasing	–	3,882	4,677	3,779
Education services	–	1,885	2,806	4,307
Health care and social assistance	–	21,993	31,110	39,503
All middle-wage		155,896	175,000	142,515
High-Wage				
Mining	–	261	359	159
Utilities	–	1,249	1,032	665
Wholesale trade	–	16,773	19,373	18,299
Information	–	5,843	8,019	5,521
Professional, scientific, and technical services	–	9,305	12,654	10,736
Management of companies and enterprises	–	3,683	6,982	7,434
All high-wage		37,114	48,419	42,814

NOTE: (1) Data on the 80/20 household income ratio, the Gini coefficient, and percentage households by income level for 1980–2000 are based on surveys during those years but actually reflect incomes during the year prior to the survey. Poverty-related measures rely on income from the year prior to the survey as well, but incorporate information on family composition during the survey year. (2) Certain measures reported in the 2010 column actually reflect averages across annual surveys covering 2008–2012. These include data on percentage foreign-born (and citizenship), unemployment rate (and by race/ethnicity), percentage households by income level, and all measures of segregation, spatial poverty, and poverty concentration. (3) Data on educational attainment for 1980 is estimated based on years of schooling; for other years it is based on degrees earned.

TABLE B.8 SELECT DEMOGRAPHIC AND ECONOMIC DATA FOR THE FRESNO REGION

Metropolitan characteristics	1980	1990	2000	2010
DEMOGRAPHY & IMMIGRATION				
Regional population	514,621	667,490	799,407	930,450
Principal cities	284,038	383,728	457,099	494,665
Suburbs	230,583	283,762	342,308	435,785
Regional net population growth over previous decade	–	30%	20%	16%
Principal cities	–	35%	19%	8%
Suburbs	–	23%	21%	27%
Race/ethnicity (%)				
White	62%	51%	40%	33%
Black	5%	5%	5%	5%
Latino	29%	35%	44%	50%
Asian/Pacific Islander	3%	8%	8%	9%
Native American	1%	1%	1%	1%
Other	1%	0%	3%	2%
Net population growth attributable to people of color over previous decade	–	86%	116%	110%
Percentage foreign-born	11%	18%	22%	22%
Of which, naturalized US citizen	9%	7%	10%	17%
Of which, non-citizen	10%	13%	32%	38%
REGIONAL ECONOMY				
Total jobs	275,120	342,583	404,091	426,263
Job growth over previous decade	–	25%	18%	5%
Jobs-to-population ratio	0.53	0.51	0.50	0.46
Average annual earnings per job (2010 dollars)	$42,270	$40,908	$42,831	$46,369
Growth over previous decade	–	–3%	5%	8%
GDP per job (2010 dollars)	$57,911	$59,549	$58,875	$71,479
Growth over previous decade	–	3%	–1%	21%
Ratio of GDP per job to earnings per job	1.37	1.46	1.37	1.54
Unemployment rate (civilian labor force ages 25–64)	8%	8%	10%	12%
By race/ethnicity				
White	5%	4%	5%	9%
Black	11%	14%	13%	20%
Latino	16%	15%	16%	14%
Asian/Pacific Islander	5%	10%	7%	11%
Native American	–	7%	10%	–
Other	–	–	7%	15%
INCOME & POVERTY				
Poverty rate (% persons)	14%	21%	23%	27%
Principal cities	15%	23%	26%	30%
Suburbs	14%	19%	19%	23%

TABLE B.8 (Continued)

Metropolitan characteristics	1980	1990	2000	2010
80/20 household income ratio	4.47	4.51	4.54	5.31
Gini coefficient (household income)	0.41	0.43	0.47	0.46
Percentage households by income level (middle class analysis)				
Lower income	30%	32%	34%	36%
Middle income	40%	41%	40%	37%
Upper income	30%	27%	26%	27%
Income differentials				
Median Black household income relative to median white household income	52%	55%	54%	44%
Median Latino household income relative to median white household income	64%	68%	65%	58%
Median Asian household income relative to median white household income	109%	69%	73%	88%
SPATIAL SEGREGATION BY RACE & INCOME				
Principal cities–suburbs job distribution				
Percentage of jobs in principal cities	58%	64%	63%	62%
Percentage of jobs in suburbs	42%	36%	37%	38%
Spatial segregation by race				
Black–white dissimilarity index	0.63	0.56	0.54	0.52
Latino–white dissimilarity index	0.46	0.49	0.48	0.46
All people of color–white dissimilarity index	0.43	0.46	0.43	0.42
Spatial segregation by income *(percentage population by income level of census tract)*				
Poor	13%	25%	25%	33%
Low income	16%	13%	22%	12%
Low-mid income	23%	26%	18%	19%
High-mid income	31%	16%	13%	12%
High income	6%	7%	7%	8%
Affluent	11%	13%	14%	15%
Spatial poverty				
Percentage of CBSA population in high poverty tracts (poverty rate > 20%)	27%	43%	52%	57%
Percentage of CBSA population in very high poverty tracts (poverty rate > 40%)	2%	16%	15%	22%
Poverty concentration				
Percentage of CBSA poor in high poverty tracts (poverty rate > 20%)	51%	71%	78%	82%
Percentage of CBSA poor in very high poverty tracts (poverty rate > 40%)	5%	34%	32%	40%
Poverty dissimilarity index	0.30	0.36	0.34	0.35

(Continued)

TABLE B.8 (Continued)

Metropolitan characteristics	1980	1990	2000	2010
EDUCATION & EMPLOYMENT				
Educational attainment				
(Population 25 years and older)				
Less than high school	36%	34%	32%	26%
High school only	26%	22%	21%	22%
Some college	23%	28%	29%	31%
Bachelor's degree	11%	12%	12%	13%
Graduate or professional degree	5%	5%	6%	7%
Workers by industry (% distribution)				
(Total employed population 16 years and older)				
Agriculture and mining	18%	17%	16%	12%
Construction	5%	5%	5%	4%
Manufacturing	9%	7%	7%	6%
Transportation, warehousing, and utilities	3%	3%	3%	4%
Wholesale trade	5%	4%	3%	3%
Retail trade	11%	11%	10%	10%
Finance, insurance, and real estate	8%	7%	7%	8%
Professional services	6%	7%	9%	11%
Health services	7%	8%	9%	11%
Information	1%	1%	1%	1%
Education	1%	1%	1%	1%
Other services	11%	12%	13%	13%
Government – civilian	15%	15%	15%	16%
Government – military	1%	1%	0%	0%
INDUSTRY WAGE STRUCTURE				
Share of jobs by industry wage level				
Low-wage	–	40%	42%	41%
Middle-wage	–	45%	45%	45%
High-wage	–	16%	14%	14%
Job growth by industry wage level over previous decade				
Low-wage	–	–	20%	–2%
Middle-wage	–	–	14%	1%
High-wage	–	–	0%	2%
Earnings growth by industry wage level over previous decade				
(Growth in real earnings per worker)				
Low-wage	–	–9%	–1%	14%
Middle-wage	–	–12%	0%	10%
High-wage	–	–13%	6%	11%

(Continued)

TABLE B.8 (Continued)

Metropolitan characteristics	1980	1990	2000	2010
INDUSTRY WAGE STRUCTURE				
Average earnings per job by industry wage level	–			
Low-wage		$18,476	$18,345	$20,842
Middle-wage		$36,200	$36,131	$39,832
High-wage		$46,583	$49,285	$54,752
Total jobs by industry wage level				
Low-Wage				
Agriculture, forestry, fishing, and hunting	–	52,942	56,304	45,946
Administrative and support and waste management and remediation services	–	8,252	12,677	14,273
Education services	–	1,502	2,130	4,263
Arts, entertainment, and recreation	–	2,161	3,913	2,942
Accommodation and food services	–	16,513	21,351	23,418
Other services (except public administration)	–	11,058	14,578	17,456
All low-wage		92,428	110,953	108,298
Middle-Wage				
Construction	–	14,992	14,965	11,947
Manufacturing	–	25,436	27,576	24,441
Retail trade	–	31,897	32,084	32,844
Transportation and warehousing	–	6,840	7,537	8,525
Real estate and rental and leasing	–	3,679	4,304	4,021
Management of companies and enterprises	–	668	4,290	2,116
Health care and social assistance	–	20,750	27,867	35,347
All middle-wage		104,262	118,623	119,241
High-Wage				
Mining	–	650	317	174
Utilities	–	1,882	1,435	1,928
Wholesale trade	–	12,592	12,058	11,462
Information	–	4,315	5,022	3,555
Finance and insurance	–	9,436	9,144	9,246
Professional, scientific, and technical services	–	7,253	8,067	10,536
All high-wage		36,128	36,043	36,901

NOTE: (1) Data on the 80/20 household income ratio, the Gini coefficient, and percentage households by income level for 1980–2000 are based on surveys during those years but actually reflect incomes during the year prior to the survey. Poverty-related measures rely on income from the year prior to the survey as well, but incorporate information on family composition during the survey year. (2) Certain measures reported in the 2010 column actually reflect averages across annual surveys covering 2008–2012. These include data on percentage foreign-born (and citizenship), unemployment rate (and by race/ethnicity), percentage households by income level, and all measures of segregation, spatial poverty, and poverty concentration. (3) Data on educational attainment for 1980 is estimated based on years of schooling; for other years it is based on degrees earned.

TABLE B.9   SELECT DEMOGRAPHIC AND ECONOMIC DATA FOR THE SAN ANTONIO
REGION

Metropolitan characteristics	1980	1990	2000	2010
DEMOGRAPHY & IMMIGRATION				
Regional population	1,152,724	1,407,745	1,711,703	2,142,508
Principal cities	849,750	1,003,663	1,154,915	1,327,407
Suburbs	302,974	404,082	556,788	815,101
Regional net population growth over previous decade	–	22%	22%	25%
Principal cities	–	18%	15%	15%
Suburbs	–	33%	38%	46%
Race/ethnicity (%)				
White	48%	46%	41%	36%
Black	6%	6%	6%	6%
Latino	44%	47%	50%	54%
Asian/Pacific Islander	1%	1%	1%	2%
Native American	0%	0%	0%	0%
Other	0%	0%	1%	1%
Net population growth attributable to people of color over previous decade	–	66%	82%	82%
Percentage foreign-born	7%	8%	10%	12%
Of which, naturalized US citizen	14%	17%	21%	32%
Of which, non-citizen	17%	30%	68%	70%
REGIONAL ECONOMY				
Total jobs	557,276	723,234	981,473	1,180,418
Job growth over previous decade	–	30%	36%	20%
Jobs-to-population ratio	0.48	0.51	0.57	0.55
Average annual earnings per job (2010 dollars)	$38,009	$39,033	$46,636	$45,923
Growth over previous decade	–	3%	19%	–2%
GDP per job (2010 dollars)	$60,036	$59,123	$65,122	$69,665
Growth over previous decade	–	–2%	10%	7%
Ratio of GDP per job to earnings per job	1.58	1.51	1.40	1.52
Unemployment rate (civilian labor force ages 25–64)	4%	6%	4%	6%
By race/ethnicity				
White	3%	5%	3%	5%
Black	6%	9%	5%	9%
Latino	5%	8%	5%	7%
Asian/Pacific Islander	5%	5%	2%	3%
Native American	–	–	–	–
Other	–	–	5%	8%

TABLE B.9 (Continued)

Metropolitan characteristics	1980	1990	2000	2010
INCOME & POVERTY				
Poverty rate (% persons)	18%	20%	15%	16%
Principal cities	20%	22%	17%	19%
Suburbs	14%	15%	11%	12%
80/20 household income ratio	4.19	4.42	4.20	4.65
Gini coefficient (household income)	0.41	0.44	0.45	0.45
Percentage households by income level				
(middle class analysis)				
Lower income	30%	32%	33%	35%
Middle income	40%	40%	41%	39%
Upper income	30%	28%	26%	27%
Income differentials				
Median Black household income relative to median white household income	70%	68%	67%	63%
Median Latino household income relative to median white household income	71%	70%	64%	66%
Median Asian household income relative to median white household income	91%	97%	83%	89%
SPATIAL SEGREGATION BY RACE & INCOME				
Principal cities–suburbs job distribution				
Percentage of jobs in principal cities	80%	78%	75%	77%
Percentage of jobs in suburbs	20%	22%	25%	23%
Spatial segregation by race				
Black–white dissimilarity index	0.63	0.57	0.54	0.49
Latino–white dissimilarity index	0.55	0.53	0.50	0.46
All people of color–white dissimilarity index	0.52	0.50	0.47	0.43
Spatial segregation by income				
(percentage population by income level				
of census tract)				
Poor	18%	23%	23%	29%
Low income	17%	19%	17%	12%
Low-mid income	23%	18%	20%	17%
High-mid income	19%	18%	19%	17%
High income	13%	11%	7%	12%
Affluent	10%	11%	13%	13%

(Continued)

TABLE B.9 (Continued)

Metropolitan characteristics	1980	1990	2000	2010
Spatial poverty				
Percentage of CBSA population in high poverty tracts (poverty rate > 20%)	37%	41%	31%	34%
Percentage of CBSA population in very high poverty tracts (poverty rate > 40%)	7%	10%	3%	5%
Poverty concentration				
Percentage of CBSA poor in high poverty tracts (poverty rate > 20%)	67%	72%	58%	63%
Percentage of CBSA poor in very high poverty tracts (poverty rate > 40%)	18%	26%	10%	14%
Poverty dissimilarity index	0.36	0.38	0.34	0.35
EDUCATION & EMPLOYMENT				
Educational attainment				
(Population 25 years and older)				
Less than high school	38%	28%	23%	18%
High school only	26%	26%	25%	26%
Some college	20%	28%	30%	32%
Bachelor's degree	10%	12%	14%	16%
Graduate or professional degree	5%	7%	8%	9%
Workers by industry (% distribution)				
(Total employed population 16 years and older)				
Agriculture and mining	4%	3%	2%	2%
Construction	7%	5%	7%	7%
Manufacturing	10%	7%	6%	4%
Transportation, warehousing, and utilities	2%	2%	3%	2%
Wholesale trade	4%	3%	3%	3%
Retail trade	12%	12%	11%	10%
Finance, insurance, and real estate	9%	10%	9%	11%
Professional services	8%	10%	13%	13%
Health services	6%	8%	9%	11%
Information	2%	2%	3%	2%
Education	1%	1%	1%	2%
Other services	11%	14%	15%	16%
Government – civilian	18%	17%	14%	14%
Government – military	8%	5%	0%	3%

TABLE B.9 (Continued)

Metropolitan characteristics	1980	1990	2000	2010
INDUSTRY WAGE STRUCTURE				
Share of jobs by industry wage level				
Low-wage	–	42%	42%	42%
Middle-wage	–	35%	36%	36%
High-wage	–	23%	22%	22%
Job growth by industry wage level over previous decade				
Low-wage	–	–	45%	11%
Middle-wage	–	–	48%	13%
High-wage	–	–	42%	12%
Earnings growth by industry wage level over previous decade				
(Growth in real earnings per worker)				
Low-wage	–	26%	8%	5%
Middle-wage	–	–6%	11%	4%
High-wage	–	6%	31%	14%
Average earnings per job by industry wage level	–			
Low-wage		$21,421	$23,168	$24,366
Middle-wage		$34,498	$38,396	$40,058
High-wage		$43,687	$57,173	$64,948
Total jobs by industry wage level				
Low-Wage				
Agriculture, forestry, fishing, and hunting	–	1,984	2,395	2,142
Retail trade	–	74,167	90,429	94,556
Administrative and support and waste management and remediation services	–	23,912	55,266	52,467
Arts, entertainment, and recreation	–	8,148	10,089	11,693
Accommodation and food services	–	44,676	67,683	90,539
Other services (except public administration)	–	18,313	23,228	26,129
All low-wage		*171,200*	*249,090*	*277,526*
Middle-Wage				
Utilities	–	749	705	958
Construction	–	23,054	40,989	43,551
Manufacturing	–	45,412	56,559	43,718
Transportation and warehousing	–	10,389	19,429	20,169
Real estate and rental and leasing	–	11,142	13,553	13,330
Education services	–	5,764	8,131	12,634
Health care and social assistance	–	47,299	73,975	107,734
All middle-wage		*143,809*	*213,341*	*242,094*

TABLE B.9 (Continued)

Metropolitan characteristics	1980	1990	2000	2010
High-Wage				
Mining	–	2,916	2,556	3,363
Wholesale trade	–	20,710	26,727	28,084
Information	–	15,677	25,051	18,351
Finance and insurance	–	32,510	42,015	51,756
Professional, scientific, and technical services	–	19,981	31,887	37,976
Management of companies and enterprises	–	1,381	3,819	8,156
All high-wage		*93,175*	*132,055*	*147,686*

NOTE: (1) Data on the 80/20 household income ratio, the Gini coefficient, and percentage households by income level for 1980–2000 are based on surveys during those years but actually reflect incomes during the year prior to the survey. Poverty-related measures rely on income from the year prior to the survey as well, but incorporate information on family composition during the survey year. (2) Certain measures reported in the 2010 column actually reflect averages across annual surveys covering 2008–2012. These include data on percentage foreign-born (and citizenship), unemployment rate (and by race/ethnicity), percentage households by income level, and all measures of segregation, spatial poverty, and poverty concentration. (3) Data on educational attainment for 1980 is estimated based on years of schooling; for other years it is based on degrees earned.

TABLE B.10 SELECT DEMOGRAPHIC AND ECONOMIC DATA FOR THE SILICON VALLEY REGION

Metropolitan characteristics	1980	1990	2000	2010
DEMOGRAPHY & IMMIGRATION				
Regional population	1,320,076	1,534,274	1,735,819	1,836,911
Principal cities	1,067,739	1,241,094	1,401,188	1,466,052
Suburbs	252,337	293,180	334,631	370,859
Regional net population growth over previous decade	–	16%	13%	6%
Principal cities	–	16%	13%	5%
Suburbs	–	16%	14%	11%
Race/ethnicity (%)				
White	70%	58%	44%	35%
Black	3%	3%	3%	2%
Latino	18%	22%	25%	28%
Asian/Pacific Islander	7%	16%	25%	31%
Native American	0%	0%	0%	0%
Other	1%	0%	3%	3%
Net population growth attributable to people of color over previous decade	–	117%	159%	219%
Percentage foreign-born	14%	23%	34%	37%
Of which, naturalized US citizen	7%	6%	6%	10%
Of which, non-citizen	8%	10%	21%	22%
REGIONAL ECONOMY				
Total jobs	814,698	1,052,577	1,295,091	1,136,759
Job growth over previous decade	–	29%	23%	−12%
Jobs-to-population ratio	0.61	0.69	0.74	0.62
Average annual earnings per job (2010 dollars)	$50,039	$59,105	$100,997	$89,221
Growth over previous decade	–	18%	71%	−12%
GDP per job (2010 dollars)	$66,598	$83,578	$134,861	$137,157
Growth over previous decade	–	25%	61%	2%
Ratio of GDP per job to earnings per job	1.33	1.41	1.34	1.54
Unemployment rate (civilian labor force ages 25–64)	3%	4%	3%	8%
By race/ethnicity				
White	2%	3%	2%	7%
Black	5%	6%	4%	11%
Latino	8%	7%	5%	10%
Asian/Pacific Islander	2%	4%	3%	8%
Native American	7%	4%	8%	–
Other	–	–	4%	9%
INCOME & POVERTY				
Poverty rate (% persons)	7%	8%	8%	11%
Principal cities	7%	8%	8%	11%
Suburbs	7%	6%	7%	10%

(Continued)

TABLE B.10 (Continued)

Metropolitan characteristics	1980	1990	2000	2010
80/20 household income ratio	3.64	3.43	3.90	4.91
Gini coefficient (household income)	0.35	0.38	0.43	0.45
Percentage households by income level (middle class analysis)				
Lower income	30%	31%	37%	39%
Middle income	40%	41%	37%	33%
Upper income	30%	28%	26%	27%
Income differentials				
Median Black household income relative to median white household income	77%	76%	75%	58%
Median Latino household income relative to median white household income	74%	74%	70%	54%
Median Asian household income relative to median white household income	98%	105%	104%	116%
SPATIAL SEGREGATION BY RACE & INCOME				
Principal cities–suburbs job distribution				
Percentage of jobs in principal cities	83%	85%	84%	87%
Percentage of jobs in suburbs	17%	15%	16%	13%
Spatial segregation by race				
Black–white dissimilarity index	0.48	0.46	0.44	0.41
Latino–white dissimilarity index	0.45	0.49	0.51	0.48
All people of color–white dissimilarity index	0.38	0.40	0.41	0.39
Spatial segregation by income *(percentage population by income level of census tract)*				
Poor	11%	13%	14%	21%
Low income	11%	13%	16%	12%
Low-mid income	27%	27%	29%	21%
High-mid income	32%	30%	25%	24%
High income	12%	9%	9%	13%
Affluent	7%	7%	8%	9%
Spatial poverty				
Percentage of CBSA population in high poverty tracts (poverty rate > 20%)	4%	8%	4%	10%
Percentage of CBSA population in very high poverty tracts (poverty rate > 40%)	0%	0%	0%	0%
Poverty concentration				
Percentage of CBSA poor in high poverty tracts (poverty rate > 20%)	12%	24%	13%	27%
Percentage of CBSA poor in very high poverty tracts (poverty rate > 40%)	0%	0%	0%	0%
Poverty dissimilarity index	0.29	0.34	0.30	0.32

TABLE B.10 (Continued)

Metropolitan characteristics	1980	1990	2000	2010
EDUCATION & EMPLOYMENT				
Educational attainment				
(Population 25 years and older)				
Less than high school	21%	18%	17%	14%
High school only	25%	19%	16%	16%
Some college	28%	31%	27%	25%
Bachelor's degree	17%	20%	24%	26%
Graduate or professional degree	9%	12%	16%	20%
Workers by industry (% distribution)				
(Total employed population 16 years and older)				
Agriculture and mining	1%	1%	1%	1%
Construction	4%	4%	5%	4%
Manufacturing	30%	25%	21%	14%
Transportation, warehousing, and utilities	2%	2%	2%	2%
Wholesale trade	3%	4%	4%	4%
Retail trade	10%	10%	9%	8%
Finance, insurance, and real estate	8%	7%	6%	8%
Professional services	14%	17%	22%	20%
Health services	4%	5%	6%	9%
Information	3%	3%	4%	4%
Education	2%	2%	3%	4%
Other services	9%	10%	11%	13%
Government – civilian	10%	9%	8%	8%
Government – military	1%	1%	0%	0%
INDUSTRY WAGE STRUCTURE				
Share of jobs by industry wage level				
Low-wage	–	28%	29%	31%
Middle-wage	–	20%	19%	24%
High-wage	–	53%	52%	46%
Job growth by industry wage level over previous decade				
Low-wage	–	–	27%	−14%
Middle-wage	–	–	21%	−1%
High-wage	–	–	21%	−29%
Earnings growth by industry wage level over previous decade				
(Growth in real earnings per worker)				
Low-wage	–	149%	28%	−3%
Middle-wage	–	203%	28%	12%
High-wage	–	194%	113%	−7%

(Continued)

TABLE B.10 (Continued)

Metropolitan characteristics	1980	1990	2000	2010
Average earnings per job by industry wage level	–			
Low-wage		$28,499	$36,374	$35,384
Middle-wage		$47,282	$60,702	$68,050
High-wage		$70,114	$149,658	$139,734
Total jobs by industry wage level				
Low-Wage				
Agriculture, forestry, fishing, and hunting	–	1,724	2,772	2,244
Retail trade	–	83,832	93,883	78,674
Administrative and support and waste management and remediation services	–	45,885	78,160	46,966
Arts, entertainment, and recreation	–	11,572	10,724	12,304
Accommodation and food services	–	46,850	62,519	62,822
Other services (except public administration)	–	24,974	25,822	31,437
All low-wage		214,837	273,880	234,447
Middle-Wage				
Mining	–	688	642	869
Construction	–	36,331	49,508	32,202
Transportation and warehousing	–	8,984	16,747	12,894
Finance and insurance	–	22,306	19,109	18,153
Real estate and rental and leasing	–	14,086	15,444	13,462
Education services	–	20,785	23,143	28,856
Health care and social assistance	–	50,462	61,799	77,388
All middle-wage		153,642	186,392	183,824
High-Wage				
Utilities	–	2,175	2,578	1,996
Manufacturing	–	264,362	256,162	152,784
Wholesale trade	–	45,287	42,220	34,994
Information	–	22,650	42,601	43,762
Professional, scientific, and technical services	–	65,945	127,891	107,395
Management of companies and enterprises	–	7,895	24,267	8,938
All high-wage		408,314	495,719	349,869

NOTE: (1) Data on the 80/20 household income ratio, the Gini coefficient, and percentage households by income level for 1980–2000 are based on surveys during those years but actually reflect incomes during the year prior to the survey. Poverty-related measures rely on income from the year prior to the survey as well, but incorporate information on family composition during the survey year. (2) Certain measures reported in the 2010 column actually reflect averages across annual surveys covering 2008–2012. These include data on percentage foreign-born (and citizenship), unemployment rate (and by race/ethnicity), percentage households by income level, and all measures of segregation, spatial poverty, and poverty concentration. (3) Data on educational attainment for 1980 is estimated based on years of schooling; for other years it is based on degrees earned.

TABLE B.11   SELECT DEMOGRAPHIC AND ECONOMIC DATA FOR
THE RALEIGH-DURHAM REGION

Metropolitan characteristics	1980	1990	2000	2010
DEMOGRAPHY & IMMIGRATION				
Regional population	694,400	885,725	1,223,564	1,634,847
Principal cities	342,189	441,968	582,671	767,456
Suburbs	352,211	443,757	640,893	867,391
Regional net population growth over previous decade	–	28%	38%	34%
Principal cities	–	29%	32%	32%
Suburbs	–	26%	44%	35%
Race/ethnicity (%)				
White	73%	73%	67%	61%
Black	25%	24%	23%	22%
Latino	1%	1%	6%	10%
Asian/Pacific Islander	1%	2%	3%	4%
Native American	0%	0%	0%	0%
Other	0%	0%	1%	2%
Net population growth attributable to people of color over previous decade	–	28%	48%	57%
Percentage foreign-born	2%	4%	9%	12%
Of which, naturalized US citizen	45%	36%	24%	31%
Of which, non-citizen	55%	64%	76%	69%
REGIONAL ECONOMY				
Total jobs	395,349	595,780	854,656	1,015,627
Job growth over previous decade	–	51%	43%	19%
Jobs-to-population ratio	0.57	0.67	0.69	0.62
Average annual earnings per job (2010 dollars)	$36,789	$42,914	$52,851	$54,801
Growth over previous decade	–	17%	23%	4%
GDP per job (2010 dollars)	$52,396	$63,594	$78,659	$94,307
Growth over previous decade	–	21%	24%	20%
Ratio of GDP per job to earnings per job	1.42	1.48	1.49	1.72
Unemployment rate	3%	3%	3%	7%
(civilian labor force ages 25–64)				
By race/ethnicity				
White	2%	2%	2%	5%
Black	5%	5%	5%	10%
Latino	–	3%	5%	9%
Asian/Pacific Islander	–	3%	3%	5%
Native American	–	–	–	–
Other	–	–	3%	6%
INCOME & POVERTY				
Poverty rate (% persons)	13%	11%	10%	15%
Principal cities	12%	11%	11%	17%
Suburbs	14%	11%	10%	13%

(*Continued*)

TABLE B.11 (Continued)

Metropolitan characteristics	1980	1990	2000	2010
80/20 household income ratio	4.33	4.06	4.07	4.64
Gini coefficient (household income)	0.39	0.41	0.44	0.45
Percentage households by income level (middle class analysis)				
Lower income	30%	30%	33%	36%
Middle income	40%	41%	40%	37%
Upper income	30%	29%	27%	27%
Income differentials				
Median Black household income relative to median white household income	58%	58%	61%	56%
Median Latino household income relative to median white household income	66%	81%	64%	53%
Median Asian household income relative to median white household income	67%	81%	106%	118%
SPATIAL SEGREGATION BY RACE & INCOME				
Principal cities–suburbs job distribution				
Percentage of jobs in principal cities	54%	58%	59%	63%
Percentage of jobs in suburbs	46%	42%	41%	37%
Spatial segregation by race				
Black–white dissimilarity index	0.46	0.47	0.46	0.45
Latino–white dissimilarity index	0.21	0.34	0.43	0.41
All people of color–white dissimilarity index	0.43	0.43	0.39	0.37
Spatial segregation by income (percentage population by income level of census tract)				
Poor	17%	17%	17%	20%
Low income	12%	16%	16%	12%
Low-mid income	33%	22%	23%	27%
High-mid income	16%	25%	23%	18%
High income	10%	9%	10%	10%
Affluent	12%	11%	10%	12%
Spatial poverty				
Percentage of CBSA population in high poverty tracts (poverty rate > 20%)	21%	15%	11%	22%
Percentage of CBSA population in very high poverty tracts (poverty rate > 40%)	1%	3%	2%	5%
Poverty concentration				
Percentage of CBSA poor in high poverty tracts (poverty rate > 20%)	38%	37%	30%	48%
Percentage of CBSA poor in very high poverty tracts (poverty rate > 40%)	2%	7%	5%	13%
Poverty dissimilarity index	0.31	0.36	0.35	0.36

TABLE B.11 (Continued)

Metropolitan characteristics	1980	1990	2000	2010
EDUCATION & EMPLOYMENT				
Educational attainment				
(Population 25 years and older)				
Less than high school	33%	21%	15%	10%
High school only	24%	24%	21%	20%
Some college	18%	25%	26%	28%
Bachelor's degree	17%	20%	24%	26%
Graduate or professional degree	9%	11%	14%	15%
Workers by industry (% distribution)				
(Total employed population 16 years and older)				
Agriculture and mining	5%	2%	1%	1%
Construction	6%	7%	7%	5%
Manufacturing	17%	14%	11%	7%
Transportation, warehousing, and utilities	3%	3%	2%	2%
Wholesale trade	3%	4%	3%	3%
Retail trade	10%	11%	11%	9%
Finance, insurance, and real estate	8%	7%	7%	9%
Professional services	9%	13%	16%	16%
Health services	5%	6%	8%	11%
Information	2%	3%	3%	3%
Education	1%	2%	2%	3%
Other services	9%	12%	12%	14%
Government – civilian	21%	17%	15%	15%
Government – military	1%	1%	0%	0%
INDUSTRY WAGE STRUCTURE				
Share of jobs by industry wage level				
Low-wage	–	34%	36%	37%
Middle-wage	–	31%	32%	36%
High-wage	–	34%	31%	27%
Job growth by industry wage level over previous decade				
Low-wage	–	–	57%	10%
Middle-wage	–	–	55%	19%
High-wage	–	–	36%	−6%
Earnings growth by industry wage level over previous decade				
(Growth in real earnings per worker)				
Low-wage	–	–	27%	−4%
Middle-wage	–	–	19%	9%
High-wage	–	–	46%	10%

(Continued)

TABLE B.11 (Continued)

Metropolitan characteristics	1980	1990	2000	2010
Average earnings per job by industry wage level	–			
Low-wage		$20,536	$26,135	$25,143
Middle-wage		$39,182	$46,589	$50,588
High-wage		$50,374	$73,563	$80,982
Total jobs by industry wage level				
Low-Wage				
Agriculture, forestry, fishing, and hunting	–	2,716	3,162	2,662
Retail trade	–	52,013	76,028	79,028
Administrative and support and waste management and remediation services	–	23,236	48,473	48,521
Arts, entertainment, and recreation	–	4,085	7,591	11,303
Accommodation and food services	–	33,790	47,493	60,919
Other services (except public administration)	–	13,058	19,500	20,739
All low-wage		*128,898*	*202,247*	*223,172*
Middle-Wage				
Construction	–	26,174	41,020	34,570
Transportation and warehousing	–	11,543	14,666	11,443
Information	–	11,338	23,719	20,358
Finance and insurance	–	17,051	21,302	27,046
Real estate and rental and leasing	–	6,220	9,976	10,690
Education services	–	3,922	12,541	19,221
Health care and social assistance	–	41,388	58,607	92,648
All middle-wage		*117,636*	*181,831*	*215,976*
High-Wage				
Mining	–	846	1,180	482
Utilities	–	5,879	3,716	2,380
Manufacturing	–	74,236	89,921	61,838
Wholesale trade	–	18,494	24,731	28,165
Professional, scientific, and technical services	–	23,734	48,514	61,090
Management of companies and enterprises	–	6,523	8,380	11,353
All high-wage		*129,712*	*176,442*	*165,308*

NOTE: (1) Data on the 80/20 household income ratio, the Gini coefficient, and percentage households by income level for 1980–2000 are based on surveys during those years but actually reflect incomes during the year prior to the survey. Poverty-related measures rely on income from the year prior to the survey as well, but incorporate information on family composition during the survey year. (2) Certain measures reported in the 2010 column actually reflect averages across annual surveys covering 2008–2012. These include data on percentage foreign-born (and citizenship), unemployment rate (and by race/ethnicity), percentage households by income level, and all measures of segregation, spatial poverty, and poverty concentration. (3) Data on educational attainment for 1980 is estimated based on years of schooling; for other years it is based on degrees earned.

TABLE B.12 SELECT DEMOGRAPHIC AND ECONOMIC DATA FOR THE SEATTLE
REGION

Metropolitan characteristics	1980	1990	2000	2010
DEMOGRAPHY & IMMIGRATION				
Regional population	2,093,112	2,559,164	3,043,878	3,439,809
Principal cities	868,579	965,868	1,084,926	1,215,777
Suburbs	1,224,533	1,593,296	1,958,952	2,224,032
Regional net population growth over previous decade	–	22%	19%	13%
Principal cities	–	11%	12%	12%
Suburbs	–	30%	23%	14%
Race/ethnicity (%)				
White	88%	85%	76%	68%
Black	4%	5%	5%	5%
Latino	2%	3%	5%	9%
Asian/Pacific Islander	4%	6%	9%	12%
Native American	1%	1%	1%	1%
Other	1%	0%	4%	5%
Net population growth attributable to people of color over previous decade	–	30%	71%	93%
Percentage foreign-born	7%	8%	13%	17%
Of which, naturalized US citizen	13%	17%	17%	23%
Of which, non-citizen	16%	29%	55%	50%
REGIONAL ECONOMY				
Total jobs	1,159,285	1,653,020	2,048,170	2,148,487
Job growth over previous decade	–	43%	24%	5%
Jobs-to-population ratio	0.55	0.64	0.67	0.62
Average annual earnings per job (2010 dollars)	$48,914	$48,034	$63,154	$63,107
Growth over previous decade	–	−2%	31%	0%
GDP per job (2010 dollars)	$74,603	$80,578	$97,970	$108,345
Growth over previous decade	–	8%	22%	11%
Ratio of GDP per job to earnings per job	1.53	1.68	1.55	1.72
Unemployment rate (civilian labor force ages 25–64)	5%	4%	4%	7%
By race/ethnicity				
White	5%	4%	3%	6%
Black	9%	9%	7%	11%
Latino	9%	5%	7%	9%
Asian/Pacific Islander	5%	5%	4%	6%
Native American	11%	8%	9%	10%
Other	–	–	5%	9%
INCOME & POVERTY				
Poverty rate (% persons)	8%	8%	9%	12%
Principal cities	11%	12%	12%	15%
Suburbs	7%	6%	7%	10%

(Continued)

TABLE B.12 (Continued)

Metropolitan characteristics	1980	1990	2000	2010
80/20 household income ratio	4.08	3.61	3.69	4.30
Gini coefficient (household income)	0.38	0.39	0.43	0.44
Percentage households by income level (middle class analysis)				
Lower income	30%	30%	33%	35%
Middle income	40%	43%	42%	39%
Upper income	30%	27%	25%	27%
Income differentials				
Median Black household income relative to median white household income	65%	68%	67%	61%
Median Latino household income relative to median white household income	76%	84%	74%	68%
Median Asian household income relative to median white household income	92%	90%	92%	105%

SPATIAL SEGREGATION BY RACE & INCOME

	1980	1990	2000	2010
Principal cities–suburbs job distribution				
Percentage of jobs in principal cities	63%	59%	55%	56%
Percentage of jobs in suburbs	37%	41%	45%	44%
Spatial segregation by race				
Black–white dissimilarity index	0.64	0.58	0.53	0.49
Latino–white dissimilarity index	0.23	0.27	0.32	0.33
All people of color–white dissimilarity index	0.40	0.36	0.32	0.31
Spatial segregation by income *(percentage population by income level of census tract)*				
Poor	10%	11%	11%	18%
Low income	11%	12%	16%	11%
Low-mid income	24%	27%	23%	23%
High-mid income	36%	29%	31%	25%
High income	14%	13%	12%	14%
Affluent	6%	7%	7%	9%
Spatial poverty				
Percentage of CBSA population in high poverty tracts (poverty rate > 20%)	6%	7%	6%	14%
Percentage of CBSA population in very high poverty tracts (poverty rate > 40%)	1%	2%	1%	1%
Poverty concentration				
Percentage of CBSA poor in high poverty tracts (poverty rate > 20%)	18%	24%	18%	33%
Percentage of CBSA poor in very high poverty tracts (poverty rate > 40%)	3%	8%	4%	4%
Poverty dissimilarity index	0.27	0.32	0.30	0.32

TABLE B.12 (Continued)

Metropolitan characteristics	1980	1990	2000	2010
EDUCATION & EMPLOYMENT				

Educational attainment
(Population 25 years and older)

	1980	1990	2000	2010
Less than high school	20%	13%	11%	9%
High school only	33%	26%	23%	21%
Some college	25%	33%	34%	33%
Bachelor's degree	15%	19%	22%	24%
Graduate or professional degree	7%	8%	11%	13%

Workers by industry (% distribution)
(Total employed population 16 years and older)

	1980	1990	2000	2010
Agriculture and mining	1%	1%	1%	1%
Construction	5%	6%	6%	5%
Manufacturing	17%	15%	11%	8%
Transportation, warehousing, and utilities	4%	4%	4%	3%
Wholesale trade	5%	5%	4%	4%
Retail trade	11%	11%	11%	10%
Finance, insurance, and real estate	9%	9%	9%	9%
Professional services	10%	12%	14%	15%
Health services	6%	7%	8%	10%
Information	3%	3%	4%	4%
Education	1%	1%	1%	2%
Other services	11%	13%	13%	14%
Government – civilian	13%	12%	12%	12%
Government – military	4%	3%	0%	2%

INDUSTRY WAGE STRUCTURE				

Share of jobs by industry wage level

	1980	1990	2000	2010
Low-wage	–	22%	25%	27%
Middle-wage	–	46%	45%	45%
High-wage	–	33%	30%	29%

Job growth by industry wage level over previous decade

	1980	1990	2000	2010
Low-wage	–	–	49%	3%
Middle-wage	–	–	25%	−1%
High-wage	–	–	18%	−7%

Earnings growth by industry wage level over previous decade
(Growth in real earnings per worker)

	1980	1990	2000	2010
Low-wage	–	−1%	25%	9%
Middle-wage	–	−3%	20%	7%
High-wage	–	13%	63%	−4%

(Continued)

TABLE B.12 (Continued)

Metropolitan characteristics	1980	1990	2000	2010
Average earnings per job by industry wage level	–			
Low-wage		$22,007	$27,507	$30,062
Middle-wage		$39,921	$47,715	$51,074
High-wage		$56,222	$91,553	$88,300
Total jobs by industry wage level				
Low-Wage				
Real estate and rental and leasing	–	24,690	31,292	29,742
Administrative and support and waste management and remediation services	–	52,429	92,650	83,307
Education services	–	10,809	17,506	22,487
Arts, entertainment, and recreation	–	17,677	27,079	28,670
Accommodation and food services	–	90,867	117,617	124,772
Other services (except public administration)	–	39,784	65,989	75,465
All low-wage		236,256	352,133	364,443
Middle-Wage				
Agriculture, forestry, fishing, and hunting	–	8,077	6,742	4,574
Construction	–	70,716	93,011	77,682
Wholesale trade	–	66,746	79,965	75,979
Retail trade	–	141,984	176,654	165,666
Transportation and warehousing	–	50,066	59,482	53,159
Finance and insurance	–	53,720	67,099	57,078
Health care and social assistance	–	102,230	135,330	175,396
All middle-wage		493,539	618,283	609,534
High-Wage				
Mining	–	778	1,318	702
Utilities	–	3,621	2,165	1,961
Manufacturing	–	231,668	211,368	165,546
Information	–	34,558	79,013	87,178
Professional, scientific, and technical services	–	67,229	100,185	109,587
Management of companies and enterprises	–	16,521	22,816	24,623
All high-wage		354,375	416,865	389,597

NOTE: (1) Data on the 80/20 household income ratio, the Gini coefficient, and percentage households by income level for 1980–2000 are based on surveys during those years but actually reflect incomes during the year prior to the survey. Poverty-related measures rely on income from the year prior to the survey as well, but incorporate information on family composition during the survey year. (2) Certain measures reported in the 2010 column actually reflect averages across annual surveys covering 2008–2012. These include data on percentage foreign-born (and citizenship), unemployment rate (and by race/ethnicity), percentage households by income level, and all measures of segregation, spatial poverty, and poverty concentration. (3) Data on educational attainment for 1980 is estimated based on years of schooling; for other years it is based on degrees earned.

Case-Study Interviews

The organization named is the one our informant was with at the time of the interview.

CHARLOTTE, NC

Debra Campbell, *Charlotte-Mecklenburg Planning Department*
Ron Carlee, *City Manager, City of Charlotte*
Robert Cook, *Mecklenburg-Union Metropolitan Planning Organization*
Dianne English, *Community Building Initiative*
Mike Manis, *Centralina Council of Governments*
Pat McCoy, *Action NC*
Jeff Michael, *UNC Charlotte Urban Institute*
Bob Morgan, *Charlotte Chamber of Commerce*
Sushil Nepal, *Centralina Council of Governments*
Mary Newsom, *UNC Charlotte Urban Institute*
Luis Rodriguez, *Action NC*
Tim Rorie, *Southern Piedmont Central Labor Council*
Héctor Vaca, *Action NC*

FRESNO, CA

Elliott Balch, *Downtown Revitalization, City of Fresno*
Jose Barraza, *Southeast Fresno Community Economic Development Association*
Keith Bergthold, *Development and Resource Management, City of Fresno*
Tony Boren, *Fresno Council of Governments*
Mike Dozier, *Office of Community and Economic Development, California State University, Fresno*

Elizabeth Jonasson, *Coalition for Clean Air*
Rey León, *San Joaquin Valley Latino Environmental Advancement and Policy Project (LEAP)*
Andy Levine, *Faith in Community (PICO)*
Deborah J. Nankivell, *Fresno Business Council*
Jenny Saklar, *Central Valley Air Quality Coalition*
Phoebe Seaton, *Leadership Counsel for Justice and Accountability*
Sarah Sharpe, *Fresno Metro Ministry*
Mayor Ashley Swearengin, *City of Fresno*
Peter Weber, *Fresno Business Council*

GRAND RAPIDS, MI

Rick Baker, *Grand Rapids Area Chamber of Commerce*
Jordan Bruxvoort, *The Micah Center*
John Canepa, *Grand Action*
Sam Cummings, *CWD Real Estate*
James Edwards, *Dorothy A. Johnson Center for Philanthropy*
Abed Itani, *Grand Valley Metropolitan Council*
Michael Johnston, *Work in Progress West Michigan*
Lisa Mitchell, *Partners for a Racism-Free Community*
Greg Northrup, *West Michigan Strategic Alliance*
Jon Nunn, *Grand Action*
Darel Ross, *LINC (Lighthouse Communities, Inc.)*

GREENSBORO, NC

R. Cameron Cooke, *Affordable Housing Management, Inc.*
Mike Fox, *North Carolina Department of Transportation*
Lindy Garnette, *YWCA of Greensboro*
April Harris, *Action Greensboro*
Reverend Virginia Herring, *Holy Trinity Episcopal Church*
Dan Lynch, *Greensboro Economic Development Alliance*
Beth McKee-Huger, *Greensboro Housing Coalition*
Lillian Plummer, *Greensboro/High Point/Guilford Workforce Development Board*
Robin Rhyne, *Greensboro Economic Development Alliance*
Terri Shelton, *Research and Economic Development, University of North Carolina at Greensboro*
John Shoffner, *Economic Development, City of Greensboro*
Stephanie M. Walker, *Impact Greensboro / Center for Creative Leadership*

OKLAHOMA CITY, OK

Nancy Anthony, *Oklahoma Community Foundation*
Rueben Aragon, *Latino Community Development Agency*
Nathaniel Batchelder, *The Peace House Oklahoma City*
Russell Claus, *Planning Department, City of Oklahoma City*

Mayor Mick Cornett, *City of Oklahoma City*
Eddie Foreman, *Central Oklahoma Workforce Investment Board*
Aubrey Hammontree, *Planning Department, City of Oklahoma City*
Blair Humphreys, *Institute for Quality Communities, University of Oklahoma*
Senator Constance Johnson, *District 48, Oklahoma State Senate*
John Johnson, *Association of Central Oklahoma Governments*
Patrick Raglow, *Catholic Charities of the Archdiocese of Oklahoma*
Steve Rhodes, *Planning Department, City of Oklahoma City*
John Sharp, *Association of Central Oklahoma Governments*
Crystal Stuhr, *United Way of Central Oklahoma*
William Tabbernee, *Oklahoma Conference of Churches*
Roy Williams, *Greater Oklahoma City Chamber*

RALEIGH-DURHAM, NC

Mark Ahrendsen, *Department of Transportation, City of Durham*
James Andrews, *North Carolina State AFL-CIO*
Allan Freyer, *North Carolina Justice Center*
Bonnie Gordon, *MDC*
Natalie Griffith, *Regional Transportation Alliance*
Charles Hayes, *Research Triangle Regional Partnership*
Sean Kosofsky, *Blueprint NC*
Greg McNamara, *Greater Raleigh Chamber of Commerce*
Joe Milazzo II, *Regional Transportation Alliance*
Tazra Mitchell, *North Carolina Justice Center*
Lee Anne B. Nance, *Research Triangle Regional Partnership*
Felix Nwoko, *Department of Transportation, City of Durham*
Shun Robertson, *MDC*
Kevin Rogers, *Action NC*
Max Rose, *MDC*
James Sauls, *Greater Raleigh Chamber of Commerce*
Stephen Scott, *Wake Technical Community College*
Barbara Zelter, *Department of Social Work, North Carolina State University*

SACRAMENTO, CA

David Butler, *NextEd*
Richard Dana, *Mutual Assistance Network*
Barbara Hayes, *Sacramento Area Trade and Commerce Organization (SACTO)*
Chet Hewitt, *Sierra Health Foundation*
Bill Kennedy, *Legal Services of Northern California*
Kathy Kossick, *Sacramento Employment and Training Organization*
Pat Fong Kushida, *California Asian Pacific Chamber of Commerce*
Howard Lawrence, *Sacramento Area Congregations Together (Sacramento ACT)*
Jonathan London, *Center for Regional Change, University of California, Davis*
Charles Mason Jr., *Ubuntu Green / Coalition for Regional Equity*
Mike McKeever, *Sacramento Area Council of Governments (SACOG)*

Bill Mueller, *Valley Vision*
Roger Niello, *Sacramento Metro Chamber*
Council Member Jay Schenirer, *District 5, Sacramento City Council*
Supervisor Phil Serna, *Sacramento County Board of Supervisors*
James Shelby, *Greater Sacramento Urban League*
Christine Tien, *The California Endowment*

SALT LAKE CITY, UT

Pamela Atkinson
Deborah S. Bayle, *United Way of Salt Lake*
Bishop H. David Burton, *Church of Jesus Christ of Latter-day Saints*
Dale Cox, *Utah AFL-CIO*
Lew Cramer, *World Trade Center Utah*
Reverend France A. Davis, *Calvary Baptist Church*
Brandon Dew, *Operating Engineers Local Union 3*
Spencer P. Eccles, *Utah Governor's Office of Economic Development*
Maria Garciaz, *NeighborWorks Salt Lake*
Luis Garza, *Comunidades Unidas*
Dayne Goodwin, *Wasatch Coalition for Peace and Justice*
Gladys Gonzalez, *HMC La Agency*
Robert Grow, *Envision Utah*
Dan Lofgren, *Cowboy Partners*
Alan Matheson, *Governor's Office*
Jason Mathis, *Downtown Alliance*
Brenda Scheer, *College of Architecture and Planning, University of Utah*
Senator Luz Robles, *District 1, Utah State Senate*
Kristine Widner, *Envision Utah*

SAN ANTONIO, TX

Becky Bridges Dinnin, *San Antonio Chamber of Commerce*
Darryl Byrd, *SA2020*
Ramiro Cavazos, *San Antonio Hispanic Chamber of Commerce*
Secretary Henry Cisneros, *CityView*
Ernie Cortes, *Industrial Areas Foundation*
Tom Cummins, *San Antonio AFL-CIO*
John Dugan, *Urban Planning Department, City of San Antonio*
Will Garrett, *San Antonio Chamber of Commerce*
Mario Hernandez, *San Antonio Economic Development Foundation*
Gabriella Lohan, *Sisters of the Holy Spirit—C.O.P.S. / Metro Alliance*
Dennis Noll, *San Antonio Area Foundation*
Sister Pearl Caesar, *Project QUEST*
Eyra Perez, *San Antonio Educational Partnership*
Richard Perez, *San Antonio Chamber of Commerce*
Mike Phillips, *First Unitarian Universalist—C.O.P.S. / Metro Alliance*
Judy Ratlief, *Eastside Promise Neighborhood / Tynan Early Childhood Center*

Ricardo Romo, *University of Texas at San Antonio*
Jeanne Russell, *SA2020*

SEATTLE, WA

Josh Brown, *Puget Sound Regional Council*
Executive Dow Constantine, *King County*
Joe Chrastil, *Industrial Areas Foundation / Sound Alliance*
David Freiboth, *King County Central Labor Council*
Paula Harris-White, *King County Equity and Social Justice*
Marty Kooistra, *Housing Development Consortium*
Susannah Malarkey, *Technology Alliance*
Gordon McHenry Jr., *Solid Ground: Building Community to End Poverty*
Norman Rice, *The Seattle Foundation*
David Rolf, *SEIU Local 775NW*
Sili Savusa, *White Center Community Development Association*
Marléna Sessions, *Workforce Development Council of Seattle—King County*
Hilary Stern, *Casa Latina*
Rich Stolz, *OneAmerica*
Matias Valenzuela, *King County Equity and Social Justice*
David West, *Puget Sound Sage*
Maiko Winkler-Chin, *Seattle Chinatown International District Preservation and Development Authority*
Victoria Woodards, *City of Tacoma / Urban League*

SILICON VALLEY, CA

Alex Andrade, *Silicon Valley Community Foundation*
Chris Block, *American Leadership Forum-Silicon Valley*
Bob Brownstein, *Working Partnerships USA*
Ben Field, *South Bay Labor Council*
Gina Gates, *People Acting in Community Together (PACT)*
Eleanor Clement Glass, *Silicon Valley Community Foundation*
Ron Gonzales, *Hispanic Foundation of Silicon Valley*
Russell Hancock, *Joint Venture Silicon Valley*
Gregory Kepferle, *Catholic Charities of Santa Clara County*
Derecka Mehrens, *Working Partnerships USA*
Manny Santamaria, *Silicon Valley Community Foundation*
Patrick Soricone, *United Way Silicon Valley*
Kris Stadelman, *NOVA Workforce Board*
Bruce Wagstaff, *Social Services Agency of Santa Clara County*
Kim Walesh, *Economic Development, City of San Jose*
Jessica Zenk, *Silicon Valley Leadership Group*

Notes

1. CAN'T WE ALL JUST GET ALONG?

1. US Bureau of Economic Analysis annualized quarterly GDP growth rates.

2. For updated data, see Emmanuel Saez's website, http://elsa.berkeley.edu/~saez/.

3. *State of Working America,* http://stateofworkingamerica.org/chart/swa-wages-table-4-2-average-hourly-pay-inequality/.

4. *State of Working America,* http://stateofworkingamerica.org/chart/swa-wages-table-4-14-hourly-wages-education/.

5. *Polling Report,* www.pollingreport.com/CongJob1.htm.

6. In fact, when asked whether they had a higher opinion of Congress or a series of unpleasant or disliked things, voters said they had a higher opinion of root canals, NFL replacement refs, political pundits, used-car salesmen, cockroaches, head lice, and colonoscopies than of Congress (Easley 2013).

7. According to the Brookings Institute's Vital Statistics on Congress, the legislative productivity of Congress—at least as measured by the number of public bills passed and signed into low—has fallen consistently over the past 50 years. In the 1950s and 1960s, in a typical two-year session of Congress, nearly 800 bills were passed. By the 1990s and 2000s, this had fallen closer to 400. In the 112th Congress of 2011–12, only 283 total public bills were passed and signed into law, and the 113th Congress did only slightly better with 296 (http://dailysignal.com/2014/12/30/turns-113th-congress-wasnt-least-productive/).

8. Newspaper Association of America, www.naa.org/Trends-and-Numbers/Readership/Age-and-Gender.aspx.

9. We calculated the 2012 share of voters in landslide counties using the same methods and data described in Bishop and Cushing (2008, 10), first calculating measures for 1988, 1992, and 2000 to insure that our new series would be consistent with what these authors report.

10. Pew Research Religion & Public Life Project, www.pewforum.org/Politics-and-Elections/Little-Voter-Discomfort-with-Romney%E2%80%99s-Mormon-Religion.aspx.

11. Scripps Survey Research Center at Ohio University, http://newspolls.org/articles/19604.

12. There is a now a vast literature on regional knowledge networks, especially as they relate to regional innovation systems (Markusen 1999). While we return to these issues at the end of the book, particularly the interconnection between such networks and epistemic communities, here the focus is on the impact on policy rather than on firm-level economic activity.

13. The elaboration is that we add a time dimension that was largely missing in Haas's formulations but has been explored in subsequent work by Antoniades (2010), who distinguished between ad hoc communities focused on specific policy problems and those that develop a more constant and holistic character. For Antoniades, these more holistic communities—which are closer to our notion of diverse and dynamic epistemic communities—are aimed at the establishment and perpetuation of beliefs and visions as dominant social discourse, and are rooted more in social interactions and struggles than in particular policy problems.

2. DRIVING THAT TRAIN: CAN CLOSING THE GAP FACILITATE SUSTAINED GROWTH?

1. See also the working paper by Levine, Frank, and Dijk (2010), which looks at the effects of income inequality on "expenditure cascades" and finds that the US counties with the highest levels of income inequality were the most likely to experience financial distress.

2. While this is the full sample, we lacked key variables for all 181 regions. We were, for example, unable to calculate Gini coefficients for ten smaller CBSAs (less than 500,000 population), and unionization rates for fifteen smaller CBSAs are not reported. In regressions with those variables, we are actually analyzing 287 growth spells in 160 regions.

3. For the three cases without any growth spells, average employment and wage growth were relatively high—but that was due to averaging one spectacular performer, one dismal performer, and one middle-range performer.

4. Berg et al. (2012) report time ratios rather than hazard ratios; the two measures move in opposite directions. We report hazard ratios because they might be more familiar to readers and because the Cox procedure is built into SPSS, our program of choice for this exercise. To check our results, we also did all the regressions in Stata, using the Streg command with the accelerated-time-to-failure option (the exact method used in Berg et al. 2012). We report those results in a footnote when we consider the integrated model; suffice it to say here that everything moves in a very similar direction.

5. Another measure that we tried—and discarded—was a dummy variable indicating whether the regional growth spell ended during a period of national economic recession (54% of our growth spells did). As it turned out, this recession dummy variable was highly significant, entered either by itself or in con-

junction with the percentage of time still growing while the nation was in recession, but the sign suggested that a growth spell that ends in a national recession is likely to be longer than one that doesn't. While this seems like an anomaly, it isn't. The average length of spells that ended in a recession is actually greater (26.77 versus 24.59) than those that ended outside of a national recession. The way to think about this is that a region that takes a national recession to get knocked off its growth spell is actually more shock-resilient, so its growth spells will be longer. Because a consideration of the features that explain this is exactly what we are trying to get at with our other variables, we do not include the recession-at-end variable either here or in our final multivariate specifications (although the results do not change much if we do).

6. In addition, the gross regional product measure used as the numerator is taken from another source, so we get some unrealistically high export shares. We logged the variable to reduce that problem and get a more normal distribution, but the result made little difference to the regression outcomes and was not parallel with the other share variables utilized later. Hence, we report the results for the straightforward share measure. Since we are not primarily concerned here with the size of the effect but its direction, we were not worried about what is likely a consistent overestimation of export shares.

7. Center for Metropolitan Studies, University of Pittsburgh, www.metrostudies.pitt.edu/Projects/MetropolitanPowerDiffusionIndex/tabid/1321/.

8. In particular, we used data on household income from the 1990 and 2000 5-percent Public Use Microdata Samples, applying trapezoidal integration to calculate the Gini coefficient for each year.

9. We used categorical household-income information by race of householder from the 1990 and 2000 censuses, and defined the middle class to include households with income between 80 and 120 percent of the overall regional median. All households falling in income brackets entirely contained within the resulting income boundaries for the middle class were included, and, for the income brackets "split" by the income boundaries, linear interpolation was used to estimate the number of households in such brackets falling in the middle class. This variable is a bit of a hang-over from our work on the determinants of equity and growth in Benner and Pastor (2012) and may be less reflective of the social-distance measures we are mainly exploring in this exercise, a point we mention in the discussion of the multivariate analysis.

10. The ratio is calculated for the so-called principal cities of a metro area relative to other areas.

11. Most economic institutions either do not vary substantially from region to region across the United States, or the nature of the differences is difficult to capture quantitatively (such as variances in economic development strategies). There are some state-level differences, such as minimum-wage or right-to-work legislation (used for example in Hill et al. 2012), but with multiple metro regions in single states, and some metropolitan regions crossing state boundaries, it seemed more appropriate to consider one economic institution that does vary by region: the percentage of unionization.

12. We reran the individual Cox regressions with the Gini coefficient and the Gini residual from this exercise; both were highly significant, but, as one

might expect, the hazard ratio for the modified Gini coefficient on its own was lower (since some of the underlying explanatory power from the education structure—that is, its role in postponing the "hazard" of an end to a growth spell—has been set to one side).

13. Because we were worried about the impacts of the Great Recession on our results—after all, part of the reason we weren't worried about right-censoring is that nearly all the growth spells were clipped by the end of the period we examined—we reran the full model with a dummy variable set to 1 if the growth spell ended in the official recession period (December 2007 to June 2009, so fourth quarter of 2007 to second quarter of 2009). The variable itself was not significant, and the only other variable that lost just a bit of its significance was the percentage of the workforce in construction, a sensible turn of events given the role that that sector played in the most recent turndown.

14. As mentioned in an earlier note, we also ran the model in Stata using Streg with an accelerated-time-to-failure option to obtain results more directly parallel to those in Berg et al. (2012). We specified the Weibull distribution, as did they. The only difference of note in the individual regressions is that the growth-shortening effect of the share of the population with a BA or better was more significant (although the high school-to-AA variable was still growth-promoting and much more significant). In the integrated model, virtually everything was identical in terms of significance, with a few minor exceptions. MPDI and the dissimilarity index were less significant, and the city–suburb poverty ratio was more significant, suggesting that the competition for significance of these similar variables winds up with slightly different results outside the Cox specification. The share of the workforce in construction also became insignificant, although it was signed as expected. As noted in the text, the time-ratio coefficient we obtain from this regression for our Gini measure (the only exactly parallel right-hand-side variable between the Berg et al. study and ours) is virtually identical to the value they obtain for the Gini.

15. To investigate that, we dropped the spatial-sorting variable, and the city–suburb poverty ratio did indeed return to significance.

3. WHERE TO GO, WHAT TO ASK: SELECTING AND DESIGNING THE CASE STUDIES

1. The reason is that we built up the various income ratios for the metro regions by adding up data from the census tracts. Because we worked with summary data, not micro-data, this data is actually recorded as the number of *households* in various preset income categories. To get at the exact income breaks for the 80/20 ratio at a regional level, we summed the number of households in each break across tracts for each metro area, approximating the distribution of household income. We then identified the income brackets containing the 80th and 20th income percentiles and applied a Pareto interpolation to choose the exact level of the 80th and 20th percentiles. This process helped us estimate the tails, but more effectively when there are many brackets; in 1980, the income categories were few in number, so we thought that estimates at the 90th and 10th percentiles would be less reliable than estimates at the 80th and

20th percentiles. The 80/20 ratio is also used in econometric work by Hill et al. (2012), and we took a similar approach in Benner and Pastor (2012).

2. We realize that including the whole time period as well as the various separate decades might seem like double-counting, but essentially we were trying to reward a region for highly consistent performance; see the discussion of the method in Benner and Pastor (2012).

3. While looking at 2010 made sense because it correlated with the time period being used for the trajectory analysis, we were concerned that this might be viewed as an odd and perhaps biased or unrepresentative ending point because of the ways in which the impacts of the Great Recession may have varied across different metropolitan economies. We therefore experimented with several other end points, including 2007 (right before the onset of the Great Recession) and an average of the years 2006–2010 (to smooth out business-cycle effects and perhaps get at a "true" value). As it turns out, no important differences in the characterizations of income and inequality resulted, so we stuck with the more intuitively obvious (and seemingly consistent) 2010. Also, while we considered both per capita income and median household income for our measure of end-point economic well-being, we decided to use only median household income. In part, this was because household income seems to be a better indicator of people's access to economic resources. But this decision was also made in part because Latino households have a significantly higher-than-average household size compared with other racial groups, meaning that the per capita income figures shifted somewhat disproportionately in regions with a growing percentage of Latino households (a compositional effect). We could see no logical reason to introduce what seemed to us a bias against selecting Latinizing regions, particularly given that the demographic changes going on in the country make the examination of such regions especially important for lessons for the future. Our equity measure was an easier choice. Since we were already using income ratios in our measures of change over time, we decided to use the Gini coefficient of household income.

4. This process resulted in a number of other region types that we ended up not using in our selection process but which might be of interest in other research. These included *valley,* or up-down-up: "good" in at least three-quarters of changes in the 1980s, "bad" in at least three-quarters of changes in the 1990s, and "good" in at least three-quarters of changes in the 2000s; *mountain,* or down-up-down: "bad" in at least three-quarters of changes in the 1980s, "good" in at least three-quarters of changes in the 1990s, and "bad" in at least three-quarters of changes in the 2000s; and *fall back*: "good" in at least three-quarters of the changes in the 1980s and 1990s and "bad" in at least three-quarters of the changes in the 2000s, or "good" in at least three-quarters of the changes in the 1980s and "bad" in at least three-quarters of the changes in the 1990s and 2000s.

4. PARKS AND RECREATION: PLANNING THE EPISTEMIC COMMUNITY

1. We define the Salt Lake City region using the December 2003 US Census CBSA definition of Salt Lake City, UT, consisting of Salt Lake County, Summit

County, and Tooele County. Note that this is different from Envision Utah's definition, which covers the entire Wasatch Front, north and south of Salt Lake City, as well.

2. The Church of Jesus Christ of Latter-day Saints, www.lds.org/bc/content/shared/content/english/pdf/welfare/2011-welfare-services-fact-sheet.pdf.

3. As of 2014, only men are allowed to be ordained as bishops in the LDS Church, though there is a growing movement for more gender equality in the church (Ordain Women, http://ordainwomen.org).

4. Newsroom, Church of Jesus Christ of Latter-day Saints, www.mormonnewsroom.org/article/church-supports-principles-of-utah-compact-on-immigration.

5. Local Area Unemployment and Employment Statistics, US Bureau of Labor Statistics.

6. We define the Sacramento region using the December 2003 US Census CBSA definition of Sacramento–Arden Arcade–Roseville, CA, consisting of El Dorado County, Placer County, Sacramento County, and Yolo County.

7. Interviews, Bill Mueller, executive director, Valley Vision, March 18, 2011, and Barbara Hayes, president and CEO, Sacramento Area Commerce and Trade Organization, March 17, 2011, by C. Benner.

8. SACOG's jurisdictional boundaries differ slightly from the CBSA definition we use in this book. In addition to El Dorado County, Placer County, Sacramento County, and Yolo County, SACOG also includes Yuba County and Sutter County.

9. Interview with Mike McKeever, SACOG, by Madeline Wander and Mirabai Auer, September 18, 2013.

5. BUSINESS KNOWS BEST: ELITE-DRIVEN REGIONAL STEWARDSHIP

1. Association of Chamber of Commerce Executives, www.acce.org/ars/about-the-alliance-for-regional-stewardship/.

2. We define the Grand Rapids region using the December 2003 US Census CBSA definition of Grand Rapids-Wyoming, MI, consisting of Barry County, Ionia County, Kent County, and Newaygo County.

3. We should note that the Brookings report defines the Grand Rapids region slightly differently than we do: it uses the federal definition of the Grand Rapids-Muskegon-Holland Combined Statistical Area, which includes the counties of Allegan, Barry, Ionia, Kent, Muskegon, Newaygo, and Ottawa.

4. Interviews, March 2013.

5. Interviews, March 2013

6. Interviews, March 2013.

7. We define the Charlotte region using the December 2003 US Census CBSA definition of Charlotte-Gastonia-Concord, NC-SC, consisting of Anson County, Cabarrus County, Gaston County, Mecklenburg County, and Union County in North Carolina, and York County in South Carolina.

8. "Regional leaders study best practices in Charlotte," Tulsa Regional Chamber, http://site7.cubicdev.com/nlarchive2/15837/monday-memo#4.

9. In *Regions that Work: How Cities and Suburbs Can Grow Together* (Pastor et al. 2000), Charlotte's strong regional identity and dual emphasis on equity and economic growth were lifted up as an example of an inclusive form of regionalism.

10. Center City Partners, www.charlottecentercity.org/live/neighborhoods/fourth-ward/ (accessed May 15, 2014).

11. Bank of America, http://newsroom.bankofamerica.com/press-releases/community/bank-america-announces-5-million-gift-foundation-carolinas; North Carolina Community Foundation, www.fftc.org/DukeGrants (accessed May 17, 2014).

12. As just one indicator, the 2012 national directory of the National Association of Latino Elected Officials lists only two Latino elected officials in the entire state of North Carolina, and both are in Raleigh, not Charlotte. The only states with fewer members are Arkansas, Oklahoma, and Vermont.

13. We define the Oklahoma City region using the December 2003 US Census CBSA definition of Oklahoma City, OK, consisting of Cleveland County, Grady County, Lincoln County, Logan County, McClain County, and Oklahoma County.

14. *Oklahoman*, "City Planning to be Aired," December 11, 1958, http://dougdawg.blogspot.com/2008/12/oklahoma-city-area-history.html.

15. http://boathousedistrict.org/training-site/.

16. City of Oklahoma City, www.okc.gov/maps3/mapshistory.html, accessed May 20, 2014; Greater Oklahoma City, www.okcchamber.com/index.php?submenu=ChamberHistory&src=gendocs&ref=ChamberHistory&category=About, accessed May 23, 2014.

17. NewsOK, http://newsok.com/maps3 (accessed July 15, 2013).

18. We have been unable to find a study documenting what proportion of sales tax revenue in Oklahoma City comes from nonresidents, but in our interviews, multiple people said that 25–30 percent was a good rule of thumb.

6. STRUGGLE AND THE CITY: CONFLICT-INFORMED COLLABORATION

1. We define the Greensboro region using the December 2003 US Census CBSA definition of Greensboro-High Point, NC, consisting of Guilford County, Randolph County, and Rockingham County. The Piedmont Triad is a broader region of north-central North Carolina which includes the cities of Greensboro, High Point, and Winston-Salem.

2. "History of Greensboro," www.greensboro-nc.gov/index.aspx?page=142 (accessed January 23, 2014). Since as far back as the 1850s, the region has been a logistics center thanks to the numerous railways (and later freeways) that cut through it.

3. "North Carolina in the Global Economy: Furniture," www.soc.duke.edu/NC_GlobalEconomy/furniture/overview.shtml, accessed January 23, 2014.

4. "About Us," Cone Denim, www.conedenim.com/about-us-2/, accessed January 23, 2014.

5. Greensboro Partnership, "Industry Clusters," http://www.greensboropartnership.org/economic-development/industry-clusters, accessed January 23, 2014.

6. Achieve Guilford, www.achieveguilford.org/parents_community/ (accessed December 15, 2013).

7. Civil Rights Greensboro, "Black Power in Greensboro," http://libcdm1.uncg.edu/cdm/essayblackpower/collection/CivilRights, accessed January 23, 2014.

8. Civil Rights Greensboro, "An Overview of Greensboro Race Relations, 1808–1980," http://libcdm1.uncg.edu/cdm/essaygreensboro/collection/CivilRights, accessed January 23, 2014.

9. Civil Rights Greensboro, "The Greensboro Massacre," http://libcdm1.uncg.edu/cdm/essay1979/collection/CivilRights, accessed January 23, 2014.

10. We define the Fresno region using the December 2003 US Census CBSA definition for Fresno, CA, which consists of Fresno County.

11. The strong agricultural presence in the region also contributes to other destructive social dynamics. The San Joaquin Valley has apparently now become the country's center of the manufacture and use of methamphetamine, with an estimated 80 percent of the nation's meth labs and 97 percent of "superlabs" located there, driven by the particular combination of rural and poverty-stricken conditions, the possibility of acquiring key toxic ingredients from the agriculture industry, and close access to major urban centers (Winter 2011).

12. American Factfinder, American Community Survey 2012 Five-Year file, http://factfinder.census.gov.

13. Community Alliance, http://fresnoalliance.com/wordpress/, accessed January 23, 2014.

14. We define the San Antonio region using the December 2003 US Census CBSA definition of San Antonio, TX, consisting of Atascosa County, Bandera County, Bexar County, Comal County, Guadalupe County, Kendall County, Medina County, and Wilson County.

15. San Antonio Economic Development Foundation, "Industry Clusters," www.sanantonioedf.com/industry-clusters, accessed January 23, 2014; City of San Antonio, "San Antonio Industry Clusters," www.sanantonio.gov/IID/IndustryClusters.aspx, accessed January 23, 2014.

16. Project QUEST, www.questsa.org, accessed January 23, 2014.

17. SA 2020 actually builds on Target '90, a similar effort at citywide goal-setting undertaken in the 1980s under then-mayor Henry Cisneros.

7. THE NEXT FRONTIER: COLLABORATION IN THE NEW ECONOMY

1. We define the Silicon Valley region using the December 2003 US Census CBSA definition of San Jose–Sunnyvale–Santa Clara, CA, consisting of San Benito County and Santa Clara County.

2. Joint Venture Silicon Valley, www.jointventure.org/index.php?option=com_content&view=article&id=325&Itemid=330, accessed May 2, 2014.

3. Even before that rechristening in 1998, the organization was known for two decades as the Santa Clara Valley Manufacturing Group (www.bizjournals.com/sanjose/stories/1998/01/19/tidbits.html).

4. Silicon Valley Leadership Group, http://svlg.org/about-us/accomplishments, accessed May 19, 2014.

5. Silicon Valley Leadership Group, http://svlg.org/policy-areas/housing, accessed May 12, 2014.

6. The Living Wage Ordinance was passed in November 1998, making Silicon Valley the highest living wage city in the country at the time. In November 2012, San Jose voters passed the Minimum Wage Ordinance, which set a minimum wage of $10.00 an hour and required that it increase annually with the cost of living. By 2015, it had reached $10.30 an hour. The public-sector pension reform initiative was favored by approximately 70 percent of San Jose voters and approved in June 2012.

7. Moyers & Company, http://billmoyers.com/segment/bill-moyers-essay-the-united-states-of-inequality/.

8. Social Capital Community Benchmark Survey, www.hks.harvard.edu/saguaro/communitysurvey/ca5c.html.

9. We define the Raleigh-Durham region by combining the December 2003 US Census CBSA definitions of Raleigh-Cary, NC (consisting of Franklin County, Johnston County, and Wake County and Durham, NC (consisting of Chatham County, Durham County, Orange County, and Person County).

10. We define the Seattle region using the December 2003 US Census CBSA definition of Seattle-Tacoma-Bellevue, WA, consisting of King County, Pierce County, and Snohomish County.

11. *Puget Sound Business Journal*, www.bizjournals.com/seattle/subscriber-only/2013/07/26/boeing-tops-the-list-of-washington.html.

12. *Puget Sound Business Journal*, www.bizjournals.com/seattle/subscriber-only/2013/07/26/boeing-tops-the-list-of-washington.html.

13. See the November 13, 2009, KCTS interview with Larry Gossett, Roberto Maestas, and Bob Santos at www.youtube.com/watch?v=eCGeWRxEwxM.

14. Gossett, Maestas, and Santos interview.

15. Puget Sound Regional Council, www.psrc.org/growth/tod/, accessed May 8, 2014. The region received two federal grants to help integrate equity into regional planning: a Sustainable Communities Initiative grant and a Growing Transit Communities grant. It is also important to note that the region has an easier time than others planning for the integration of economic development and transportation because the Puget Sound Regional Council acts as both the region's Metropolitan Planning Organization and the Economic Development District as the results of a memorandum of understanding developed in 2003. Also see the Puget Sound Regional Council, "History," www.psrc.org/assets/3305/timeline.pdf.

16. Both out-of-state US-born and foreign-born residents of the Seattle region have higher levels of educational attainment (44 and 38 percent have at least a bachelor's degree, respectively) than those Seattle residents born in Washington (only 30 percent of whom have a bachelor's degree or higher). We should note, however, that Seattle's foreign-born also exhibit lower levels of high school graduation than the Washington-born. The region's immigrant population, it seems, works in both high-tech and low-wage service sectors.

8. STEPPING BACK: THEORIZING DIVERSE AND DYNAMIC EPISTEMIC COMMUNITIES

1. A more recent faith-based initiative called MOSES (Metropolitan Organizing Strategy Enabling Strength) has explicitly engaged in a number of regional advocacy campaigns. Though it was founded in the late 1990s, its efforts have yet to result in substantial change in regional governance, which remains fragmented and divided on race and income lines.

9. LOOKING FORWARD: A BELOVED (EPISTEMIC) COMMUNITY?

1. US Department of Housing and Urban Development, http://portal.hud.gov/hudportal/HUD?src=/hudprograms/sci.

2. US Department of Housing and Urban Development, http://portal.hud.gov/hudportal/HUD?src=/program_offices/economic_resilience/sustainable_communities_regional_planning_grants.

APPENDIX B: DATA SOURCES AND METHODS FOR REGIONAL PROFILES

1. Available at http://socds.huduser.org/Census/Census_Home.html.

2. The formula used to calculate it is well established, and made available by the US Census Bureau at www.census.gov/hhes/www/housing/housing_patterns/app_b.html.

Bibliography

Acs, Zoltan. 2000. *Regional Innovation, Knowledge and Global Change.* London: Pinter.

Adler, Emanual, and Peter Haas. 1992. "Epistemic Communities, World Order and the Creation of a Reflective Research Program." *International Organization* 46 (1): 367–90.

Aghion, Philippe, Eve Caroli, and Cecilia García-Peñalosa. 1999. "Inequality and Economic Growth: The Perspective of the New Growth Theories." *Journal of Economic Literature* 37 (4): 1615–60.

Aguiar, Mark, and Gita Gopinath. 2007. "Emerging Market Business Cycles: The Cycle Is the Trend." *Journal of Political Economy* 115 (1): 69–102. doi: http://dx.doi.org/10.1086/511283.

Akerlof, George A., and Rachel Kranton. 2010. *Identity Economics: How Our Identities Shape Our Work, Wages, and Well-Being.* Princeton, NJ: Princeton University Press.

Albetta, Gloria, and Matias Valenzuela. 2010. *King County Equity Impact Review Tool.* King County, WA. www.kingcounty.gov/exec/equity/toolsandresources.aspx.

Alesina, Alberto, and Roberto Perotti. 1996. "Income Distribution, Political Instability, and Investment." *European Economic Review* 40: 1203–28.

Alesina, A., and D. Rodrik. 1994. "Distributive Politics and Economic Growth." *Quarterly Journal of Economics* 109 (2): 465–90.

Alexeeff, George V., John B. Faust, Laura Meehan August, Carmen Milanes, Karen Randles, Lauren Zeise, and Joan Denton. 2012. "A Screening Method for Assessing Cumulative Impacts." *International Journal of Environmental Research and Public Health* 9 (2): 648–59. doi: http://dx.doi.org/10.3390/ijerph9020648.

Allison, Paul David. 2012. *Survival Analysis Using SAS: A Practical Guide.* Cary, NC: SAS Institute.

Alvaredo, Facundo, Anthony B. Atkinson, Thomas Piketty, and Emmanuel Saez. 2013. "The Top 1 Percent in International and Historical Perspective." *Journal of Economic Perspectives* 27 (3): 3–20. doi: http://dx.doi.org/10.1257/jep.27.3.3.

Amdurksy, Robert S. 1968. "A Public-Private Partnership for Urban Progress." *Journal of Urban Law* 46: 199–215.

Amin, Ash, and Patrick Cohendet. 2004. *Architectures of Knowledge: Firms, Capabilities, and Communities.* Oxford: Oxford University Press.

Anderson, Benedict. 1983. *Imagined Communities: Reflections on the Origin and Spread of Nationalism.* New York: Verso.

Antoniades, Andreas. 2010. "Epistemic Communities, Epistemes and the Construction of (World) Politics." *Global Society* 17 (1): 21–38.

Arax, Mark. 1995. "Trouble in California's Heartland." *Los Angeles Times,* December 6. http://articles.latimes.com/1995-12-06/news/mn-10860_1_fresno-county.

———. 2009. *West of the West: Dreamers, Believers, Builders, and Killers in the Golden State.* New York: PublicAffairs.

Asheim, Bjorn, Philip Cooke, and Ron Martin. 2013. *Clusters and Regional Development: Critical Reflections and Explorations.* New York: Routledge.

Atkinson, Anthony B., Thomas Piketty, and Emmanuel Saez. 2011. "Top Incomes in the Long Run of History." *Journal of Economic Literature* 49 (1): 3–71. doi: http://dx.doi.org/10.1257/jel.49.1.3.

Atkins, Patricia, Pamela Blumenthal, Leah Curran, Adrienne Edisis, Alec Friedhoff, Lisa Lowry, Travis St Clair, Howard Wial, and Harold Wolman. 2011. *Responding to Manufacturing Job Loss: What Can Economic Development Policy Do?* Metro Economy Series. Metropolitan Policy Program, Brookings Institution. www.brookings.edu/research/papers/2011/06/manufacturing-job-loss.

Autor, David H., Lawrence F. Katz, and Melissa S. Kearney. 2006. "The Polarization of the U.S. Labor Market." *American Economic Review* 96 (2): 189–94. doi: http://dx.doi.org/10.1257/000282806777212620.

Bardacke, Frank. 2012. *Trampling out the Vintage: Cesar Chavez and the Two Souls of the United Farm Workers.* New York: Verso.

Barnes, William R., and Larry C. Ledebur. 1998. *The New Regional Economies: The U.S. Common Market and the Global Economy.* Thousand Oaks, CA: Sage.

Baxter, Jamie. 2010. "Case Studies in Qualitative Research." In *Qualitative Research Methods in Human Geography,* edited by Ian Hay, 3rd ed. London: Oxford University Press.

Bellini, Elena, Gianmarco I.P. Ottaviano, Dino Pinelli, and Giovanni Prarolo. 2013. "Cultural Diversity and Economic Performance: Evidence from European Regions." In *Geography, Institutions and Regional Economic Performance,* edited by Riccardo Crescenzi and Marco Percoco, 121–41. Advances in Spatial Science. Berlin: Springer. http://link.springer.com/chapter/10.1007/978-3-642-33395-8_7.

Bender, Richard, and John Parman. 2005. "New Campuses for New Communities: The University and Exurbia [Research and Debate]." *Places* 17 (1). http://escholarship.org/uc/item/6x92x7d9.

Benhamou, Eric. 2000. "Valley Must Narrow the Wage Gap." *San Jose Mercury News*, May 31.

Benkler, Yochai. 2006. *The Wealth of Networks: How Social Production Transforms Markets and Freedom.* New Haven, CT: Yale University Press.

———. 2011. *The Penguin and the Leviathan: The Triumph of Cooperation over Self-Interest.* New York: Crown Business.

Benner, Chris. 1996. *Growing Together or Drifting Apart? Working Families and Business in the New Economy.* San Jose, CA: Working Partnerships USA, with the Economic Policy Institute.

———. 2002. *Work in the New Economy: Flexible Labor Markets in Silicon Valley.* Oxford: Blackwell Press.

———. 2003. "Learning Communities in a Learning Region: The Soft Infrastructure of Cross-Firm Learning Networks in Silicon Valley." *Environment & Planning A* 35 (10): 1809–30.

Benner, Chris, and Amy Dean. 2000. "Labor in the New Economy: Lessons from Labor Organizing in Silicon Valley." In *Nonstandard Work: The Nature and Challenges of Changing Employment Arrangements.* Champaign, IL: Industrial Relations Research Association.

Benner, Chris, and Manuel Pastor. 2012. *Just Growth: Inclusion and Prosperity in America's Metropolitan Regions.* New York: Routledge.

———. 2014. "Brother, Can You Spare Some Time? Sustaining Prosperity and Social Inclusion in America's Metropolitan Regions." *Urban Studies*, September.

———. 2015. "Collaboration, Conflict and Community-Building at the Regional Scale: Implications for Advocacy Planning." *Journal of Planning Education and Research*, online preview, doi: http://dx.doi.org/10.1177/0739456X15580024.

Berg, Andrew G., and Jonathan D. Ostry. 2011. *Inequality and Unsustainable Growth: Two Sides of the Same Coin?* Washington, DC: International Monetary Fund. www.imf.org/external/pubs/cat/longres.aspx?sk=24686.

Berg, Andrew, Jonathan D. Ostry, and Jeromin Zettelmeyer. 2012. "What Makes Growth Sustained?" *Journal of Development Economics* 98 (2): 149–66. doi: http://dx.doi.org/10.1016/j.jdeveco.2011.08.002.

Bergthold, Keith. 2012. "City of Fresno: Fresno General Plan Alternative 'A' Story." California Pan-Ethnic Health Network. http://cpehn.org/sites/default/files/hbdcityoffresnopresentation4-13.pdf.

Berube, Alan. 2007. *MetroNation: How U.S. Metropolitan Areas Fuel American Prosperity.* Washington DC: Brookings Institution Metropolitan Policy Program. http://www.brookings.edu/~/media/research/files/reports/2007/11/06%20metronation%20oberube/metronationbp.pdf.

Berube, Alan, and Bruce Katz. 2005. *Katrina's Window: Confronting Concentrated Poverty Across America.* Washington, DC: Brookings Institution.

Beugelsdijk, Sjoerd, and Sjak Smulders. 2009. *Bonding and Bridging Social Capital and Economic Growth.* Paper 1402697. Rochester, NY: Social Science Research Network. http://papers.ssrn.com/abstract=1402697.

Birdsall, N., D. Ross, and R. Sabot. 1995. "Inequality and Growth Reconsidered: Lessons from East Asia." *World Bank Economic Review* 9 (3): 477.

Bischoff, Kendra, and Sean F. Reardon. 2013. *Residential Segregation by Income, 1970–2009*. US2010 Discover America in a New Century. Providence, RI: Brown University. http://www.s4.brown.edu/us2010/Data/Report/report10162013.pdf.

Bishop, Bill, and Robert G. Cushing. 2008. *The Big Sort: Why the Clustering of Like-Minded America Is Tearing Us Apart*. Boston, MA: Houghton Mifflin Harcourt.

Bogliacino, Francesco, and Marco Vivarelli. 2010. *The Job Creation Effect of R&D Expenditures*. Paper 1549204. Rochester, NY: Social Science Research Network. http://papers.ssrn.com/abstract=1549204.

Bollens, Scott. 2003. "In through the Back Door: Social Equity and Regional Governance." *Housing Policy Debate* 13 (4): 631–57.

Bolman, Lee G., and Terrence E. Deal. 2013. *Reframing Organizations: Artistry, Choice, and Leadership*. Hoboken, NJ: John Wiley & Sons.

Borgsdorf, Del. 1995. "Charlotte's City Within A City: The Community Problem-Solving Approach." *National Civic Review* 84 (3): 218–24.

Boushey, Heather, and Adam S. Hersh. 2012. *The American Middle Class, Income Inequality, and the Strength of Our Economy: New Evidence in Economics*. Washington, DC: Center for American Progress. http://www.americanprogress.org/issues/economy/report/2012/05/17/11628/the-american-middle-class-income-inequality-and-the-strength-of-our-economy/.

Bowles, Samuel. 2012. *The New Economics of Inequality and Redistribution*. Cambridge: Cambridge University Press.

Braczyk, Hans-Joachim, Philip Cooke, and Martin Heidenreich. 1998. *Regional Innovation Systems*. London: University College Long Press.

Brandenburger, Adam M., and Barry J. Nalebuff. 2011. *Co-Opetition*. New York: Crown Business.

Braunstein, Leslie. 2012. "Bank of America Legend Hugh McColl Charts Charlotte's Future." *Urban Land Magazine*, May 17. http://urbanland.uli.org/capital-markets/bank-of-america-legend-hugh-mccoll-charts-charlotte-s-future/.

Brod, Andrew. 2007. "Yes, Regionalism Is Hard Work." *Greensboro News & Record*, November 11. https://web.uncg.edu/bae/documents/cber/articlemuEQltRVCL.pdf.

Brooks, H., L. Liebman, and C. Schelling. 1984. *Public Private Partnership: New Opportunities for Meeting Social Needs*. Cambridge, MA: Ballinger. http://trid.trb.org/view.aspx?id=215895.

Brown, John Seely, and John Duguid. 1998. "Organizing Knowledge." *California Management Review* 40 (3).

Brown, John Sealy, and Paul Duguid. 2000. *The Social Life of Information*. Boston: Harvard Business School Press.

Brynjolfsson, Erik, and Andrew McAfee. 2011. *Race against the Machine: How the Digital Revolution Is Accelerating Innovation, Driving Productivity, and Irreversibly Transforming Employment and the Economy*. Cambridge, MA: Digital Frontier Press.

Brynjolfsson, Erik, and Adam Saunders. 2010. *Wired for Innovation.* Cambridge, MA: MIT Press.

Burritt, Chris. 2012. "Cone Denim's Old Factory Is Back in Fashion." *Business-Week: Companies and Industries,* May 17. http://www.businessweek.com/articles/2012-05-17/cone-denims-old-factory-is-back-in-fashion.

Cairns, John. 1967. "Living with Our Natural Water Systems." *Scientist and Citizen* 9 (2): 28–35. doi: http://dx.doi.org/10.1080/21551278.1967.10114775.

California Department of Food and Agriculture. 2012. *California Agricultural Statistics Review.* Sacramento, CA: California Department of Food and Agriculture. www.cdfa.ca.gov/Statistics/.

Campbell, Alexia Fernandez, and Reena Flores. 2014. "How Silicon Valley Created America's Largest Homeless Camp." *National Journal,* November 25. www.nationaljournal.com/next-america/population-2043/how-silicon-valley-created-america-s-largest-homeless-camp-20141125.

Canham, Matt. 2012. "Census: Share of Utah's Mormon Residents Holds Steady." *Salt Lake Tribune,* April 17. www.sltrib.com/sltrib/home3/53909710-200/population-lds-county-utah.html.csp.

Card, David, and Alan Kreuger. 1997. *Myth and Measurement: The New Economics of the Minimum Wage.* Princeton, NJ: Princeton University Press.

Carlock, Catherine. 2014a. "Frustration Fuels Talk of Re-Thinking Greensboro Economic Development Efforts." *Triad Business Journal,* January 24. www.bizjournals.com/triad/blog/2014/01/frustration-fuels-talk-of-re-thinking.html.

———. 2014b. "Exclusive: Greensboro, High Point, Guilford Leaders Discuss Uniting Economic Development Efforts—Greensboro." *Triad Business Journal,* November 26. www.bizjournals.com/triad/blog/morning-edition/2014/11/exclusive-greensboro-high-point-guilford-leaders.html.

Carter, John R., and Michael D. Irons. 1991. "Are Economists Different, and If So, Why?" *Journal of Economic Perspectives* 5 (2): 171–77. doi: http://dx.doi.org/10.1257/jep.5.2.171.

Carter, Lloyd G. 2009. "Reaping Riches in a Wretched Region: Subsidized Industrial Farming and Its Link to Perpetual Poverty." *Golden Gate University Environmental Law Journal* 3: 5.

Castells, Manuel. 1996. *The Rise of the Network Society.* Cambridge, MA: Blackwell.

———. 1997. *The Power of Identity.* Malden, MA: Blackwell.

———. 2009. *Communication Power.* New York: Oxford University Press.

Castree, Noel. 2005. "The Epistemology of Particulars: Human Geography, Case Studies and 'Context.'" *GeoForum* 36: 541–44.

Chapple, Karen. 2005. *Building Institutions from the Region Up: Regional Workforce Development Collaboratives in California.* Working paper 2005-01. Institute for Urban and Regional Development, University of California, Berkeley. http://escholarship.org/uc/item/93d1h1vt.

Chapple, Karen, and Elizabeth Mattiuzzi. 2013. *Planting the Seeds for a Sustainable Future: HUD's Sustainable Communities Initiative.* Center for Community Innovation, University of California, Berkeley. http://communityinnovation.berkeley.edu/SCIRPGFinal%28080713%29.pdf.

Charlotte Magazine. 2010, August. "Where Are They Now?: The Group." www.charlottemagazine.com/Charlotte-Magazine/August-2010/Where-are-They-Now/The-Group/.

Checkoway, Barry. 1994. "Paul Davidoff and Advocacy Planning in Retrospect." *Journal of the American Planning Association* 60 (2): 139–43.

Chesser, John. 2011. "You're Not from Around Here, Are You?" *UNC Charlotte Urban Institute.* November 18. http://ui.uncc.edu/story/youre-not-around-here-are-you.

Chilvers, Jason. 2008. "Environmental Risk, Uncertainty and Participation: Mapping an Emergent Epistemic Community." *Environment & Planning A* 40(12):2990–3008.

Chinni, Dante, and James Gimpel. 2011. *Our Patchwork Nation: The Surprising Truth about the "Real" America.* New York: Penguin.

Chittum, Ryan. 2005. "Oklahoma City's Revival: Ten Years after the Bombing, Downtown Sees a Renaissance; No More 'Inferiority Complex.'" *Wall Street Journal,* April 23, sec. Property Report. http://online.wsj.com/article/0,,SB111334506692305140,00.html.

Choi, Brian. 2011. "Banktown: Assessing Blame for the Near-Collapse of Charlotte's Biggest Banks." *North Carolina Banking Institute Journal* 15: 423.

Christensen, Rob. 2011. "Many Hail North Carolina Annexation Law." *News & Observer,* March 27.

City of Seattle. 2014a. "Race and Social Justice Initiative (RSJI)." www.seattle.gov/rsji/about.

———. 2014b. "Seattle Challenge Grant." www.seattle.gov/housing/ChallengeGrant/.

———. 2014c. "Seattle Housing Levy." www.seattle.gov/housing/levy/.

Clark, Jennifer. 2013. *Working Regions: Reconnecting Innovation and Production in the Knowledge Economy.* Regions and Cities 66. Abingdon: Routledge.

Conway, Maureen, and Robert Giloth, eds. 2014. *Connecting People to Work: Workforce Intermediaries and Sector Strategies.* Washington, DC: Aspen Institute.

Cooke, Philip, and Kevin Morgan. 1998. *The Associational Economy: Firms, Regions, and Innovation.* New York: Oxford University Press.

Copeland, Michael. 2006. "The Mighty Micro-Multinational." *Business 2.0,* July 28. http://money.cnn.com/magazines/business2/business2_archive/2006/07/01/8380230/.

Cornwall, Marie. 2001. "The Institutional Role of Mormon Women." In *Contemporary Mormonism: Social Science Perspectives,* edited by Marie Cornwall, Tim B. Heaton, and Lawrence Alfred Young, 239–64. Champaign: University of Illinois Press.

Cross, Mai'a K. Davis. 2013. "Rethinking Epistemic Communities Twenty Years Later." *Review of International Studies* 39 (01): 137–60. doi: http://dx.doi.org/10.1017/S0260210512000034.

Crum, William. 2014. "Oklahoma City's Mick Cornett Wins Fourth Term as Mayor." *The Oklahoman,* March 4. http://newsok.com/oklahoma-citys-mick-cornett-wins-fourth-term-as-mayor/article/3940020.

Cunningham, David, Colleen Nugent, and Caitlin Slodden. 2010. "The Durability of Collective Memory: Reconciling the 'Greensboro Massacre.'" *Social Forces* 88 (4): 1517–42.

Cytron, Naomi. 2009. *The Enduring Challenge of Concentrated Poverty in America: Case Study of Fresno, California*. Federal Reserve Bank of San Francisco. www.frbsf.org/community-development/files/fresno_case_study.pdf.

Dalesio, Emery. 2009. "Changing Focus Leads Dell to Close NC Plant." *USA Today*, October 8. http://usatoday30.usatoday.com/tech/techinvestor/corporatenews/2009-10-08-dell-close-north-carolina_N.htm.

Daly, M., and L. Delaney. 2013. "The Scarring Effect of Unemployment throughout Adulthood on Psychological Distress at Age 50: Estimates Controlling for Early Adulthood Distress and Childhood Psychological Factors." *Social Science & Medicine* 80 (March): 19–23. doi: http://dx.doi.org/10.1016/j.socscimed.2012.12.008.

Daukas, Nancy. 2006. "Epistemic Trust and Social Location." *Episteme* 3 (1–2): 109–24. doi: http://dx.doi.org/10.3366/epi.2006.3.1-2.109.

———. 2011. "Altogether Now: A Virtue-Theoretic Approach to Pluralism in Feminist Epistemology." In *Feminist Epistemology and Philosophy of Science: Power in Knowledge*, edited by Heidi E. Grasswick, 45–68. New York: Springer.

Davidoff, Paul. 1965. "Advocacy and Pluralism in Planning." *Journal of the American Planning Association* 31 (4): 331–38.

DealBook. 2008. "Wells Fargo to Buy Wachovia in $15.1 Billion Deal." *New York Times*, October 3. http://dealbook.nytimes.com/2008/10/03/wells-fargo-to-merge-with-wachovia/.

Dean, Amy, and David B. Reynolds. 2009. *A New New Deal: How Regional Activism Will Reshape the American Labor Movement*. Ithaca, NY: ILR Press.

De la Mothe, John, and Gilles Paquet. 1998. *Local and Regional Systems of Innovation*. Boston: Kluwer Academic.

De Langhe, Rogier. 2014. "A Unified Model of the Division of Cognitive Labor." *Philosophy of Science* 81 (3): 444–59.

Deninger, K., and L. Squire. 1996. "Measuring Income Inequality: A New Database." *World Bank Economic Review* 10 (3): 565–91.

DeVos, Rich. 2014. *Simply Rich: Life and Lessons from the Cofounder of Amway: A Memoir*. New York: Simon and Schuster.

Dolan, Drew A. 1990. "Local Government Fragmentation: Does It Drive up the Cost of Government?" *Urban Affairs Review* 26 (1): 28–45. doi: http://dx.doi.org/10.1177/004208169002600102.

Donnor, Jamel K., and Adrienne Dixson. 2013. *The Resegregation of Schools: Education and Race in the Twenty-First Century*. Abingdon: Routledge.

Doran, Jeanette. 2012. *What North Carolina's Annexation Law Reforms Mean to You!* Raleigh, NC: North Carolina Institute for Constitutional Law. http://ncicl.org/article/710.

Dreier, Peter. 2013. "Activists to Watch: Rev. Dr. William J. Barber II." *BillMoyers.com*, October 24. http://billmoyers.com/content/rev-william-j-barber/.

Drennan, Matthew P. 2005. "Possible Sources of Wage Divergence among Metropolitan Areas of the United States." *Urban Studies* 42 (9): 1609–20. doi: http://dx.doi.org/10.1080/00420980500185538.

DuBois, Linda. 2011. "Bird's-Eye View: A Former Military Base Turned Thriving Business Park." *Comstock's* 23, no. 1. www.comstocksmag.com/article/birds-eye-view.

Dutzik, Tony, and Brian Imus. 2002. *Coordinated Planning in Michigan: Three Case Studies*. Ann Arbor, MI: Public Interest Research Group in Michigan. www.greaterlansingurbanservice.org/documents/Coordinated%20Planning%20in%20Michigan.pdf.

Dymski, Gary A., and Manuel Pastor. 1991. "Bank Lending, Misleading Signals, and the Latin American Debt Crisis." *International Trade Journal* 6 (2): 151–91. doi: http://dx.doi.org/10.1080/08853909108523737.

Eaken, Amanda, Justin Horner, and Gloria Ohland. 2012. *A Bold Plan for Sustainable California Communities: A Report on the Implementation of Senate Bill 375*. San Francisco, CA: Natural Resources Defense Council.

Easley, Jason. 2013. "Congress Is Now Less Popular than Lice but More Popular than Meth Labs and Lindsey Lohan." *PoliticusUSA*, January 8. www.politicususa.com/2013/01/08/congress-popular-lice-popular-meth-labs-lindsey-lohan.html.

Eberlein, Sven. 2013. "What's the Matter with 'The Google Bus?'" *Daily Kos*, April 12. www.dailykos.com/story/2013/04/12/1201298/-What-s-the-matter-with-The-Google-Bus.

Eberts, Randall, George Erickcek, and Jack Kleinhenz. 2006. *Dashboard Indicators for the Northeast Ohio Economy: Prepared for the Fund for Our Economic Future, Working Paper 06–05*. Cleveland, OH: Federal Reserve Bank of Cleveland. www.clevelandfed.org/Research/Workpaper/2006/wp06–05.pdf.

Emrich, Anne Bond. 2008. "Downtown Renaissance Took 'Money People,' Vision." *Crain's Detroit Business*, October 5. www.crainsdetroit.com/article/20081005/BRIDGING96/810060310.

Envision Utah. 2013. *The History of Envision Utah*. Salt Lake: Envision Utah. http://envisionutah.org/about/mission-history.

Eskenazi, Stuart. 2001. "Familiar Landscape Lured Scandinavians." *Seattle Times*, November 4. http://old.seattletimes.com/news/local/seattle_history/articles/scandinavians.html.

Faust, Steve, and Elaine Cogan. 2010. *Innovative Civic Engagement Tools and Practices in Land Use Decision-Making*. Primer prepared for the inaugural meeting of the Intermountain West Funder Network.

Finkelstein, Dianne M. 1986. "A Proportional Hazards Model for Interval-Censored Failure Time Data." *Biometrics* 42 (4): 845–54. doi: http://dx.doi.org/10.2307/2530698.

Fleck, Ludwik. 2012. *Genesis and Development of a Scientific Fact*. Chicago: University of Chicago Press.

Forester, John. 1989. *Planning in the Face of Power*. Berkeley, CA: University of California Press.

Foucault, Michel. 1970. *The Order of Things: An Archaeology of the Human Sciences*. New York: Pantheon.

Fourcade, Marion, Etienne Ollion, and Yann Algan. 2014. *The Superiority of Economists.* 14/3. Discussion Paper 14/3. Max Planck Sciences Po Center on Coping with Instability in Market Societies. http://pubman.mpdl.mpg. de/pubman/item/escidoc:2071743:4/component/escidoc:2076000/mpifg_mpdp14_3.pdf.

Frank, Robert H. 2012. *The Darwin Economy: Liberty, Competition, and the Common Good.* Princeton, NJ: Princeton University Press.

Freedman, Michael, and Tim Ransdell. 2005. *California Institute Special Report: California's Past Base Closure Experiences and the 2005 BRAC Round.* Washington, DC: California Institute for Federal Policy Research.

Fulton, William B. 2001. *The Reluctant Metropolis: The Politics of Urban Growth in Los Angeles.* Baltimore, MD: Johns Hopkins University Press.

Ganz, Marshall. 2009. *Why David Sometimes Wins: Leadership, Organization, and Strategy in the California Farm Worker Movement.* New York: Oxford University Press.

George, Carmen. 2013. "Bus Tour Examines Disparities in Fresno's 'Tale of Two Cities.'" *Fresno Bee,* September 25, Local News.

Gertler, Meric S. 2003. "Tacit Knowledge and the Economic Geography of Context, or The Undefinable Tacitness of Being (There)." *Journal of Economic Geography* 3 (1): 75–99. doi: http://dx.doi.org/10.1093/jeg/3.1.75.

Glaser, Barney G., and Anselm L. Strauss. 1967. *The Discovery of Grounded Theory.* Chicago, IL: Aldine.

Godwin, R. Kenneth, Suzanne M. Leland, Andrew D. Baxter, and Stephanie Southworth. 2006. "Sinking Swann: Public School Choice and the Resegregation of Charlotte's Public Schools." *Review of Policy Research* 23 (5): 983–97. doi: http://dx.doi.org/10.1111/j.1541-1338.2006.00246.x.

Goodman, J. S. 1980. *The Dynamics of Urban Growth and Politics.* New York: Macmillan.

Gottlieb, Paul D. 2000. "The Effects of Poverty on Metropolitan Area Economic Performance." In *Urban-Suburban Interdependence: New Directions for Research and Policy,* edited by Wim Wiewel and Roz Greenstein, 21–48. Cambridge, MA: Lincoln Institute for Land Policy.

Grady, Barbara. 2014. "Few Options for Homeless as San Jose Clears Camp." *New York Times,* December 4. www.nytimes.com/2014/12/05/us/driven-from-silicon-valleys-jungle-homeless-face-limited-options.html.

Grand Rapids Area Chamber of Commerce. 2013. "Leadership Grand Rapids." www.grandrapids.org/leadershipgr.

Granovetter, Mark. 1973. "The Strength of Weak Ties." *American Journal of Sociology* 78: 1360–80.

———. 1995. *Getting a Job : A Study of Contacts and Careers.* Chicago, IL: University of Chicago Press.

Grant, Gerald. 2009. *Hope and Despair in the American City: Why There Are No Bad Schools in Raleigh.* Cambridge, MA: Harvard University Press.

Grassmueck, Georg, and Martin Shields. 2010. "Does Government Fragmentation Enhance or Hinder Metropolitan Economic Growth?" *Papers in Regional Science* 89 (3): 641–57. doi: http://dx.doi.org/10.1111/j.1435-5957. 2010.00278.x.

Greenspan, Alan. 2013. "Never Saw It Coming: Why the Financial Crisis Took Economists by Surprise." *Foreign Affairs* 92 (6). www.foreignaffairs.com/articles/140161/alan-greenspan/never-saw-it-coming.

Greenwood, Davydd J. 2008. "Theoretical Research, Applied Research, and Action Research: The Deinstitutionalization of Activist Research." In *Engaging Contraditions: Theory, Politics, and Methods of Activist Scholarship*, edited by Charles R. Hale. Berkeley: University of California Press.

Haas, Peter. 1992. "Introduction: Epistemic Communities and International Policy Coordination." *International Organization* 46 (1): 1–35.

Habyarimana, James, Macartan Humphreys, Daniel N. Posner, and Jeremy M. Weinstein. 2007. "Why Does Ethnic Diversity Undermine Public Goods Provision?" *American Political Science Review* 101 (04). doi: http://dx.doi.org/10.1017/S0003055407070499.

Hakanson, Lars. 2005. "Epistemic Communities and Cluster Dynamics: On the Role of Knowledge in Industrial Districts." *Industry & Innovation* 12 (4): 433–63.

Hamilton, David K., David Y. Miller, and Jerry Paytas. 2004. "Exploring the Horizontal and Vertical Dimensions of the Governing of Metropolitan Regions." *Urban Affairs Review* 40 (2): 147–82. doi: http://dx.doi.org/10.1177/1078087404268077.

Hausmann, Ricardo, Lant Pritchett, and Dani Rodrik. 2005. "Growth Accelerations." *Journal of Economic Growth* 10 (4): 303–29. doi: http://dx.doi.org/10.1007/s10887-005-4712-0.

Hausmann, Ricardo, Francisco Rodríguez, and Rodrigo Wagner. 2006. *Growth Collapses*. Working Paper 2006–024. Department of Economics, Wesleyan University. http://ideas.repec.org/p/wes/weswpa/2006-024.html.

Henderson, Jason Mark. 2013. *Street Fight: The Politics of Mobility in San Francisco*. Amherst: University of Massachusetts Press.

Henton, Doug. 2003. *Civic Revolutionaries: Igniting the Passion for Change in America's Communities*. New York: Jossey Bass.

Henton, Douglas C., and Alliance for Regional Stewardship. 2000. *Regional Stewardship: A Commitment to Place*. Mountain View, CA: Alliance for Regional Stewardship. www.coecon.com/assets/monograph1.pdf.

Henton, Douglas, John G. Melville, and Kimberly A. Walesh. 2003. *Civic Revolutionaries: Igniting the Passion for Change in America's Communities*. San Francisco, CA: John Wiley & Sons.

———. 2004. "The Rise of the New Civic Revolutionaries: Answering the Call to Stewardship in Our Times." *National Civic Review* 93 (1): 43–49. doi: http://dx.doi.org/10.1002/ncr.40.

Hernandez, Mario. 2011. "San Antonio Industry Focus Has Grown beyond the 'Big Three.'" *Bringing Jobs 2 U*, November 7. http://blog.mysanantonio.com/edfwsa/2011/11/san-antonio-industry-focus-has-grown-beyond-the-%e2%80%9cbig-three%e2%80%9d/.

Hill, Edward, Travis St. Clair, Howard Wial, Harold Wolman, Patricia Atkins, Pamela Blumental, Sarah Ficenec, and Alec Friedhoff. 2012. "Economic Shocks and Regional Economic Resilience." In *Urban and Regional Policy and Its Effects: Building Resilient Regions*, edited by Nancy Pindus, Howard Wial, Harold Wolman, and Margaret Weir, 24–59. Washington, DC: Brookings Institution Press.

Hoig, Stan. 1984. *The Oklahoma Land Rush of 1889.* Oklahoma City: Oklahoma Historical Society. www.getcited.org/pub/102394425.

Holzner, Burkart. 1968. *Reality Construction in Society.* Cambridge: Schenkman.

Holzner, Burkart, and John Marx. 1979. *Knowledge Affiliation: The Knowledge System in Society.* Boston, MA: Allyn and Bacon.

Howells, Jeremy R. L. 2002. "Tacit Knowledge, Innovation and Economic Geography." *Urban Studies* 39 (5–6): 871–84. doi: http://dx.doi.org/10.1080/0042098022012835 4.

Huang, Ganlin, and Jonathan K. London. 2012. "Cumulative Environmental Vulnerability and Environmental Justice in California's San Joaquin Valley." *International Journal of Environmental Research and Public Health* 9 (5): 1593–1608. doi: http://dx.doi.org/10.3390/ijerph9051593.

Ingalls, Jerry, and Gary R. Rassel. 2005. "Political Fragmentation, Municipal Incorporation and Anexation in a High Growth Urban Area: The Case of Charlotte, North Carolina." *North Carolina Geographer* 13: 17–30.

Innes, Judith E. 1998. "Information in Communicative Planning." *Journal of the American Planning Association* 64 (1): 52–63. doi: http://dx.doi.org/10.1080/01944369808975956.

Innes, Judith E., and David E. Booher. 1999. "Consensus Building and Complex Adaptive Systems." *Journal of the American Planning Association* 65 (4): 412–23. doi: http://dx.doi.org/10.1080/01944369908976071.

Inwood, Joshua. 2012. "Righting Unrightable Wrongs: Legacies of Racial Violence and the Greensboro Truth and Reconciliation Commission." *Annals of the Association of American Geographers* 102 (6): 1450–67. doi: http://dx.doi.org/10.1080/00045608.2011.603647.

Irwin, Alan, and Mike Michael. 2003. *Science, Social Theory and Public Knowledge.* Philadelphia, PA: McGraw-Hill International.

ISC. 2012. "Sustainable Communities Leadership Academy: A Resource Guide for Local Leaders, V 2.0." Institute for Sustainable Communities. www.southernnevadastrong.org/files/managed/Document/43/Denver_resource_guide_-_no_bios.pdf.

Jenniges, Amy. 2004. "Rained Out? CASA Latina Causes Political Storm in Rainier Valley." *The Stranger,* December 23. www.thestranger.com/seattle/Content?oid=20175.

Jensen, K., J. Call, and M. Tomasello. 2007. "Chimpanzees Are Rational Maximizers in an Ultimatum Game." *Science* 318 (5847): 107–9. doi: http://dx.doi.org/10.1126/science.1145850.

Jerzmanowski, Michal. 2005. *Empirics of Hills, Plateaus, Mountains and Plains: A Markov-Switching Approach to Growth.* Paper 755484. Rochester, NY: Social Science Research Network. http://papers.ssrn.com/abstract=755484.

Johnson, James H., Elisa Jayne Bienenstock, and Walter C. Farrell. 1999. "Bridging Social Networks and Female Labor-Force Participation in a Multiethnic Metropolis." *Urban Geography* 20 (1): 3–30.

Jones, Benjamin F., and Benjamin A. Olken. 2008. "The Anatomy of Start-Stop Growth." *Review of Economics and Statistics* 90 (3): 582–87. doi: http://dx.doi.org/10.1162/rest.90.3.582.

JVSVN. 1992. *An Economy at Risk: The Phase I Diagnostic Report.* San Jose, CA: Joint Venture: Silicon Valley Network.

————. 1995. *The Joint Venture Way: Lessons for Regional Rejuvenation, Vol. 1*. San Jose, CA: Joint Venture: Silicon Valley Network. http://www.jointventure.org/images/stories/pdf/lessons1.pdf.

————. 1999. *Joint Venture's 1999 Index of Silicon Valley*. Palo Alto, CA: Joint Venture: Silicon Valley Network.

Kahn, Lisa B. 2010. "The Long-Term Labor Market Consequences of Graduating from College in a Bad Economy." *Labour Economics* 17 (2): 303–16. doi: http://dx.doi.org/10.1016/j.labeco.2009.09.002.

Kaldor, Nicholas. 1977. "Capitalism and Industrial Development: Some Lessons from Britain's Experience." *Cambridge Journal of Economics* 1 (2): 193–204.

Kanter, Rosabeth Moss. 1994. "Collaborative Advantage: The Art of Alliances." *Harvard Business Review* 72 (4): 96–108.

Katz, Bruce. 2014. "Seattle Uniquely Placed to Compete on Global Stage, but Success Is Not Inevitable." *Brookings Opinions*, May 12. www.brookings.edu/research/opinions/2014/05/12-global-seattle-katz.

Katz, Bruce, and Jennifer Bradley. 2013. *The Metropolitan Revolution: How Cities and Metros Are Fixing Our Broken Politics and Fragile Economy*. Washington, DC: Brookings Institution Press. www.brookings.edu/research/books/2013/the-metropolitan-revolution.

Kearl, J. R., Clayne L. Pope, Gordon C. Whiting, and Larry T. Wimmer. 1979. "A Confusion of Economists?" *American Economic Review* 69 (2): 28–37. doi: http://dx.doi.org/10.2307/1801612.

Killian, Joe. 2013. "Upscale Conflict." *Greensboro News & Record*, July 14. www.news-record.com/news/local_news/article_8069c028-ec34-11e2-99b6-0019bb30f31a.html.

Klein, John P., and Melvin L. Moeschberger. 2003. *Survival Analysis: Techniques for Censored and Truncated Data*. New York: Springer.

Kneebone, Elizabeth. 2014. *Confronting Suburban Poverty in America*. Washington, DC: Brookings Institution.

Kneebone, Elizabeth, Carey Nadeau, and Alan Berube. 2011. *The Re-Emergence of Concentrated Poverty: Metropolitan Trends in the 2000s*. Metropolitan Opportunity Series. Washington, DC: Brookings Institution. www.brookings.edu/~/media/research/files/papers/2011/11/03%20poverty%20kneebone%20nadeau%20berube/1103_poverty_kneebone_nadeau_berube.

Knight, Richard L. 1998. *Stewardship across Boundaries*. Washington, DC: Island Press.

Kuchler, Hannah. 2014. "Tale of Two Valleys: Silicon Valley Fight over Inequality." *Financial Times*, February 14. http://www.ft.com/cms/s/0/d0a260da-8dd4-11e3-bbe7-00144feab7de.html.

Kuhn, Thomas S. 2012. *The Structure of Scientific Revolutions: 50th Anniversary Edition*. Chicago, IL: University of Chicago Press.

Kuznets, Simon. 1955. "Economic Growth and Income Inequality." *American Economic Review* 45 (1): 1–28.

Lackmeyer, Steve, and Jack Money. 2006. *OKC Second Time Around: A Renaissance Story*. Oklahoma City: Full Circle Press.

Lakoff, G. 2004. *Don't Think of an Elephant!: Know Your Values and Frame the Debate: The Essential Guide for Progressives*. Hartford: Chelsea Green.

Lakoff, George, and Mark Johnson. 2008. *Metaphors We Live By*. Chicago, IL: University of Chicago Press.

Lassiter, Matthew D. 2004. "The Suburban Origins of 'Color-Blind' Conservatism: Middle-Class Consciousness in the Charlotte Busing Crisis." *Journal of Urban History* 30 (4): 549–82. doi: http://dx.doi.org/10.1177/0096144204263812.

Lawson, Clive, and Edward Lorenz. 1999. "Collective Learning, Tacit Knowledge and Regional Innovative Capacity." *Regional Studies* 33 (4): 305–17. doi: http://dx.doi.org/10.1080/713693555.

Learn NC. N.d. "Recent North Carolina." In *North Carolina History: A Digital Textbook*. University of North Carolina School of Education. www.learnnc.org/lp/editions/nchist-recent/6177.

Lee, Neil. 2011. "Ethnic Diversity and Employment Growth in English Cities." *Urban Studies* 48 (2): 407–25. doi: http://dx.doi.org/10.1177/0042098010363500.

Leonard, Dorothy, and Sylvia Sensiper. 1998. "The Role of Tacit Knowledge in Group Innovation." *California Management Review* 40 (3): 112–32.

Lesher, Dave, and Jeff Leeds. 1997. "Battles Won—and Lost—in Military Base Conversions." *Los Angeles Times*, May 31. http://articles.latimes.com/1997-05-31/news/mn-64207_1_military-base-conversions.

Lester, T. William, and Sarah Reckhow. 2013. "Network Governance and Regional Equity: Shared Agendas or Problematic Partners?" *Planning Theory* 12 (2): 115–38. doi: http://dx.doi.org/10.1177/1473095212455189.

Levine, Adam Seth, Robert H. Frank, and Oege Dijk. 2010. *Expenditure Cascades*. Paper 1690612. Rochester, NY: Social Science Research Network. http://ssrn.com/abstract=1690612.

Lewis, Paul George, and Mary Sprague. 1997. *Federal Transportation Policy and the Role of Metropolitan Planning Organizations in California*. San Francisco: Public Policy Institute of California.

Li, Huiping, Harrison Campbell, and Steven Fernandez. 2013. "Residential Segregation, Spatial Mismatch and Economic Growth across US Metropolitan Areas." *Urban Studies*, March. doi: http://dx.doi.org/10.1177/0042098013477697.

Link, Albert N., and John T. Scott. 2003. "The Growth of Research Triangle Park." *Small Business Economics* 20 (2): 167–75. doi: http://dx.doi.org/10.1023/A:1022216116063.

Logan, John R., and Harvey Luskin Molotch. 2007. *Urban Fortunes: The Political Economy of Place*. Berkeley, CA: University of California Press.

Logan, Robert K., and Louis W. Stokes. 2003. *Collaborate to Compete: Driving Profitability in the Knowledge Economy*. New York: Wiley.

London, J., G. Huang, and T. Zagofsky. 2011. *Land of Risk, Land of Opportunity: Cumulative Environmental Vulnerabilities in California's San Joaquin Valley*. Center for Regional Change, University of California, Davis, CA: http://explore.regionalchange.ucdavis.edu/ourwork/publications/ceva-sjv/full-report-land-of-risk-land-of-opportunity.

Lopez, Humberto, and Luis Serven. 2009. *Too Poor to Grow*. Policy Research Working Paper No. 5012. Washington, DC: World Bank.

Lowitt, Eric. 2013. *The Collaboration Economy: How to Meet Business, Social, and Environmental Needs and Gain Competitive Advantage*. New York: Jossey-Bass.

Lowrey, Annie. 2013. "The Low Politics of Economic Growth." *New York Times*, January 12. www.nytimes.com/2013/01/13/sunday-review/the-low-politics-of-economic-growth.html.

Magarrell, Lisa, and Joya Wesley. 2010. *Learning from Greensboro: Truth and Reconciliation in the United States*. Philadelphia: University of Pennsylvania Press.

Mann, Catherine L. 2012. *Information Technology Intensity, Diffusion, and Job Creation*. Boston, MA: Brandeis University. www.brandeis.edu/departments/economics/RePEc/brd/doc/Brandeis_WP46.pdf.

Mann, Thomas E., and Norman J. Ornstein. 2012. *It's Even Worse Than It Looks: How the American Constitutional System Collided with the New Politics of Extremism*. New York: Basic Books.

Markusen, Ann. 1999. "Fuzzy Concepts, Scanty Evidence, Policy Distance: The Case for Rigour and Policy Relevance in Critical Regional Studies." *Regional Studies* 33 (9): 869–84.

Marlowe, Steven T., and University of Alabama Dept. of Educational Leadership, Policy and Technology Studies. 2009. *Implications of the Triple Helix Model: Case Study of AIDT and "Mega Projects."* Tuscaloosa: University of Alabama.

Marquez, Benjamin. 1990. "Organizing the Mexican-American Community in Texas: The Legacy of Saul Alinsky." *Policy Studies Review* 9 (2): 355–73.

Martin, Ron, Michael Kitson, and Peter Tyler. 2012. *Regional Competitiveness*. Abingdon: Routledge.

Maskell, P., and A. Malmberg. 1999. "The Competitiveness of Firms and Regions: 'Ubiquitification' and the Importance of Localized Learning." *European Urban and Regional Studies* 6 (1): 9–25. doi: http://dx.doi.org/10.1177/096977649900600102.

Massaro, Rachel, and Alesandra Najera. 2014. *2014 Silicon Valley Index*. San Jose, CA: Joint Venture: Silicon Valley Network.

McCarty, Nolan, Keith T. Poole, and Howard Rosenthal. 2006. *Polarized America: The Dance of Ideology and Unequal Riches*. Cambridge, MA: MIT Press.

McDonald, Michael. 2010. "Voter Turnout in the 2010 Midterm Election." *The Forum* 8 (4).

McKeever, Mike. 2011. "Integrated Land Use, Transportation, and Air Quality Planning in Sacramento." In *Regional Planning for a Sustainable America: How Creative Programs Are Promoting Prosperity and Saving the Environment*. New Brunswick, NJ: Rutgers University Press.

McNeal, William R., and Thomas B. Oxholm. 2009. *A School District's Journey to Excellence: Lessons from Business and Education*. Thousand Oaks, CA: Sage.

Meyerson, Harold. 2013. "L.A. Story." *The American Prospect*, August 6. http://prospect.org/article/la-story-0.

Miller, Char. 2011. "San Antonio, TX 1989–2011." In *Cities in American Political History*, edited by Richardson Dilworth, 669–75. Washington, DC: Congressional Quarterly Press.

Miller, David Young, and Joo Hun Lee. 2009. "Making Sense of Metropolitan Regions: A Dimensional Approach to Regional Governance." *Publius:*

The Journal of Federalism 41 (1): 126–45. doi: http://dx.doi.org/10.1093/publius/pjp040.

Miller, Elena M. 2010. *2009 Annual Report of the State Oil & Gas Supervisor.* Sacramento, CA: California Department of Conservation, Division of Oil, Gas & Geothermal Resources. ftp://ftp.consrv.ca.gov/pub/oil/annual_reports/2009/.

Millner, Caille. 2013. "Why We're Invisible to Google Bus Riders." *San Francisco Chronicle,* April 26. www.sfchronicle.com/living/article/Why-we-re-invisible-to-Google-bus-riders-4467574.php.

Montalvo, Jose G., and Marta Reynal-Querol. 2005. "Ethnic Diversity and Economic Development." *Journal of Development Economics* 76: 293–323.

Montana, Jennifer Paige, and Boris Nenide. 2008. "The Evolution of Regional Industry Clusters and Their Implications for Sustainable Economic Development: Two Case Illustrations." *Economic Development Quarterly* 22 (4): 290–302. doi: http://dx.doi.org/10.1177/0891242408324084.

Moody, Fred. 2004. *Seattle and the Demons of Ambition: From Boom to Bust in the Number One City of the Future.* New York: St. Martin's Griffin.

Morantz, Alison. 1996. "Desegregation at Risk: Threat and Reaffirmation in Charlotte." In *Dismantling Desegregation: The Quiet Reversal of Brown V. Board of Education,* edited by Myron Orfield and Susan Eaton, 179–206. New York: New Press.

Mortensen, Dale T., and Christopher A. Pissarides. 1998. "Technological Progress, Job Creation, and Job Destruction." *Review of Economic Dynamics* 1 (4): 733–53. doi: http://dx.doi.org/10.1006/redy.1998.0030.

Morton, Neal. 2013. "Toyota Changed Jobs Game in S.A." *San Antonio Express-News,* February 2. www.mysanantonio.com/news/local_news/article/Toyota-changed-jobs-game-in-S-A-4246638.php.

Mroz, Thomas A., and Timothy H. Savage. 2006. "The Long-Term Effects of Youth Unemployment." *Journal of Human Resources* 41 (2): 259–93.

Muro, Mark, Bruce Katz, Sarah Rahman, and David Warren. 2008. *MetroPolicy: Shaping a New Federal Partnership for a Metropolitan Nation.* Washington, DC: Brookings Institution. www.brookings.edu/reports/2008/06_metropolicy.aspx.

National Public Radio. 2002. "California's Central Valley. Part Four: Farm Labor and Illegal Immigration." *All Things Considered.* www.npr.org/templates/story/story.php?storyId=843392.

Newport, Frank. 2013. "Congress' Job Approval Falls to 11% Amid Gov't Shutdown." *Gallup,* October 7. www.gallup.com/poll/165281/congress-job-approval-falls-amid-gov-shutdown.aspx.

Newsom, Mary. 2010. "Charlotte Does Light Rail Right." *Grist.org,* June 26. http://grist.org/article/2010-06-25-charlotte-does-light-rail-right/.

Nieves, Evelyn. 2000. "Many in Silicon Valley Cannot Afford Housing, Even at $50,000 a Year." *New York Times,* February 20.

Nowell, Paul. 1999. "McColl, Bank of America Support the Arts by Opening Mint Gallery." *Spartanburg Herald-Journal,* January 7.

O'Daniel, Adam. 2013. "An Hour with Ed Crutchfield: Fishing, Banking and Hugh McColl." *Charlotte Business Journal,* April 18.

www.bizjournals.com/charlotte/blog/bank_notes/2013/04/an-hour-with-ed-crutchfield-fishing.html.

Oreopoulos, Philip, Till von Wachter, and Andrew Heisz. 2012. "The Short- and Long-Term Career Effects of Graduating in a Recession." *American Economic Journal: Applied Economics* 4 (1): 1–29. doi: http://dx.doi.org/10.1257/app.4.1.1.

Orfield, Myron. 2002. *American Metropolitics: The New Suburban Reality.* Washington, DC: Brookings Institution Press.

Ornstein, Norman J., Thomas E. Mann, Michael J. Malbin, Andrew Rugg, and Raffaela Wakeman. 2013. "Vital Statistics on Congress." Brookings Institution. www.brookings.edu/research/reports/2013/07/vital-statistics-congress-mann-ornstein.

Ostrom, Elinor. 2000. "Collective Action and the Evolution of Social Norms." *Journal of Economic Perspectives* 14 (3): 137–58.

Ostrom, Elinor, Roger B. Parks, and Gordon P. Whitaker. 1974. "Defining and Measuring Structural Variations in Interorganizational Arrangements." *Journal of Federalism* 4(4):87–108. doi: http://dx.doi.org/10.2307/3329480.

Ostrom, Elinor, and James Walker, eds. 2005. *Trust and Reciprocity: Interdisciplinary Lessons from Experimental Research.* Russell Sage Foundation Series on Trust. New York: Russell Sage Foundation. www.russellsage.org/publications/trust-and-reciprocity.

Owen, Diana. 2012. "Media Consolidation, Fragmentation and Selective Exposure in the USA." In *The SAGE Handbook of Political Communication,* edited by Holli A Semetko and Margaret Scammell. Thousand Oaks, CA: Sage.

Packer, George. 2013. "Change the World: Silicon Valley Transfers Its Slogans and Its Money to the Realm of Politics." *New Yorker,* May 27.

Pariser, Eli. 2011. *The Filter Bubble: How the New Personalized Web Is Changing What We Read and How We Think.* New York: Penguin.

Pastor, Manuel. 2006. "Cohesion and Competitiveness: Business Leadership for Regional Growth and Social Equity." In *Competitive Cities in the Global Economy,* by OECD, 393–406. OECD. http://www.oecd-ilibrary.org/urban-rural-and-regional-development/competitive-cities-in-the-global-economy/cohesion-and-competitiveness-business-leadership-for-regional-growth-and-social-equity_9789264027091-16-en.

Pastor, Manuel, and Chris Benner. 2008. "Been Down So Long: Weak Market Cities and Regional Equity." In *Retooling for Growth: Building a 21st Century Economy in America's Older Industrial Areas,* edited by Richard M. McGahey and Jennifer S. Vey. Washington, DC: Brookings Institution Press.

———. 2011. "Planning for Equity, Fighting for Justice: Planners, Organizers, and the Fight for Metropolitan Inclusion." In *Regional Planning in America: Practice and Prospect,* edited by Ethan Seltzer and Armando Carbonell, 296. Cambridge, MA: Lincoln Institute of Land Planning.

Pastor, Manuel, Chris Benner, and Martha Matsuoka. 2009. *This Could Be the Start of Something Big: How Social Movements for Regional Equity Are Reshaping Metropolitan America.* Ithaca, NY: Cornell University Press.

———. 2011. "For What It's Worth: Regional Equity, Community Organizing, and Metropolitan America." *Community Development* 42 (4): 437–57.

Pastor, Manuel, Peter Dreier, J. Eugene Grigsby III, and Marta Lopez-Garza. 2000. *Regions That Work: How Cities and Suburbs Can Grow Together.* Minneapolis: University of Minnesota Press.

Pastor, Manuel, T. William Lester, and Justin Scoggins. 2009. "Why Regions? Why Now? Who Cares?" *Journal of Urban Affairs* 31 (3): 269–96. doi: http://dx.doi.org/10.1111/j.1467–9906.2009.00460.x.

Pastor, Manuel, and Enrico A. Marcelli. 2013. *What's at Stake for the State: Undocumented Californians, Immigration Reform, and Our Future Together.* Program for Environmental and Regional Equity, University of Southern California, Los Angeles. http://csii.usc.edu/undocumentedCA.html.

Pastor, Manuel, and John Mollenkopf. 2012. "Struggling over Strangers or Receiving with Resilience? The Metropolitics of Immigrant Incorporation." In *Urban and Regional Policy and Its Effects, Vol. 4: Building Resilient Regions,* edited by Nancy Pindus, Margaret Wier, Howard Wial, and Harold Wolman. Washington, DC: Brookings Institution Press.

Pastor, Manuel, and Michele Prichard. 2012. *LA Rising: The 1992 Civil Unrest, the Arc of Social Justice Organizing, and the Lessons for Today's Movement Building.* Program for Environmental and Regional Equity, University of Southern California, Los Angeles. http://dornsife.usc.edu/pere/larising/.

Pastor, Manuel, Justin Scoggins, T. William Lester, and Karen Chapple. 2012. *Building Resilient Regions Database: A Project of the Building Resilient Regions Network, Funded by the John D. and Catherine T. MacArthur Foundation.* Program for Environmental and Regional Equity, University of Southern California, Los Angeles.

Patterson, Thom. 2011. *After 50 Years of Racial Strife: Why Is Greensboro Still so Tense?* CNN. http://www.cnn.com/2011/US/06/07/greensboro.race/.

Pattillo, Catherine, and Sanjeev Gupta. 2006. *Sustaining Growth Accelerations and Pro-Poor Growth in Africa.* Paper 888064. Rochester, NY: Social Science Research Network. http://papers.ssrn.com/abstract=888064.

Persson, Torsten, and Guido Tabellini. 1994. "Is Inequality Harmful for Growth?" *American Economic Review* 84 (3): 600–621.

Piketty, Thomas. 2014. *Capital in the Twenty-First Century.* Translated by Arthur Goldhammer. Cambridge, MA: Belknap Press.

Piketty, Thomas, and Emmanuel Saez. 2003. "Income Inequality in the United States." *Quarterly Journal of Economics* 118(1):1–41. doi: http://dx.doi.org/10.1162/00335530360535135.

Pisani, Donald J. 1991. "Land Monopoly in Nineteenth-Century California." *Agricultural History* 65 (4): 15–37.

Porter, Michael F. 1998. "Clusters and the New Economics of Competition." *Harvard Business Review* (November-December): 77–90.

Portillo, Ely. 2011. "Chiquita Relocating Headquarters to Charlotte." *Charlotte Observer,* November 30.

———. 2014a. "Chiquita Was Exploring Merger Options in 2011, Filings Show." *Charlotte Observer,* April 30. www.charlotteobserver.com/2014/04/30/4876365/chiquita-was-exploring-merger.html.

———. 2014b. "Chiquita CEO Leaves Door Open to Incentives Repayment for Charlotte, Mecklenburg, and NC." *Charlotte Observer,* May 22. http://

www.charlotteobserver.com/2014/05/22/4926246/chiquita-ceo-leaves-door-open.html.

powell, john. 1999. "Race, Poverty, and Urban Sprawl: Access to Opportunities through Regional Strategies." *Forum for Social Economics* 28 (2): 1–20. doi: http://dx.doi.org/10.1007/BF02833980.

Racemacher, Ida, Marshall Bear, and Maureen Conway. 2001. *Project QUEST: A Case Study of a Sectoral Employment Development Approach.* Washington, DC: Aspen Institute. http://www.aspeninstitute.org/publications/project-quest-case-study-sectoral-employment-development-approach.

Reardon, Sean, and Kendra Bischoff. 2011. "Growth in the Residential Segregation of Families by Income, 1970–2009." American Communities Project, Brown University. www.s4.brown.edu/us2010/Data/Report/report111111.pdf.

Research Triangle Park. 2014. "Keeping the Promise." www.rtp.org/about-us/.

Research Triangle Regional Partnership. 2015. "Triple Helix: Research Triangle Region." www.researchtriangle.org/assets/triple-helix.

Reynolds, David B. 2012. "Review Essay." *WorkingUSA* 15 (4): 609–12. doi: http://dx.doi.org/10.1111/wusa.12019.

Riley, Michale. 2006. "Utah's Embrace: No Documents, No Problem." *Denver Post*, April 2. http://www.denverpost.com/search/ci_3663998.

Rodriguez, A. J. 2013. "New Vision for Project Quest." *San Antonio Express-News,* July 15. www.mysanantonio.com/opinion/commentary/article/New-vision-for-Project-Quest-4662688.php.

Rodrik, Dani. 1999. "Where Did All the Growth Go? External Shocks, Social Conflict, and Growth Collapses." *Journal of Economic Growth* 4 (4): 385–412. doi: http://dx.doi.org/10.1023/A:1009863208706.

Rogers, Mary Beth. 1990. *Cold Anger: A Story of Faith and Power Politics.* Denton, TX: University of North Texas Press.

Rohe, William M. 2011. *The Research Triangle: From Tobacco Road to Global Prominence.* Philadelphia: University of Pennsylvania Press.

Rolf, David. 2014. "What If We Treated Labor Like a Startup?" *The Nation,* June 18. http://www.thenation.com/article/180316/what-if-we-treated-labor-startup.

Rosales, Rodolfo. 2000. *The Illusion of Inclusion: The Untold Political Story of San Antonio.* Austin: University of Texas Press.

Rosenberg, Brett. 2010. "Oklahoma City: A Win-Win; How Oklahoma City Passed Three Transformative Tax Initiatives in Difficult Economic Times." *U.S. Mayor,* June 28.

Rothacker, Rick. 2010. *Banktown: The Rise and Struggles of Charlotte's Big Banks.* Winston-Salem, NC: John F. Blair.

Rothwell, Jonathan. 2013. *The Hidden STEM Economy.* Metropolitan Policy Program at Brookings. www.brookings.edu/research/reports/2013/06/10-stem-economy-rothwell.

Ruggie, John. 1972. "Collective Goods and Future International Collaboration." *American Political Science Review* 66 (September): 874–93.

Ruggie, John Gerard. 1975. "International Responses to Technology: Concepts and Trends." *International Organization* 29 (03): 557–83. doi: http://dx.doi.org/10.1017/S0020818300031696.

Ruggles, Steven J., J. Trent Alexander, Katie Genadek, Ronald Goeken, Matthew B. Schroeder, and Matthew Sobek. 2010. *Integrated Public Use Microdata Series: Version 5.0* [Machine-Readable Database]. Minneapolis: University of Minnesota.

Rusk, David. 1993. *Cities without Suburbs*. Washington, DC: Woodrow Wilson Center Press.

———. 2001. *Inside Game/Outside Game: Winning Strategies for Saving Urban America*. Washington, DC: Brookings Institution Press.

———. 2003. *Cities without Suburbs: A Census 2000 Update*. Washington, DC: Woodrow Wilson Center Press.

———. 2006. *Annexation and the Fiscal Fate of Cities*. Washington, DC: Brookings Institution Metropolitan Policy Program. http://www.brookings.edu/~/media/research/files/reports/2006/8/metropolitanpolicy%20rusk/20060810_fateofcities.pdf.

SACOG. 2004. "Summit Participants Support Blueprint Principles." Sacramento Area Council of Governments Regional Report. www.sacog.org/regrpt/Nov2004_RR.pdf.

———. 2012. "Metropolitan Transportation Plan / Sustainable Communities Strategy." http://sacog.org/mtpscs/files/MTP-SCS/MTPSCS%20WEB.pdf.

Sadd, James, Manuel Pastor, Rachel Morello-Frosch, Justin Scoggins, and Bill M. Jesdale. 2011. "Playing It Safe: Assessing Cumulative Impact and Social Vulnerability through an Environmental Justice Screening Method in the South Coast Air Basin, California." *International Journal of Environmental Research and Public Health* 8 (5): 1441–59. doi: http://dx.doi.org/10.3390/ijerph8051441.

Saegert, Susan, J. Phillip Thompson, and Mark R Warren. 2001. *Social Capital and Poor Communities*. New York: Russell Sage Foundation.

Safford, Sean. 2009. *Why the Garden Club Couldn't Save Youngstown: The Transformation of the Rust Belt*. Cambridge, MA: Harvard University Press.

Santos, Bob. 2005. *Hum Bows, Not Hot Dogs!* 2nd ed. Seattle, WA: International Examiner Press.

Saros, Daniel E. 2009. *Labor, Industry, and Regulation during the Progressive Era*. New York: Routledge.

Savitch, H. V., D. Collins, D. Sanders, and J. P Markham. 1993. "Ties That Bind: Central Cities, Suburbs, and the New Metropolitan Region." *Economic Development Quarterly* 7 (4): 341–57. doi: http://dx.doi.org/10.1177/089124249300700403.

Saxenian, AnnaLee. 1994. *Regional Advantage: Culture and Competition in Silicon Valley and Route 128*. Cambridge, MA: Harvard University Press.

Saxenian, AnnaLee, and Nadya Chinoy Dabby. 2004. *Creating and Sustaining Regional Collaboration in Silicon Valley? The Case of Joint Venture: Silicon Valley*. Institute of Urban and Regional Development, University of California, Berkeley.

Scheer, Brenda. 2012. *The Utah Model: Lessons for Regional Planning*. Brookings Mountain West, University of Nevada, Las Vegas. www.unlv.edu/sites/default/files/TheUtahModel_0.pdf.

Scherer, F. M., and David Ross. 2009. *Industrial Market Structure and Economic Performance.* Paper 1496716. Rochester, NY: Social Science Research Network. http://papers.ssrn.com/abstract=1496716.

Schildt, Chris. 2012. "Just Growth: Inclusion and Prosperity in American's Metropolitan Regions by Chris Benner and Manuel Pastor." *Urban Fringe,* August 3. http://ced.berkeley.edu/bpj/2012/08/just-growth-inclusion-and-prosperity-in-americans-metropolitan-regions-by-chris-benner-and-manuel-pastor/.

Schwantes, Carlos Arnaldo. 1994. *Radical Heritage: Labor, Socialism, and Reform in Washington and British Columbia, 1885–1917.* Moscow, ID: Caxton Press.

Scott, Allen, and Michael Storper. 2003. "Regions, Globalization, Development." *Regional Studies* 37 (6&7): 579–93.

Scott, Allen John. 1998. *Regions and the World Economy: The Coming Shape of Global Production, Competition, and Political Order.* Oxford: Oxford University Press.

Scott, Robert. 2003. *The High Price of "Free" Trade: NAFTA's Failure Has Cost the United States Jobs across the Nation.* Washington, DC: Economic Policy Institute. www.epi.org/publication/briefingpapers_bp147/.

Shapiro, Carl, and Hal R. Varian. 1998. *Information Rules: A Strategic Guide to the Network Economy.* Boston, MA: Harvard Business School Press.

Sheehan, Tim. 2014. "Fresno Gets New 'Scorecard' Website to Measure Quality of Life." *Fresno Bee,* June 18, Local News. www.govtech.com/internet/Fresno-Gets-New-Scorecard-Website-to-measure-quality-of-life.html.

Simon, Roger. 2013. "Government Shutdown Unleashes Racism." *Politico,* October 14. www.politico.com/story/2013/10/government-shutdown-racism-roger-simon-98272.html.

Smith, Heather, and William Graves. 2005. "Gentrification as Corporate Growth Strategy: The Strange Case of Charlotte, North Carolina and the Bank of America." *Journal of Urban Affairs* 27 (4): 403–18. doi: http://dx.doi.org/10.1111/j.0735-2166.2005.00243.x.

Smith, Russell M., and John T. Willse. 2012. "Influences on Municipal Annexation Methodology: An Intrastate Analysis of Annexation Activity in North Carolina, 2000–2010." *State and Local Government Review* 44 (3): 185–95. doi: http://dx.doi.org/10.1177/0160323X12456403.

Smith, Stephen Samuel. 1997. "Hugh Governs? Regime and Educational Policy in Charlotte, North Carolina." *Journal of Urban Affairs* 19 (3): 247–74.

———. 2010. "Development and the Politics of School Desegregation and Resegregation." In *Charlotte, NC: The Global Evolution of a New South City,* edited by William Graves and Heather A. Smith. Athens: University of Georgia Press.

Spanberg, Erik. 2007. "Voters Rally in Support of Transit Tax." *Charlotte Business Journal,* November 7. www.bizjournals.com/charlotte/stories/2007/11/05/daily27.html.

———. 2012. "Charlotte Wins $580M from Feds for Light-Rail Extension." *Charlotte Business Journal,* October 16. www.bizjournals.com/charlotte/blog/queen_city_agenda/2012/10/charlotte-wins-580m-from-obama-feds.html.

Sparber, Chad. 2010. "Racial Diversity and Macroeconomic Productivity across US States and Cities." *Regional Studies* 44 (1): 71–85. doi: http://dx.doi.org/10.1080/00343400802360436.

Stiglitz, Joseph E. 2012. *The Price of Inequality: How Today's Divided Society Endangers Our Future.* New York: W. W. Norton.

St. Onge, Paul, and Tim Funk. 2009. "Who Will Lead Charlotte Now?" *Charlotte Observer,* December 13. www.fftc.org/document.doc?id=767.

Storper, Michael. 1997. *The Regional World: Territorial Development in a Global Economy.* New York: Guilford Press.

———. 2013. *Keys to the City: How Economics, Institutions, Social Interactions, and Politics Shape Development.* Princeton, NJ: Princeton University Press.

Thomas, Mike. 2013. "San Antonio Poised to Weather Future Military Base Closures." *San Antonio Business Journal,* December 26. www.bizjournals.com/sanantonio/news/2013/12/26/san-antonio-poised-to-weather-future.html.

Triple Helix Research Group, Stanford University. 2010. "The Triple Helix Concept." http://triplehelix.stanford.edu/3helix_concept.

Ubell, Karen E. 2004. "Consent Not Required: Municipal Annexation in North Carolina." *North Carolina Law Review* 83: 1634.

United States Commission on Civil Rights. 1972. "Five Communities: Their Search for Equal Education." Washington, DC: Clearinghouse Publication. www.law.umaryland.edu/marshall/usccr/documents/cr11037.pdf.

US Environmental Protection Agency. 2013. "Geographic Area of Focus: San Joaquin Valley." Region 9 Strategic Plan, 2011–14. http://www.epa.gov/region9/strategicplan/sanjoaquin.html.

Uslaner, Eric. 2012. *Income Inequality in the United States Fuels Pessimism and Threatens Social Cohesion.* Washington, DC: Center for American Progress. www.americanprogress.org/wp-content/uploads/2012/12/Uslaner.pdf.

Vande Bunte, Matt. 2013. "Poverty Surging in Grand Rapids, Suburbs: Brookings Institution Book." *MLive.com,* May 22. www.mlive.com/news/grand-rapids/index.ssf/2013/05/poverty_surging_in_grand_rapid.html.

Varian, Hal. 2011. "Micromultinationals Will Run the World." *Foreign Policy,* October. http://www.foreignpolicy.com/articles/2011/08/15/micromultinationals_will_run_the_world.

Vey, Jennifer S. 2012. *Building from Strength: Creating Opportunity in Greater Baltimore's Next Economy.* Metropolitan Policy Program, Brookings Institution. http://www.brookings.edu/~/media/research/files/reports/2012/4/26%20baltimore%20economy%20vey/0426_baltimore_economy_vey.pdf.

Voith, Richard. 1998. "Do Suburbs Need Cities?" *Journal of Regional Science* 38 (3): 445–64. doi: http://dx.doi.org/10.1111/0022-4146.00102.

Waller, Signe. 2002. *Love and Revolution: A Political Memoir. People's History of the Greensboro Massacre, Its Setting and Aftermath.* Lanham, MD: Rowman & Littlefield.

Warren, Mark, James Defilippis, and Susan Saegert. 2008. "A Theology of Organizing: From Alinsky to the Modern IAF." In *The Community Development Reader,* ed. J. DeFilippis and S. Saegert, 194–203. New York: Routledge.

Warren, Mark R. 1998. "Community Building and Political Power: A Community Organizing Approach to Democratic Renewal." *American Behavioral Scientist* 42 (1): 78–92. doi: http://dx.doi.org/10.1177/0002764298042001007.

Weise, Karen. 2014. "How Seattle Agreed to a $15 Minimum Wage Without a Fight." *Bloomberg Businessweek*, May 8. www.businessweek.com/articles/2014-05-08/how-seattle-agreed-to-a-15-minimum-wage-without-a-fight.

Weisman, Jonathan. 2012. "Nonpartisan Tax Report Withdrawn after G.O.P. Protest." *New York Times*, November 1, Business Day. www.nytimes.com/2012/11/02/business/questions-raised-on-withdrawal-of-congressional-research-services-report-on-tax-rates.html.

Wenger, Etienne. 1998. *Communities of Practice: Learning, Meaning, and Identity*. Cambridge: Cambridge University Press.

Werbel, Richard, and Peter Haas. 2002. "Voting Outcomes of Local Tax Ballot Measures with a Substantial Rail Transit Component: Case Study of Effects of Transportation Packages." *Transportation Research Record* 1799 (January): 10–17. doi: http://dx.doi.org/10.3141/1799-02.

Whitebear, Bernie. 1994. "Taking Back Fort Lawton." *Race, Poverty and the Environment* 4: 3–6.

White, O. Kendall, and Daryl White. 1980. "Abandoning an Unpopular Policy: An Analysis of the Decision Granting the Mormon Priesthood to Blacks." *Sociology of Religion* 41 (3): 231–45. doi: http://dx.doi.org/10.2307/3710400.

Wial, Howard. 1991. "Getting a Good Job: Mobility in a Segmented Labor Market." *Industrial Relations* 30 (3): 396–416.

Winter, Ray. 2011. "New Factories in the Fields." *Boom: A Journal of California* 1 (4): 80–87.

Woo, Myungje, Catherine Ross, and Thomas Boston. 2015. "Do Megaregions Produce Greater Regional Convergence or Divergence? Implications for Spatial Planning and Infrastructure Investment." *Journal of Urban Planning and Development* 141(1):1–14. doi: http://dx.doi.org/10.1061/(ASCE)UP.1943-5444.0000198.

Zuckerberg, Mark. 2013. "Immigrants Are the Key to a Knowledge Economy." *Washington Post*, April 10. www.washingtonpost.com/opinions/mark-zuckerberg-immigrants-are-the-key-to-a-knowledge-economy/2013/04/10/aba05554-a20b-11e2-82bc-511538ae90a4_story.html.

Zuk, Miriam Zofith. 2013. "Health Equity in a New Urbanist Environment: Land Use Planning and Community Capacity Building in Fresno, CA." PhD thesis, University of California, Berkeley. http://escholarship.org/uc/item/4pq5p68j.

Index

CPSIA information can be obtained
at www.ICGtesting.com
Printed in the USA
FSOW04n1748191015
12349FS